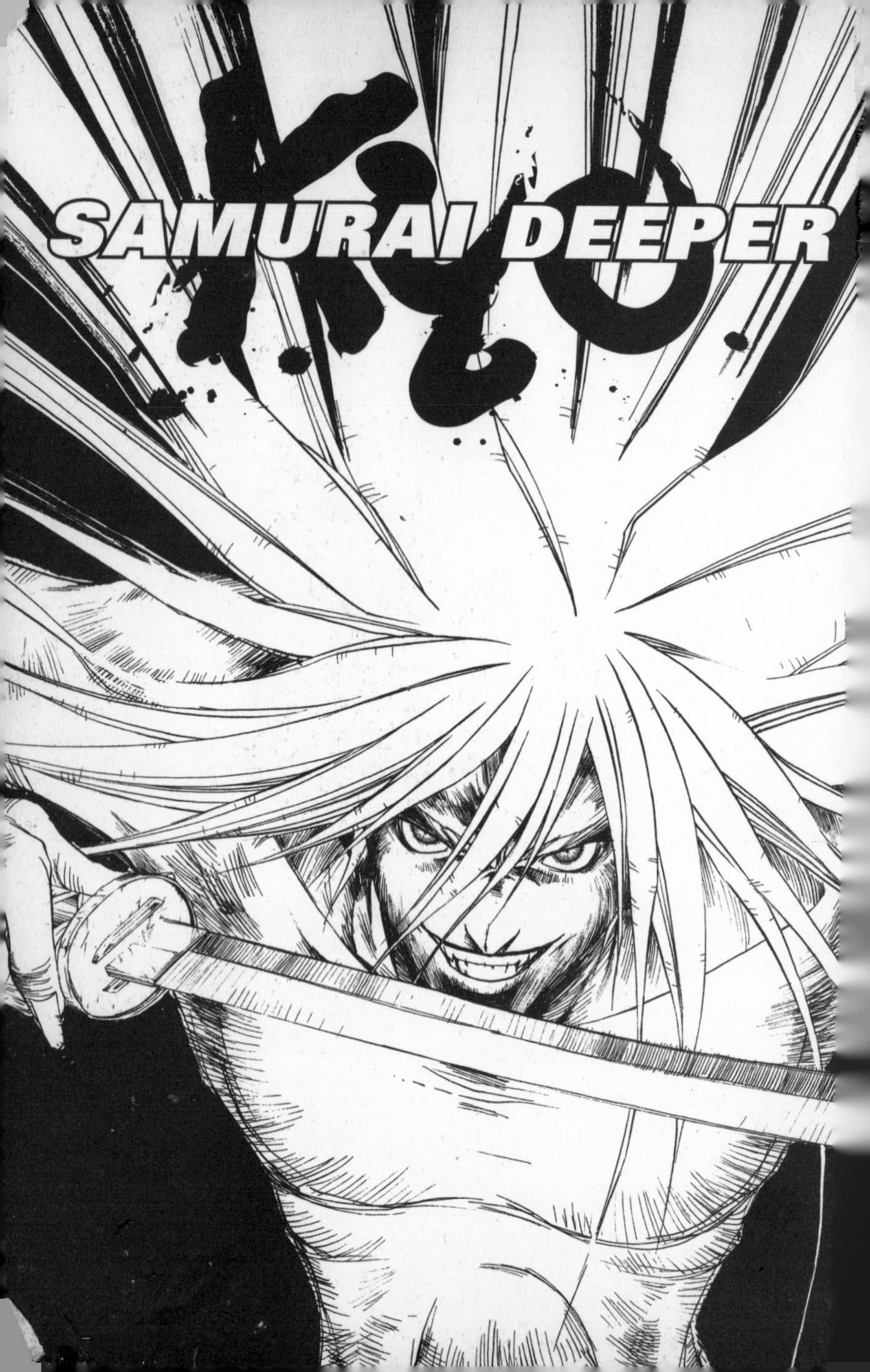
SAMURAI DEEPER
KYO

Samurai Deeper Kyo Vol. 9
Created by Akimine Kamijyo

Translation - Alexander O. Smith
Script Editor - Rich Amtower
Copy Editor - Peter Ahlstrom
Retouch and Lettering - Patrick Tran
Production Artists - Vicente Rivera, Jr. and James Lee
Cover Design - Raymond Makowski

Editor - Jake Forbes
Digital Imaging Manager - Chris Buford
Pre-Press Manager - Antonio DePietro
Production Managers - Jennifer Miller and Mutsumi Miyazaki
Art Director - Matt Alford
Managing Editor - Jill Freshney
VP of Production - Ron Klamert
President and C.O.O. - John Parker
Publisher and C.E.O. - Stuart Levy

A  Manga

TOKYOPOP Inc.
5900 Wilshire Blvd. Suite 2000
Los Angeles, CA 90036

E-mail: info@TOKYOPOP.com
Come visit us online at www.TOKYOPOP.com

©2001 Akimine Kamijyo. All rights reserved. No portion of this book may be reproduced or transmitted in any form or by any means without written permission from the copyright holders. This manga is a work of fiction. Any resemblance to actual events or locales or persons, living or dead, is entirely coincidental.

All rights reserved. First published in Japan in 2001 by Kodansha LTD., Tokyo. English language translation rights arranged by Kodansha LTD.

English text copyright ©2004 TOKYOPOP Inc.

ISBN: 1-59182-545-8

First TOKYOPOP printing: October 2004
10 9 8 7 6 5 4 3 2 1
Printed in the USA

SAMURAI DEEPER Kyo

Vol. 9
by Akimine Kamijyo

NORTHWEST

TOKYOPOP®

HAMBURG // LONDON // LOS ANGELES // TOKYO

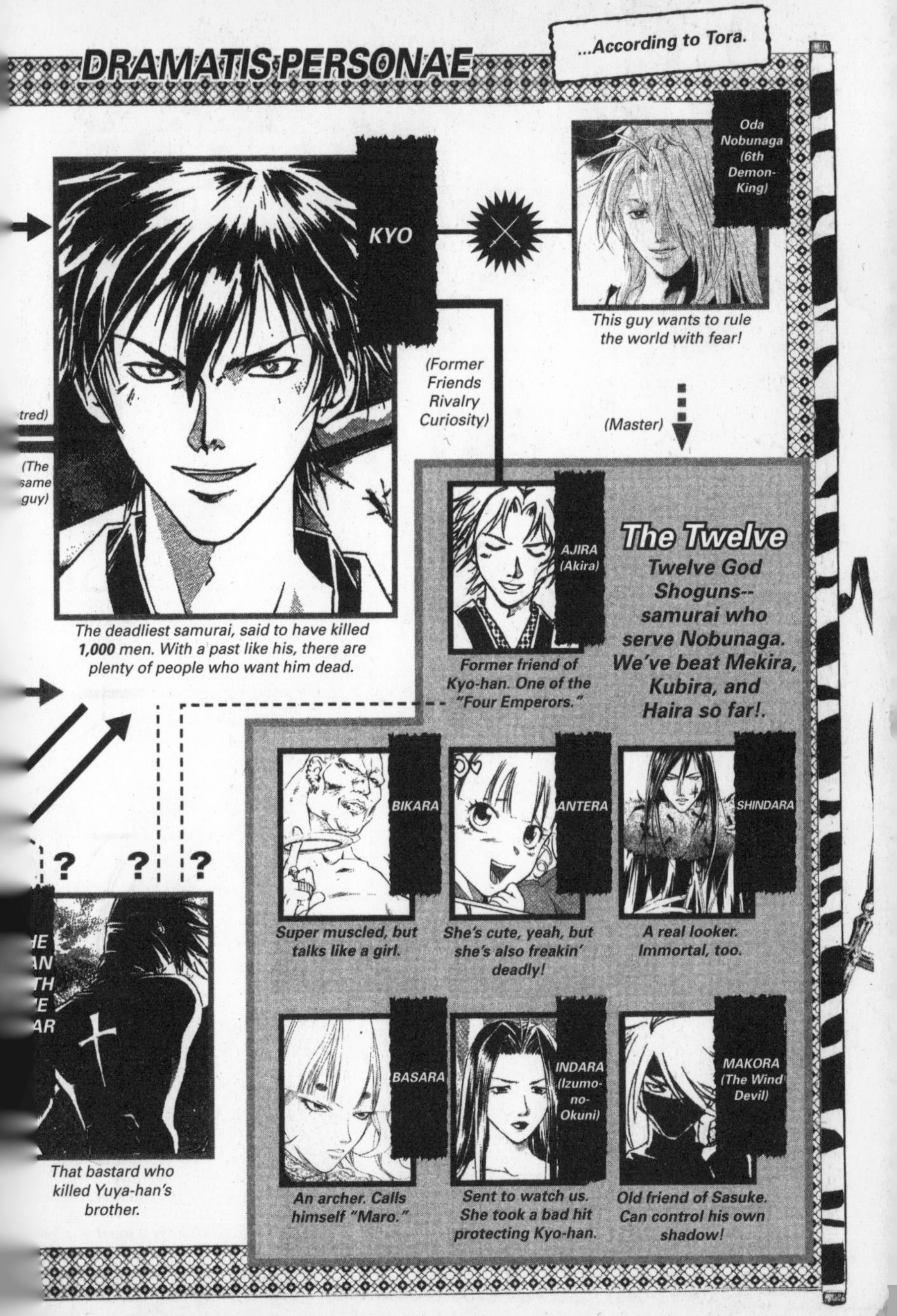
DRAMATIS PERSONAE
...According to Tora.
Oda Nobunaga (6th Demon-King)
This guy wants to rule the world with fear!
KYO
The deadliest samurai, said to have killed 1,000 men. With a past like his, there are plenty of people who want him dead.
(Former Friends Rivalry Curiosity)
(Master)
tred)
(The same guy)
AJIRA (Akira)
Former friend of Kyo-han. One of the "Four Emperors."
The Twelve
Twelve God Shoguns--samurai who serve Nobunaga. We've beat Mekira, Kubira, and Haira so far!.
BIKARA
Super muscled, but talks like a girl.
ANTERA
She's cute, yeah, but she's also freakin' deadly!
SHINDARA
A real looker. Immortal, too.
? ? ?
That bastard who killed Yuya-han's brother.
BASARA
An archer. Calls himself "Maro."
INDARA (Izumo-no-Okuni)
Sent to watch us. She took a bad hit protecting Kyo-han.
MAKORA (The Wind Devil)
Old friend of Sasuke. Can control his own shadow!

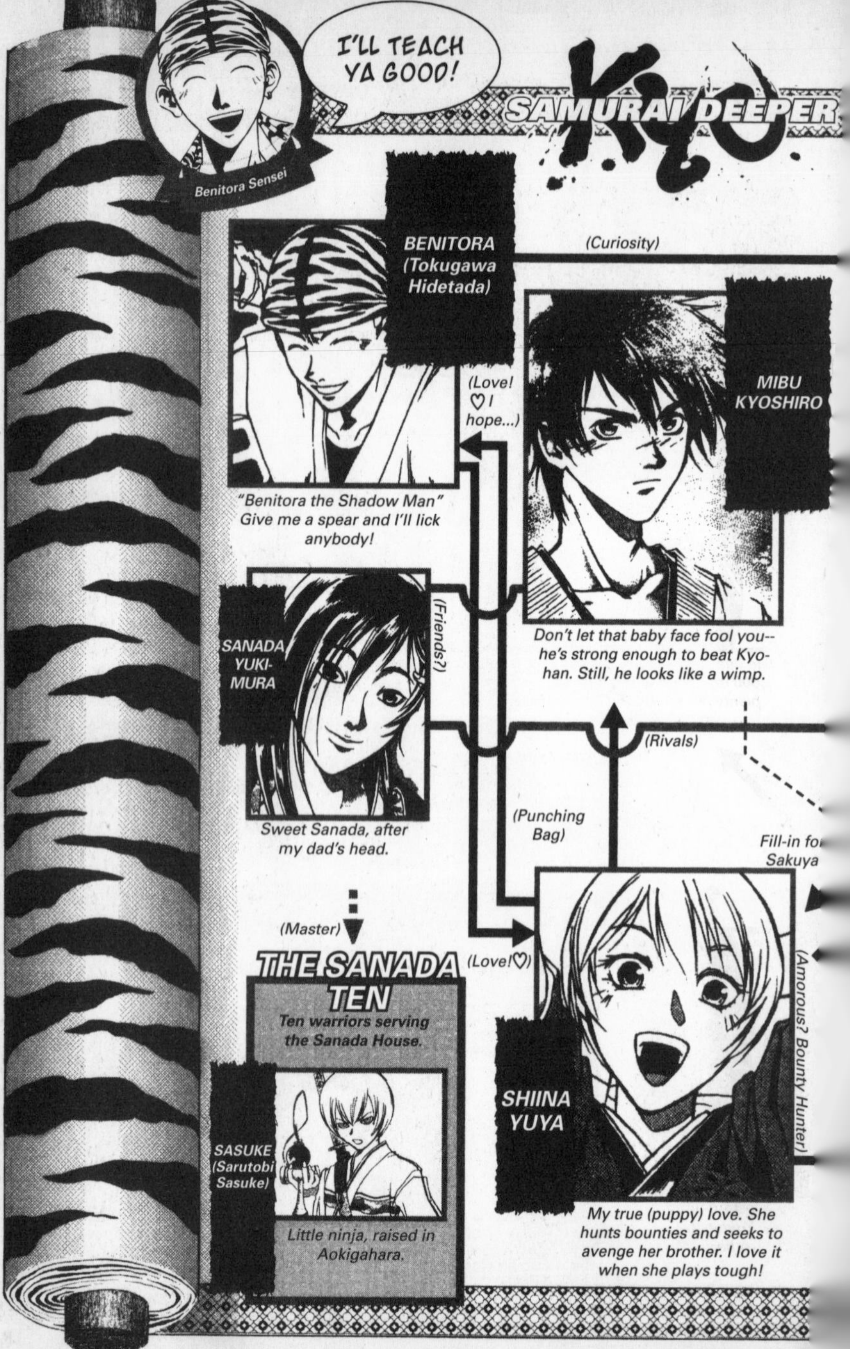
I'LL TEACH YA GOOD!
Benitora Sensei
SAMURAI DEEPER KYO
BENITORA (Tokugawa Hidetada)
"Benitora the Shadow Man" Give me a spear and I'll lick anybody!
(Curiosity)
MIBU KYOSHIRO
Don't let that baby face fool you-- he's strong enough to beat Kyo-han. Still, he looks like a wimp.
(Love! ♡ I hope...)
SANADA YUKI-MURA
(Friends?)
Sweet Sanada, after my dad's head.
(Rivals)
(Punching Bag)
Fill-in fo
Sakuya
(Master)
THE SANADA TEN
Ten warriors serving the Sanada House.
SASUKE (Sarutobi Sasuke)
Little ninja, raised in Aokigahara.
(Love!♡)
SHIINA YUYA
(Amorous? Bounty Hunter)
My true (puppy) love. She hunts bounties and seeks to avenge her brother. I love it when she plays tough!

Kyo and his companions continue to search ***Aokigahara*** Forest for Demon Eyes' true body.

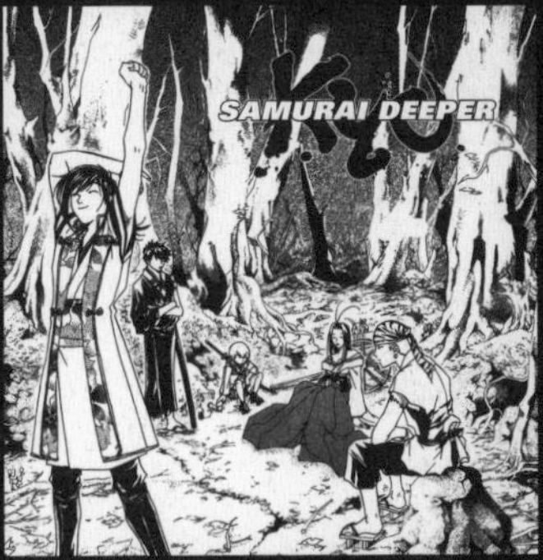
SAMURAI DEEPER
KYO

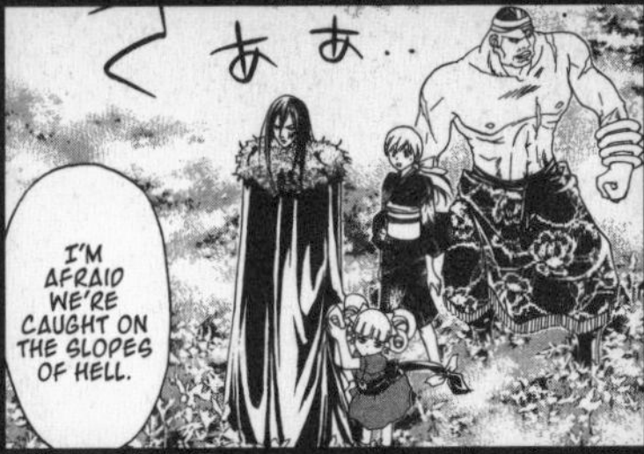
くああ...
I'M AFRAID WE'RE CAUGHT ON THE SLOPES OF HELL.

Bikara, Antera, and ***Shindara*** have taken Yuya hostage and now travel the ***Slopes of Hell,*** the path that leads to the ***Land of the Fire Lotus,*** where Kyo's body is hidden.

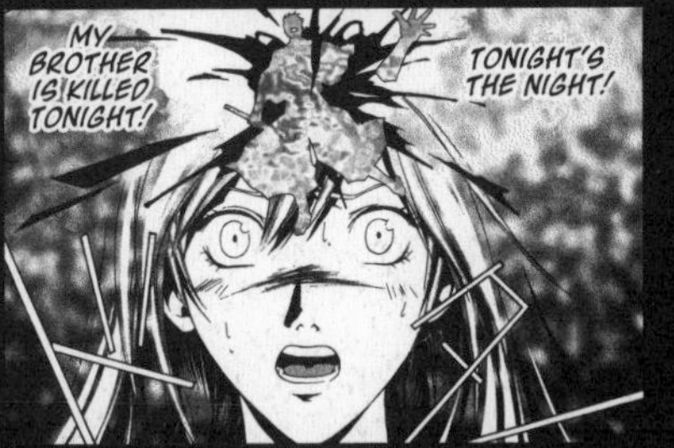
TONIGHT'S THE NIGHT!
MY BROTHER IS KILLED TONIGHT!

There, Yuya experiences a troubling vision from her past and discovers that...

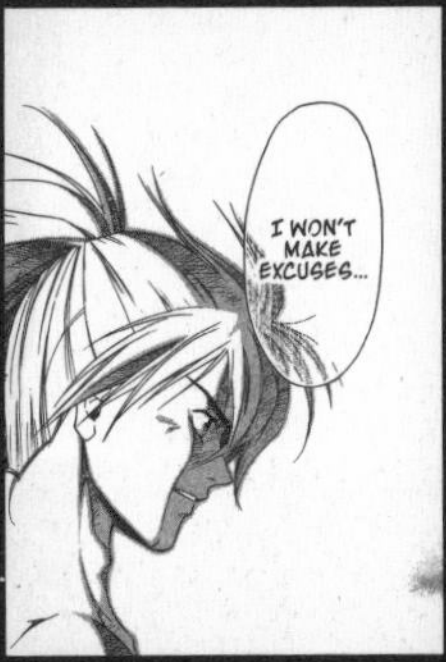
I WON'T MAKE EXCUSES...

...her brother's murderer is Kyoshiro! But before Yuya can hear Kyoshiro's cryptic words, the vision fades.

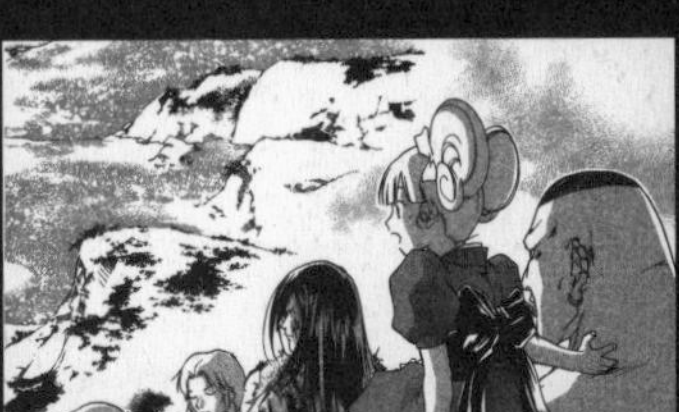

Ajira of the Twelve joins his comrades as they approach their destination... but can they trust him?

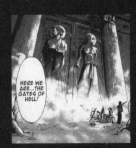

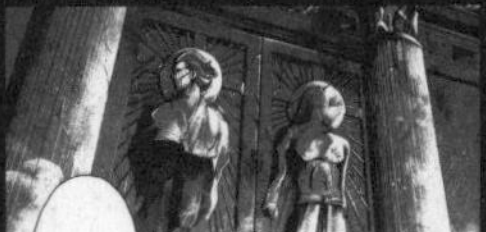
HERE WE ARE...THE GATES OF HELL!

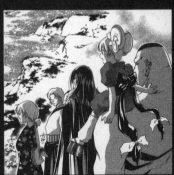

Back in the forest, Kyo's team arrives at last at the ***Gates of Hell...***

The elderly gatekeeper is convinced Kyo is her people's leader, the ***Crimson King,*** and agrees to help him.

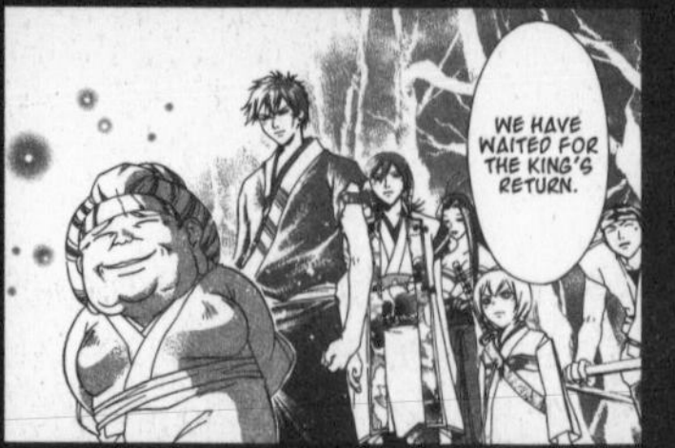
WE HAVE WAITED FOR THE KING'S RETURN.

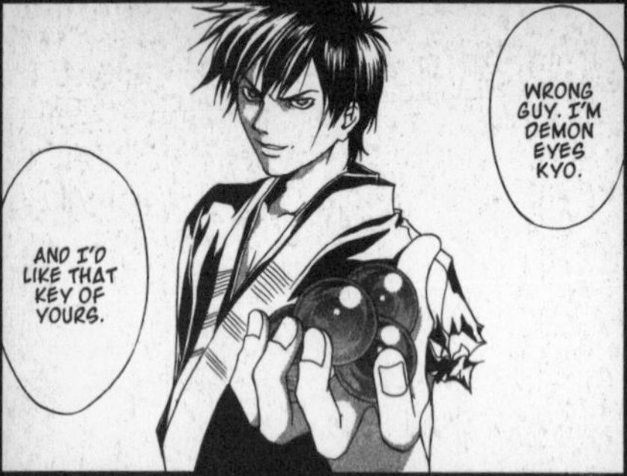
WRONG GUY. I'M DEMON EYES KYO.
AND I'D LIKE THAT KEY OF YOURS.

But Kyo tells the old woman otherwise.

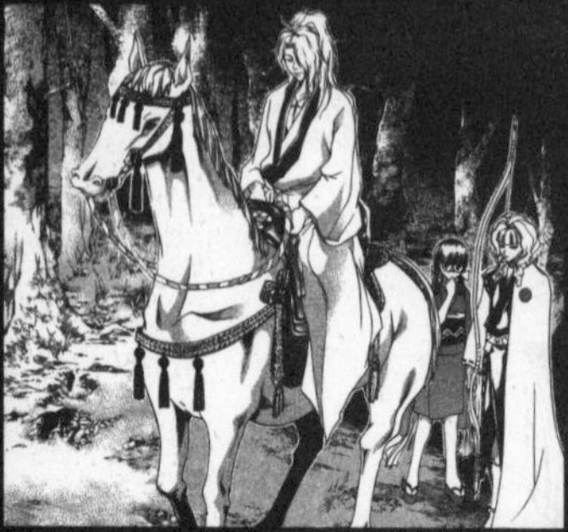

Meanwhile, another traveler has reached the gates. None other than... ***The Master!***

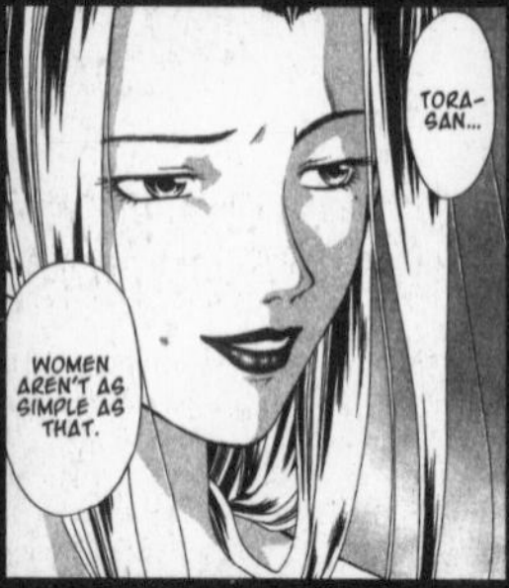
TORA-SAN...
WOMEN AREN'T AS SIMPLE AS THAT.

In a surprise announcement, Kyo and team learn that there's been a ***traitor*** in their midst all the while—***Izumo-no-Okuni*** is actually ***Indara*** of the Twelve!

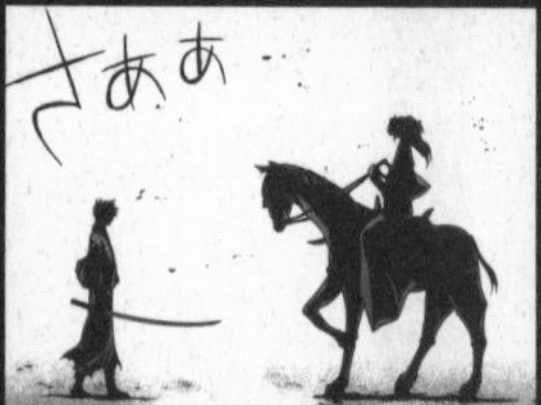
さああ

Kyo takes on the Master, but underestimates the strength of his opponent.

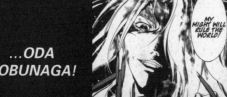

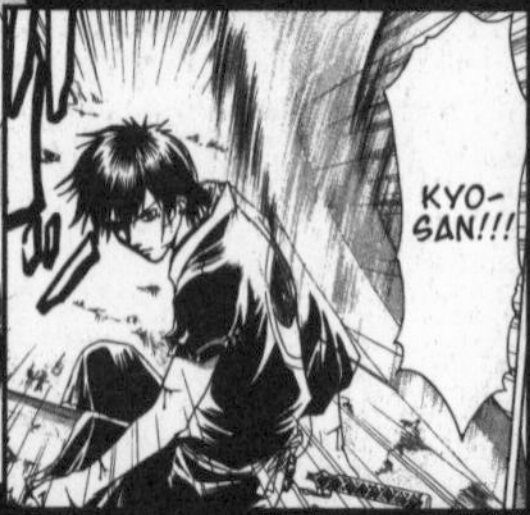
KYO-SAN!!!

The Master swings a fatal blow at Kyo...

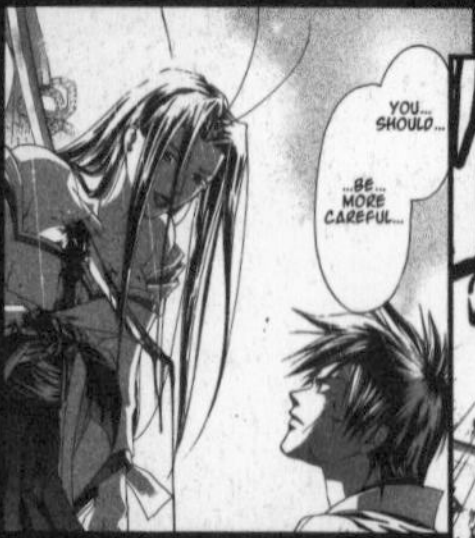
YOU... SHOULD...
...BE... MORE CAREFUL...

...but the blade is intercepted by Okuni, who sacrifices her own life for Kyo's.

Kyo is surely out of his league this time, for his opponent is none other than...

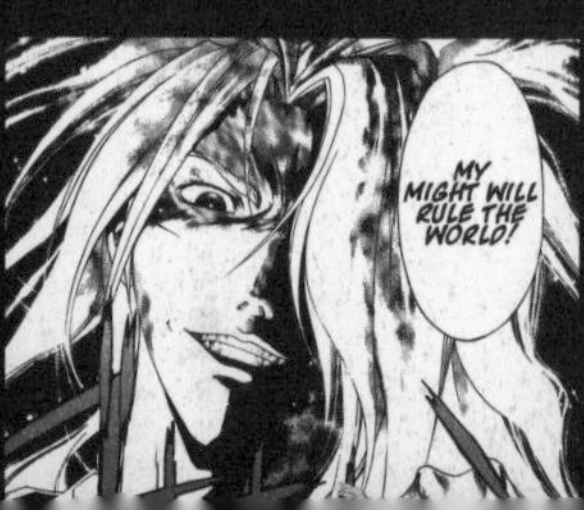
MY MIGHT WILL RULE THE WORLD!

...ODA NOBUNAGA!

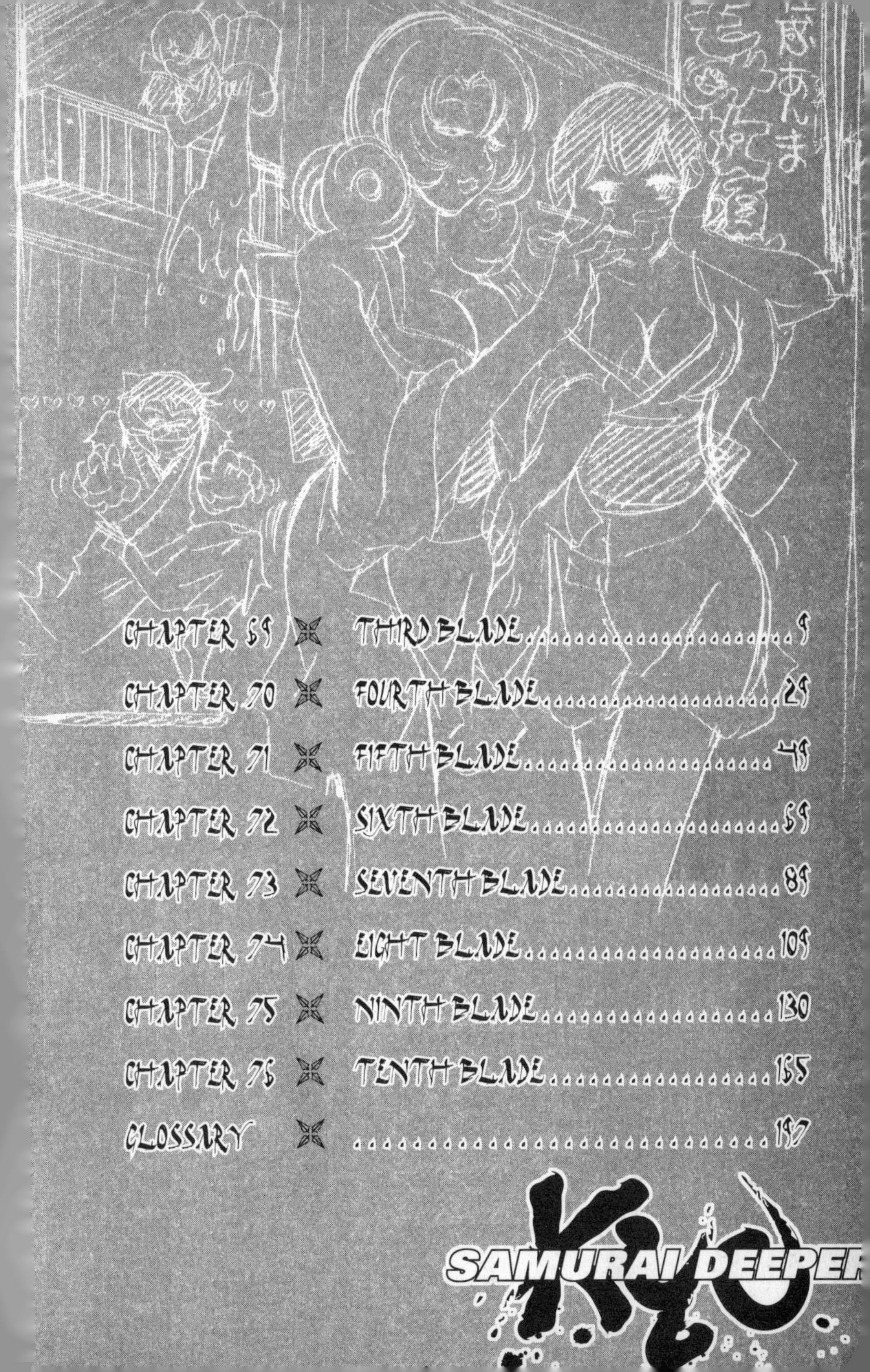

SAMURAI DEEPER KYO

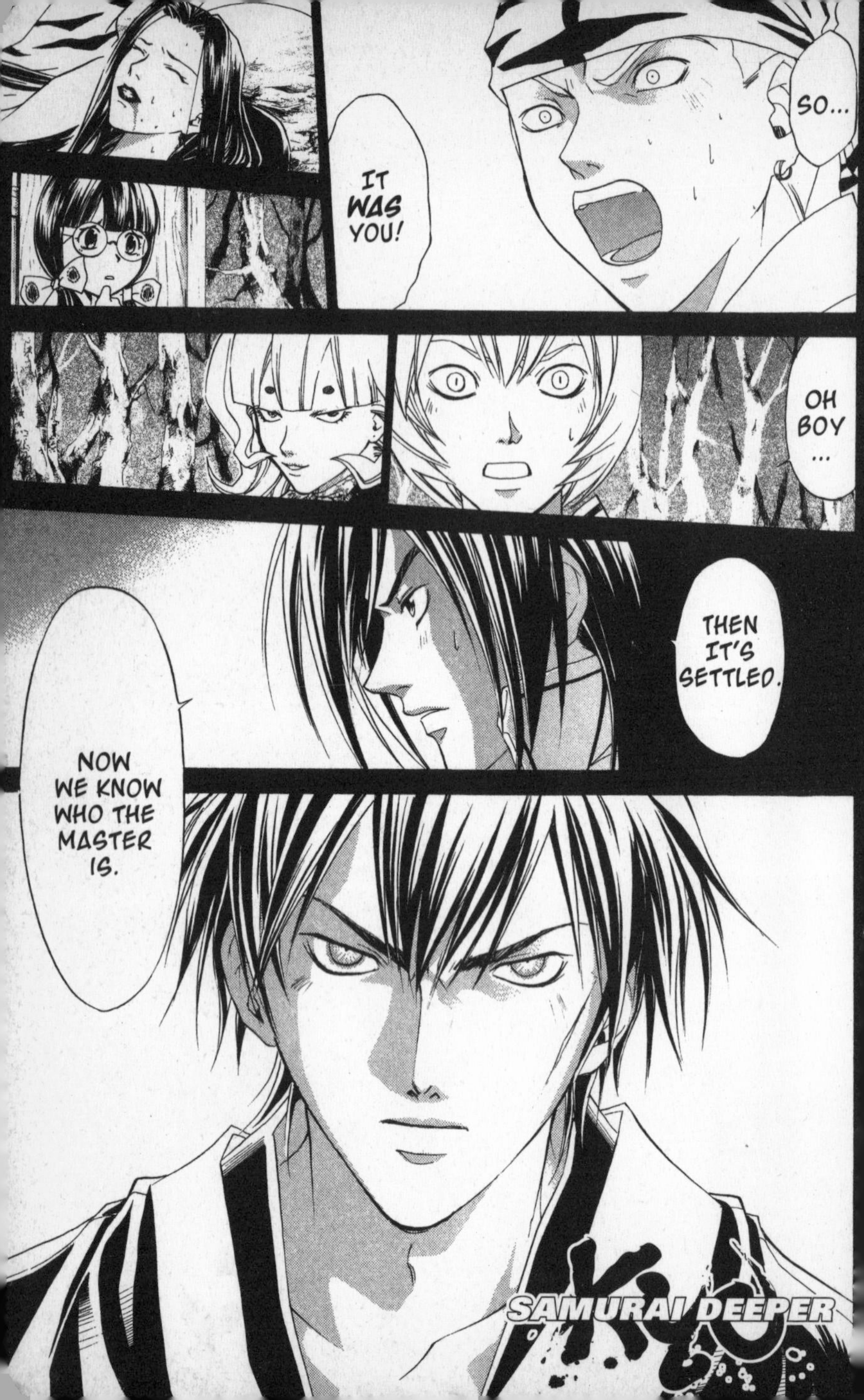
SO...
IT WAS YOU!
OH BOY ...
THEN IT'S SETTLED.
NOW WE KNOW WHO THE MASTER IS.
SAMURAI DEEPER KYO

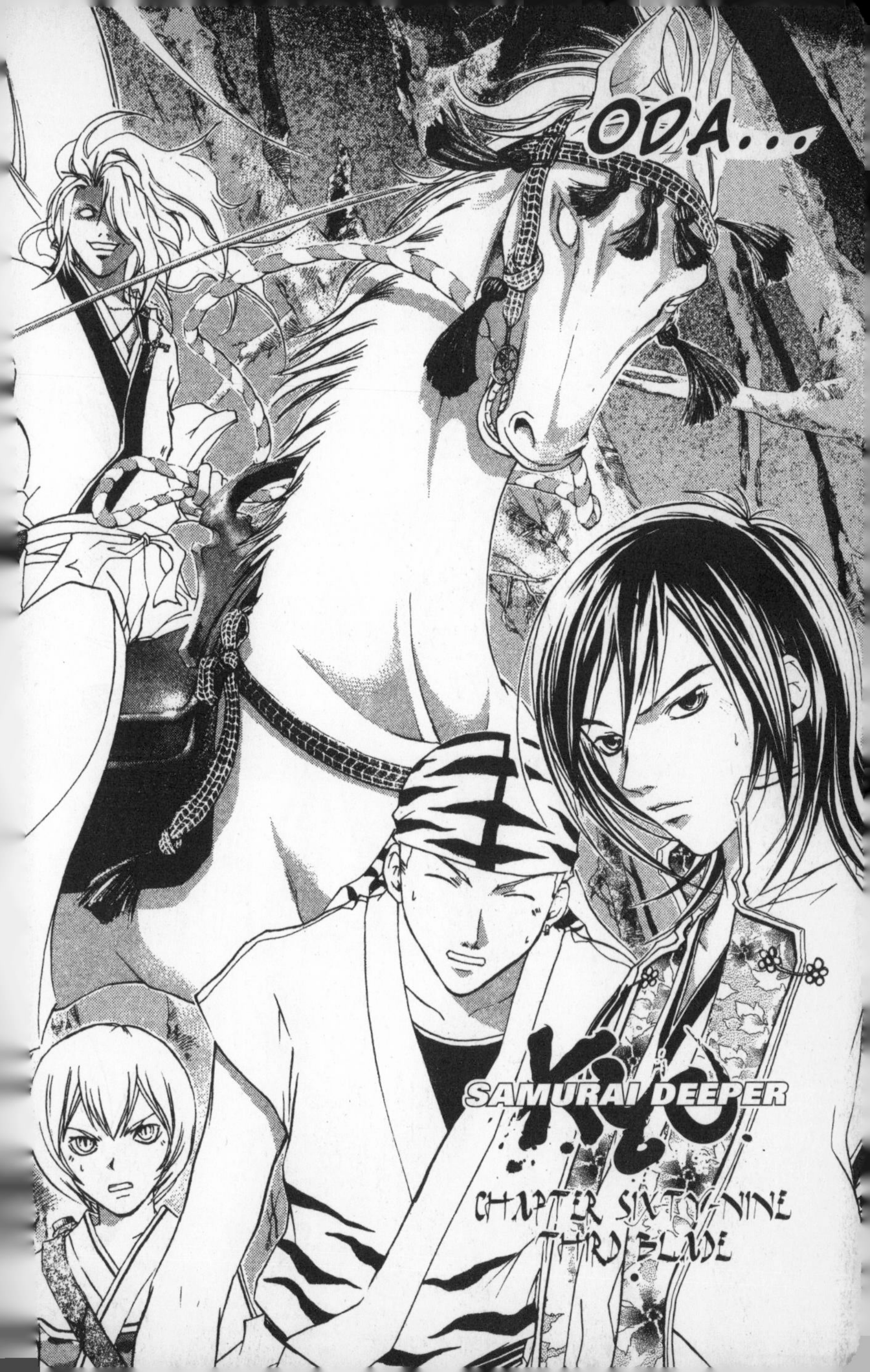
ODA...
SAMURAI DEEPER
KYO
CHAPTER SIXTY-NINE
THIRD BLADE

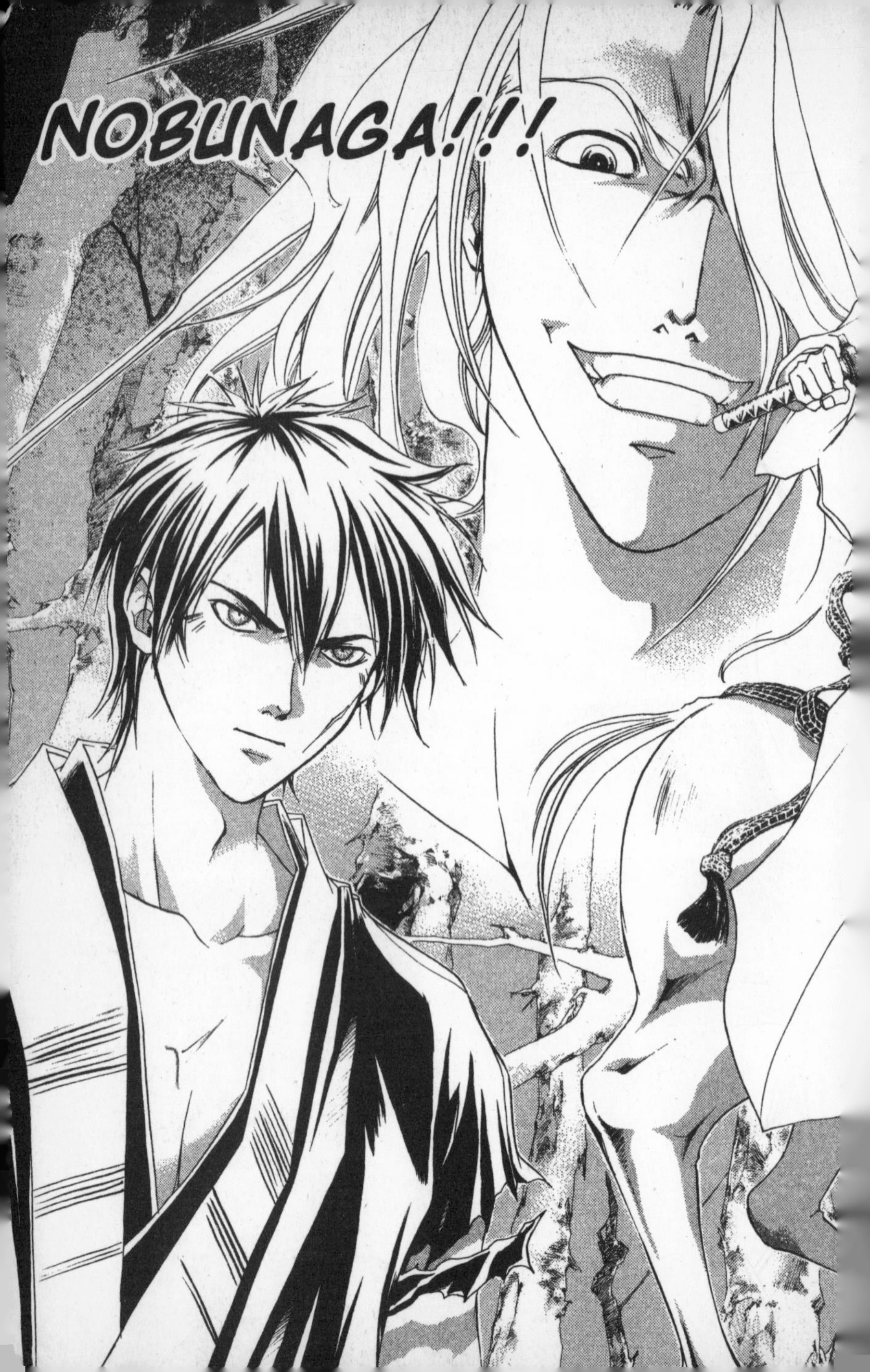
NOBUNAGA!!!!

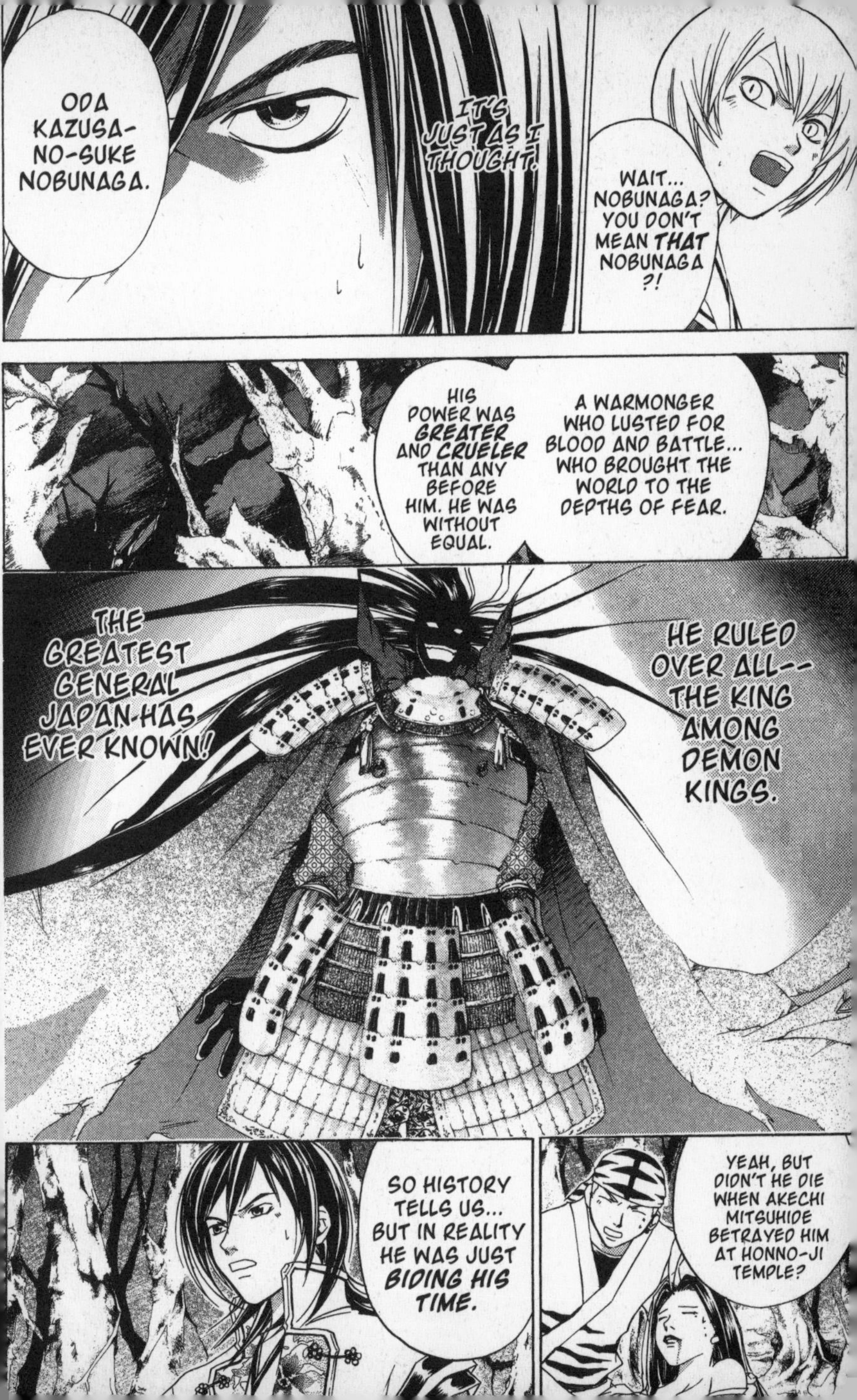
WAIT... NOBUNAGA? YOU DON'T MEAN THAT NOBUNAGA ?!
IT'S JUST AS I THOUGHT.
ODA KAZUSA-NO-SUKE NOBUNAGA.
A WARMONGER WHO LUSTED FOR BLOOD AND BATTLE... WHO BROUGHT THE WORLD TO THE DEPTHS OF FEAR.
HIS POWER WAS GREATER AND CRUELER THAN ANY BEFORE HIM. HE WAS WITHOUT EQUAL.
HE RULED OVER ALL-- THE KING AMONG DEMON KINGS.
THE GREATEST GENERAL JAPAN HAS EVER KNOWN!
YEAH, BUT DIDN'T HE DIE WHEN AKECHI MITSUHIDE BETRAYED HIM AT HONNO-JI TEMPLE?
SO HISTORY TELLS US... BUT IN REALITY HE WAS JUST BIDING HIS TIME.

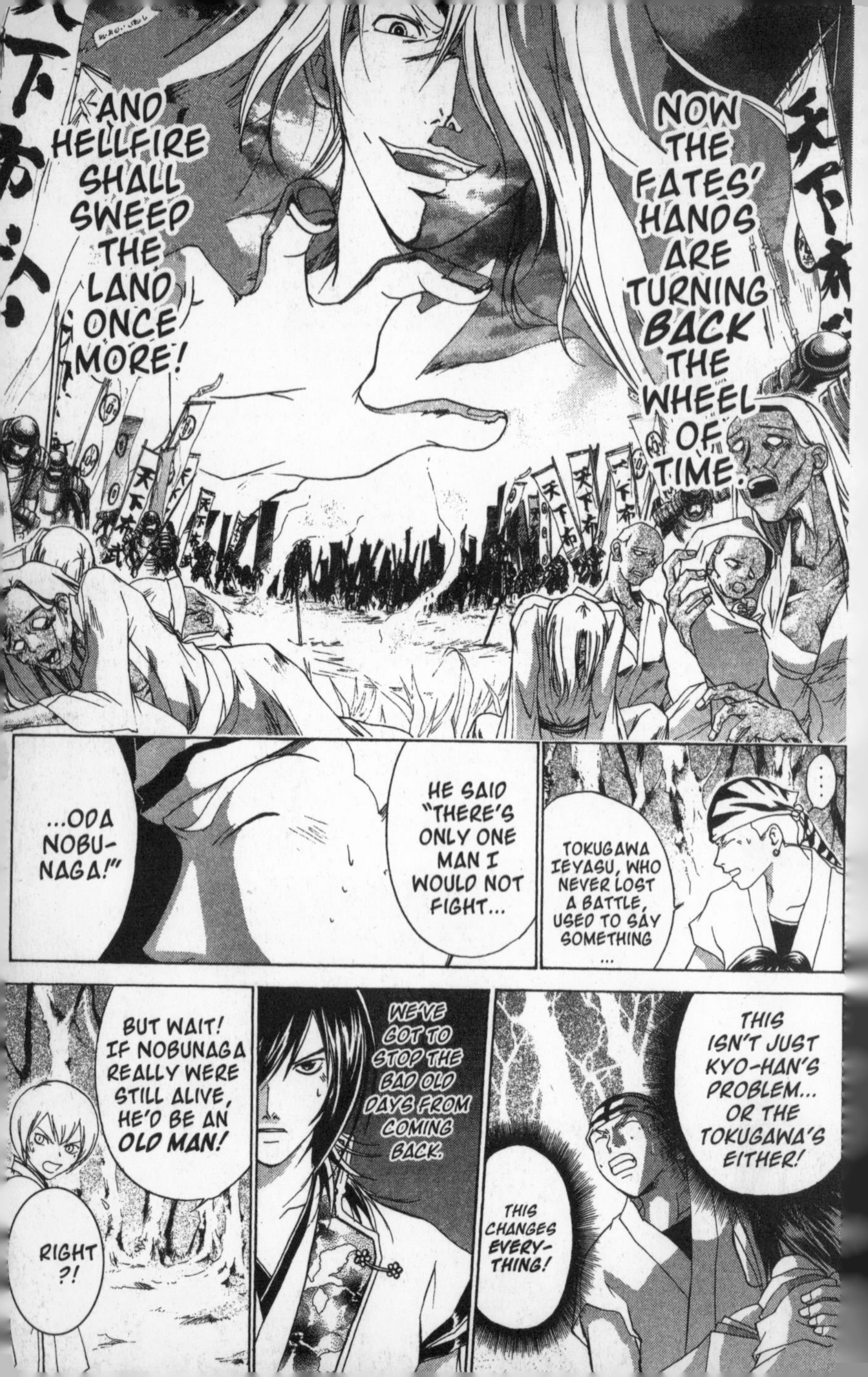
NOW THE FATES' HANDS ARE TURNING BACK THE WHEEL OF TIME.
AND HELLFIRE SHALL SWEEP THE LAND ONCE MORE!
...
TOKUGAWA IEYASU, WHO NEVER LOST A BATTLE, USED TO SAY SOMETHING ...
HE SAID "THERE'S ONLY ONE MAN I WOULD NOT FIGHT...
...ODA NOBUNAGA!"
THIS ISN'T JUST KYO-HAN'S PROBLEM... OR THE TOKUGAWA'S EITHER!
THIS CHANGES EVERY-THING!
WE'VE GOT TO STOP THE BAD OLD DAYS FROM COMING BACK.
BUT WAIT! IF NOBUNAGA REALLY WERE STILL ALIVE, HE'D BE AN OLD MAN!
RIGHT?!

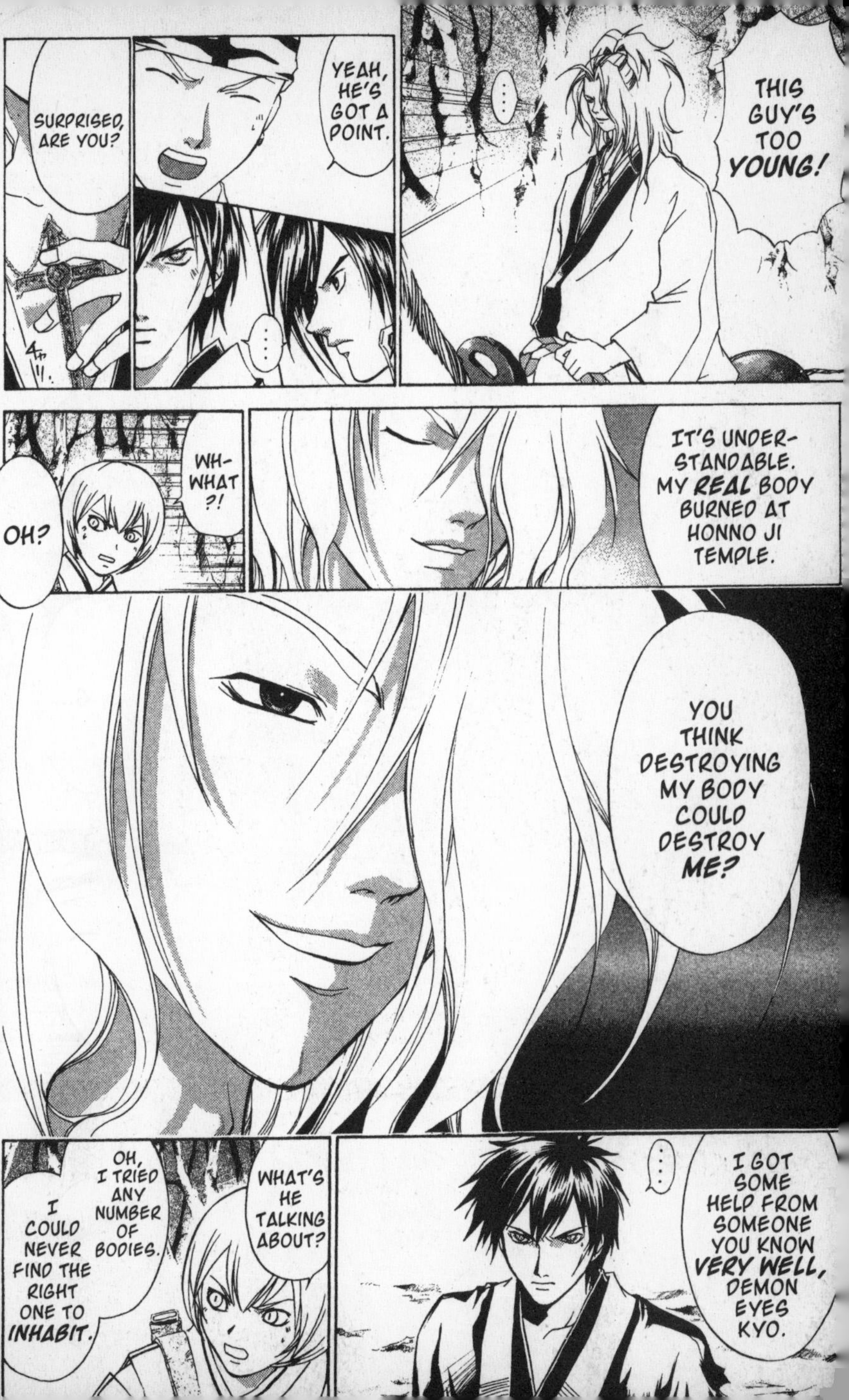
THIS GUY'S TOO YOUNG!
...
YEAH, HE'S GOT A POINT.
...
SURPRISED, ARE YOU?
IT'S UNDER-STANDABLE. MY REAL BODY BURNED AT HONNO JI TEMPLE.
WH-WHAT?!
OH?
YOU THINK DESTROYING MY BODY COULD DESTROY ME?
I GOT SOME HELP FROM SOMEONE YOU KNOW VERY WELL, DEMON EYES KYO.
...
WHAT'S HE TALKING ABOUT?
OH, I TRIED ANY NUMBER OF BODIES.
I COULD NEVER FIND THE RIGHT ONE TO INHABIT.

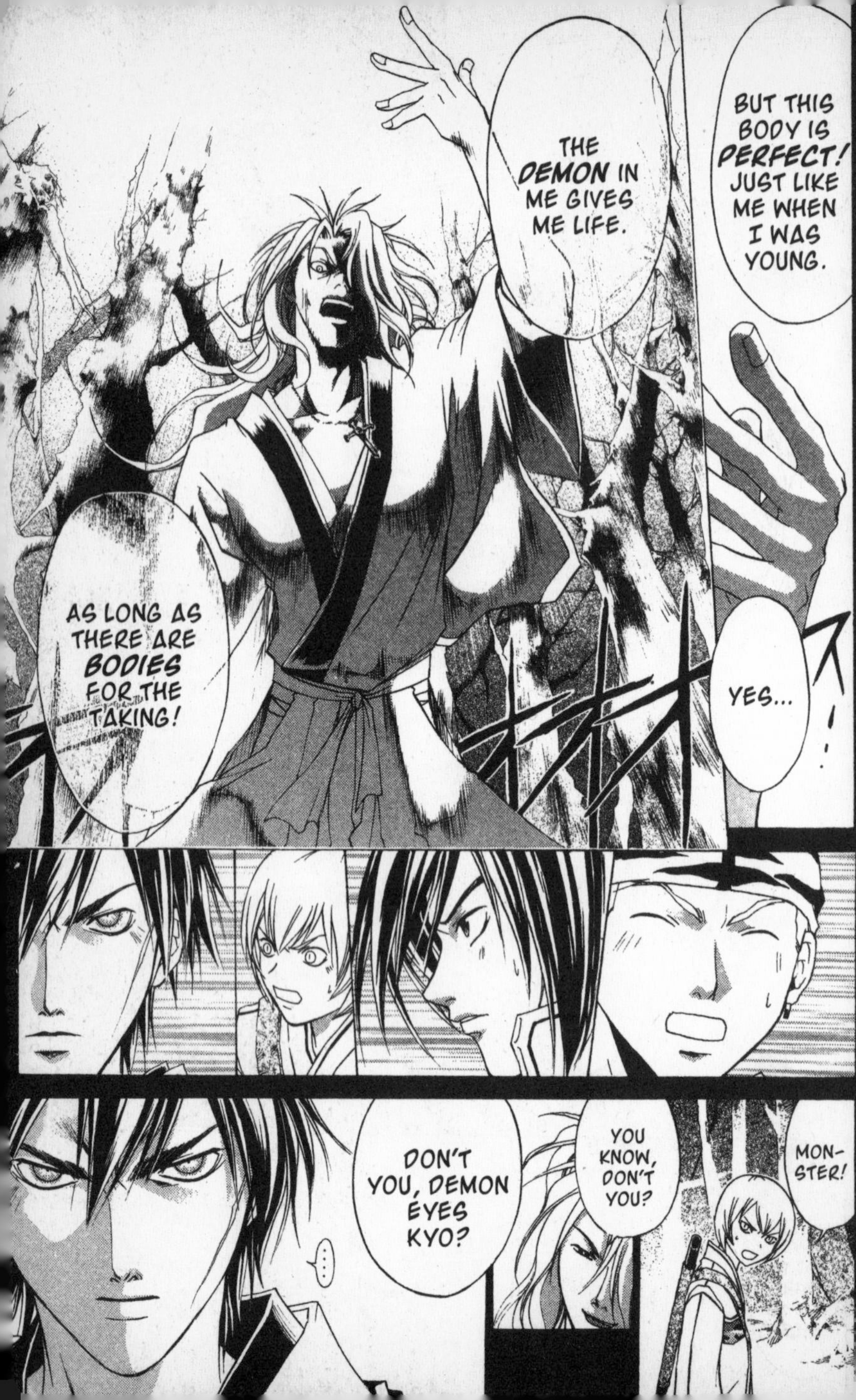
BUT THIS BODY IS PERFECT! JUST LIKE ME WHEN I WAS YOUNG.
YES...
!
THE DEMON IN ME GIVES ME LIFE.
AS LONG AS THERE ARE BODIES FOR THE TAKING!
MON-STER!
YOU KNOW, DON'T YOU?
DON'T YOU, DEMON EYES KYO?
...

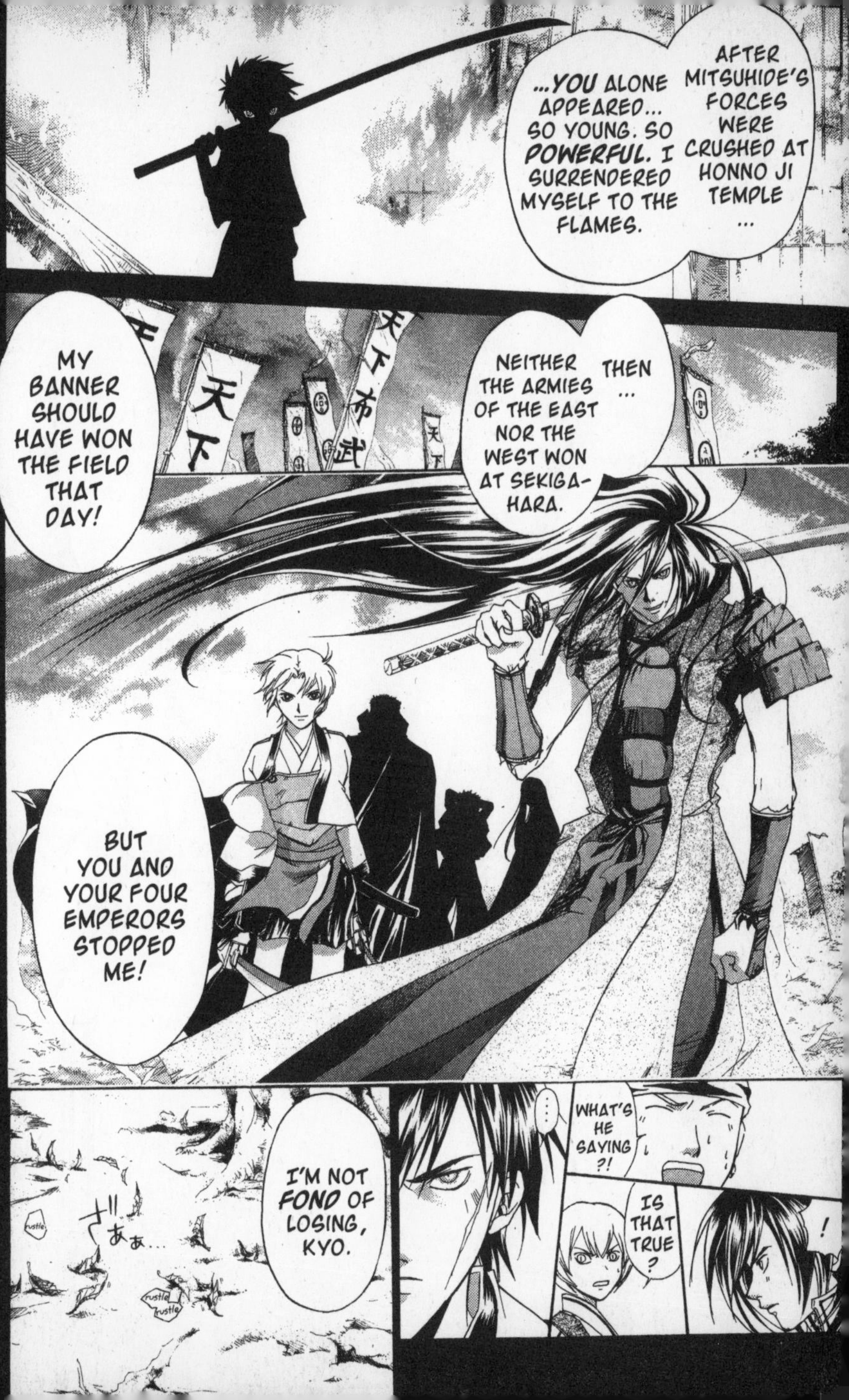
AFTER MITSUHIDE'S FORCES WERE CRUSHED AT HONNO JI TEMPLE ...
...YOU ALONE APPEARED... SO YOUNG. SO POWERFUL. I SURRENDERED MYSELF TO THE FLAMES.
THEN ...
NEITHER THE ARMIES OF THE EAST NOR THE WEST WON AT SEKIGAHARA.
MY BANNER SHOULD HAVE WON THE FIELD THAT DAY!
BUT YOU AND YOUR FOUR EMPERORS STOPPED ME!
WHAT'S HE SAYING ?!
!
IS THAT TRUE ?
...
I'M NOT FOND OF LOSING, KYO.
ざぁぁ...
rustle
rustle rustle

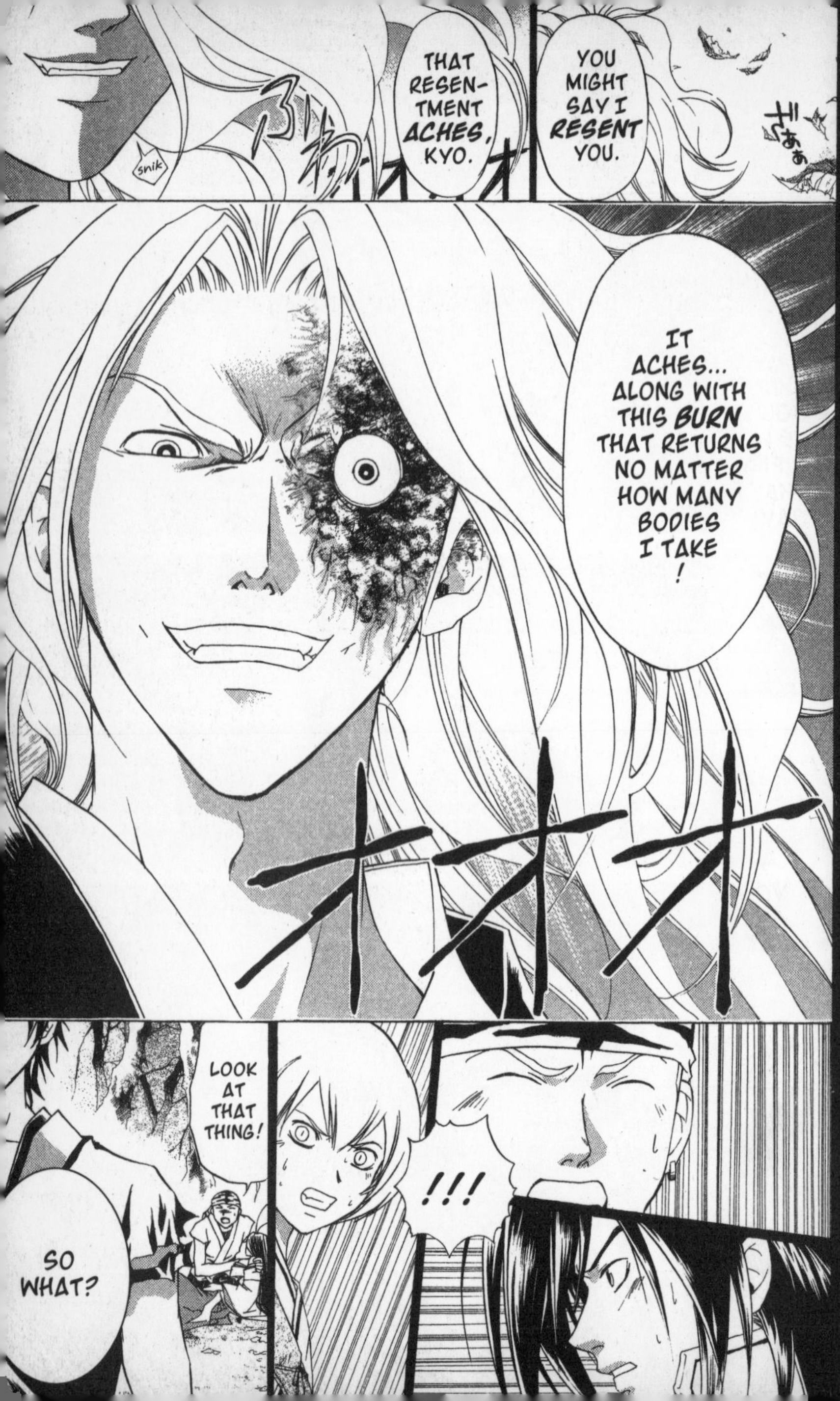
YOU MIGHT SAY I RESENT YOU.
THAT RESENTMENT ACHES, KYO.
snik
IT ACHES... ALONG WITH THIS BURN THAT RETURNS NO MATTER HOW MANY BODIES I TAKE!
オオオ
!!!
LOOK AT THAT THING!
SO WHAT?

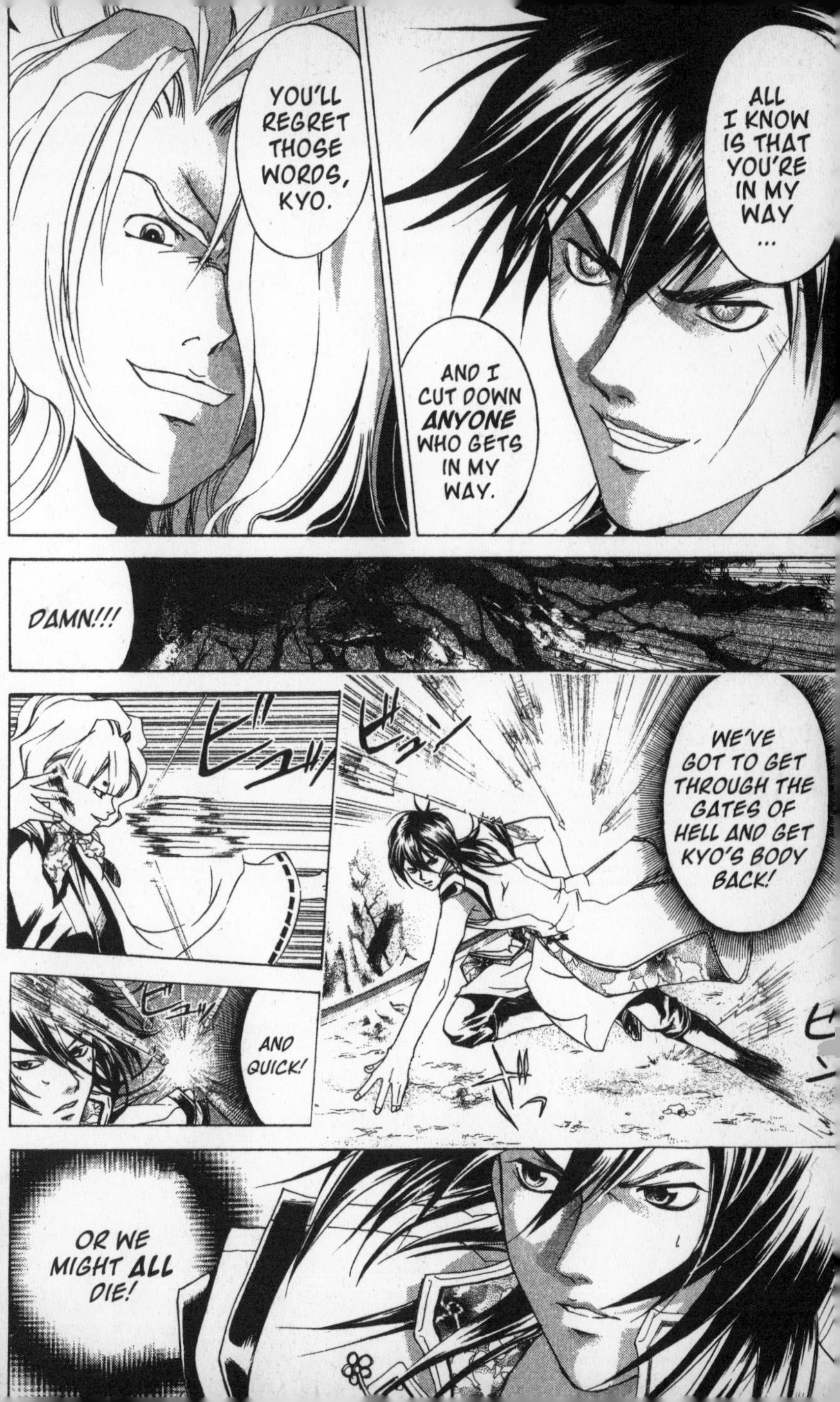
ALL I KNOW IS THAT YOU'RE IN MY WAY ...
AND I CUT DOWN ANYONE WHO GETS IN MY WAY.
YOU'LL REGRET THOSE WORDS, KYO.
DAMN!!!
WE'VE GOT TO GET THROUGH THE GATES OF HELL AND GET KYO'S BODY BACK!
AND QUICK!
OR WE MIGHT ALL DIE!

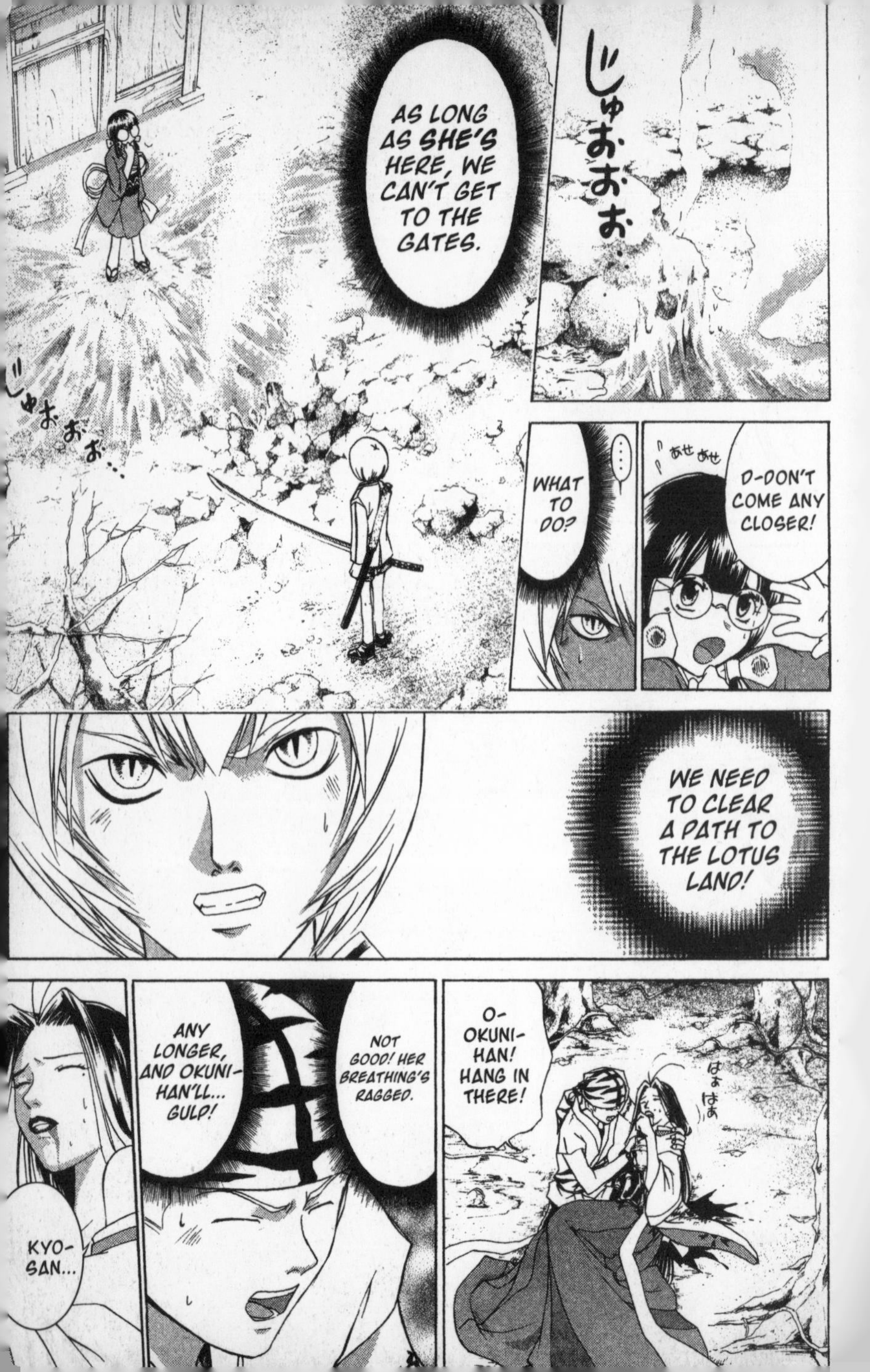
じゅおおお・・
あせ あせ
D-DON'T COME ANY CLOSER!
...
WHAT TO DO?
AS LONG AS SHE'S HERE, WE CAN'T GET TO THE GATES.
じゅおおお...
WE NEED TO CLEAR A PATH TO THE LOTUS LAND!
O-OKUNI-HAN! HANG IN THERE!
はぁ はぁ
NOT GOOD! HER BREATHING'S RAGGED.
ANY LONGER, AND OKUNI-HAN'LL... GULP!
KYO-SAN...

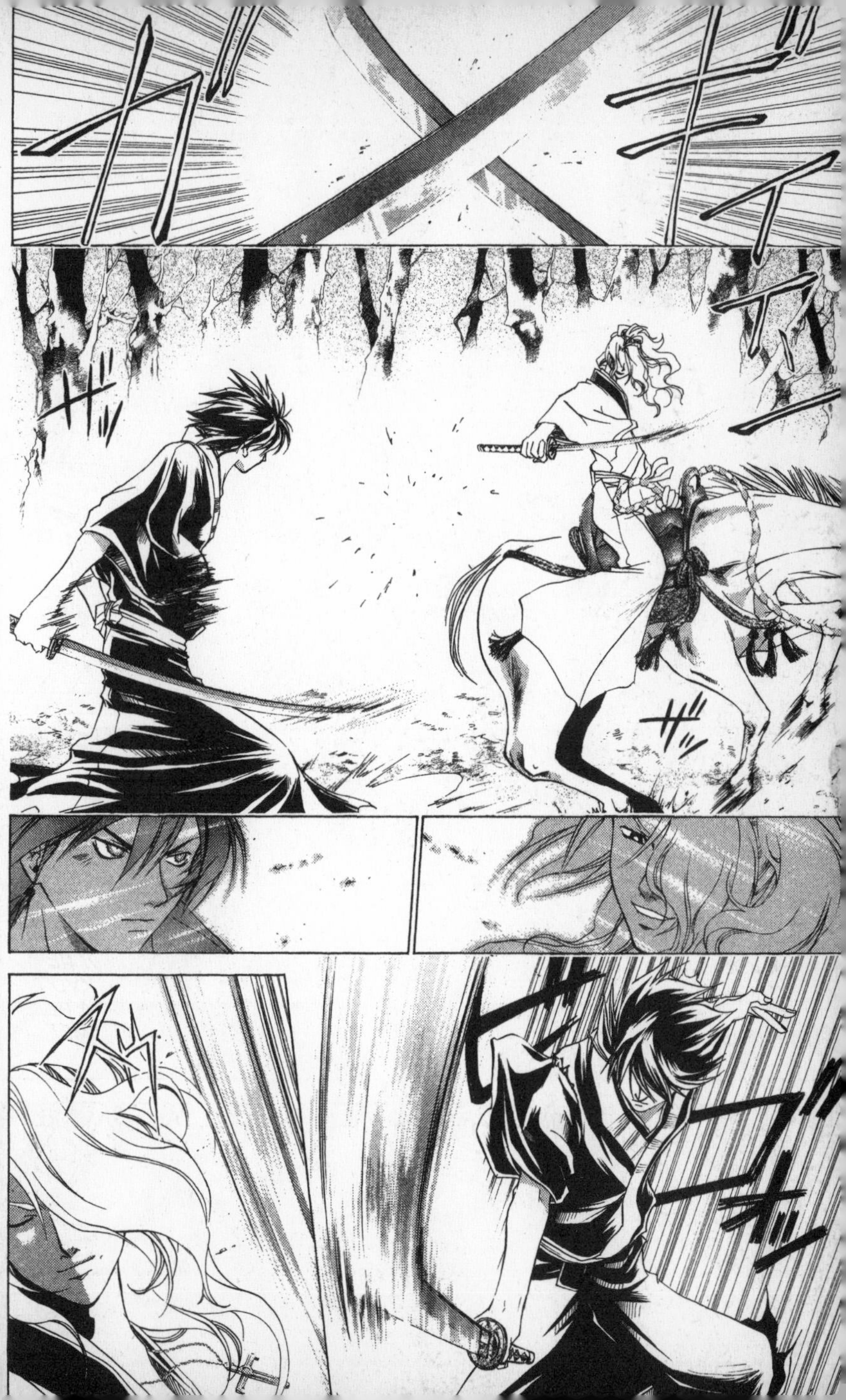
ザッ
ザッ

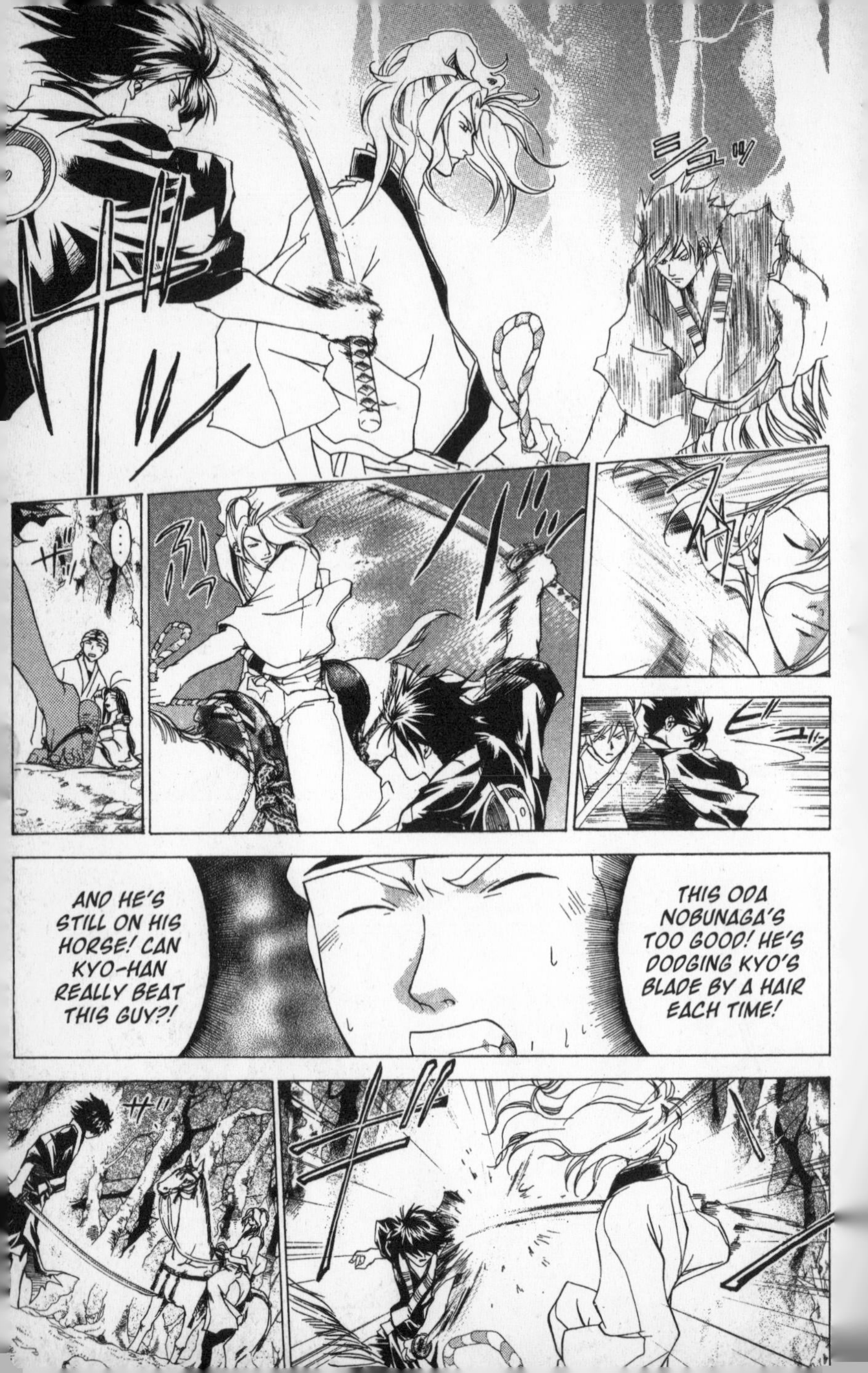
THIS ODA NOBUNAGA'S TOO GOOD! HE'S DODGING KYO'S BLADE BY A HAIR EACH TIME!
AND HE'S STILL ON HIS HORSE! CAN KYO-HAN REALLY BEAT THIS GUY?!

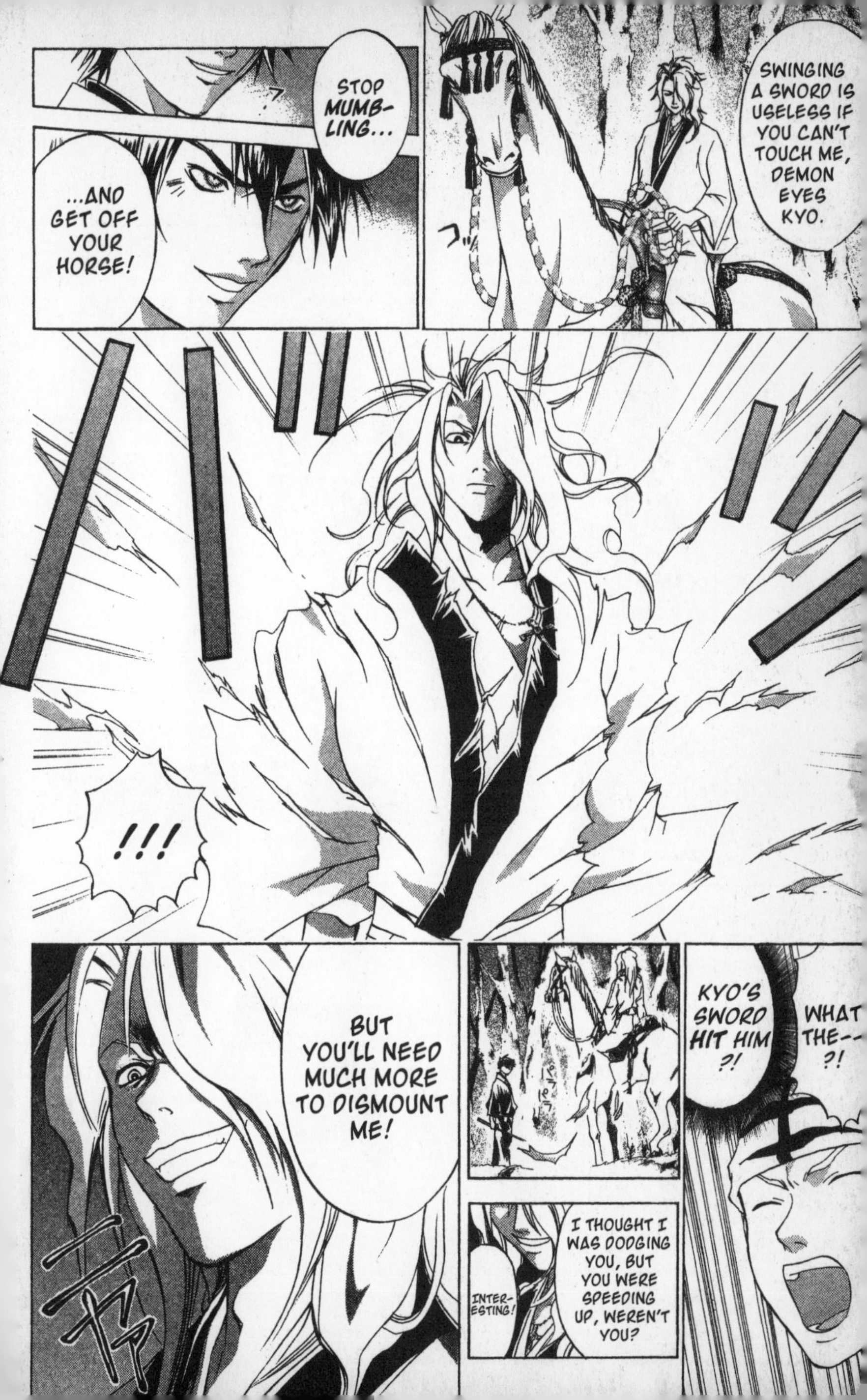
SWINGING A SWORD IS USELESS IF YOU CAN'T TOUCH ME, DEMON EYES KYO.
STOP MUMBLING...
...AND GET OFF YOUR HORSE!
!!!
WHAT THE--?!
KYO'S SWORD HIT HIM?!
I THOUGHT I WAS DODGING YOU, BUT YOU WERE SPEEDING UP, WEREN'T YOU?
INTERESTING!
BUT YOU'LL NEED MUCH MORE TO DISMOUNT ME!

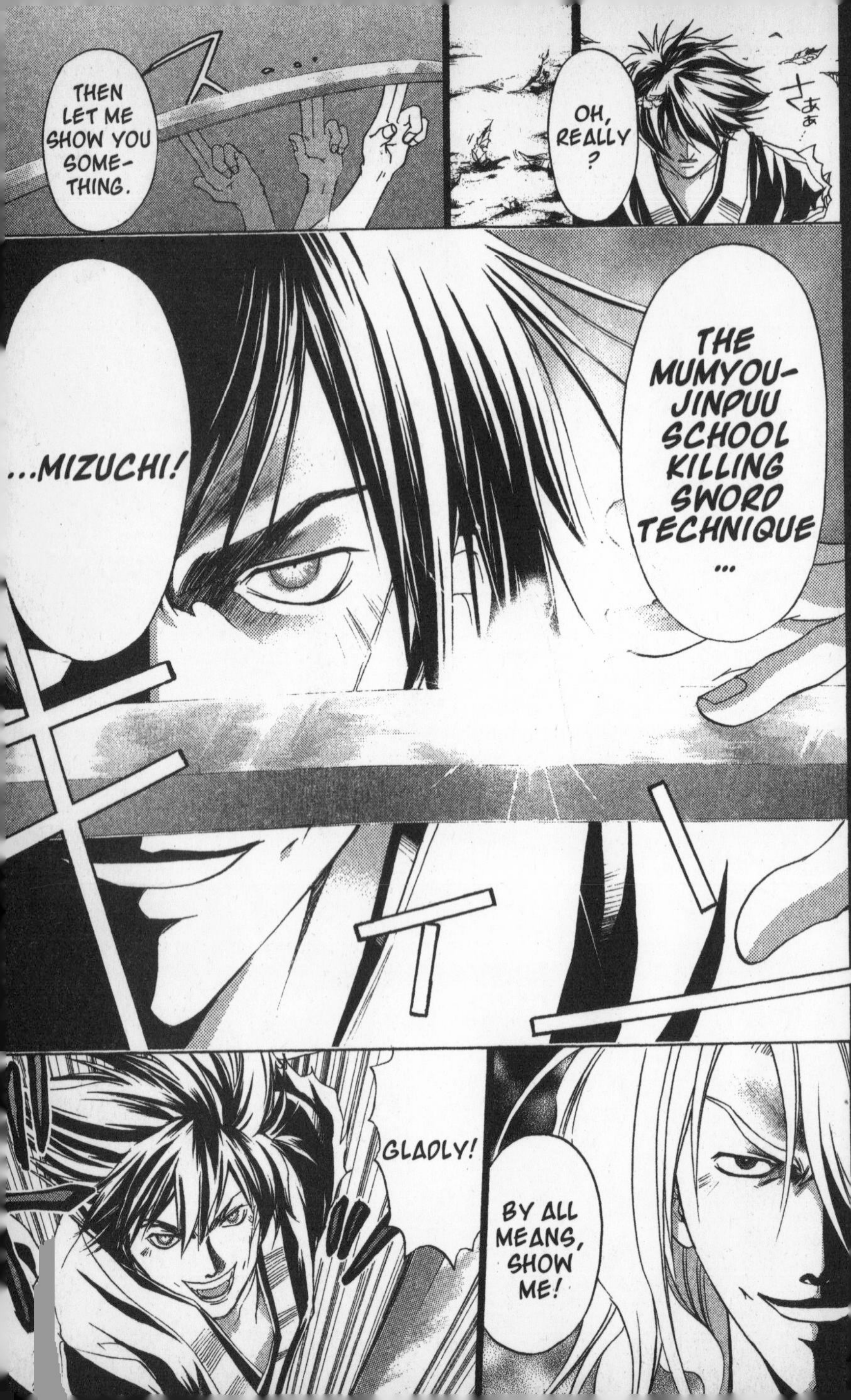
OH, REALLY?
THEN LET ME SHOW YOU SOME-THING.
THE MUMYOU-JINPUU SCHOOL KILLING SWORD TECHNIQUE...
...MIZUCHI!
BY ALL MEANS, SHOW ME!
GLADLY!

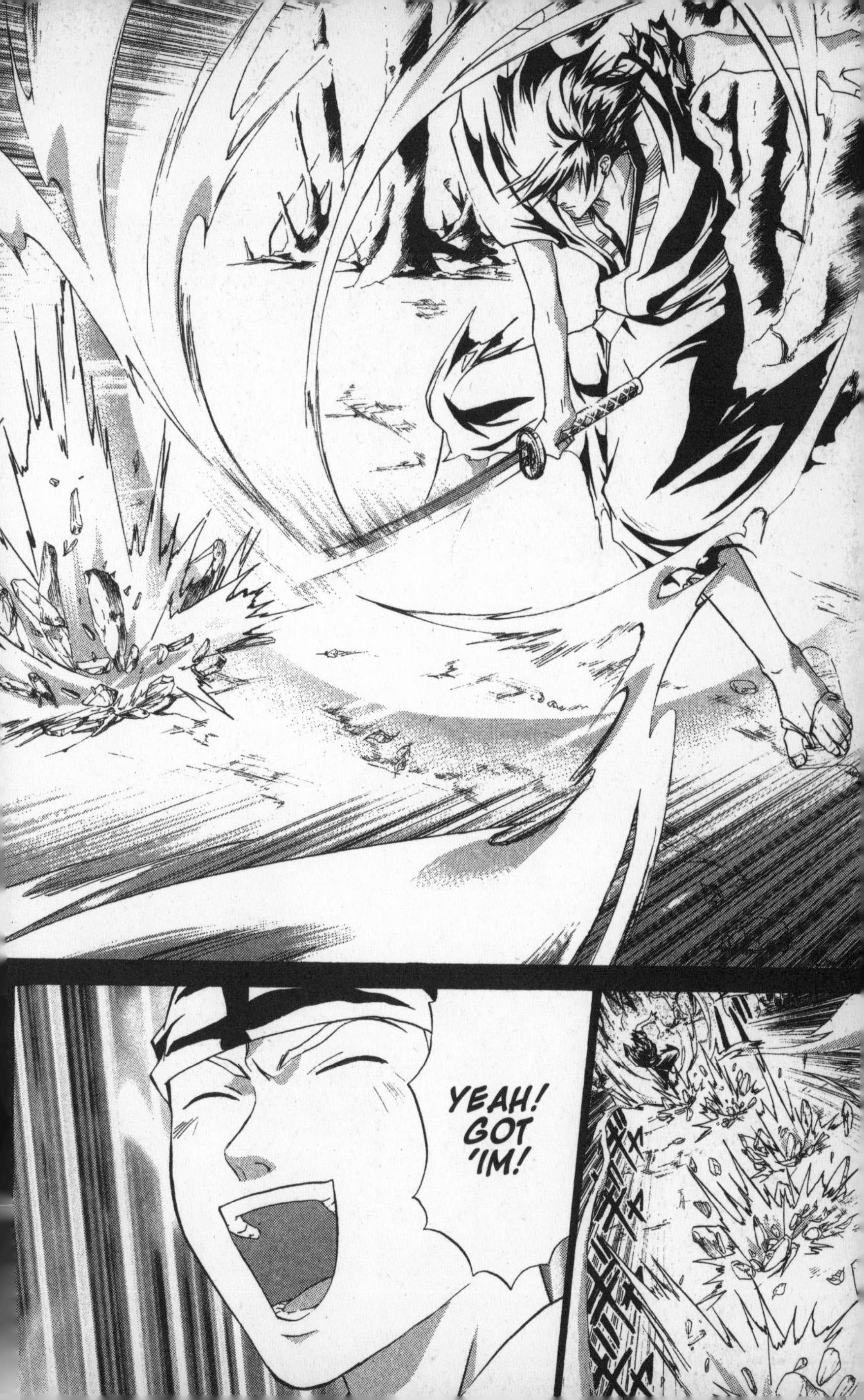
YEAH! GOT 'IM!

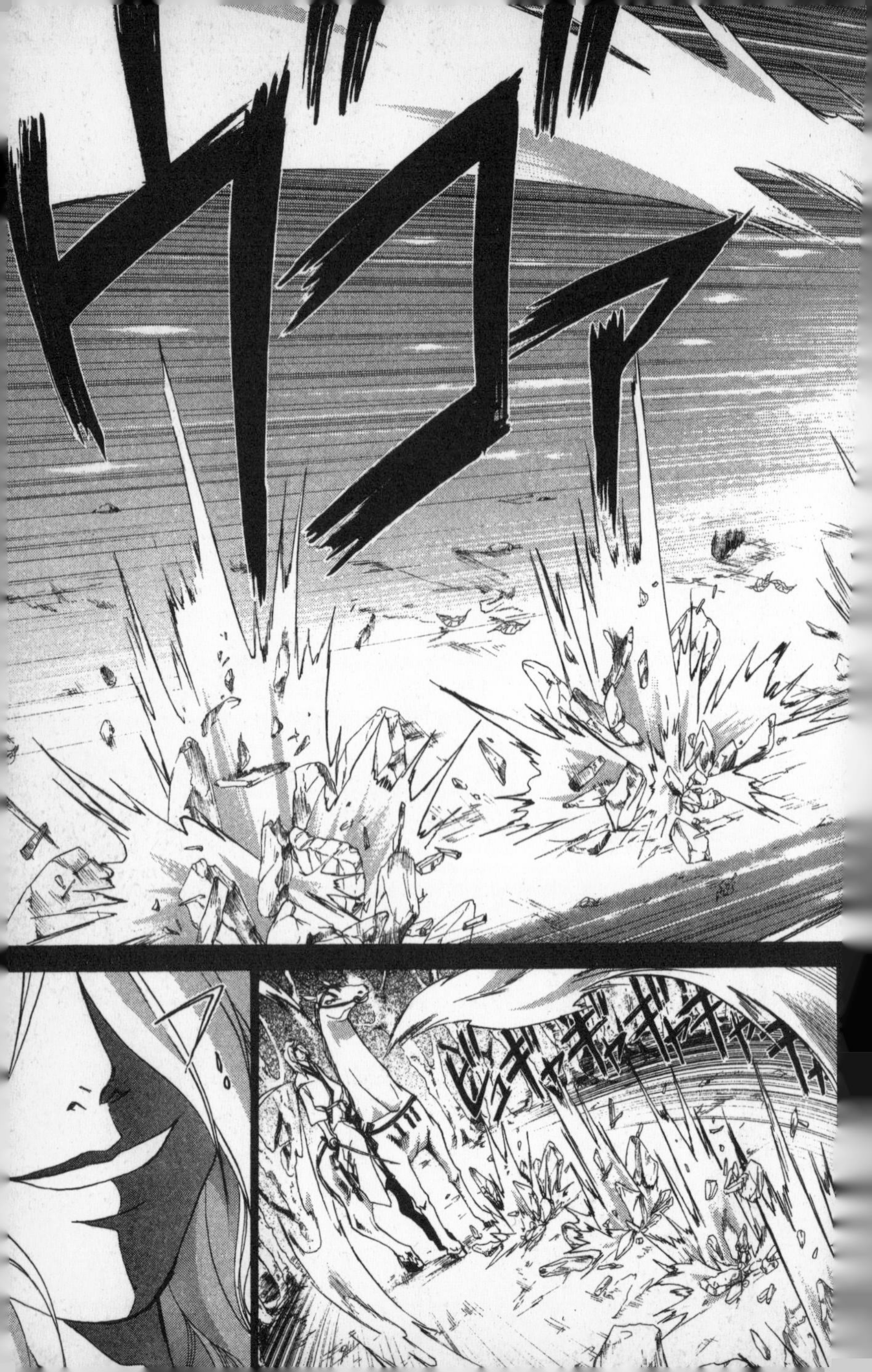
ビッギャギャギャキャキャキィ

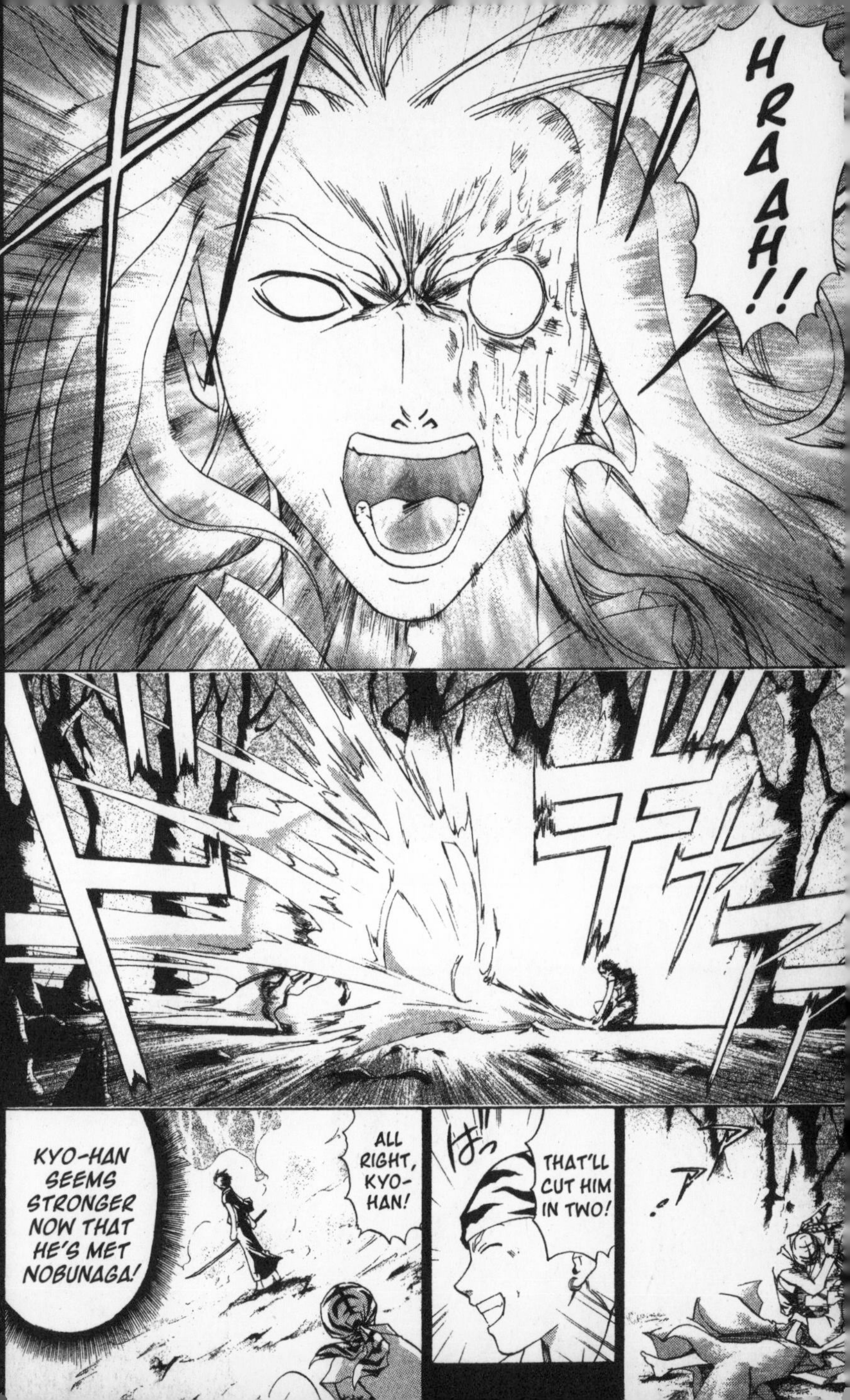
HRAAAH!!
ばっ
THAT'LL CUT HIM IN TWO!
ALL RIGHT, KYO-HAN!
KYO-HAN SEEMS STRONGER NOW THAT HE'S MET NOBUNAGA!

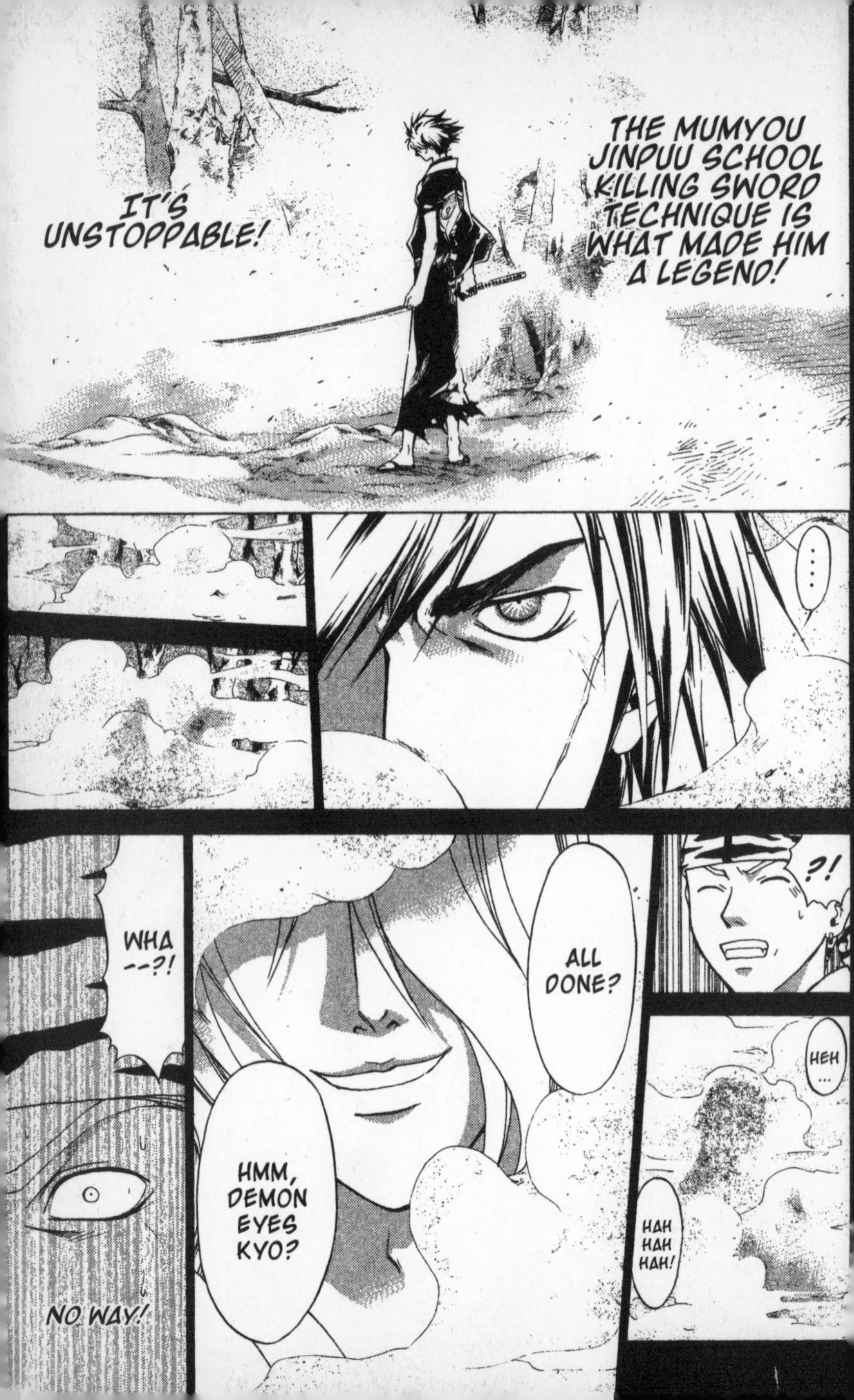
THE MUMYOU JINPUU SCHOOL KILLING SWORD TECHNIQUE IS WHAT MADE HIM A LEGEND!
IT'S UNSTOPPABLE!
...
?!
HEH...
HAH HAH HAH!
ALL DONE?
HMM, DEMON EYES KYO?
WHA--?!
NO WAY!

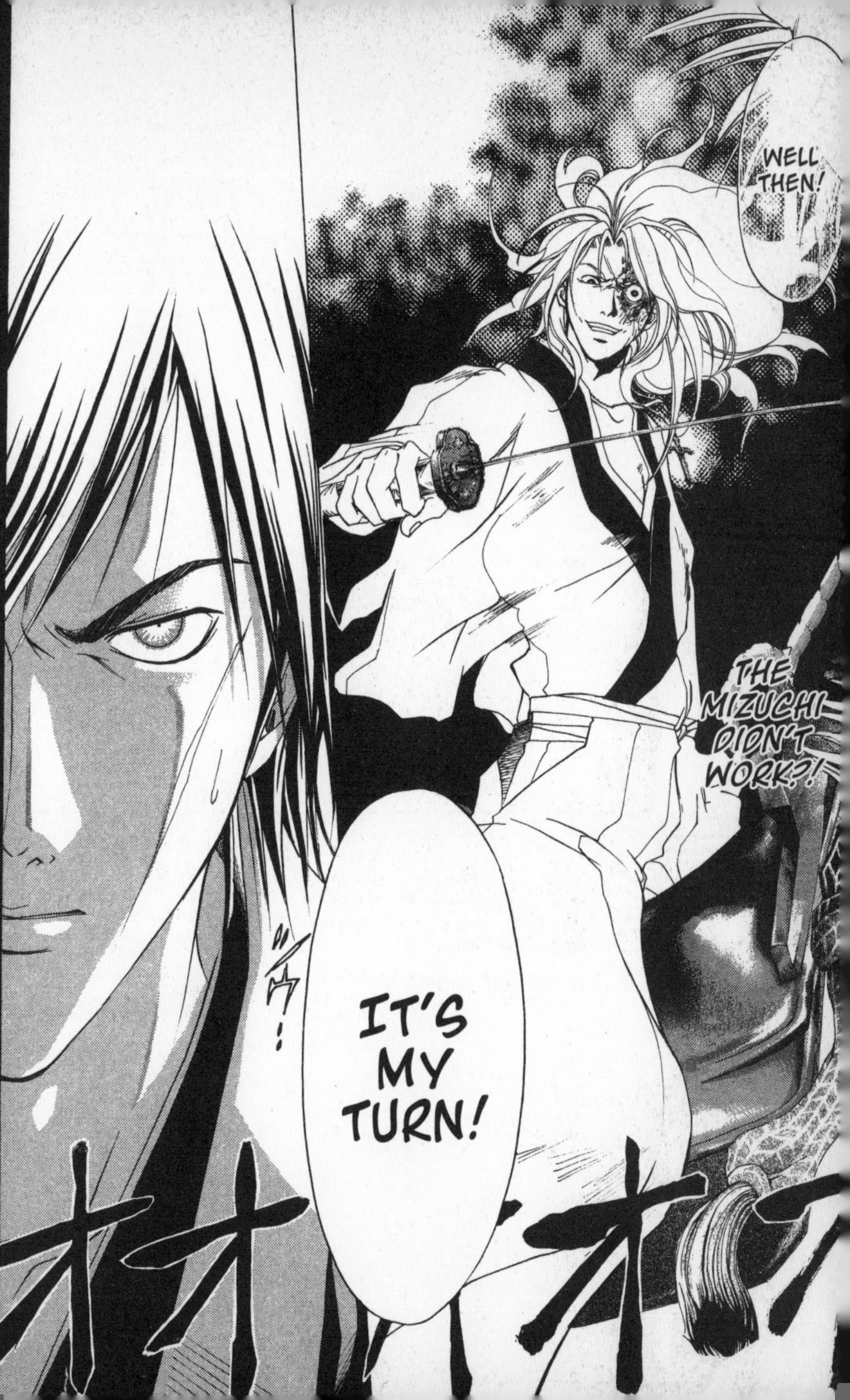
WELL THEN!
THE MIZUCHI DIDN'T WORK?!
IT'S MY TURN!

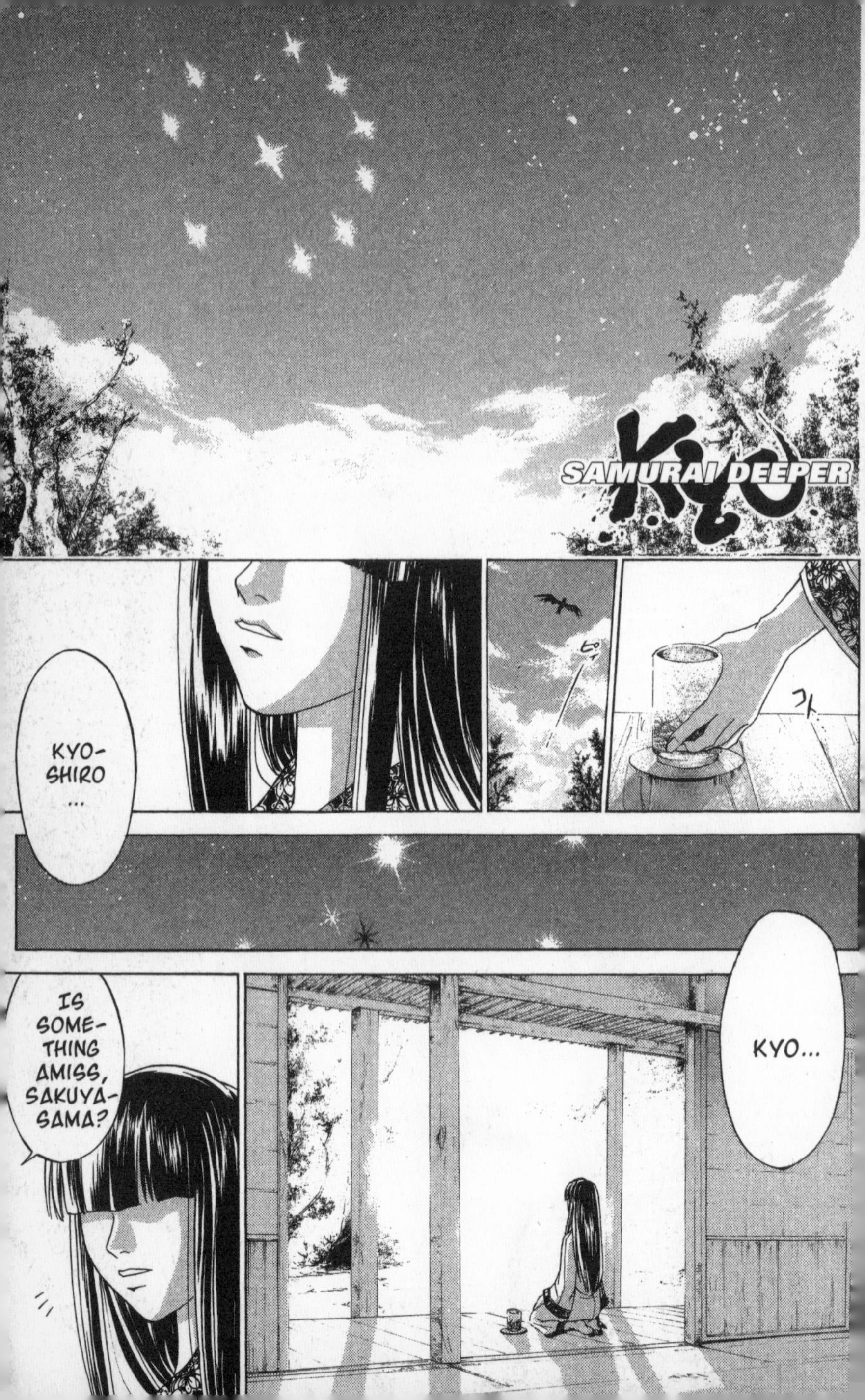
SAMURAI DEEPER
KYO
KYO-SHIRO ...
KYO...
IS SOMETHING AMISS, SAKUYA-SAMA?

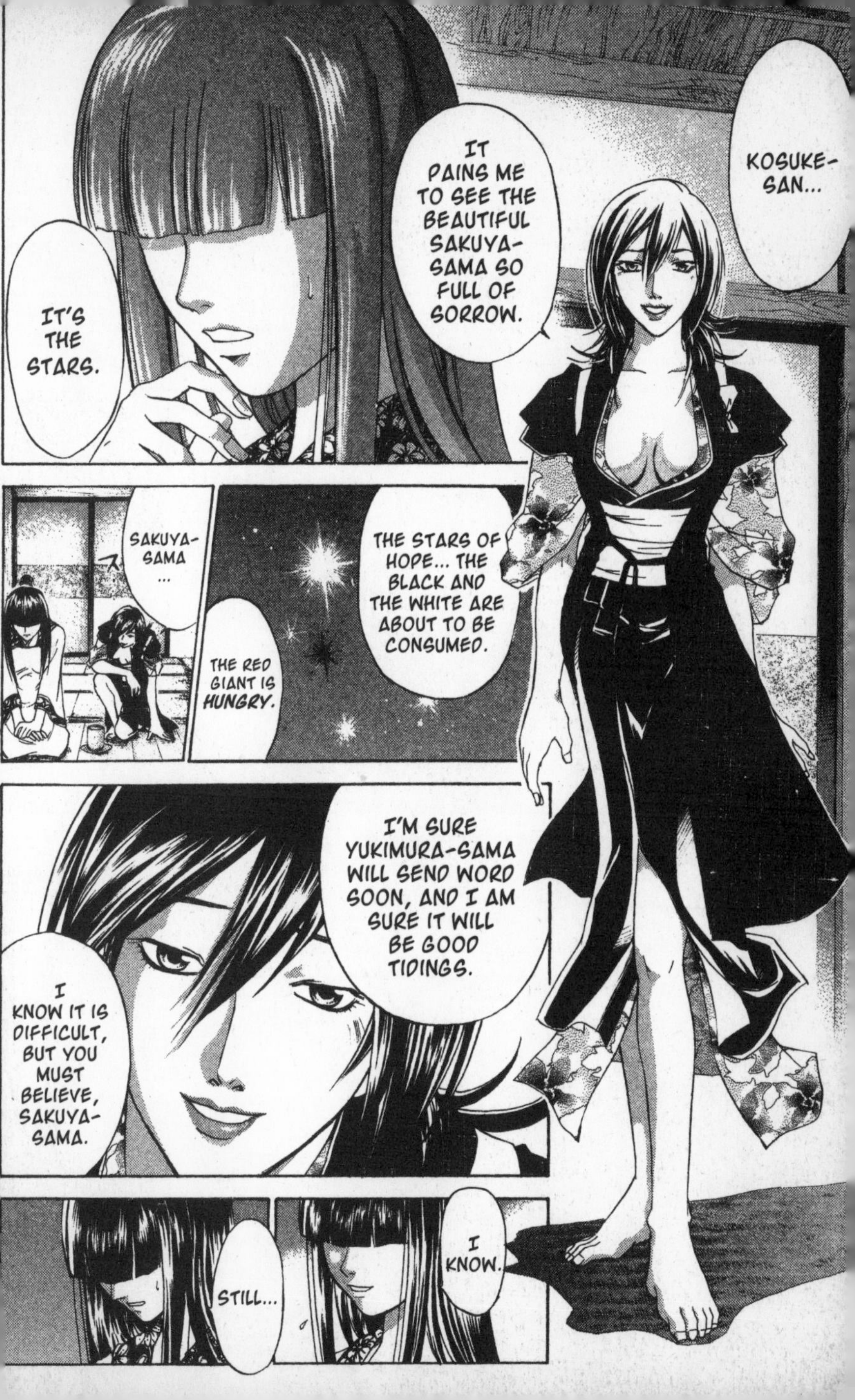

KOSUKE-SAN...
IT PAINS ME TO SEE THE BEAUTIFUL SAKUYA-SAMA SO FULL OF SORROW.
IT'S THE STARS.
THE STARS OF HOPE... THE BLACK AND THE WHITE ARE ABOUT TO BE CONSUMED.
THE RED GIANT IS HUNGRY.
SAKUYA-SAMA ...
I'M SURE YUKIMURA-SAMA WILL SEND WORD SOON, AND I AM SURE IT WILL BE GOOD TIDINGS.
I KNOW IT IS DIFFICULT, BUT YOU MUST BELIEVE, SAKUYA-SAMA.
I KNOW.
STILL...

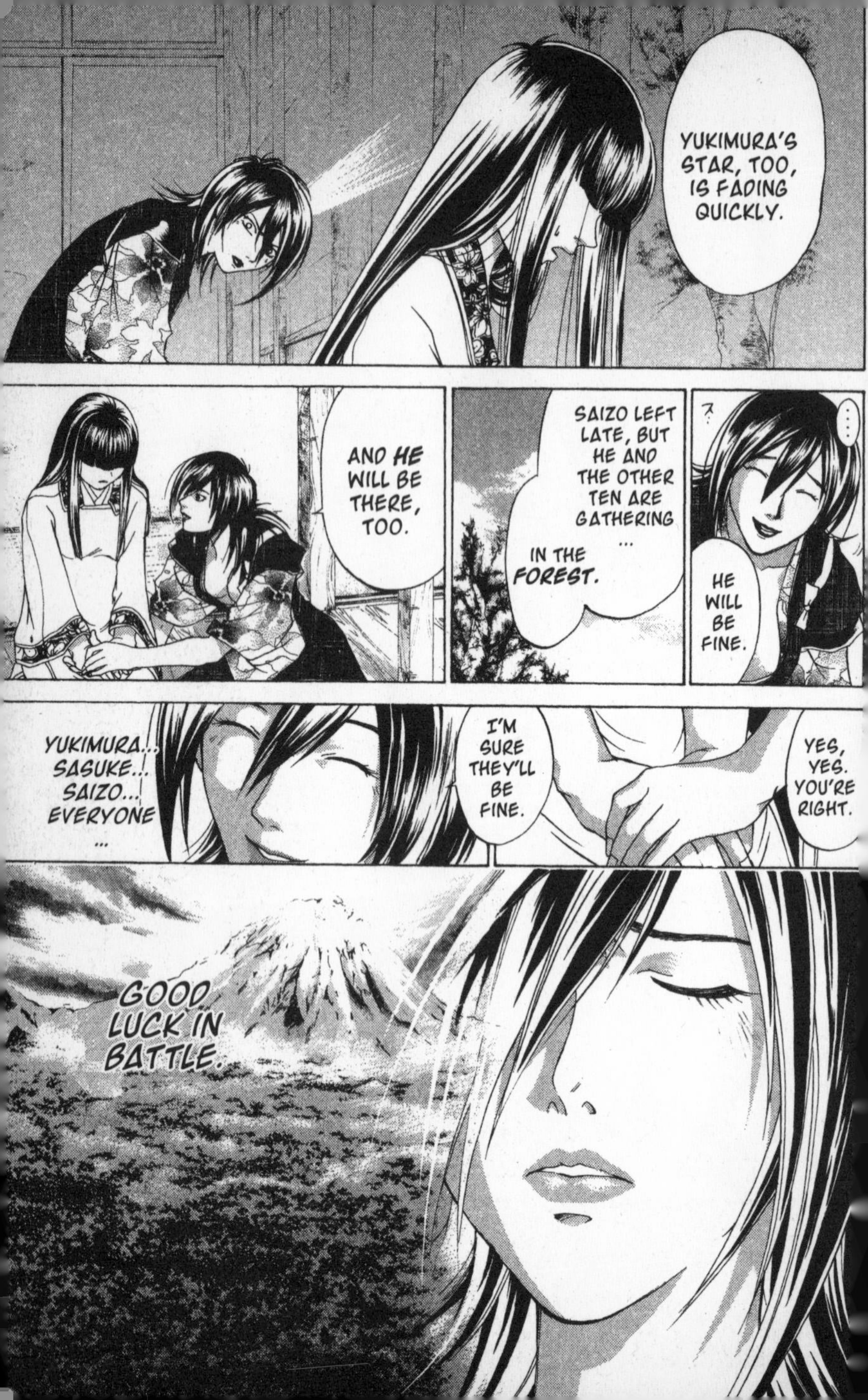
YUKIMURA'S STAR, TOO, IS FADING QUICKLY.
...
HE WILL BE FINE.
SAIZO LEFT LATE, BUT HE AND THE OTHER TEN ARE GATHERING ...
IN THE FOREST.
AND HE WILL BE THERE, TOO.
YES, YES. YOU'RE RIGHT.
I'M SURE THEY'LL BE FINE.
YUKIMURA... SASUKE... SAIZO... EVERYONE ...
GOOD LUCK IN BATTLE.

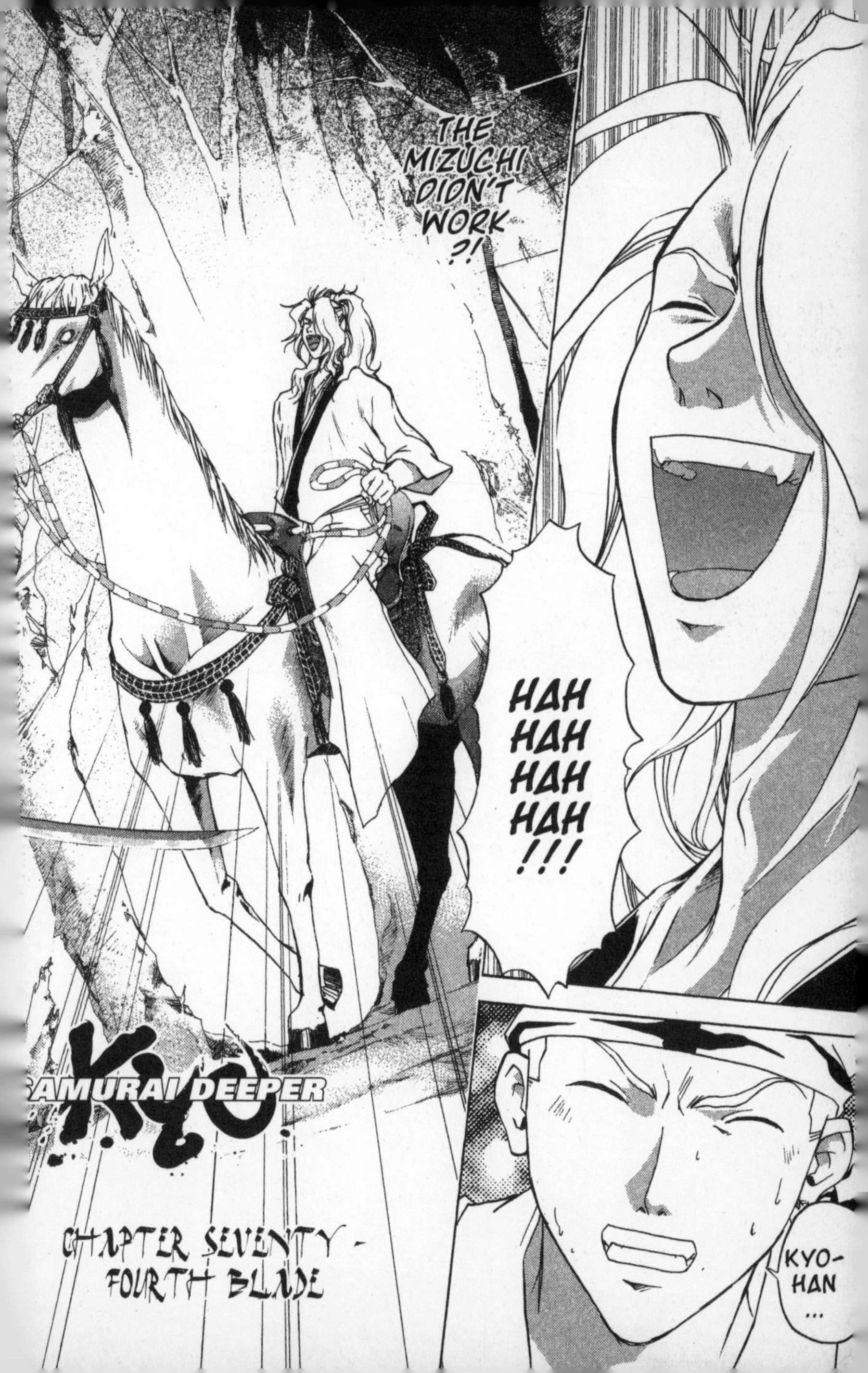
HAH HAH HAH HAH!!!
KYO-HAN...
THE MIZUCHI DIDN'T WORK?!
SAMURAI DEEPER KYO
CHAPTER SEVENTY-FOURTH BLADE

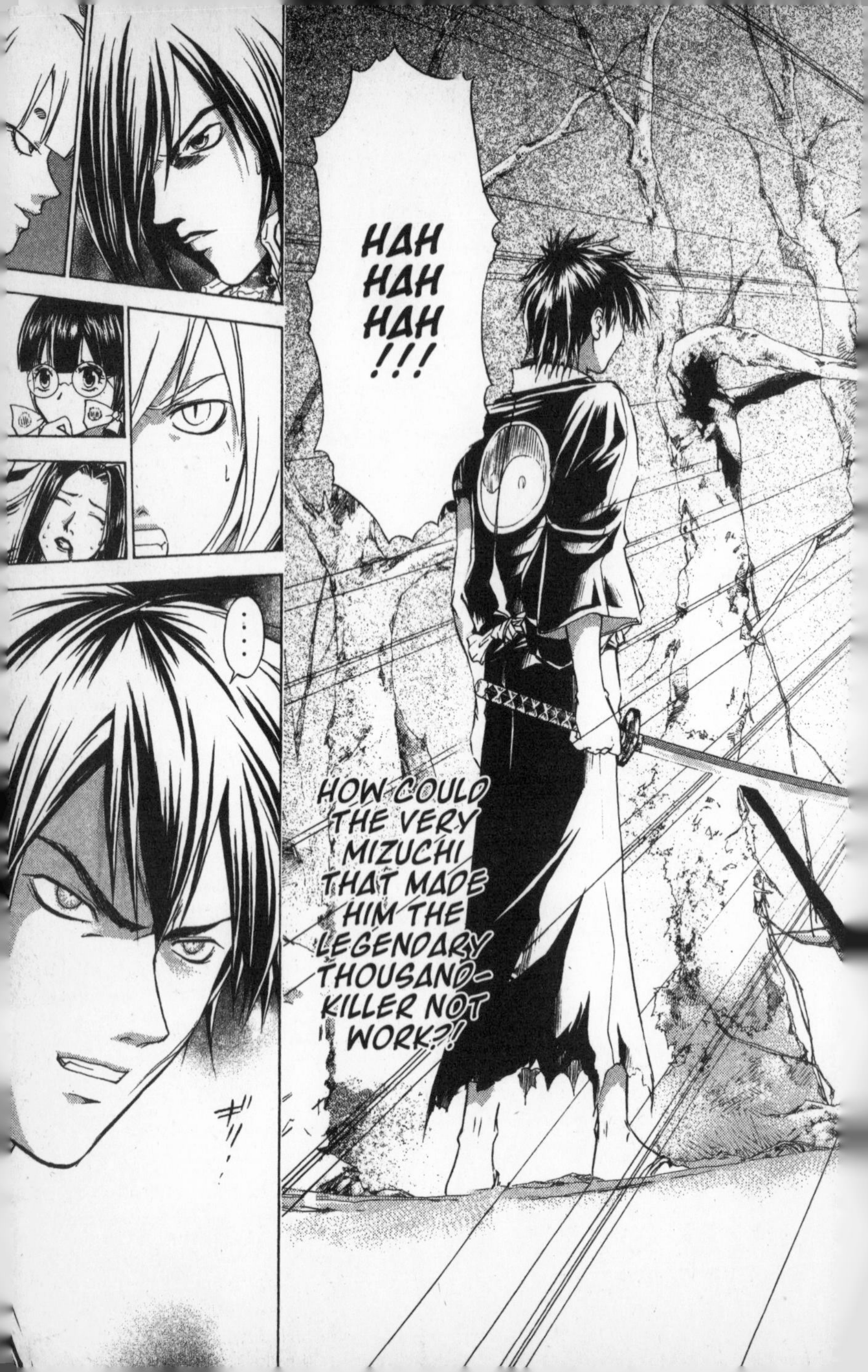
HAH HAH HAH !!!
HOW COULD THE VERY MIZUCHI THAT MADE HIM THE LEGENDARY THOUSAND-KILLER NOT WORK?!
....
ギリ

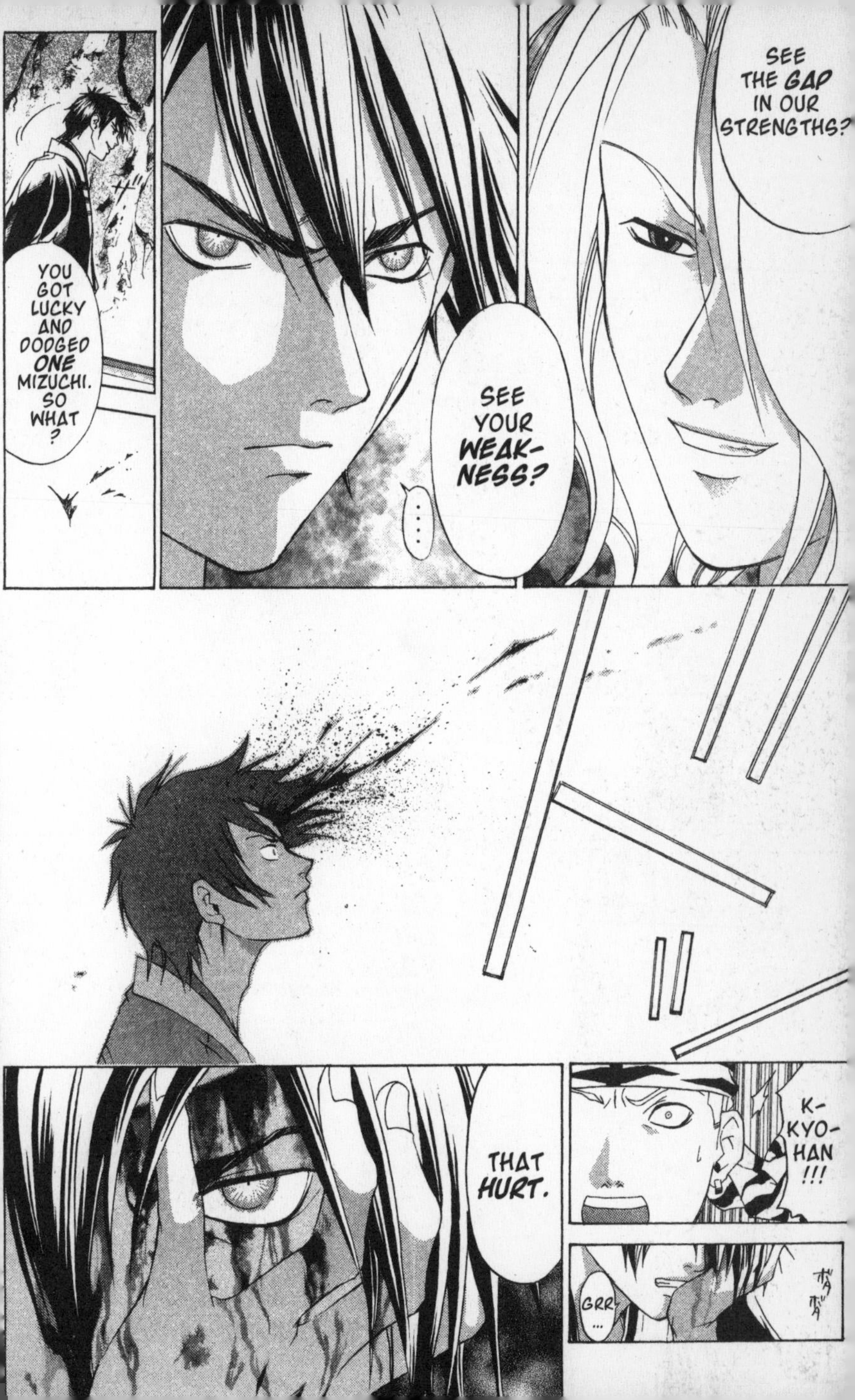
SEE THE GAP IN OUR STRENGTHS?
SEE YOUR WEAKNESS?
......
YOU GOT LUCKY AND DODGED ONE MIZUCHI. SO WHAT?
K-KYOHAN!!!
GRR...
THAT HURT.

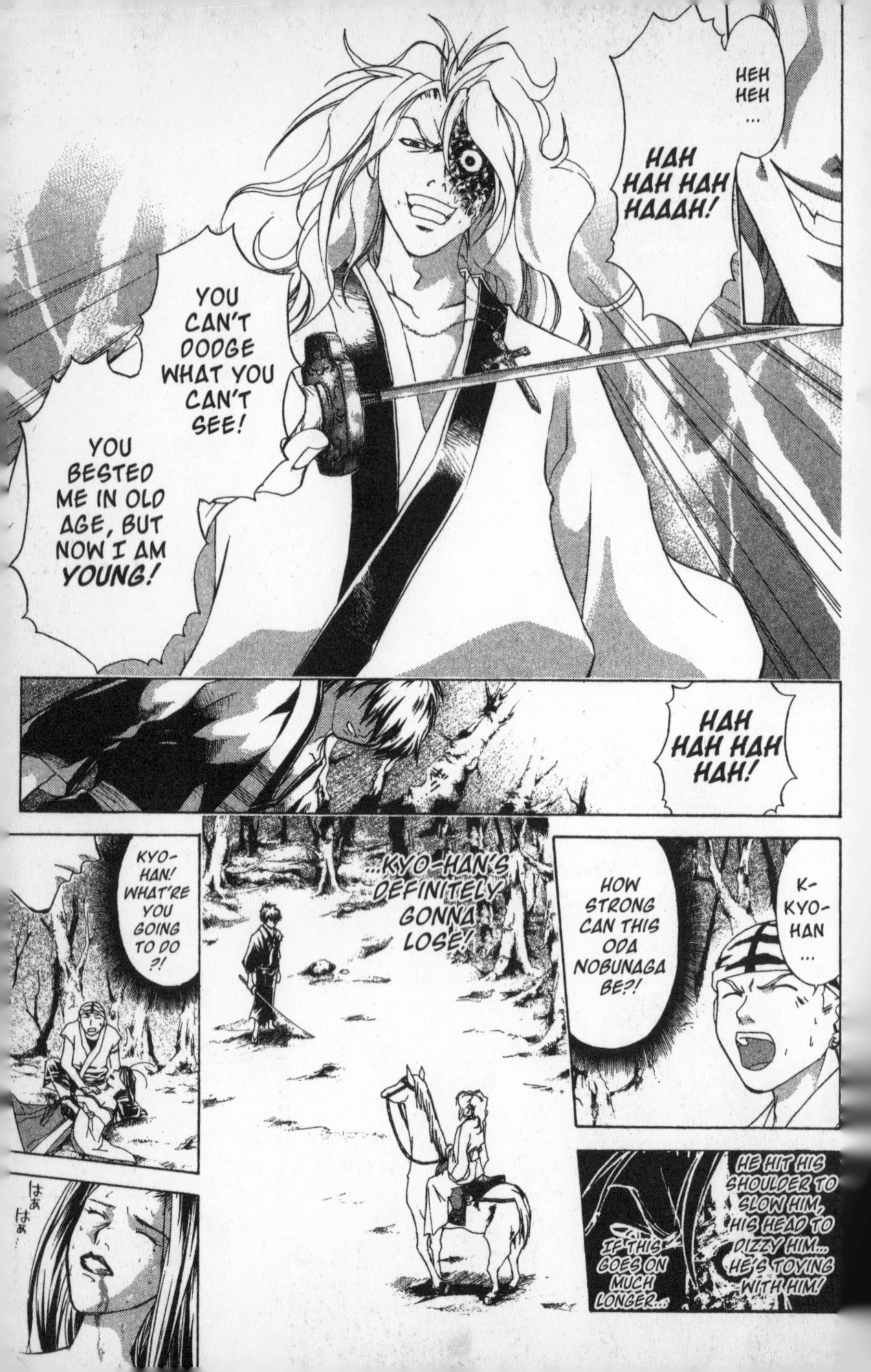
HEH HEH ...
HAH HAH HAH HAAAH!
YOU CAN'T DODGE WHAT YOU CAN'T SEE!
YOU BESTED ME IN OLD AGE, BUT NOW I AM YOUNG!
HAH HAH HAH HAH!
K-KYO-HAN ...
HOW STRONG CAN THIS ODA NOBUNAGA BE?!
HE HIT HIS SHOULDER TO SLOW HIM, HIS HEAD TO DIZZY HIM... HE'S TOYING WITH HIM!
IF THIS GOES ON MUCH LONGER...
...KYO-HAN'S DEFINITELY GONNA LOSE!
KYO-HAN! WHAT'RE YOU GOING TO DO ?!
はあ はあ…

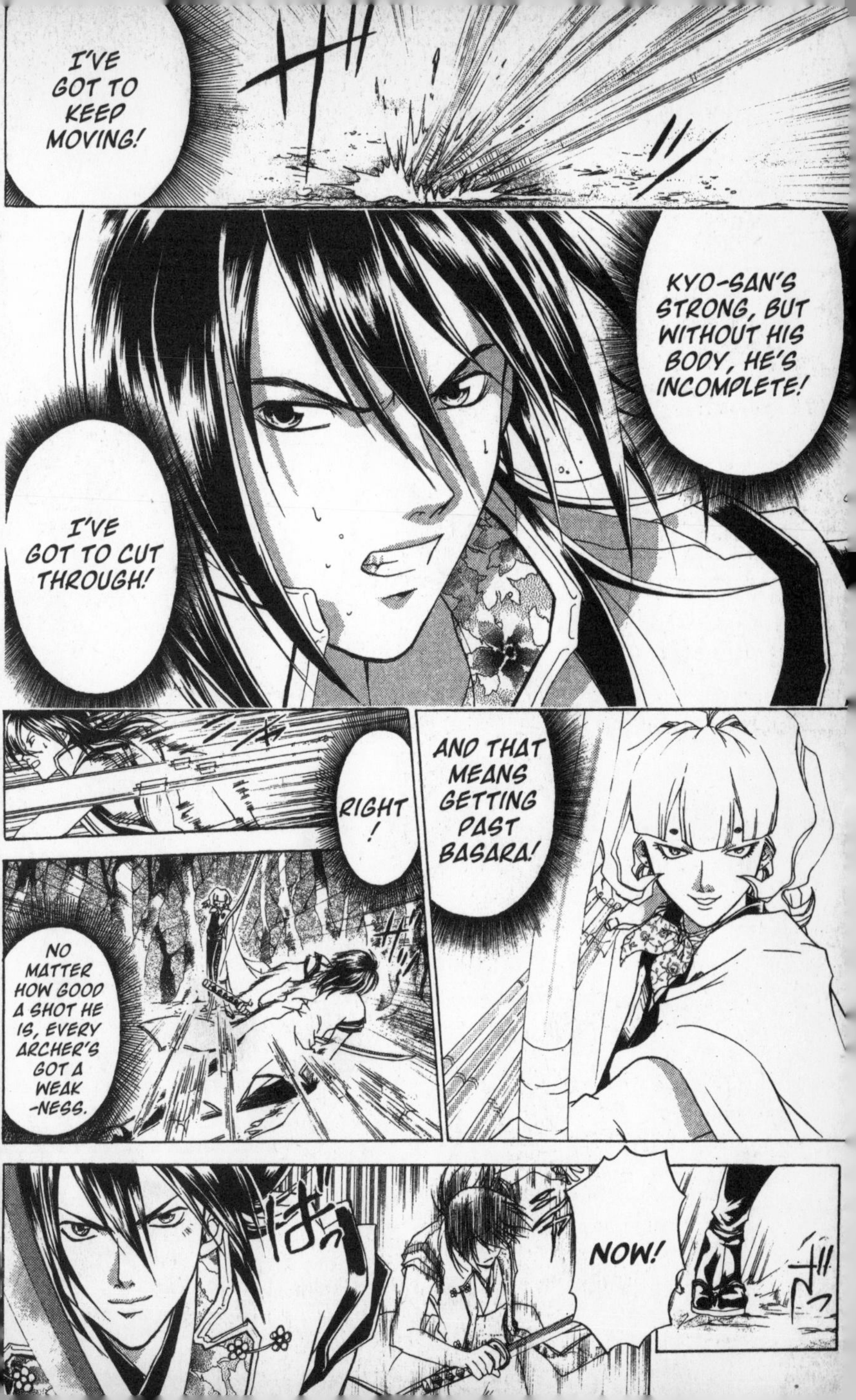

I'VE GOT TO KEEP MOVING!
KYO-SAN'S STRONG, BUT WITHOUT HIS BODY, HE'S INCOMPLETE!
I'VE GOT TO CUT THROUGH!
AND THAT MEANS GETTING PAST BASARA!
RIGHT!
NO MATTER HOW GOOD A SHOT HE IS, EVERY ARCHER'S GOT A WEAK-NESS.
NOW!
はっ

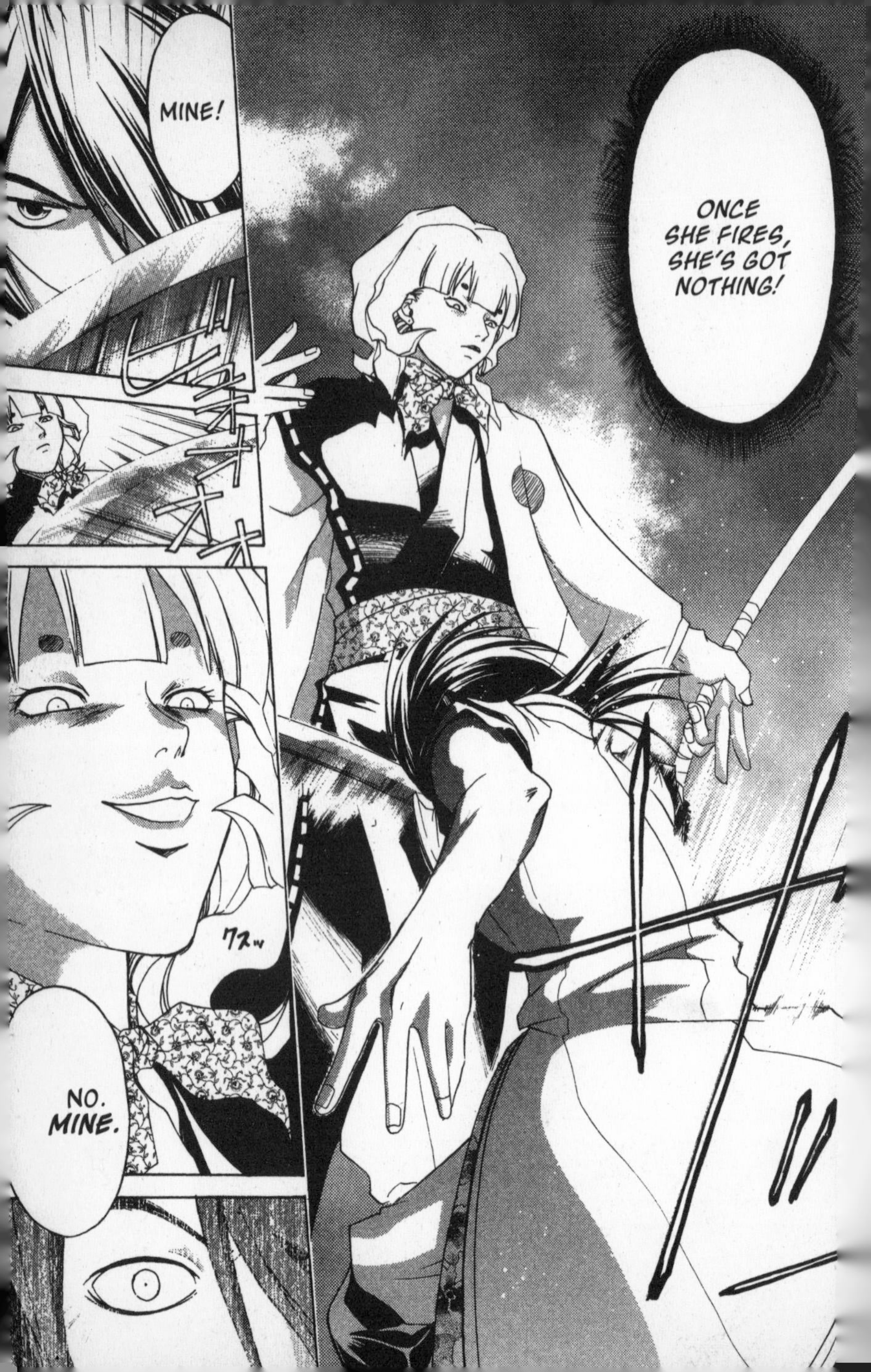
ONCE SHE FIRES, SHE'S GOT NOTHING!
MINE!
NO. MINE.

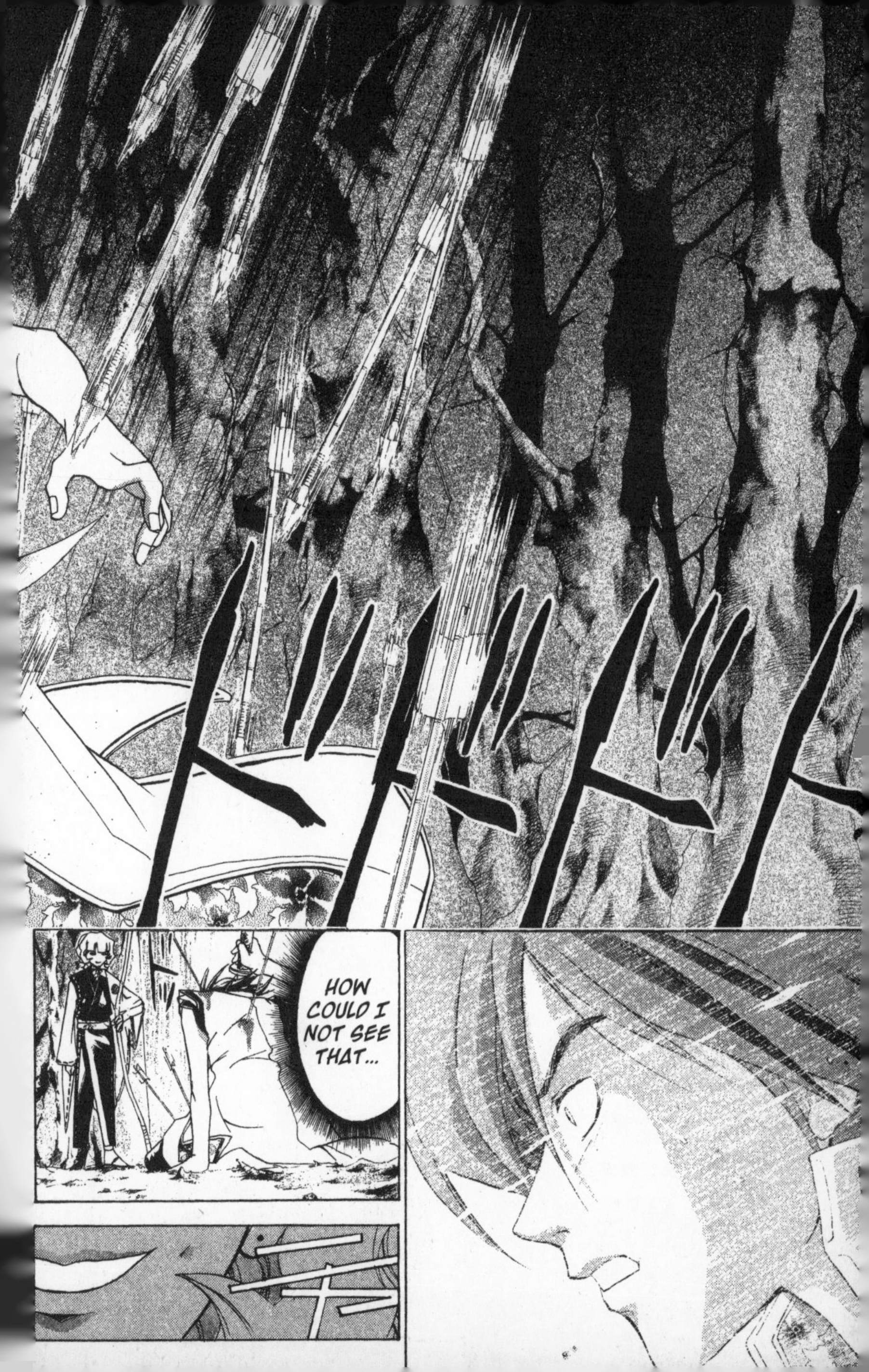
HOW COULD I NOT SEE THAT...

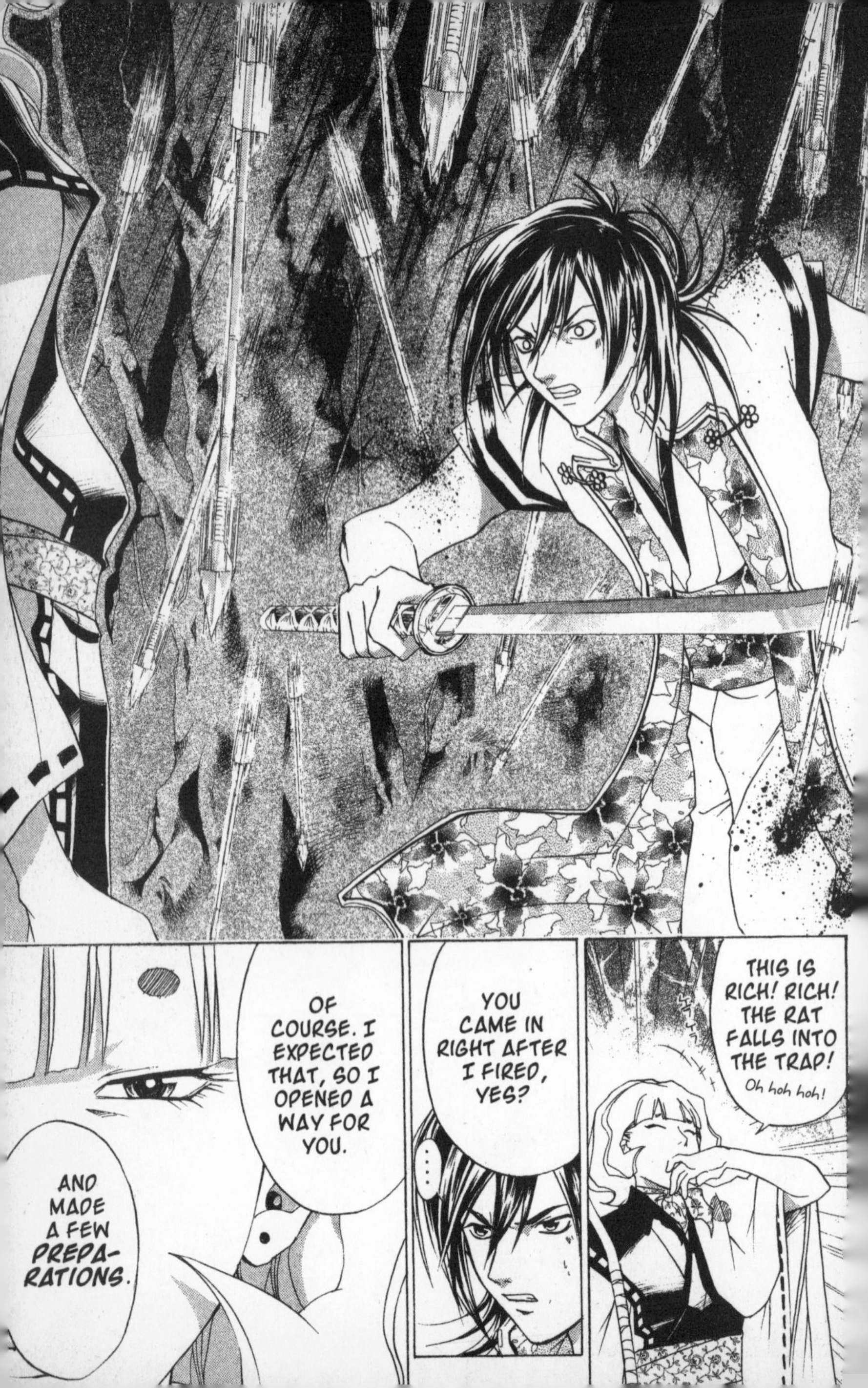
THIS IS RICH! RICH! THE RAT FALLS INTO THE TRAP!
Oh hoh hoh!
YOU CAME IN RIGHT AFTER I FIRED, YES?
...
OF COURSE. I EXPECTED THAT, SO I OPENED A WAY FOR YOU.
AND MADE A FEW PREPARATIONS.

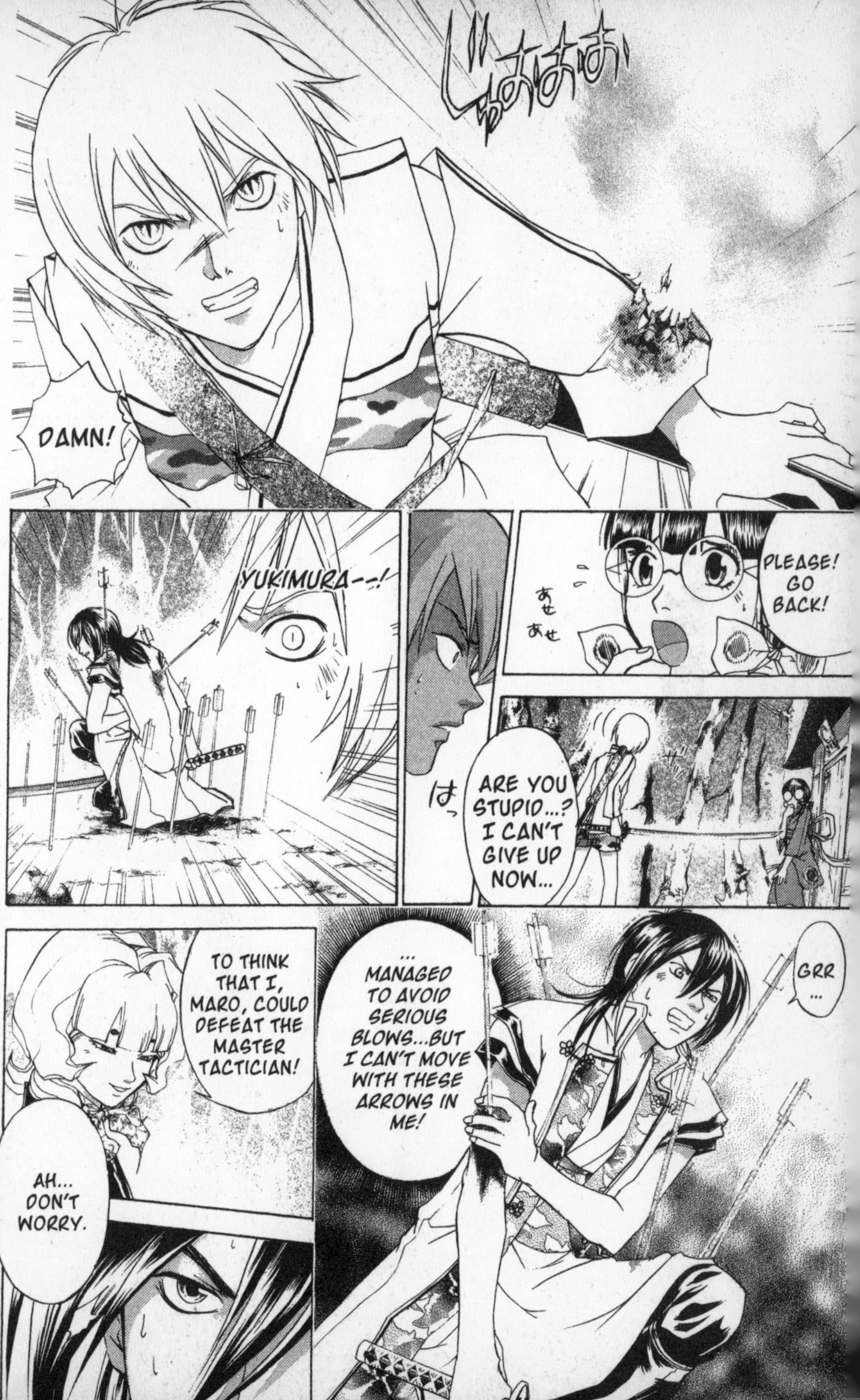

じゅおおお
DAMN!
PLEASE! GO BACK!
あせ あせ
ARE YOU STUPID...? I CAN'T GIVE UP NOW...
はっ
YUKIMURA--!
GRR ...
... MANAGED TO AVOID SERIOUS BLOWS...BUT I CAN'T MOVE WITH THESE ARROWS IN ME!
TO THINK THAT I, MARO, COULD DEFEAT THE MASTER TACTICIAN!
AH... DON'T WORRY.

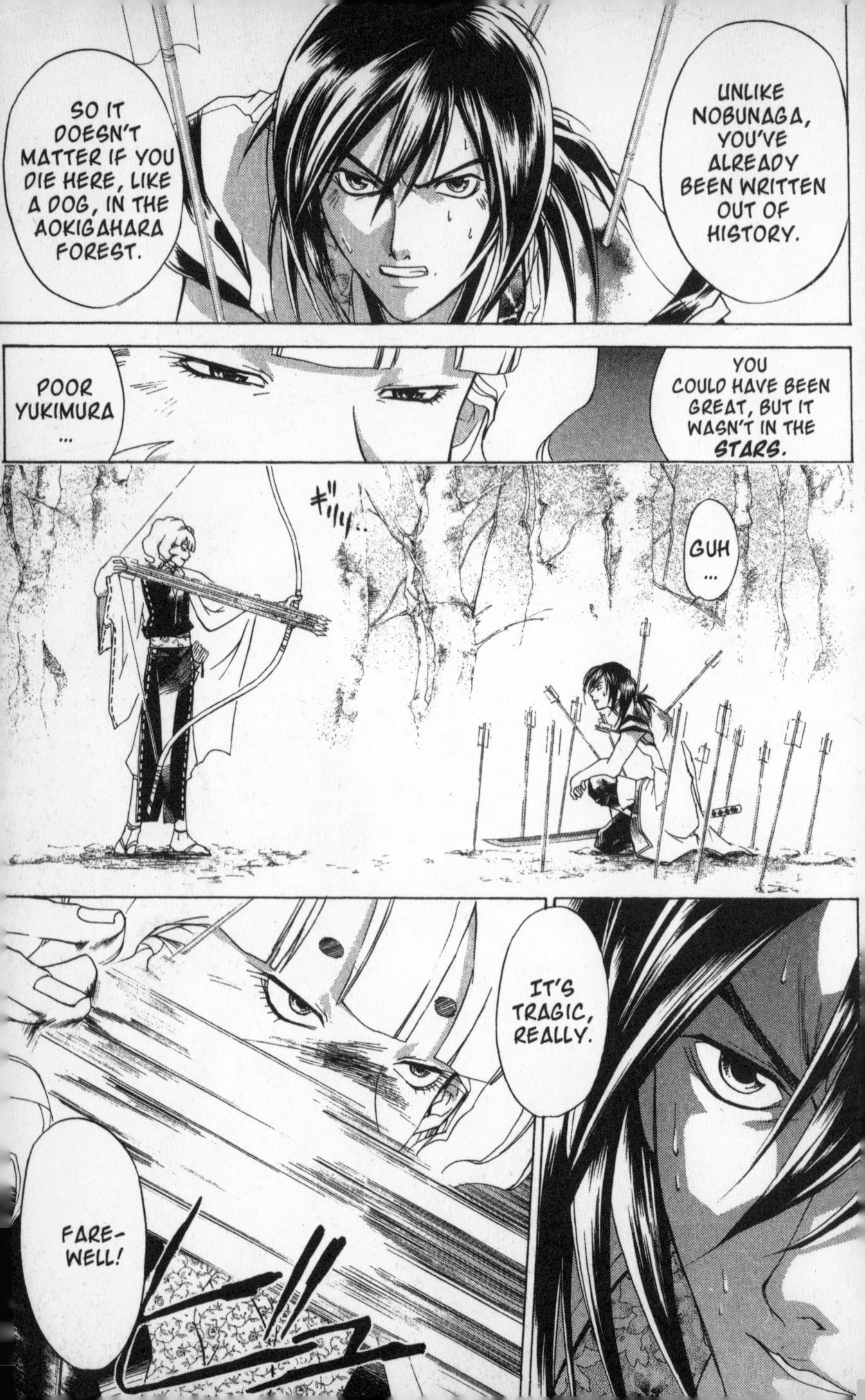
UNLIKE NOBUNAGA, YOU'VE ALREADY BEEN WRITTEN OUT OF HISTORY.
SO IT DOESN'T MATTER IF YOU DIE HERE, LIKE A DOG, IN THE AOKIGAHARA FOREST.
YOU COULD HAVE BEEN GREAT, BUT IT WASN'T IN THE STARS.
POOR YUKIMURA ...
GUH ...
ギリリ..
IT'S TRAGIC, REALLY.
FARE-WELL!

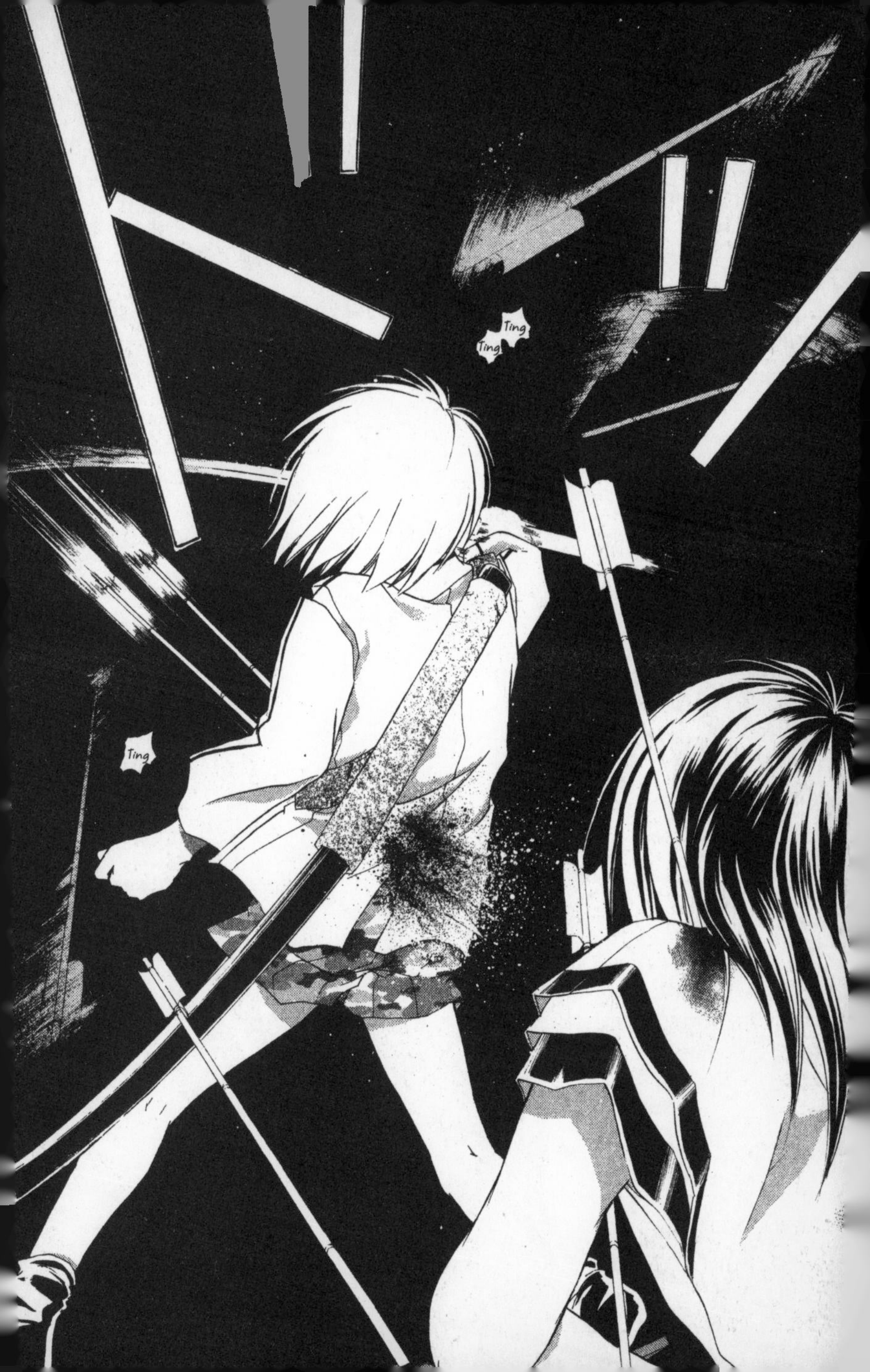
Ting
Ting
Ting

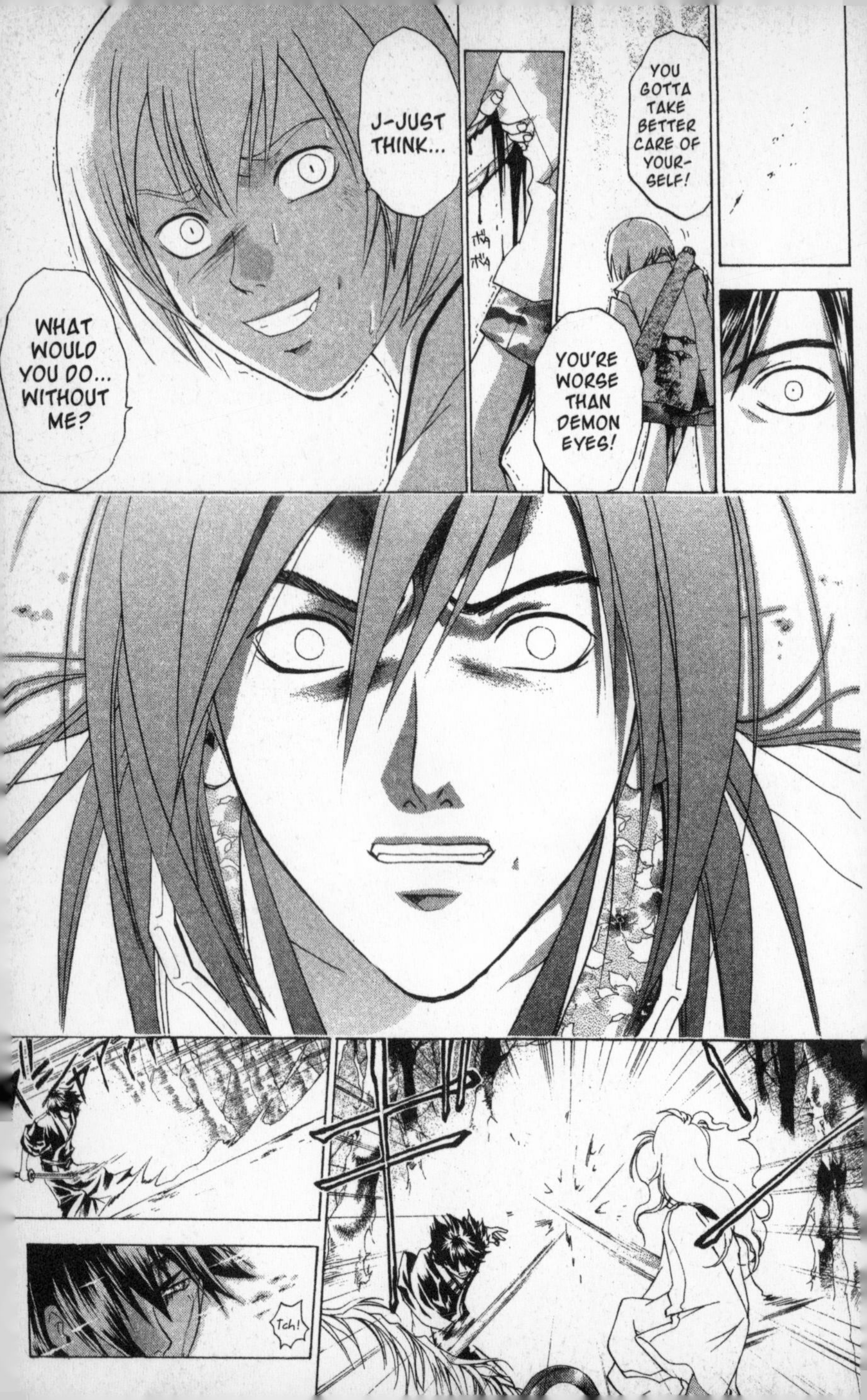
YOU GOTTA TAKE BETTER CARE OF YOUR-SELF!
YOU'RE WORSE THAN DEMON EYES!
J-JUST THINK...
WHAT WOULD YOU DO... WITHOUT ME?
Tch!

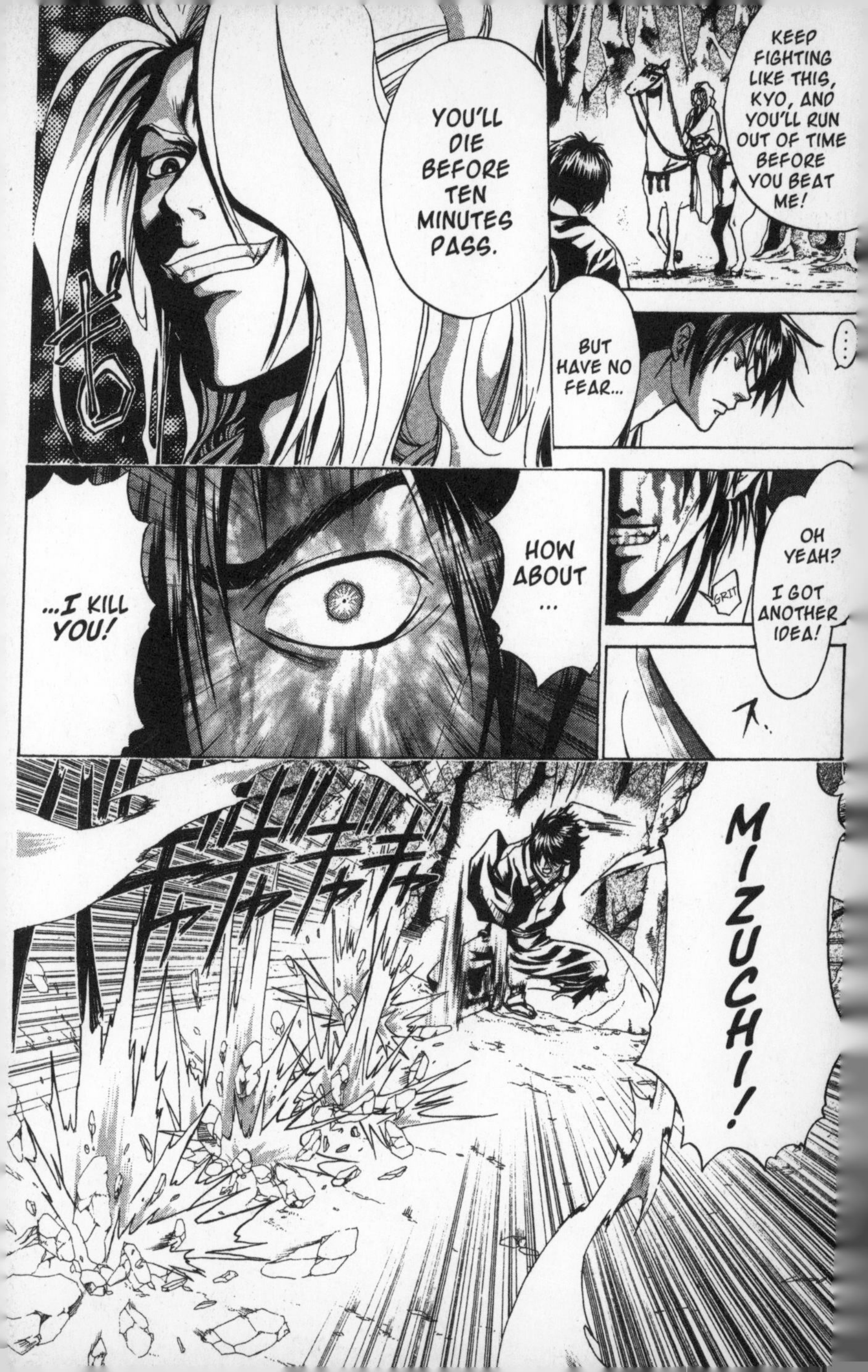
KEEP FIGHTING LIKE THIS, KYO, AND YOU'LL RUN OUT OF TIME BEFORE YOU BEAT ME!
BUT HAVE NO FEAR...
...
YOU'LL DIE BEFORE TEN MINUTES PASS.
OH YEAH?
GRIT
I GOT ANOTHER IDEA!
HOW ABOUT ...
...I KILL YOU!
MIZUCHI!!

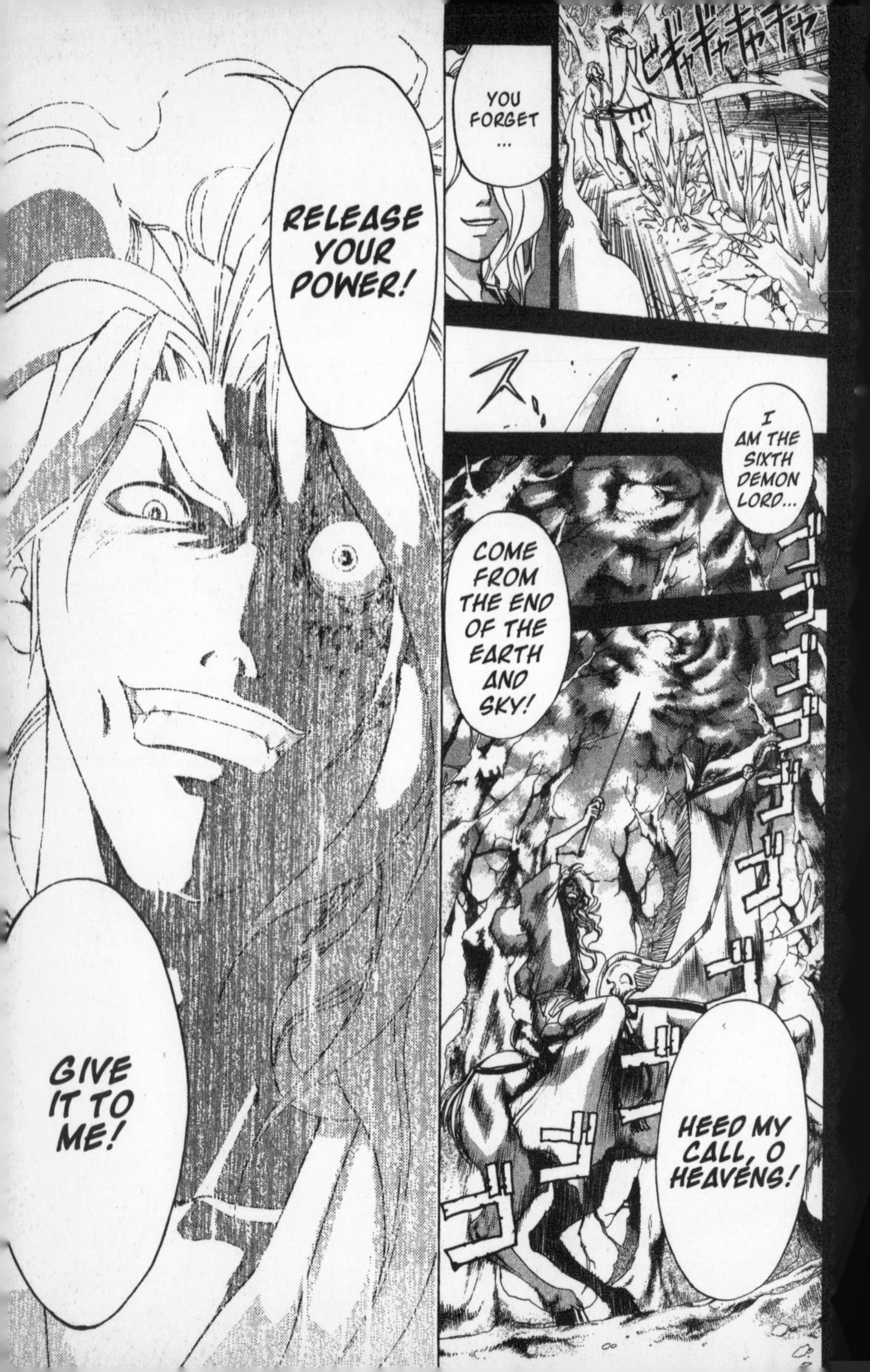
YOU FORGET ...
I AM THE SIXTH DEMON LORD...
COME FROM THE END OF THE EARTH AND SKY!
HEED MY CALL, O HEAVENS!
RELEASE YOUR POWER!
GIVE IT TO ME!

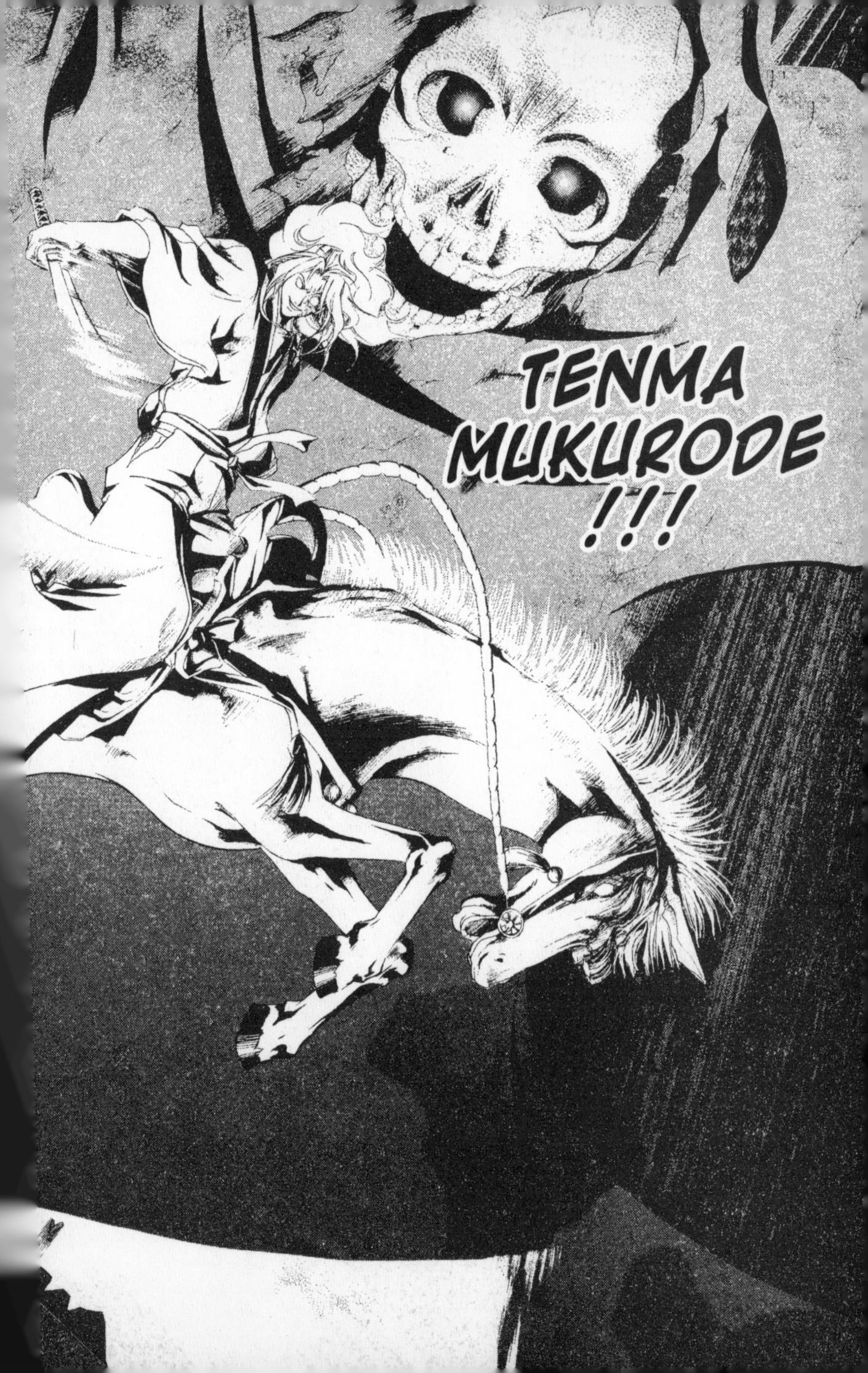
TENMA MUKURODE !!!

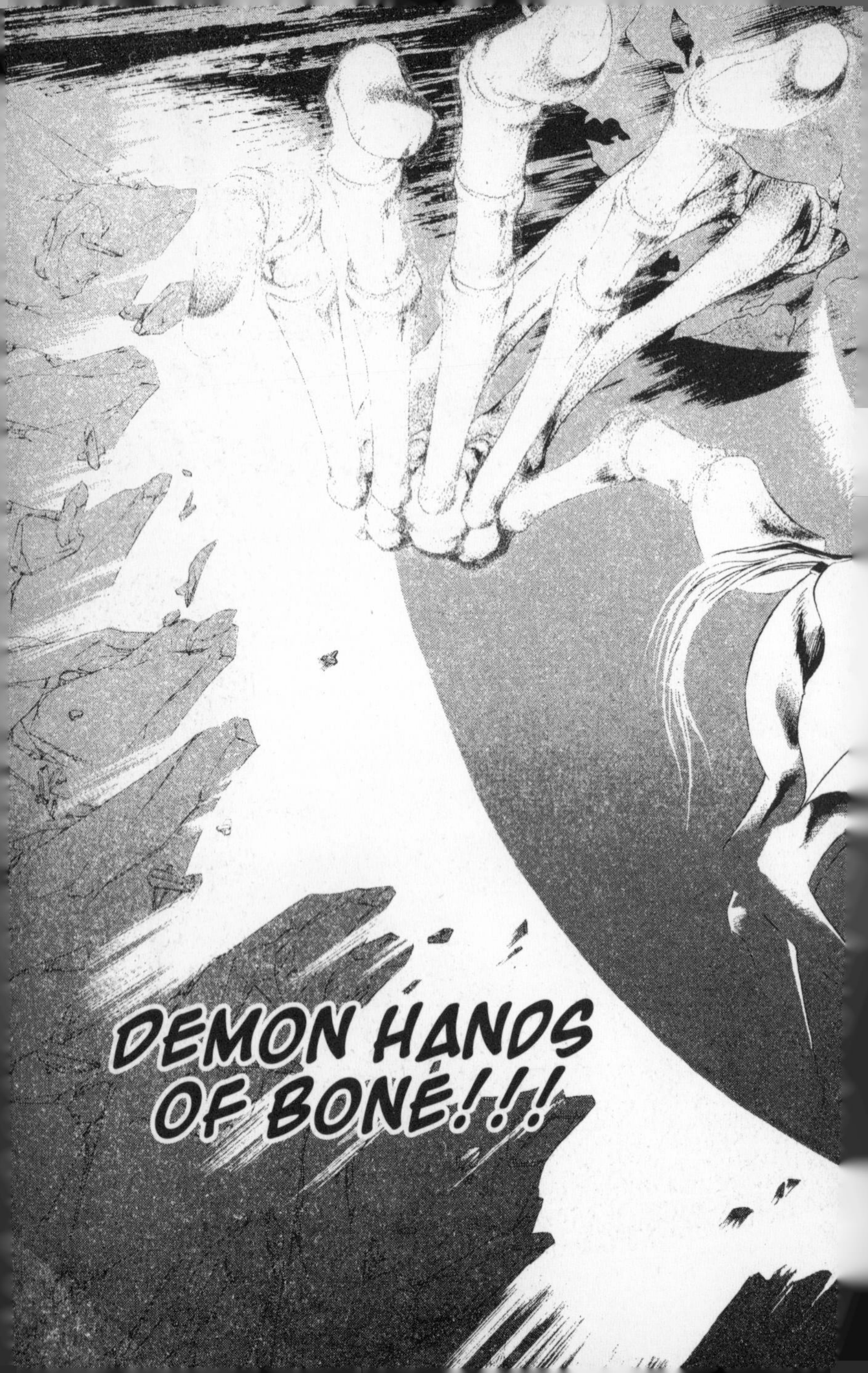
DEMON HANDS OF BONE!!!

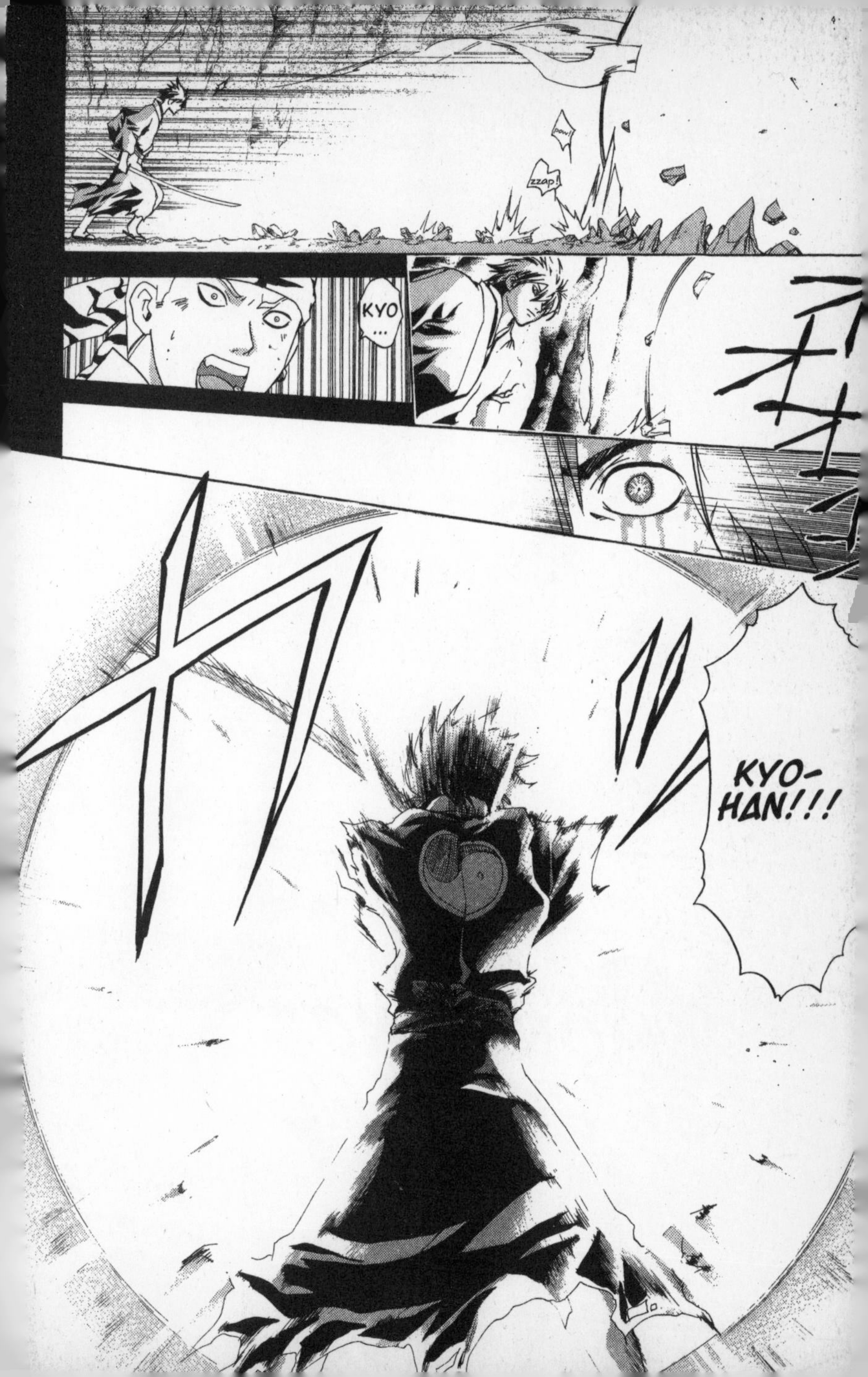
pow!
zzap!
KYO ...
KYO-HAN!!!

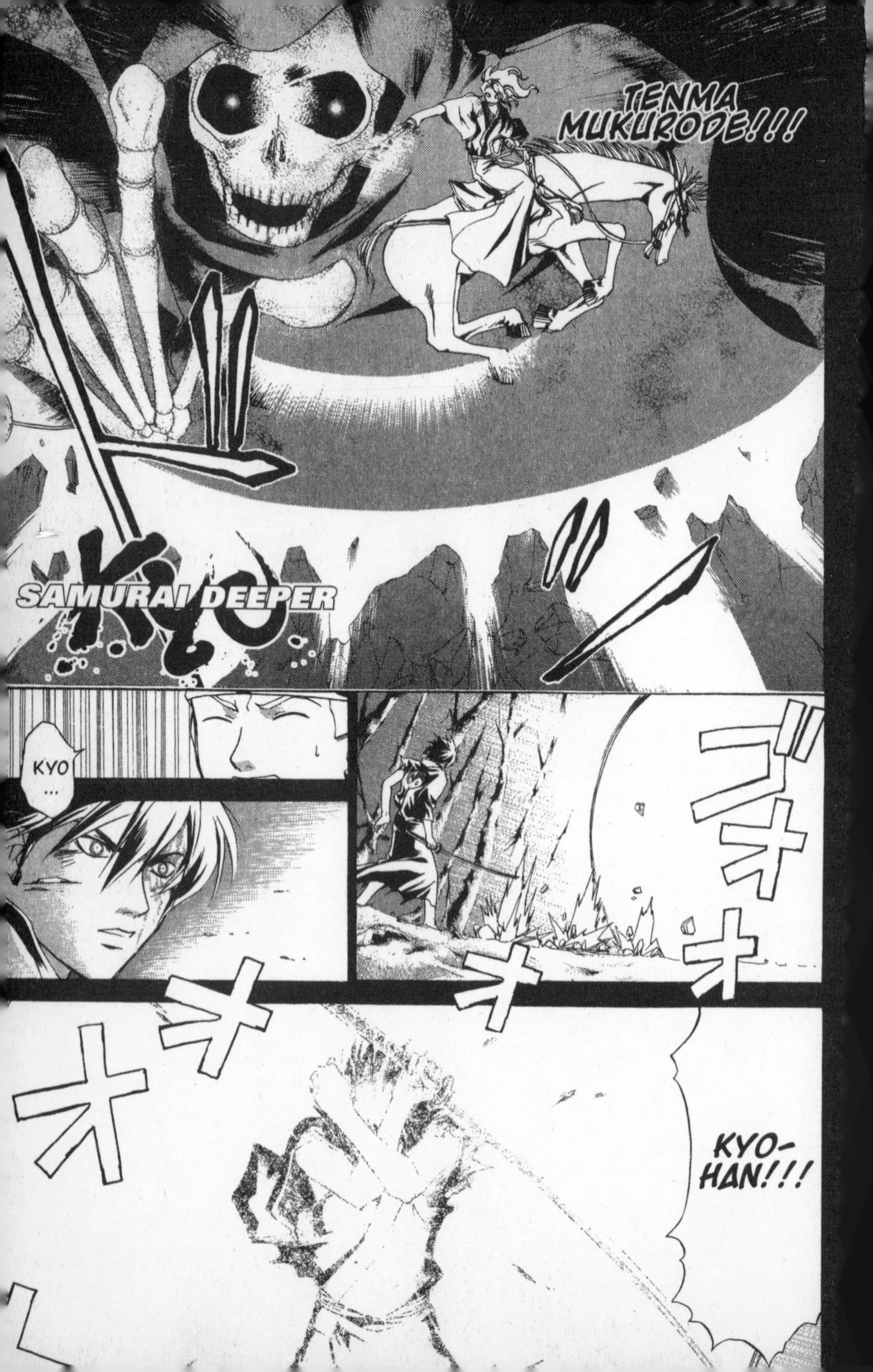
TENMA MUKURODE!!!
SAMURAI DEEPER KYO
KYO ...
KYO-HAN!!!

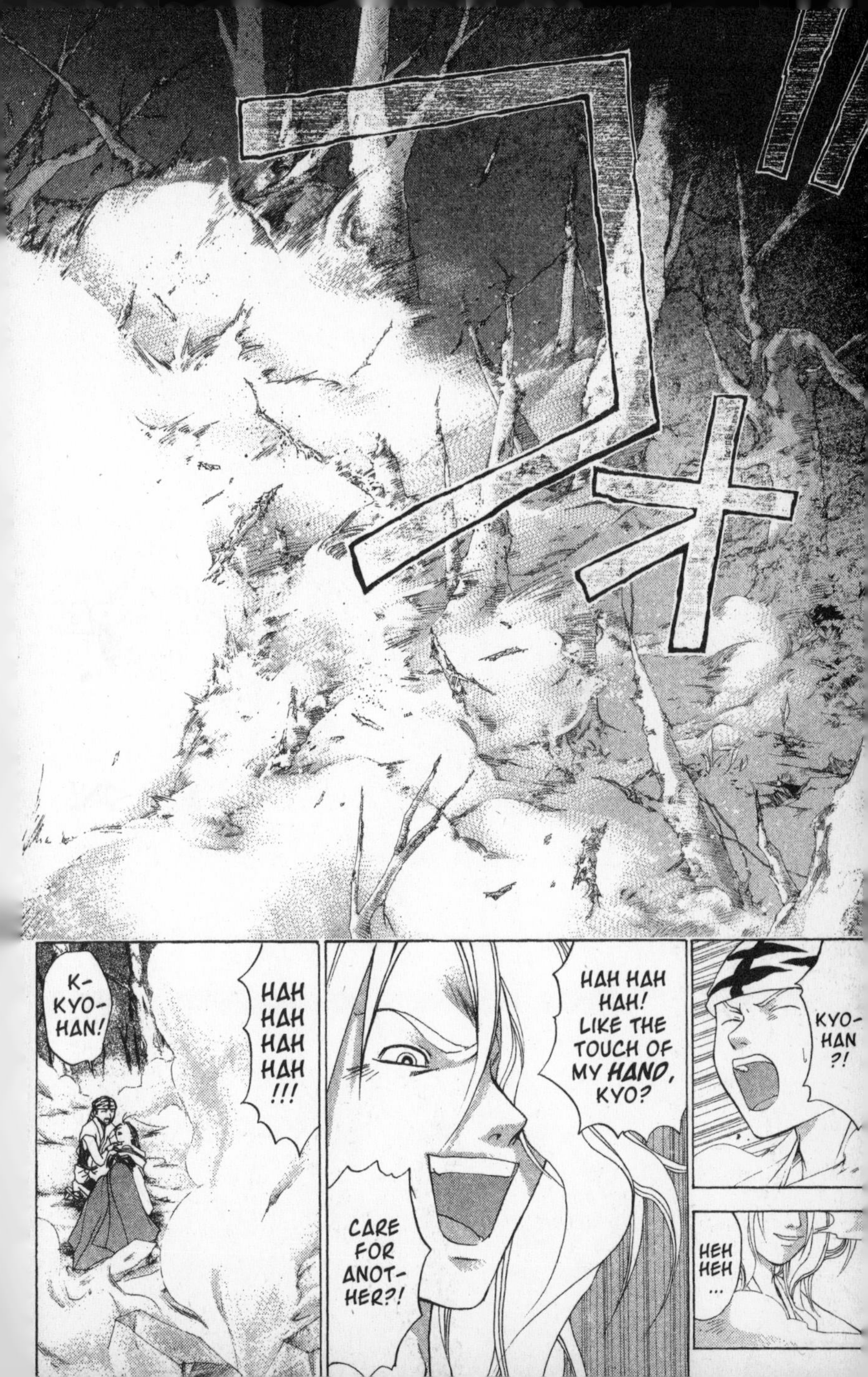
KYO-HAN?!
HEH HEH...
HAH HAH HAH! LIKE THE TOUCH OF MY *HAND*, KYO?
CARE FOR ANOT-HER?!
HAH HAH HAH HAH!!!
K-KYO-HAN!

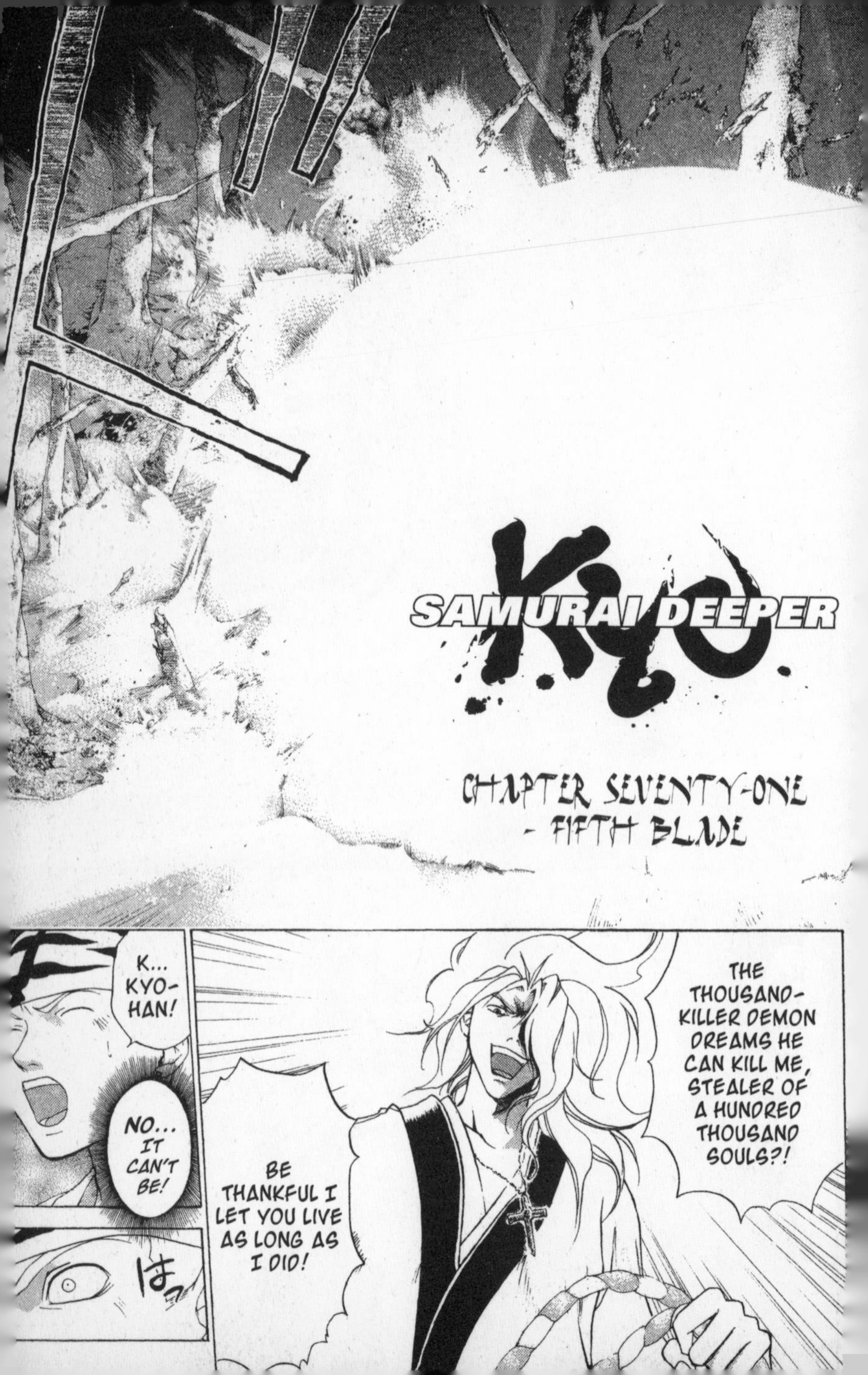
SAMURAI DEEPER KYO
CHAPTER SEVENTY-ONE - FIFTH BLADE
THE THOUSAND-KILLER DEMON DREAMS HE CAN KILL ME, STEALER OF A HUNDRED THOUSAND SOULS?!
BE THANKFUL I LET YOU LIVE AS LONG AS I DID!
K... KYO-HAN!
NO... IT CAN'T BE!
はっ

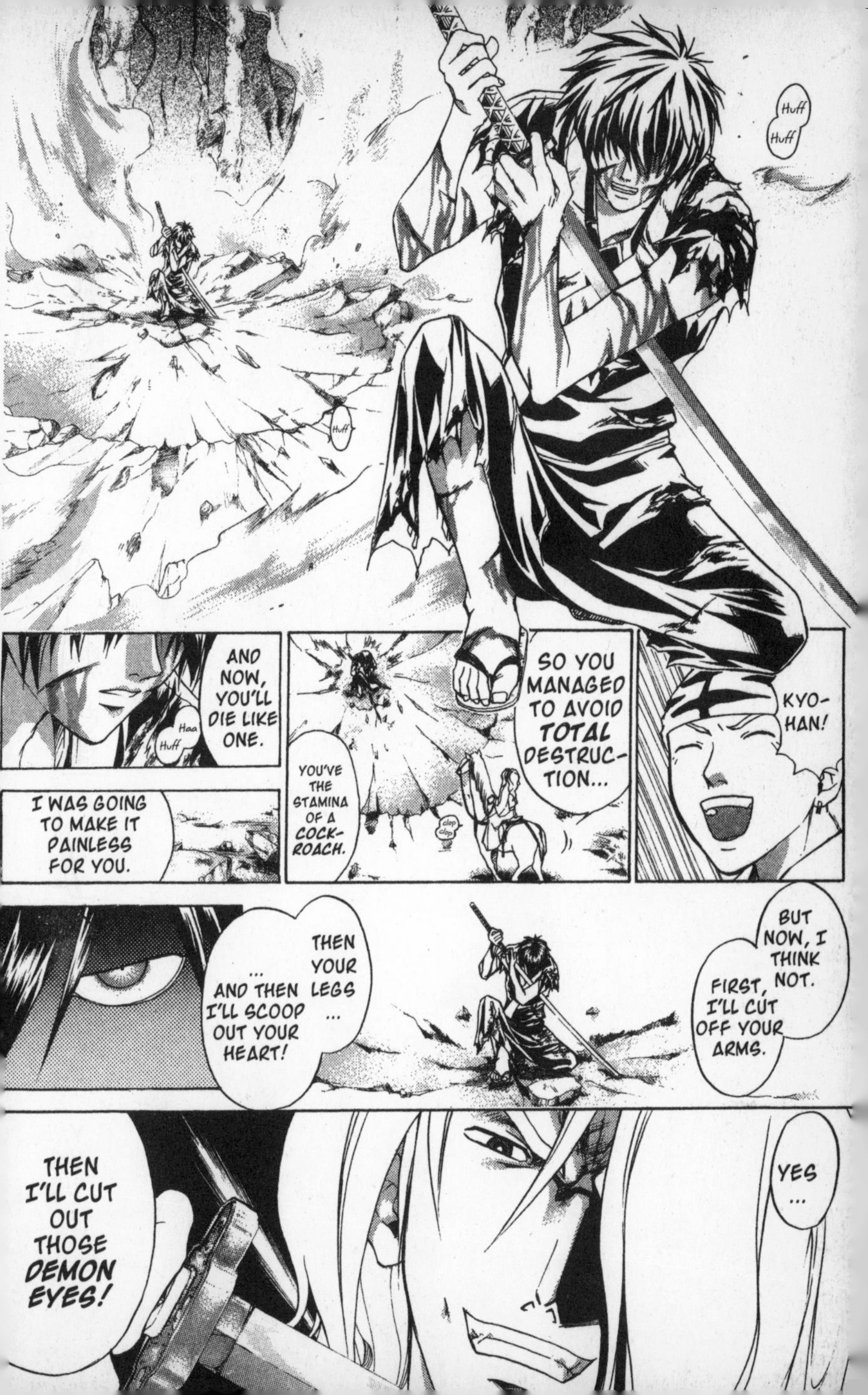
Huff
Huff
Huff
KYO-HAN!
SO YOU MANAGED TO AVOID TOTAL DESTRUCTION...
YOU'VE THE STAMINA OF A COCKROACH.
clop clop
AND NOW, YOU'LL DIE LIKE ONE.
Haa
Huff
I WAS GOING TO MAKE IT PAINLESS FOR YOU.
BUT NOW, I THINK NOT.
FIRST, I'LL CUT OFF YOUR ARMS.
THEN YOUR LEGS ...
... AND THEN I'LL SCOOP OUT YOUR HEART!
YES ...
THEN I'LL CUT OUT THOSE DEMON EYES!

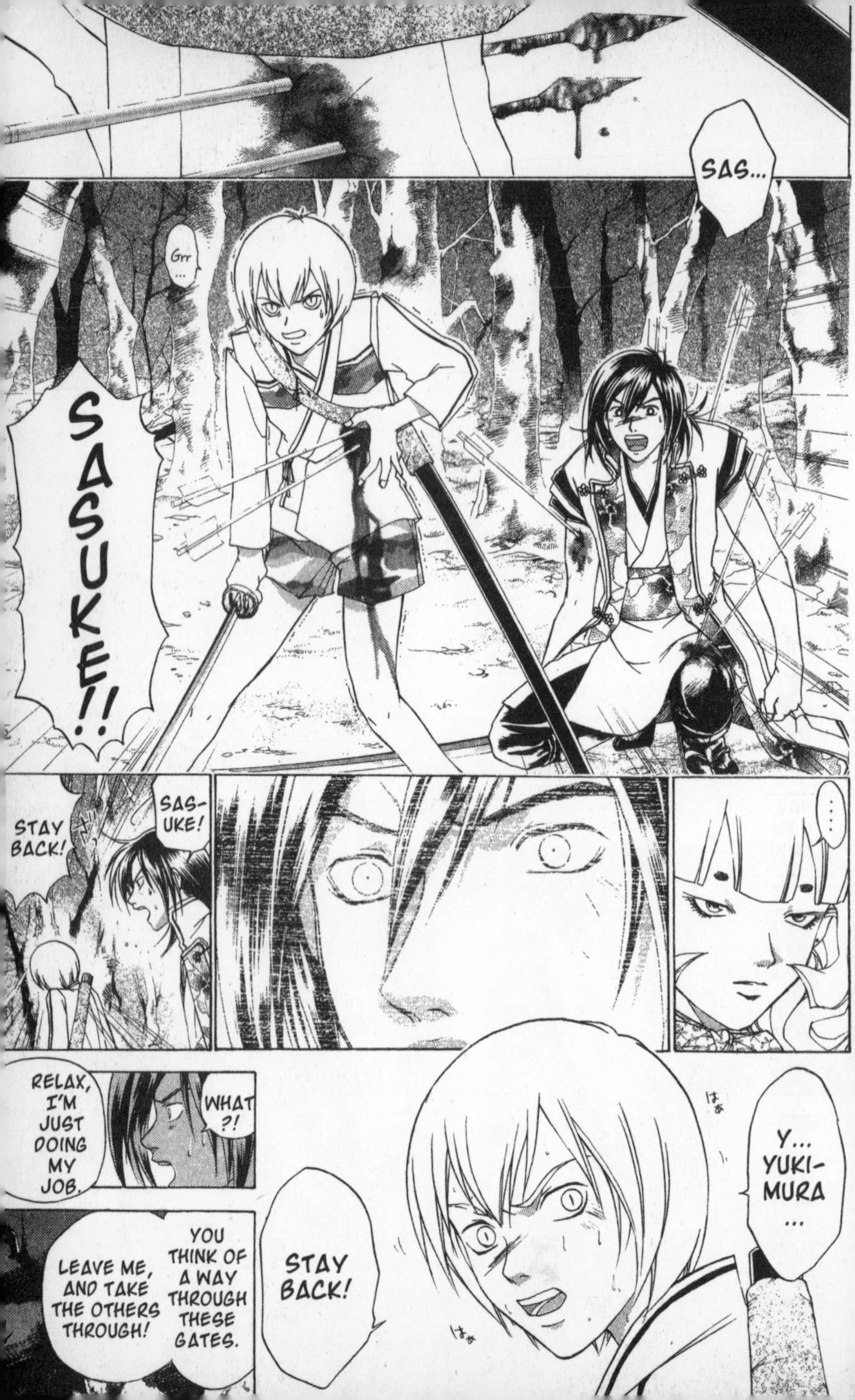
SAS...
GRR ...
SASUKE!!
...
SAS-UKE!
STAY BACK!
Y... YUKI-MURA ...
はぁ
STAY BACK!
はぁ
WHAT ?!
RELAX, I'M JUST DOING MY JOB.
YOU THINK OF A WAY THROUGH THESE GATES.
LEAVE ME, AND TAKE THE OTHERS THROUGH!

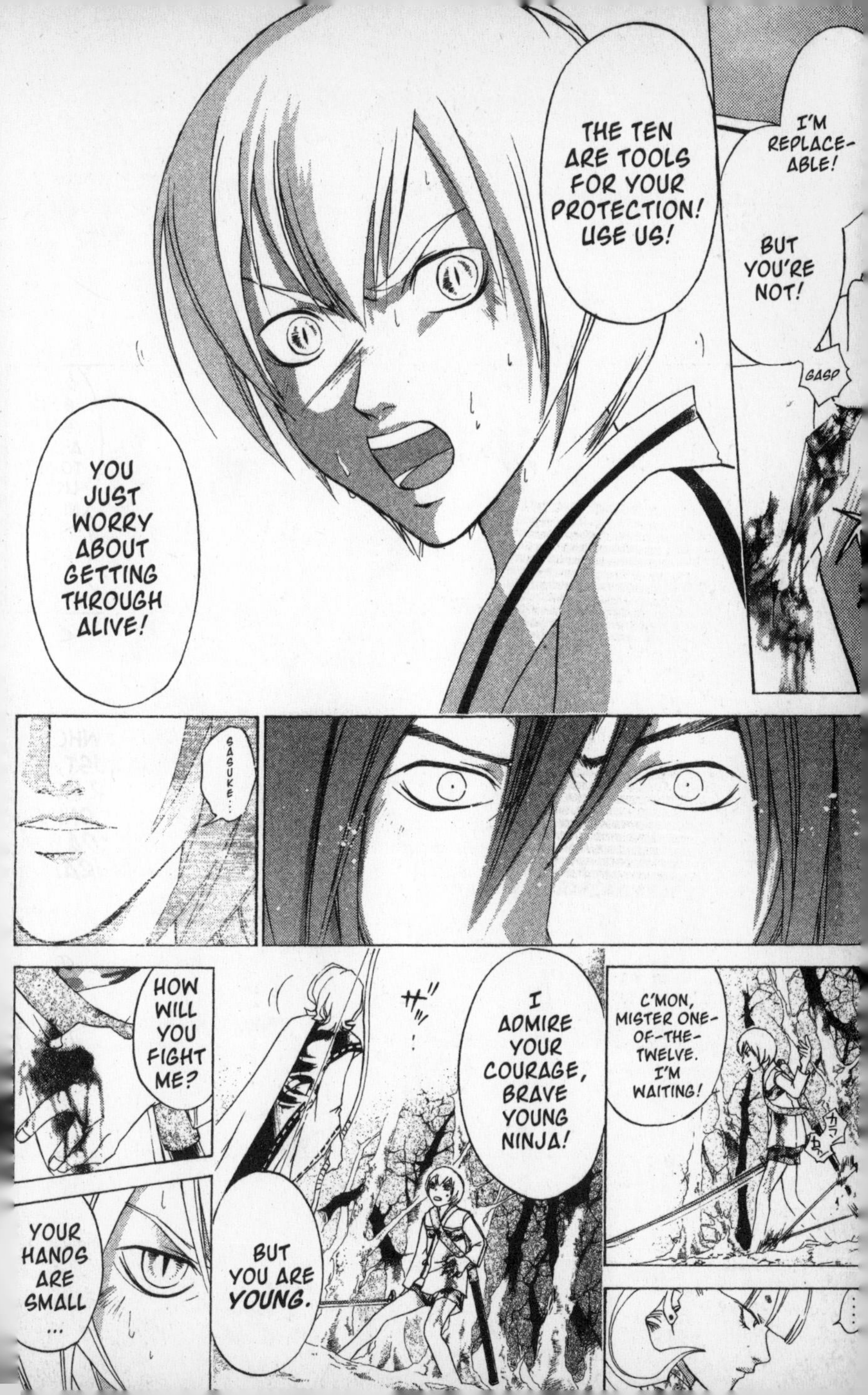
I'M REPLACE-ABLE!
BUT YOU'RE NOT!
GASP
THE TEN ARE TOOLS FOR YOUR PROTECTION! USE US!
YOU JUST WORRY ABOUT GETTING THROUGH ALIVE!
SASUKE...
C'MON, MISTER ONE-OF-THE-TWELVE. I'M WAITING!
...
I ADMIRE YOUR COURAGE, BRAVE YOUNG NINJA!
BUT YOU ARE YOUNG.
HOW WILL YOU FIGHT ME?
YOUR HANDS ARE SMALL...

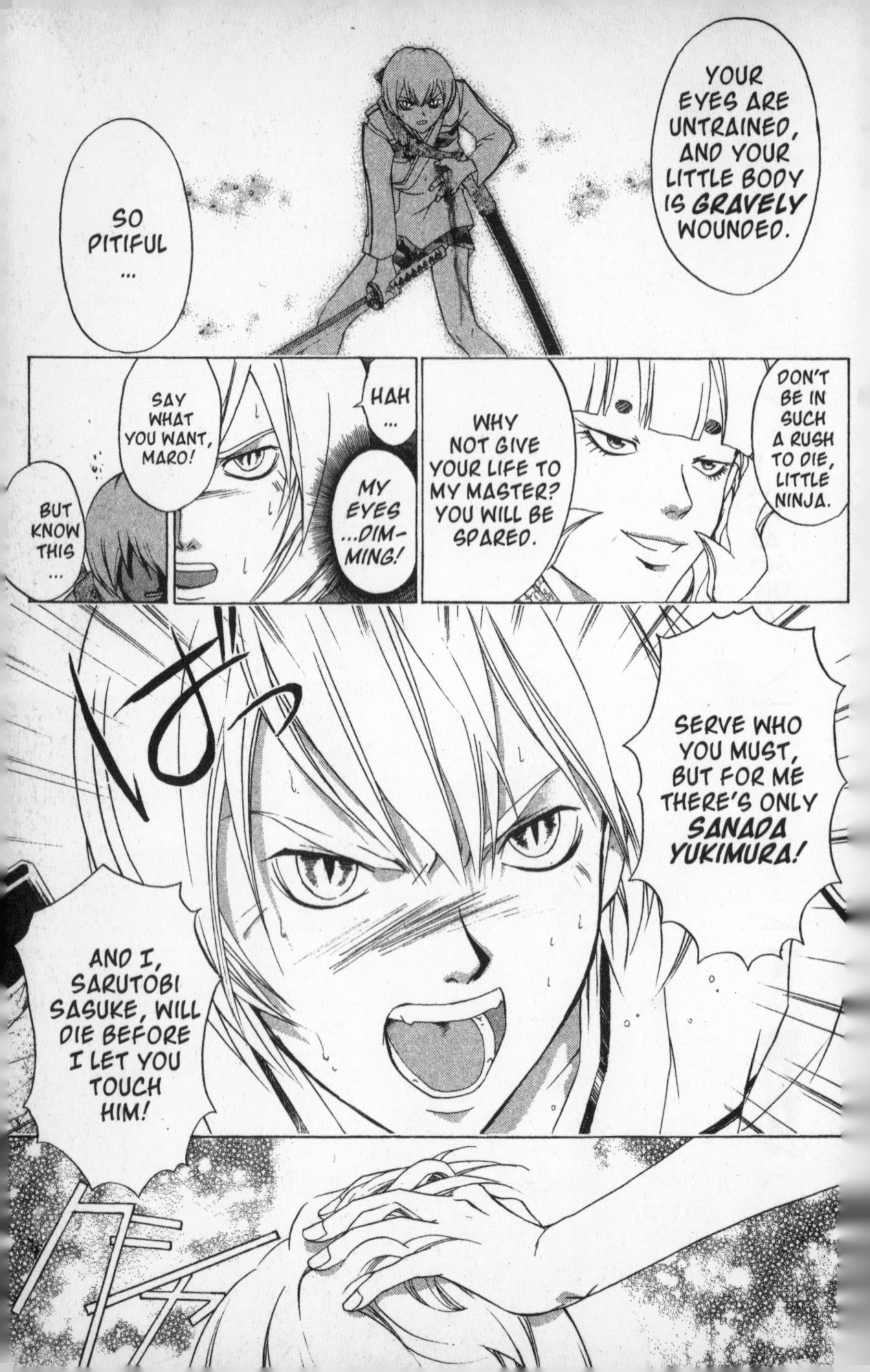
YOUR EYES ARE UNTRAINED, AND YOUR LITTLE BODY IS GRAVELY WOUNDED.
SO PITIFUL ...
DON'T BE IN SUCH A RUSH TO DIE, LITTLE NINJA.
WHY NOT GIVE YOUR LIFE TO MY MASTER? YOU WILL BE SPARED.
HAH ...
MY EYES ...DIM-MING!
SAY WHAT YOU WANT, MARO!
BUT KNOW THIS ...
SERVE WHO YOU MUST, BUT FOR ME THERE'S ONLY SANADA YUKIMURA!
AND I, SARUTOBI SASUKE, WILL DIE BEFORE I LET YOU TOUCH HIM!

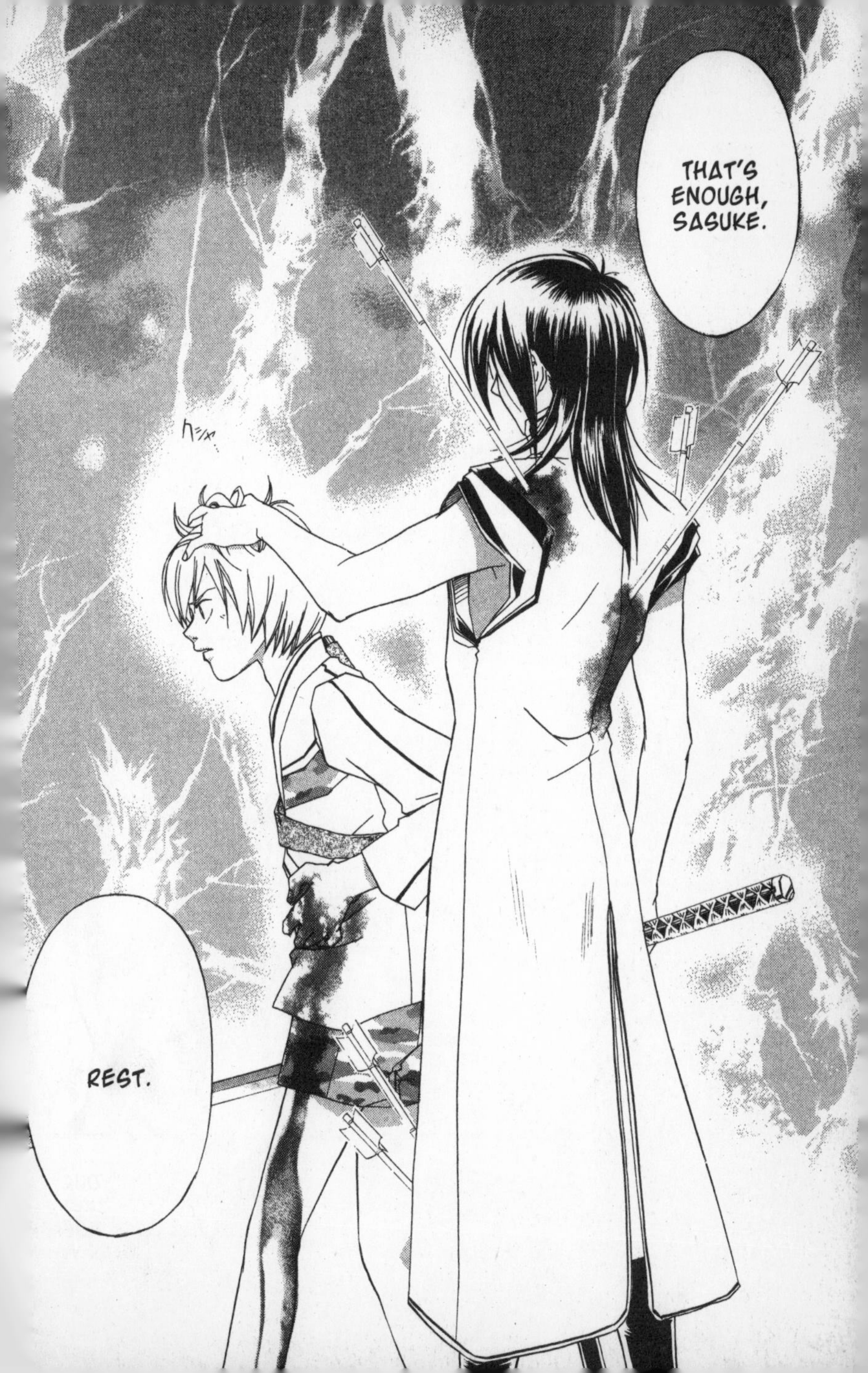
THAT'S ENOUGH, SASUKE.
クシャ…
REST.

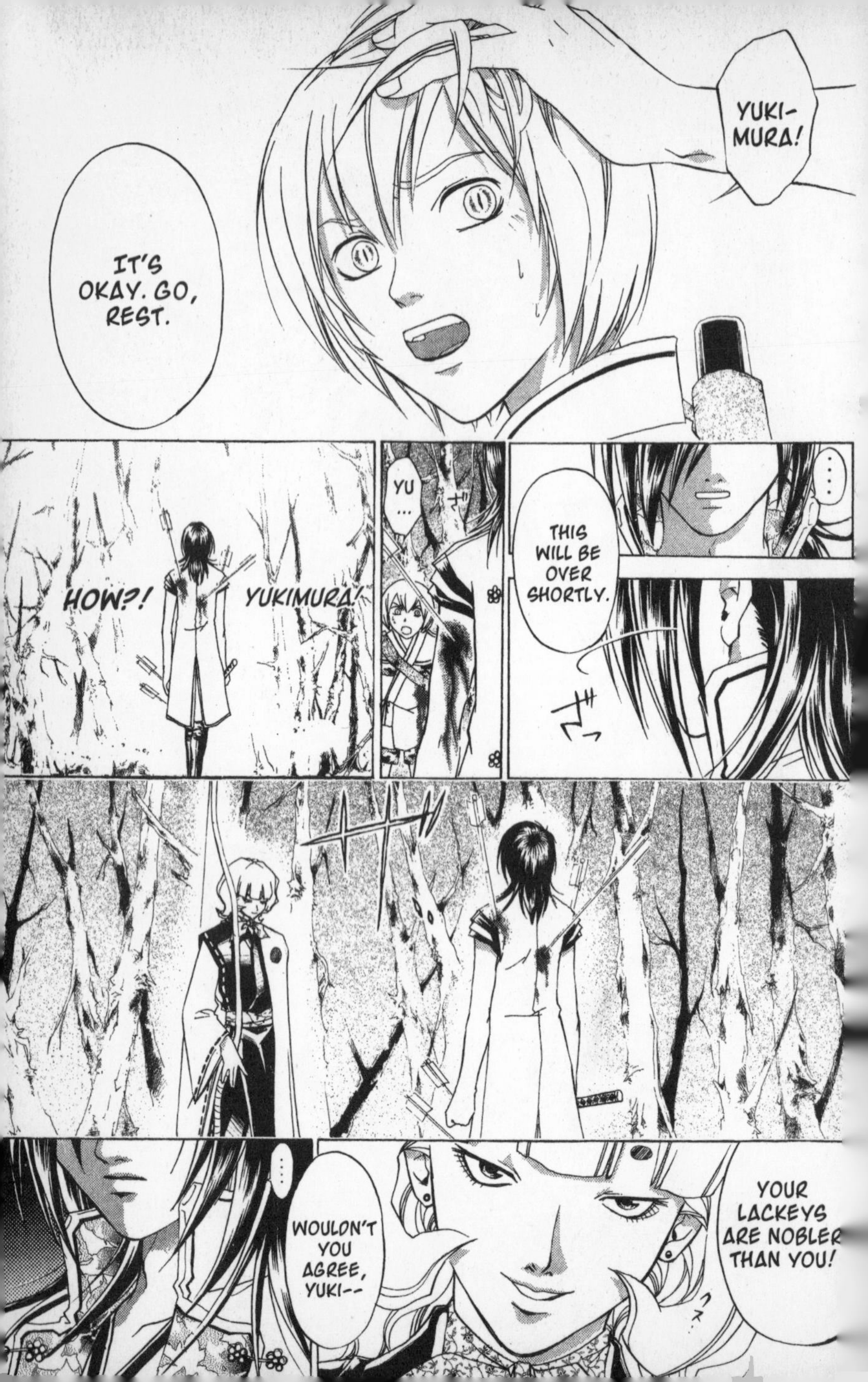
YUKI-MURA!
IT'S OKAY. GO, REST.
...
THIS WILL BE OVER SHORTLY.
YU ...
YUKIMURA!
HOW?!
YOUR LACKEYS ARE NOBLER THAN YOU!
WOULDN'T YOU AGREE, YUKI--
...

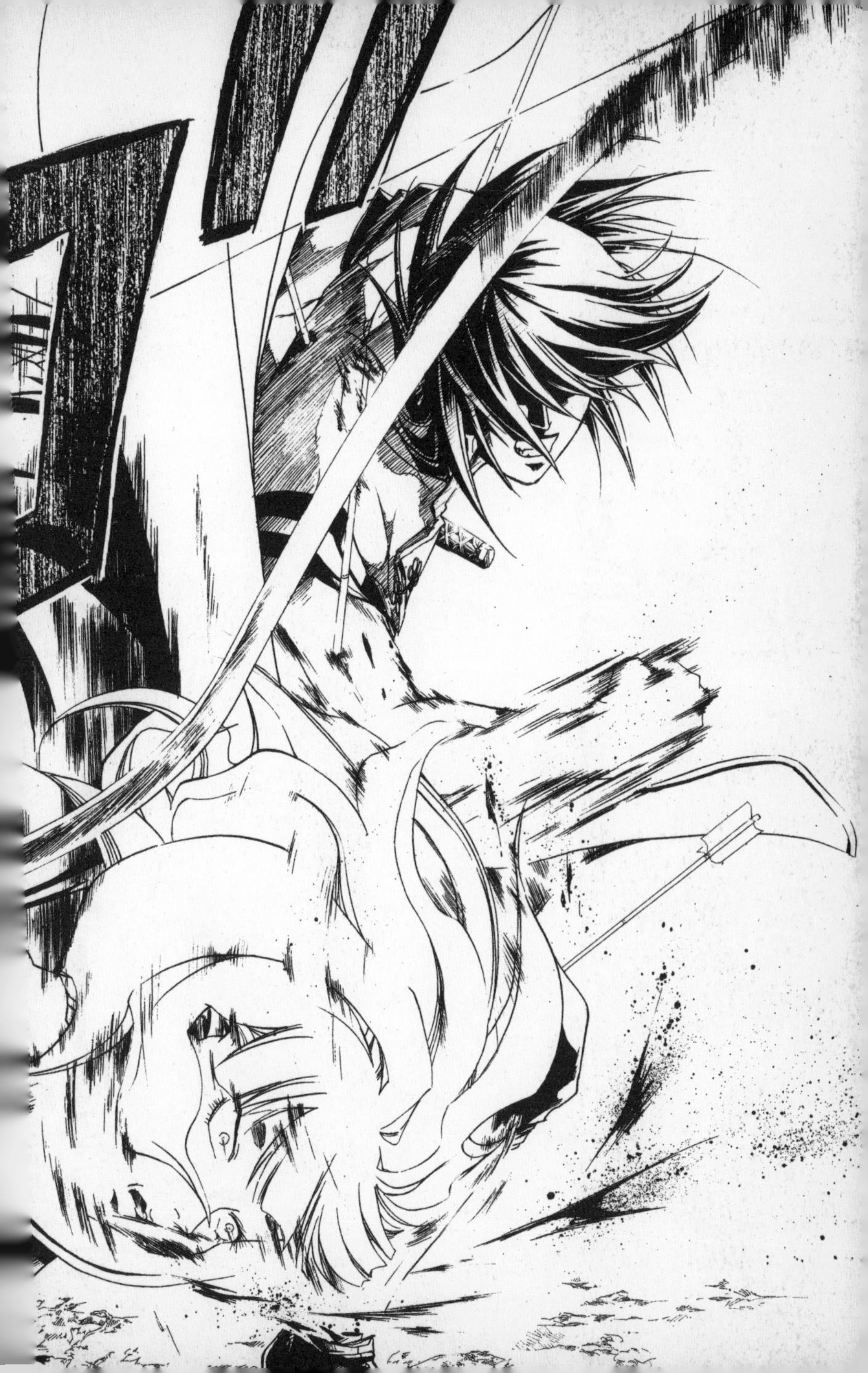

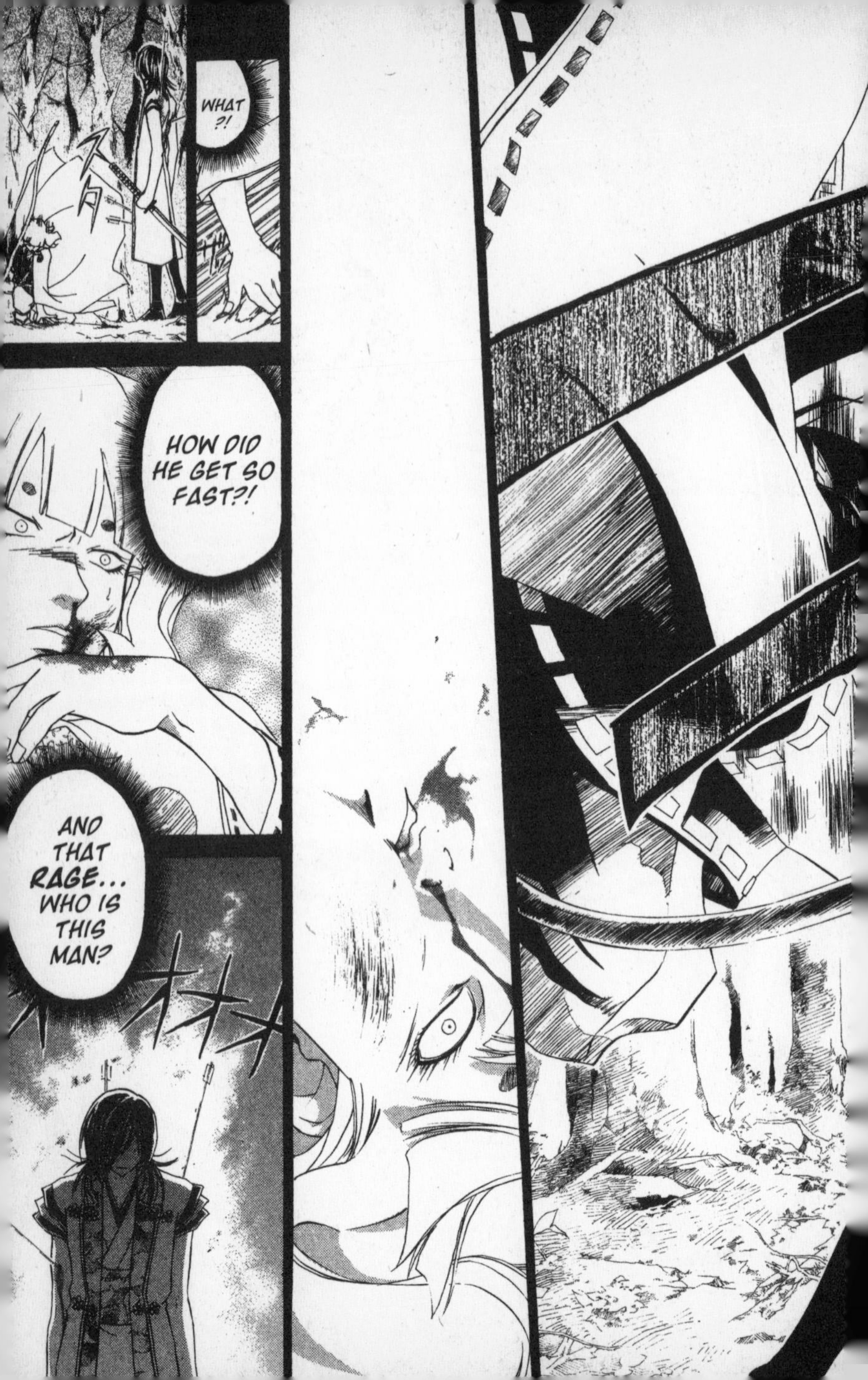
WHAT ?!
HOW DID HE GET SO FAST?!
AND THAT RAGE... WHO IS THIS MAN?

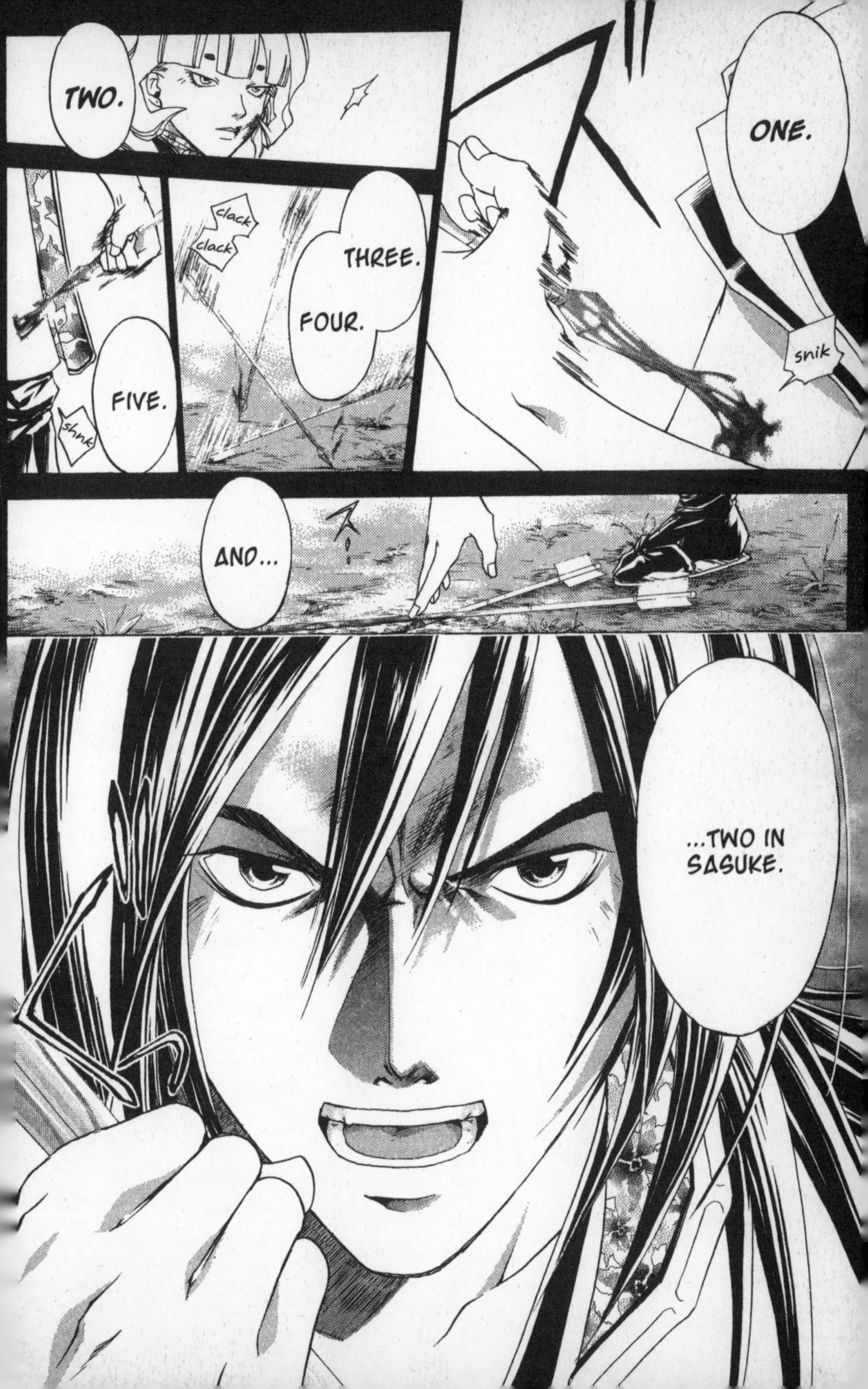
ONE.
snik
TWO.
THREE.
FOUR.
clack
clack
FIVE.
shnk
AND...
...TWO IN SASUKE.

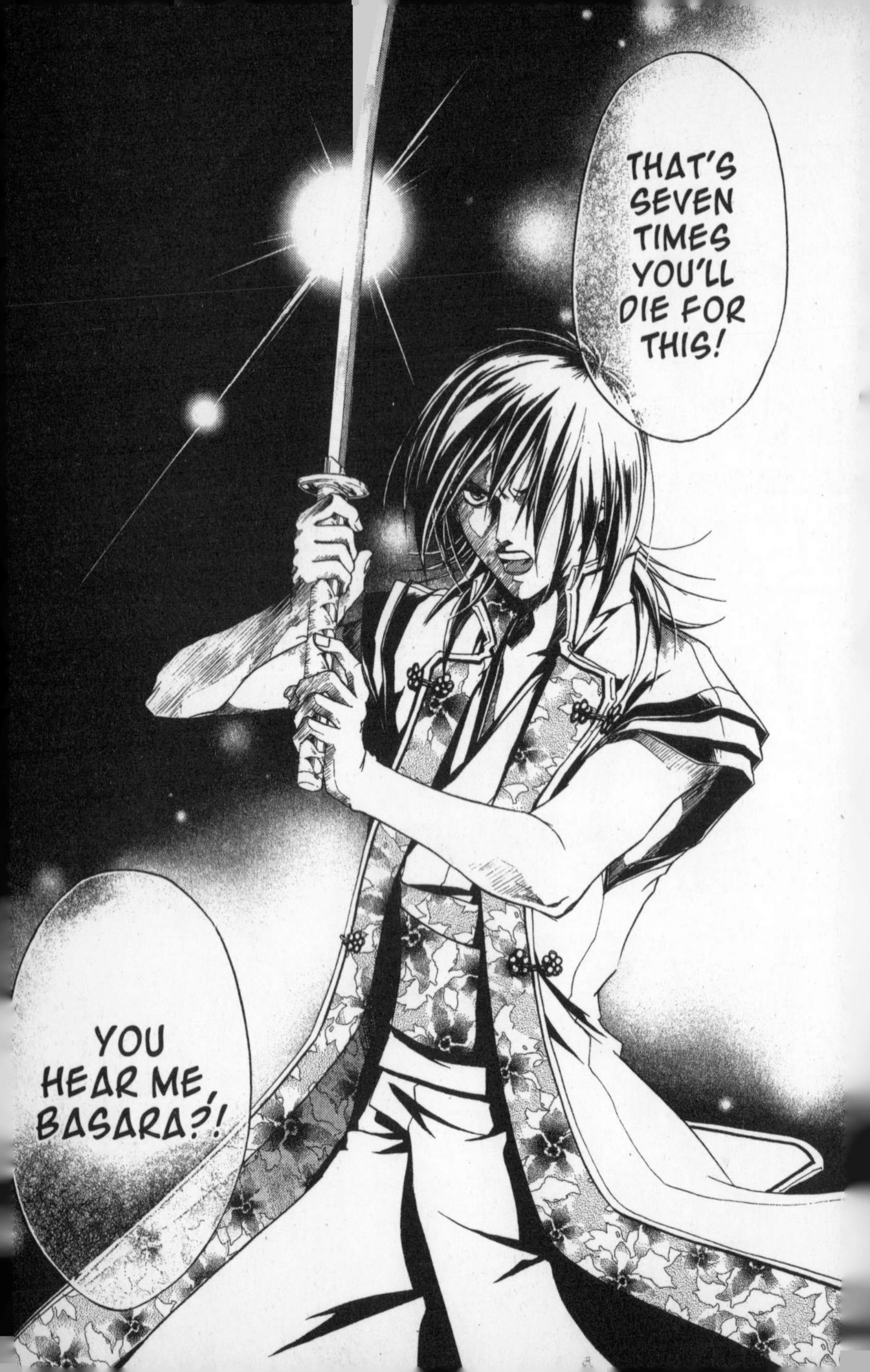
THAT'S SEVEN TIMES YOU'LL DIE FOR THIS!
YOU HEAR ME, BASARA?!

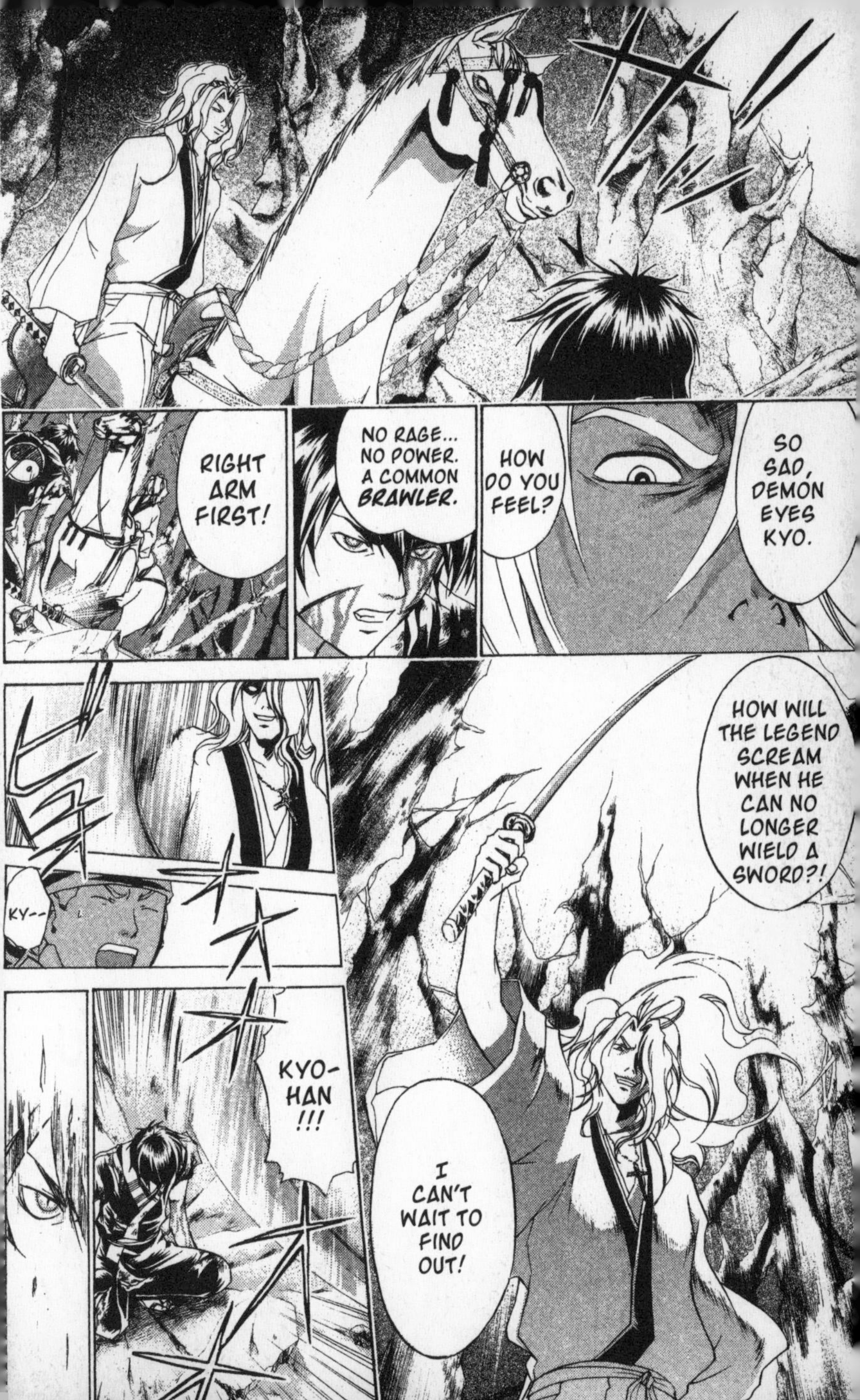
SO SAD, DEMON EYES KYO.
HOW DO YOU FEEL?
NO RAGE... NO POWER. A COMMON BRAWLER.
RIGHT ARM FIRST!
HOW WILL THE LEGEND SCREAM WHEN HE CAN NO LONGER WIELD A SWORD?!
I CAN'T WAIT TO FIND OUT!
KY--
KYO-HAN!!!

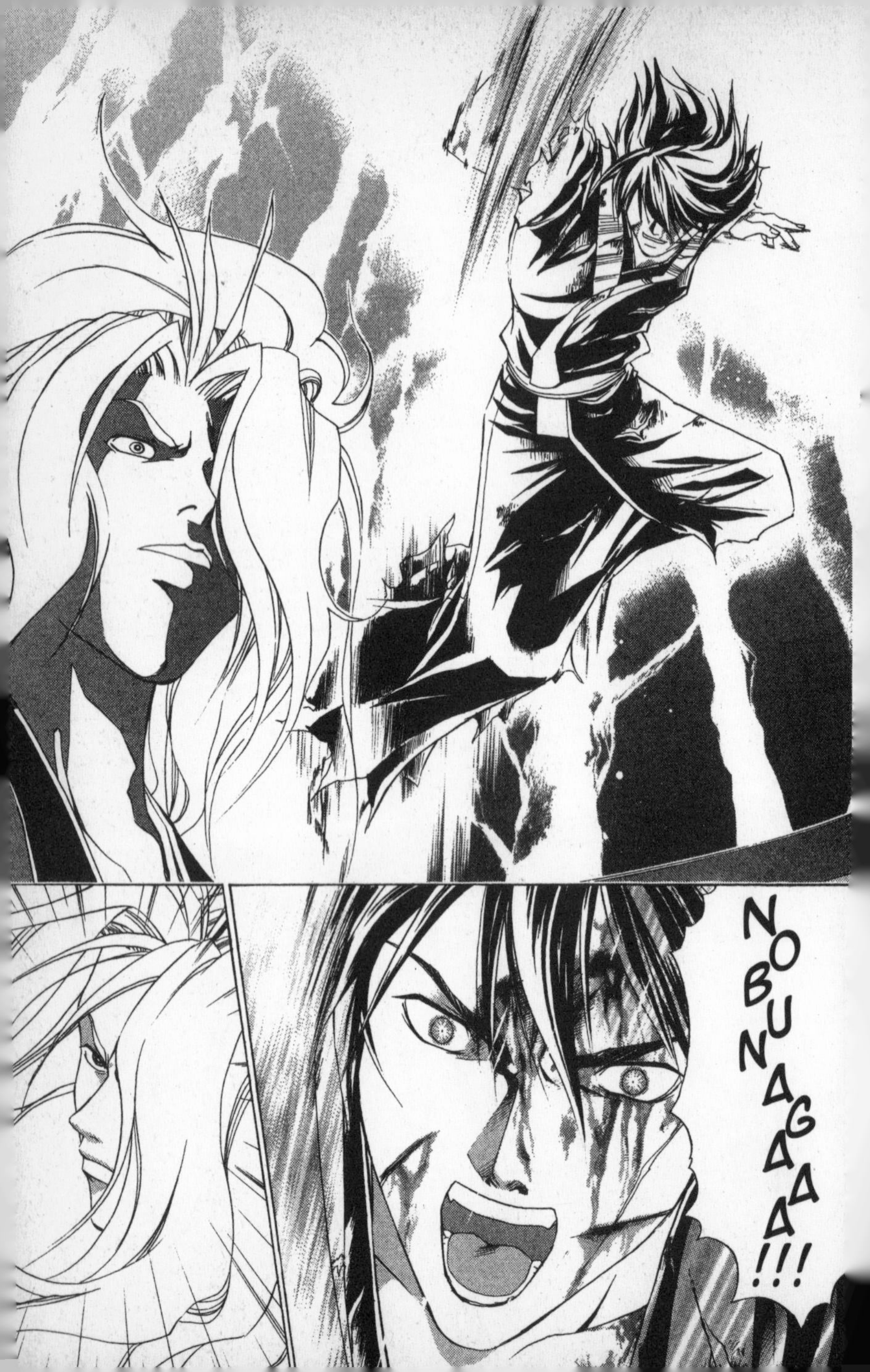
NOBUNAGAAAA!!!

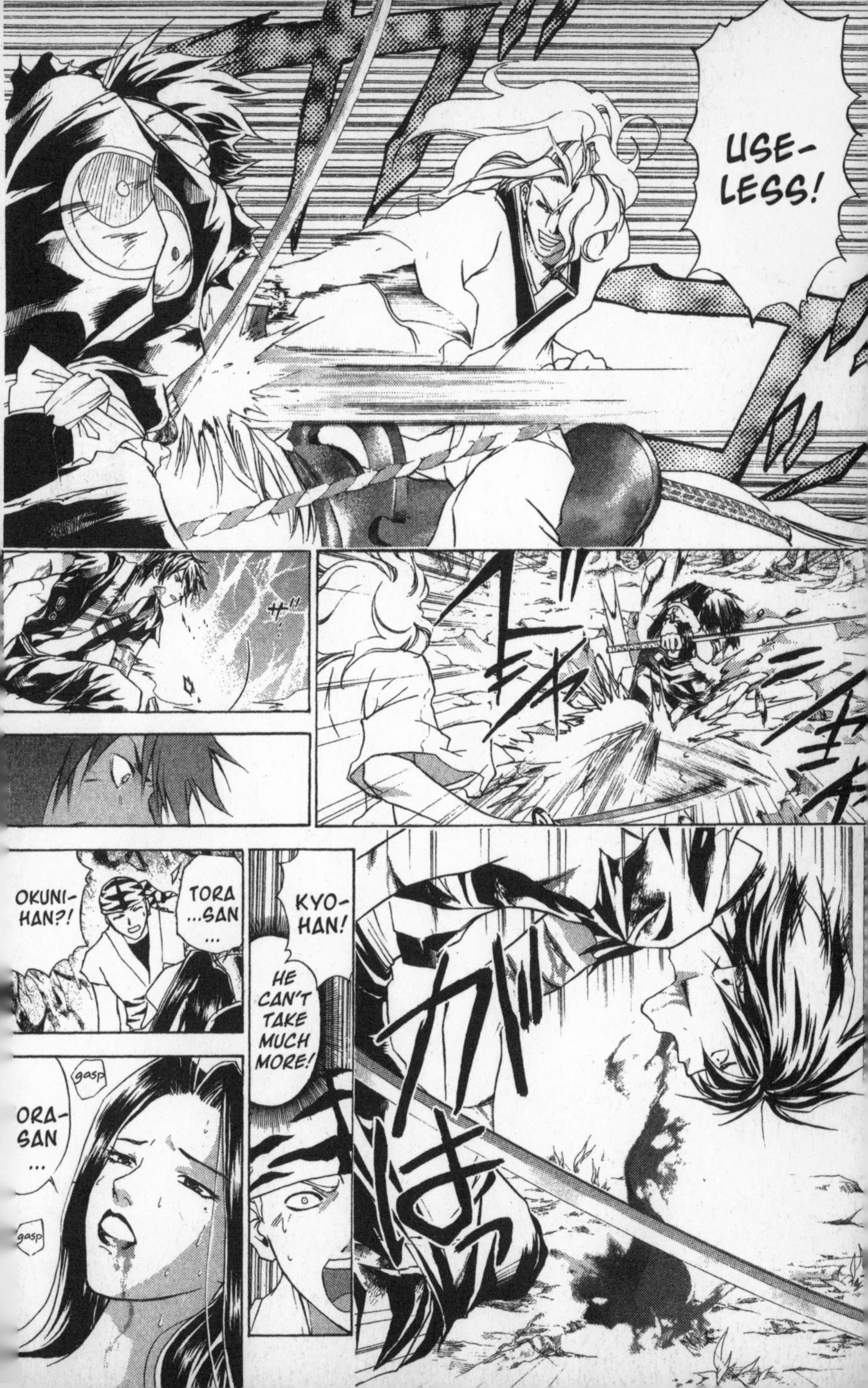
USE-LESS!
KYO-HAN!
HE CAN'T TAKE MUCH MORE!
TORA ...SAN ...
OKUNI-HAN?!
gasp
ORA-SAN ...
gasp

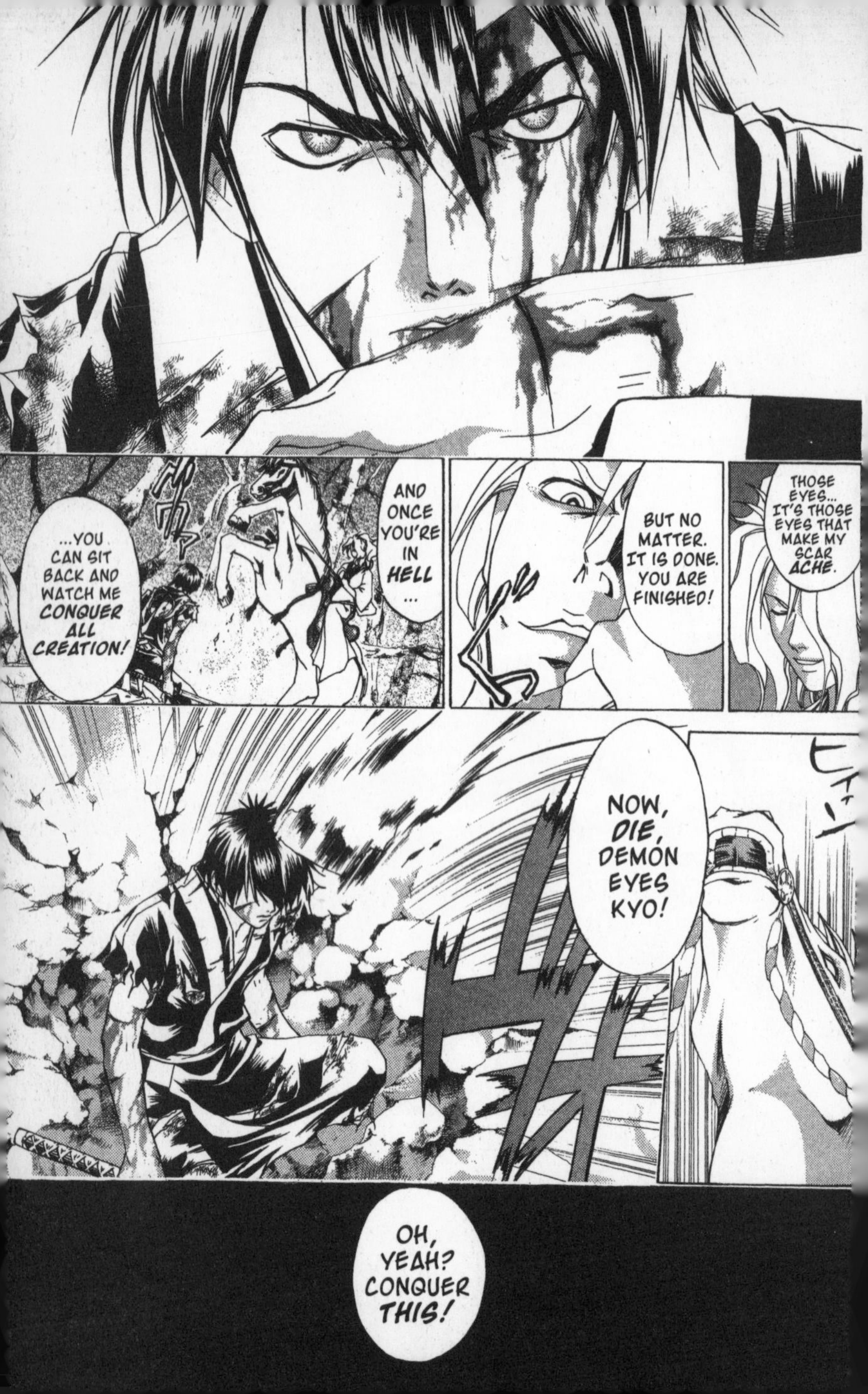
THOSE EYES... IT'S THOSE EYES THAT MAKE MY SCAR ACHE.
BUT NO MATTER. IT IS DONE. YOU ARE FINISHED!
AND ONCE YOU'RE IN HELL ...
...YOU CAN SIT BACK AND WATCH ME CONQUER ALL CREATION!
NOW, DIE, DEMON EYES KYO!
OH, YEAH? CONQUER THIS!

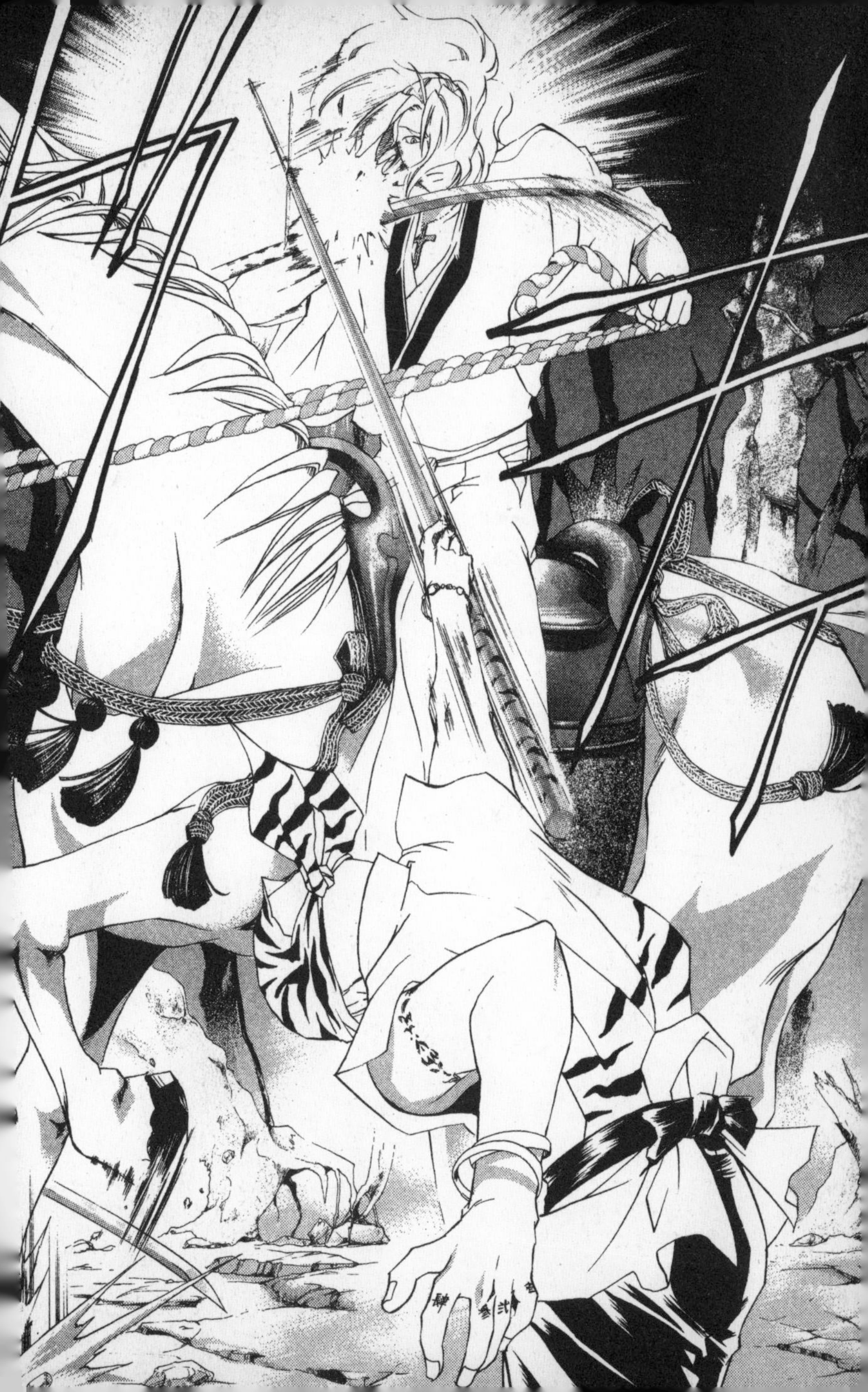
肆 参 弐 壱

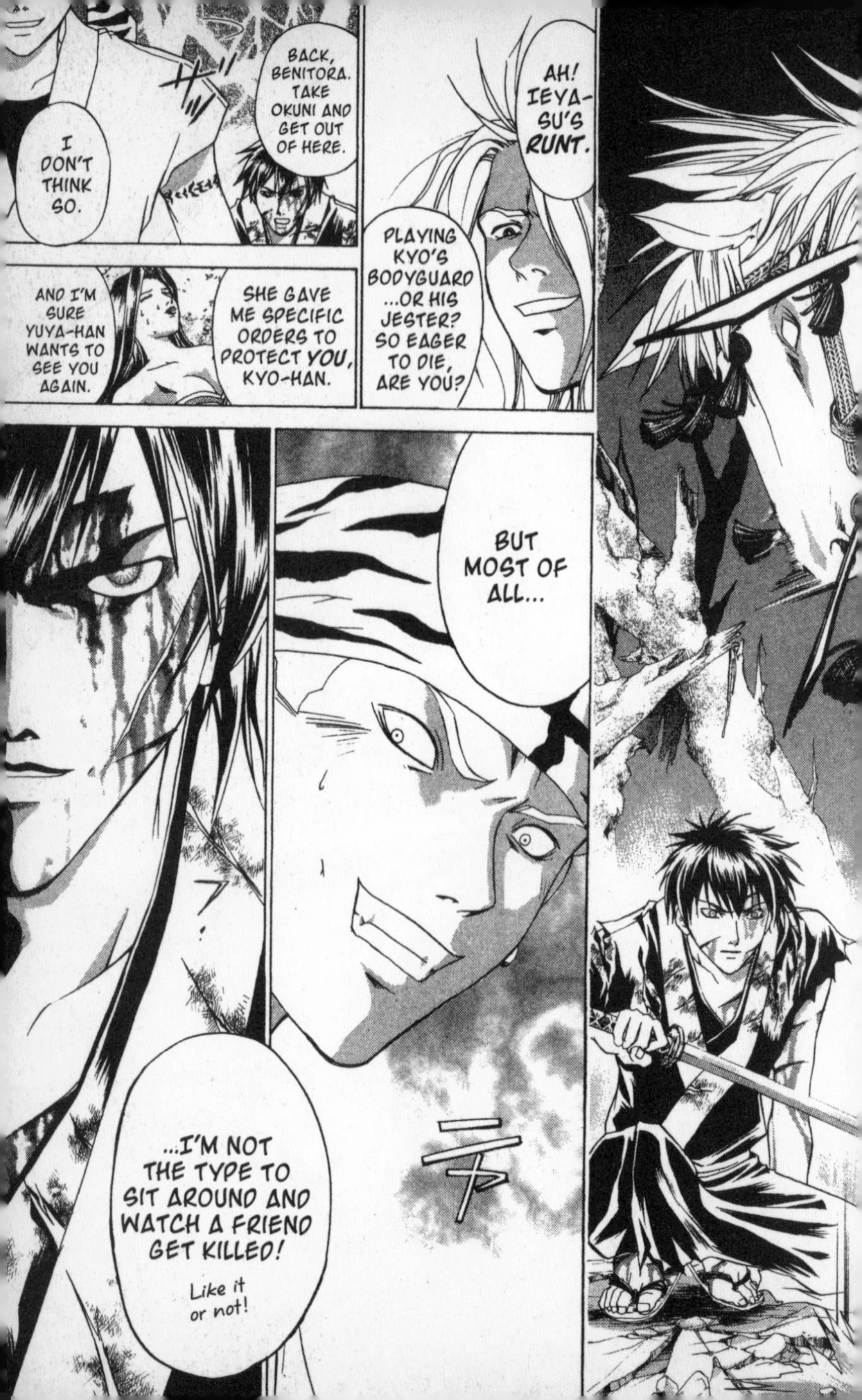
AH! IEYA-SU'S *RUNT*.
PLAYING KYO'S BODYGUARD ...OR HIS JESTER? SO EAGER TO DIE, ARE YOU?
BACK, BENITORA. TAKE OKUNI AND GET OUT OF HERE.
I DON'T THINK SO.
SHE GAVE ME SPECIFIC ORDERS TO PROTECT *YOU*, KYO-HAN.
AND I'M SURE YUYA-HAN WANTS TO SEE YOU AGAIN.
BUT MOST OF ALL...
...I'M NOT THE TYPE TO SIT AROUND AND WATCH A FRIEND GET KILLED!
Like it or not!

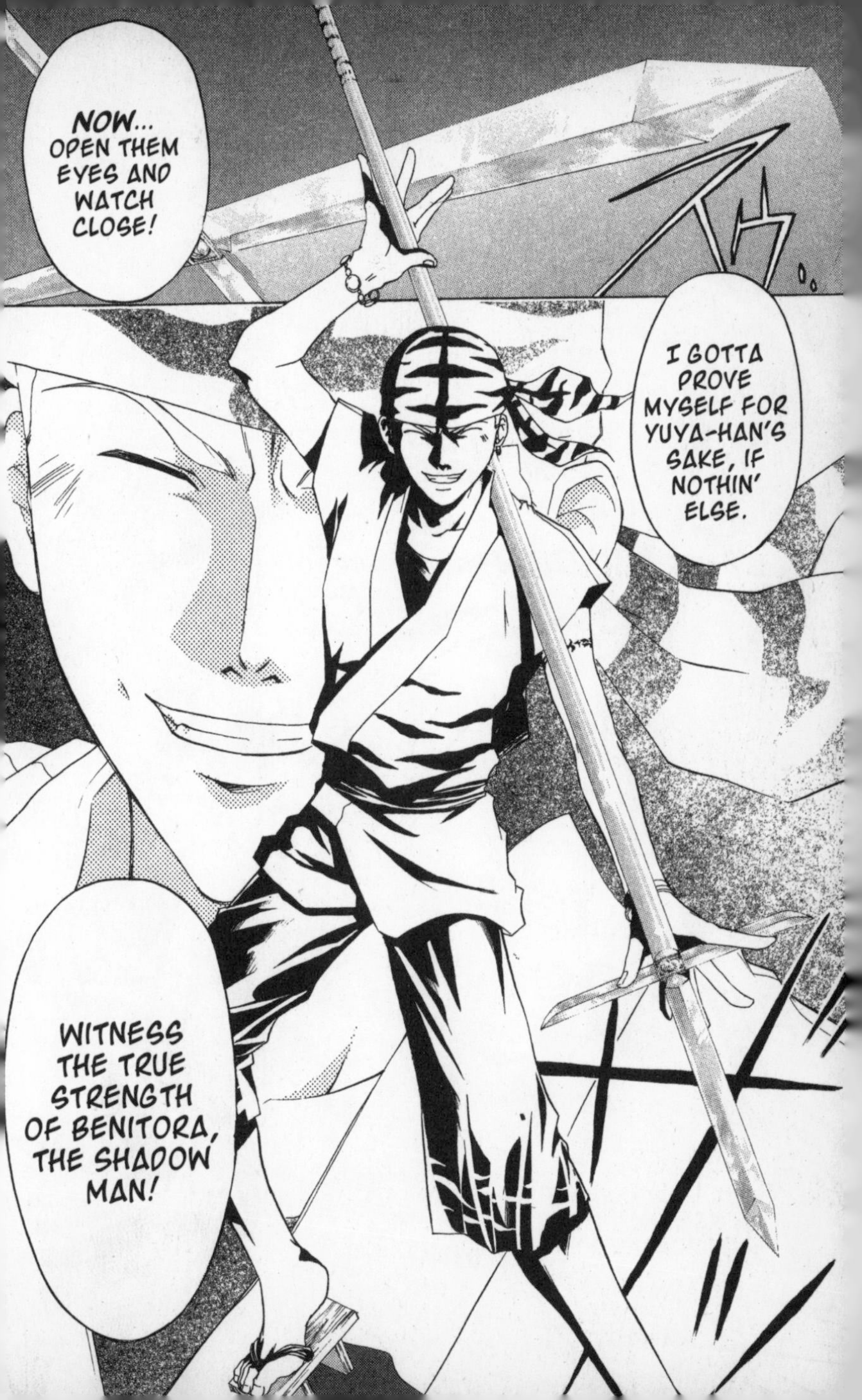
NOW... OPEN THEM EYES AND WATCH CLOSE!
I GOTTA PROVE MYSELF FOR YUYA-HAN'S SAKE, IF NOTHIN' ELSE.
WITNESS THE TRUE STRENGTH OF BENITORA, THE SHADOW MAN!

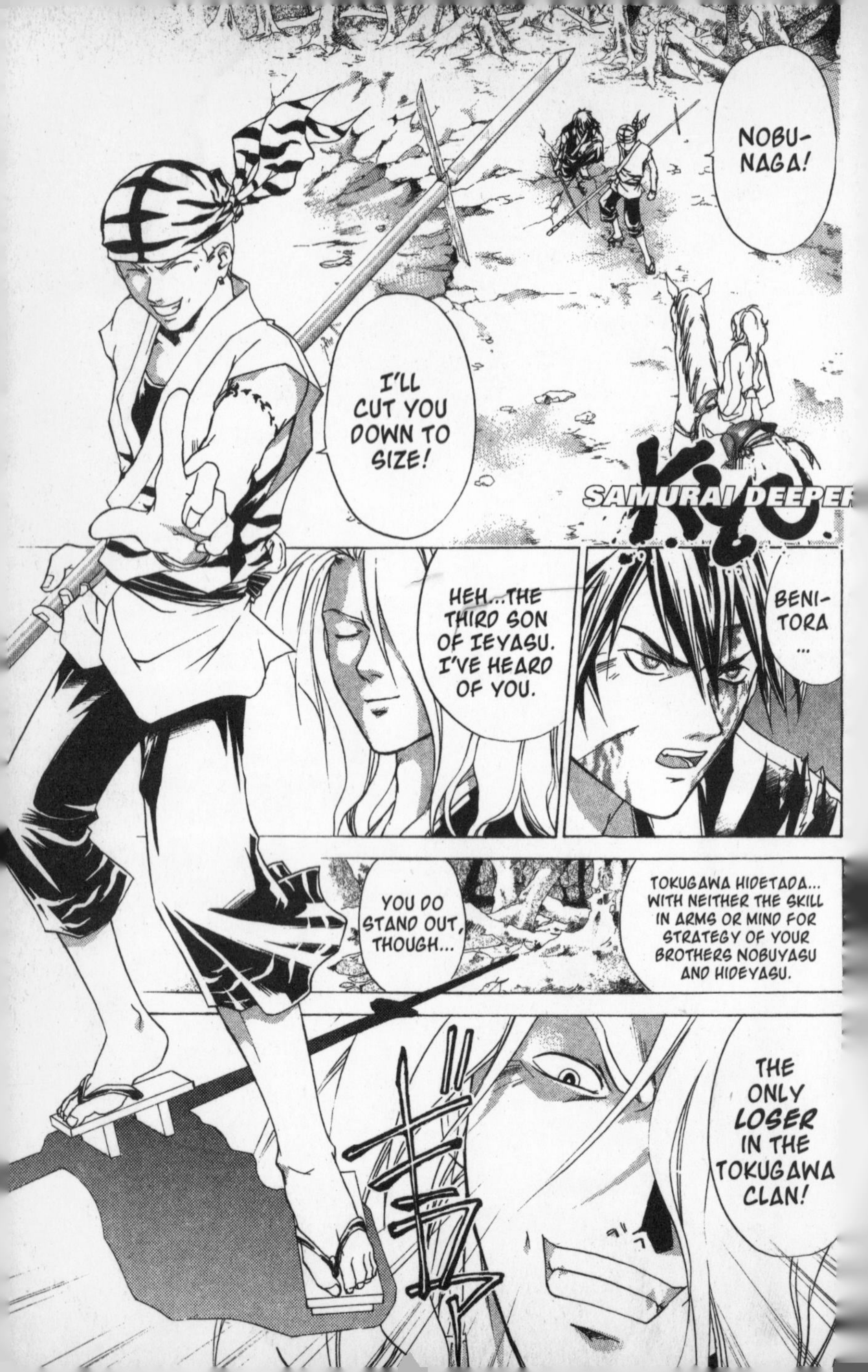
NOBU-NAGA!
SAMURAI DEEPER KYO
I'LL CUT YOU DOWN TO SIZE!
BENI-TORA...
HEH...THE THIRD SON OF IEYASU. I'VE HEARD OF YOU.
TOKUGAWA HIDETADA... WITH NEITHER THE SKILL IN ARMS OR MIND FOR STRATEGY OF YOUR BROTHERS NOBUYASU AND HIDEYASU.
YOU DO STAND OUT, THOUGH...
THE ONLY **LOSER** IN THE TOKUGAWA CLAN!

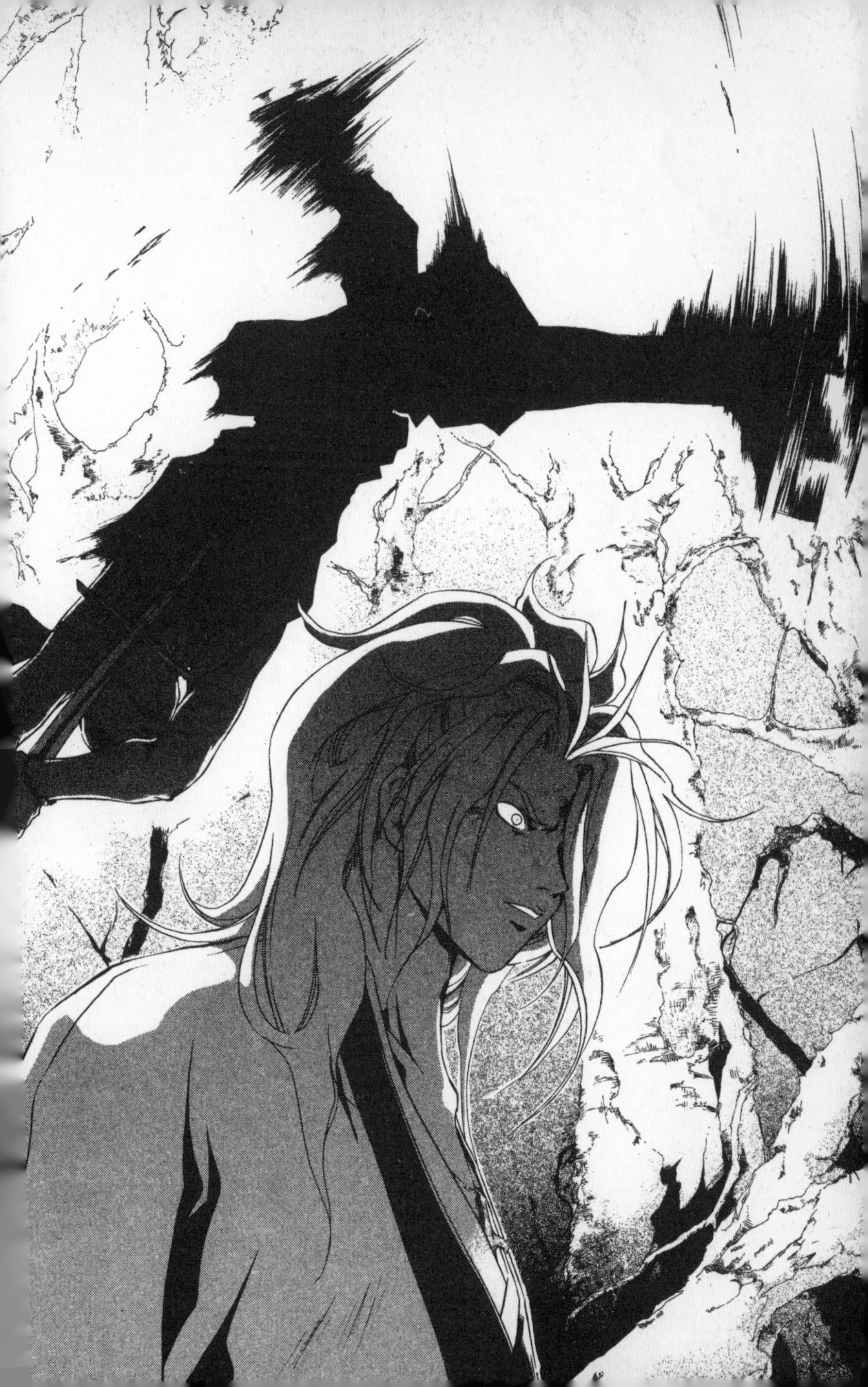

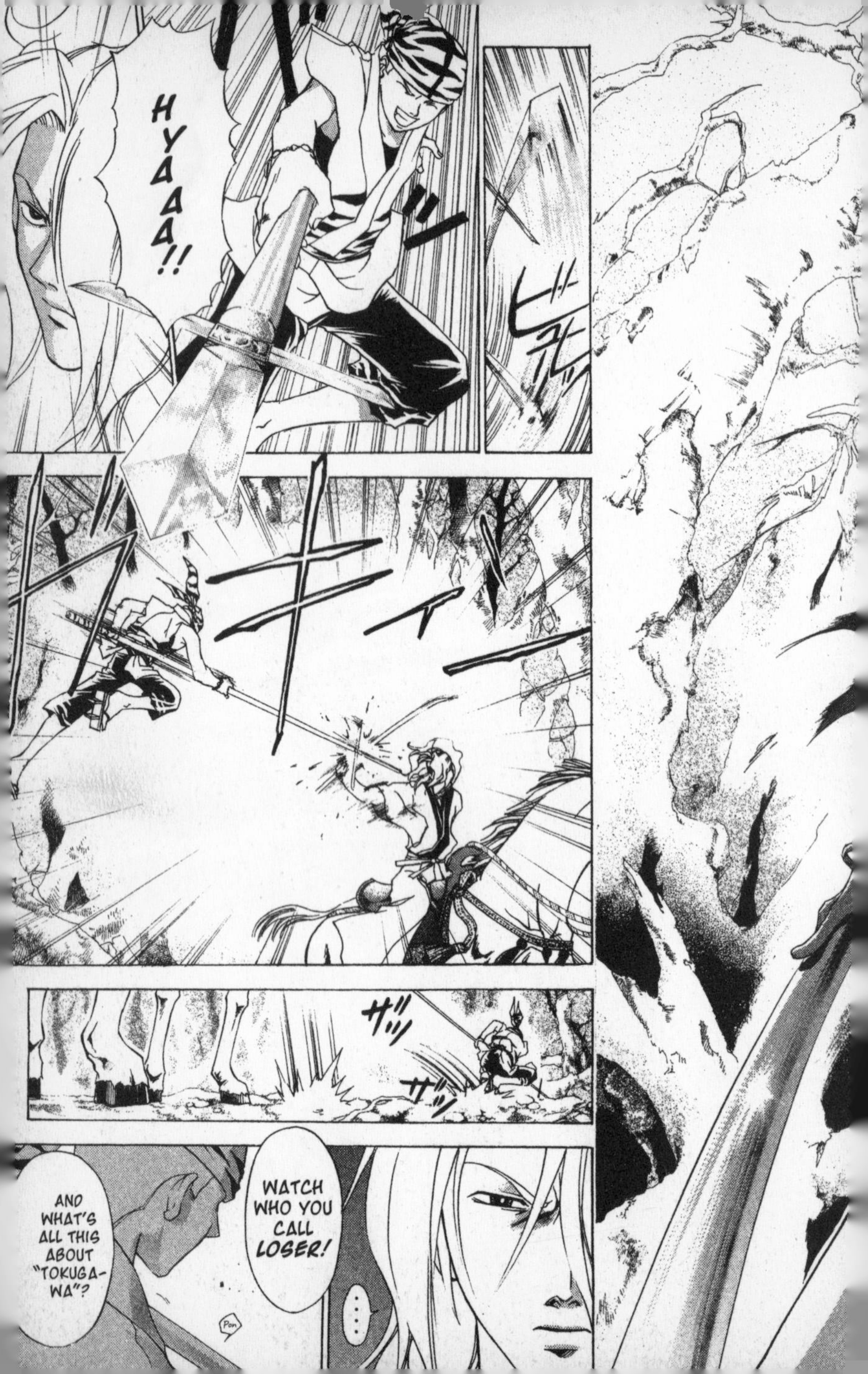
HYAAAA!!
ザッ
ザッ
WATCH WHO YOU CALL LOSER!
...
AND WHAT'S ALL THIS ABOUT "TOKUGAWA"?
Pon

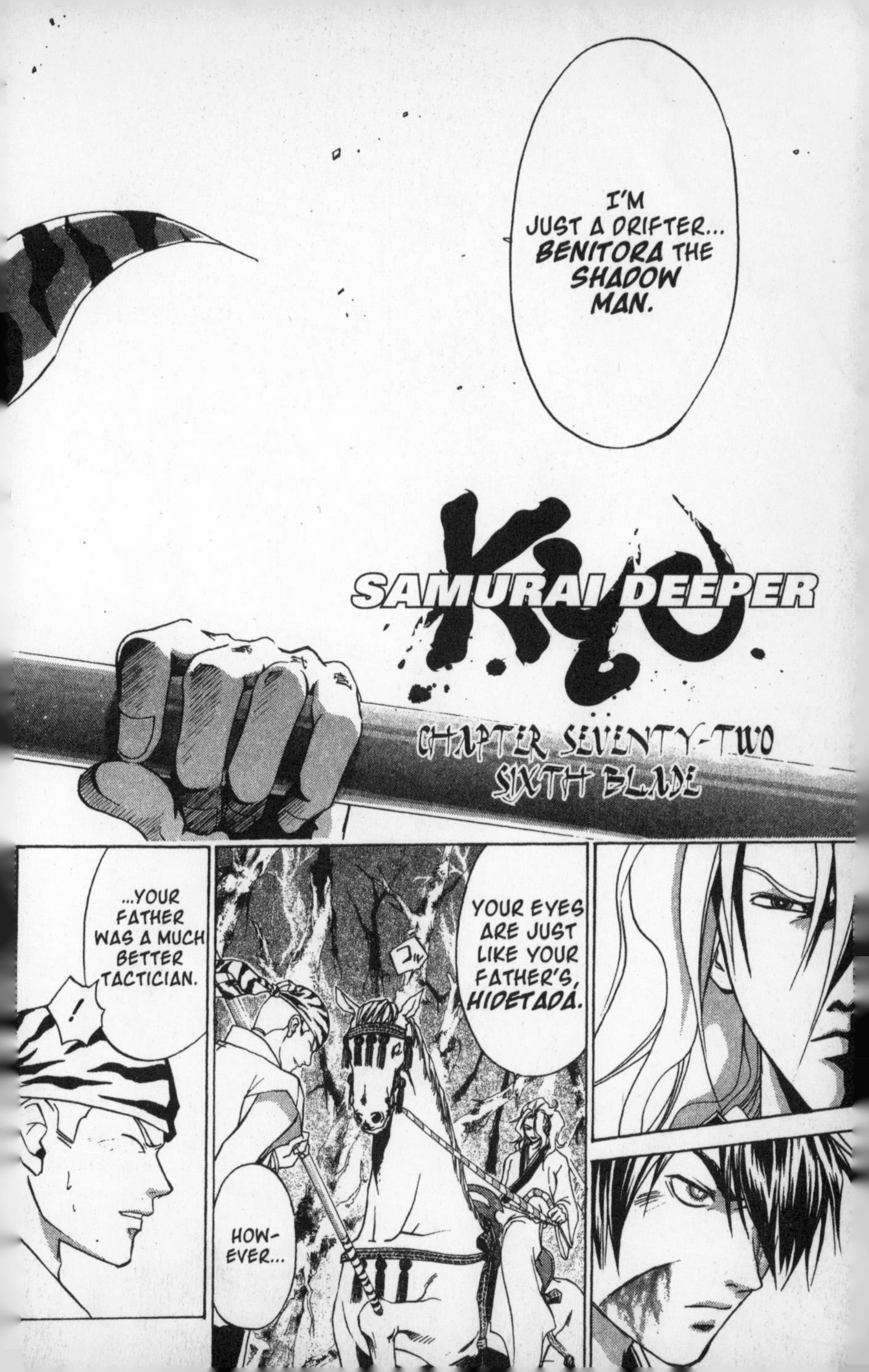
I'M JUST A DRIFTER... BENITORA THE SHADOW MAN.
SAMURAI DEEPER KYO
CHAPTER SEVENTY-TWO
SIXTH BLADE
YOUR EYES ARE JUST LIKE YOUR FATHER'S, HIDETADA.
HOW-EVER...
...YOUR FATHER WAS A MUCH BETTER TACTICIAN.
!

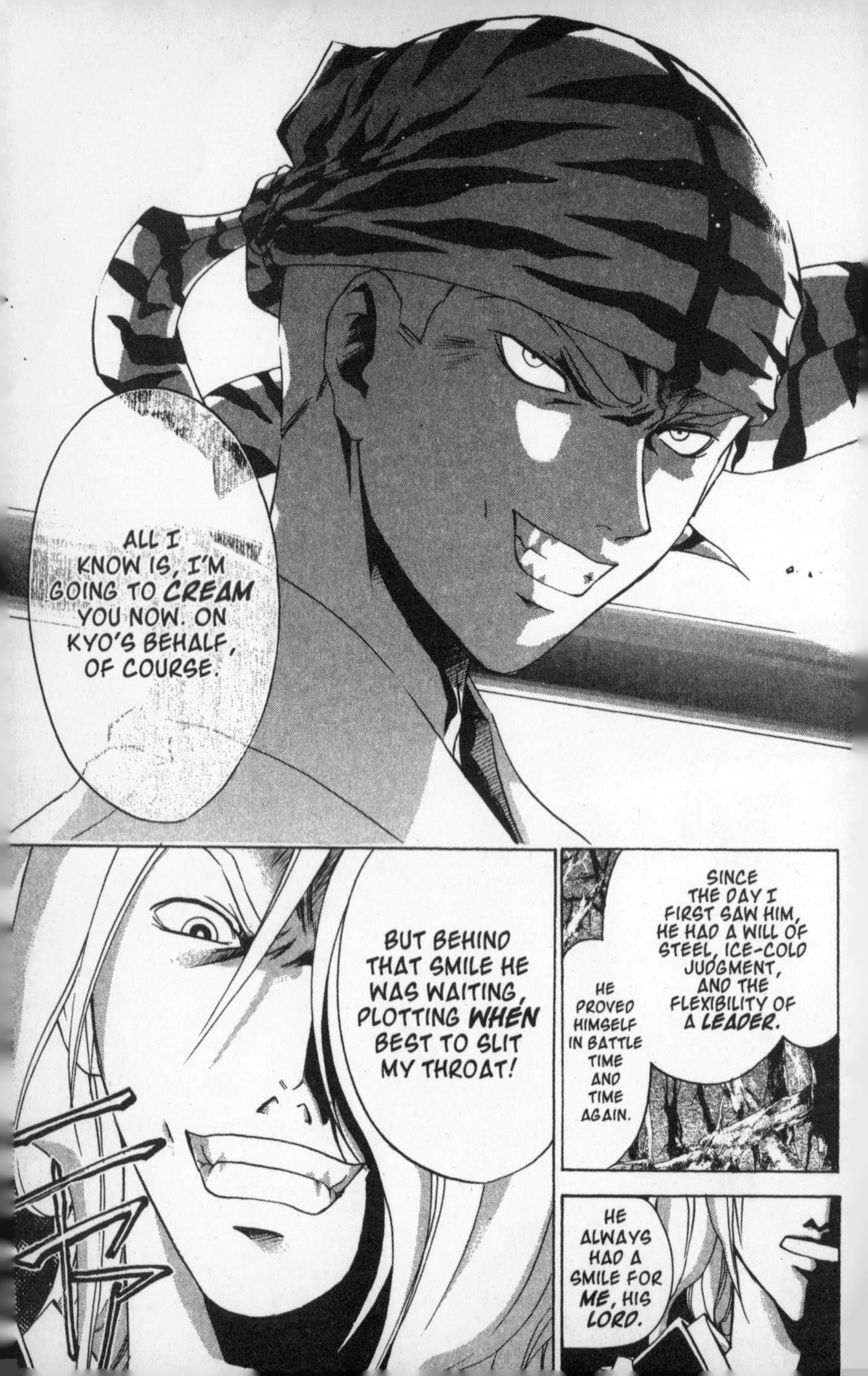
ALL I KNOW IS, I'M GOING TO **CREAM** YOU NOW. ON KYO'S BEHALF, OF COURSE.
SINCE THE DAY I FIRST SAW HIM, HE HAD A WILL OF STEEL, ICE-COLD JUDGMENT, AND THE FLEXIBILITY OF A **LEADER**.
HE PROVED HIMSELF IN BATTLE TIME AND TIME AGAIN.
HE ALWAYS HAD A SMILE FOR **ME**, HIS **LORD**.
BUT BEHIND THAT SMILE HE WAS WAITING, PLOTTING **WHEN** BEST TO SLIT MY THROAT!

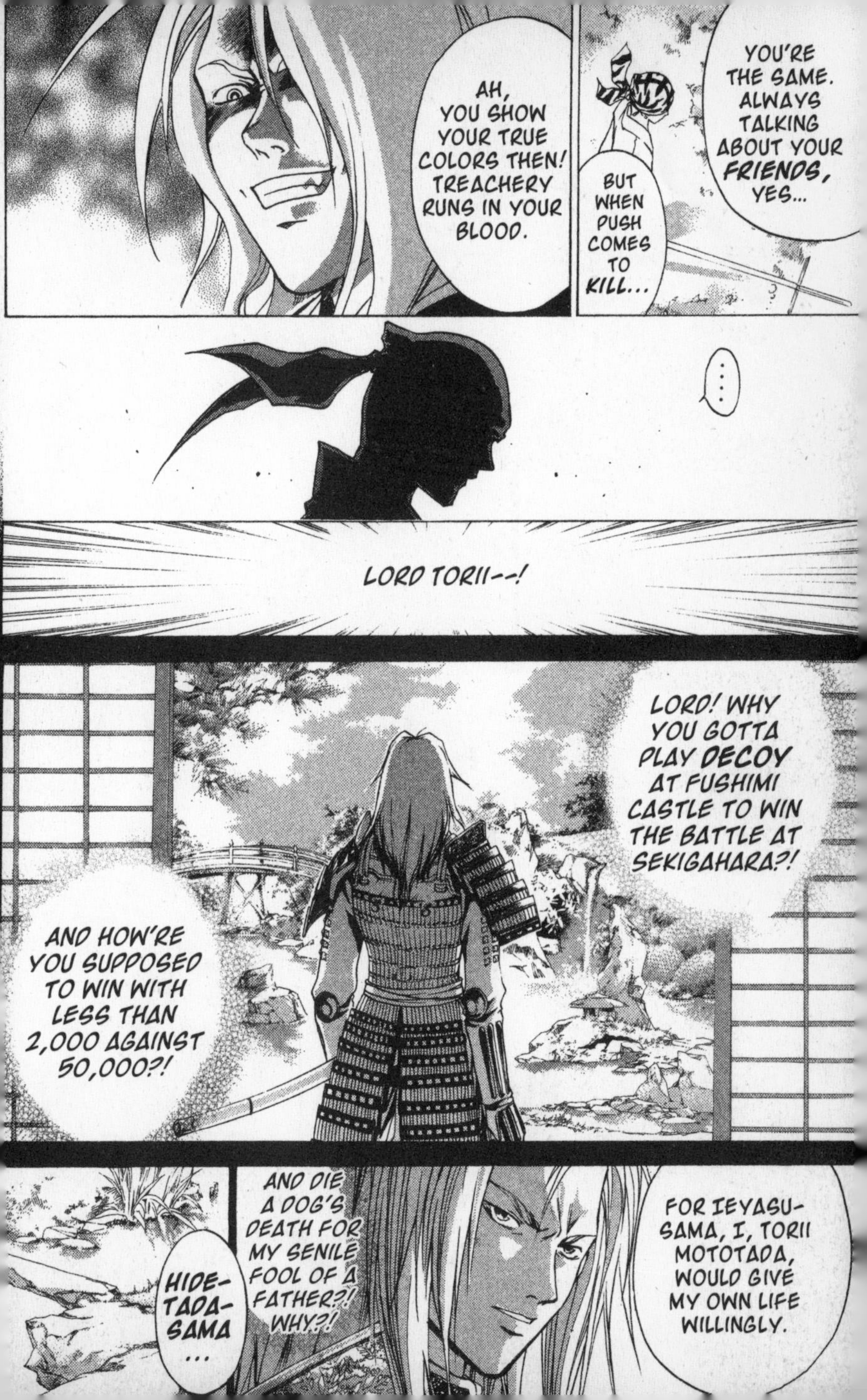
YOU'RE THE SAME. ALWAYS TALKING ABOUT YOUR FRIENDS, YES...
BUT WHEN PUSH COMES TO KILL...
AH, YOU SHOW YOUR TRUE COLORS THEN! TREACHERY RUNS IN YOUR BLOOD.
......
LORD TORII--!
LORD! WHY YOU GOTTA PLAY DECOY AT FUSHIMI CASTLE TO WIN THE BATTLE AT SEKIGAHARA?!
AND HOW'RE YOU SUPPOSED TO WIN WITH LESS THAN 2,000 AGAINST 50,000?!
AND DIE A DOG'S DEATH FOR MY SENILE FOOL OF A FATHER?! WHY?!
FOR IEYASU-SAMA, I, TORII MOTOTADA, WOULD GIVE MY OWN LIFE WILLINGLY.
HIDE-TADA-SAMA...

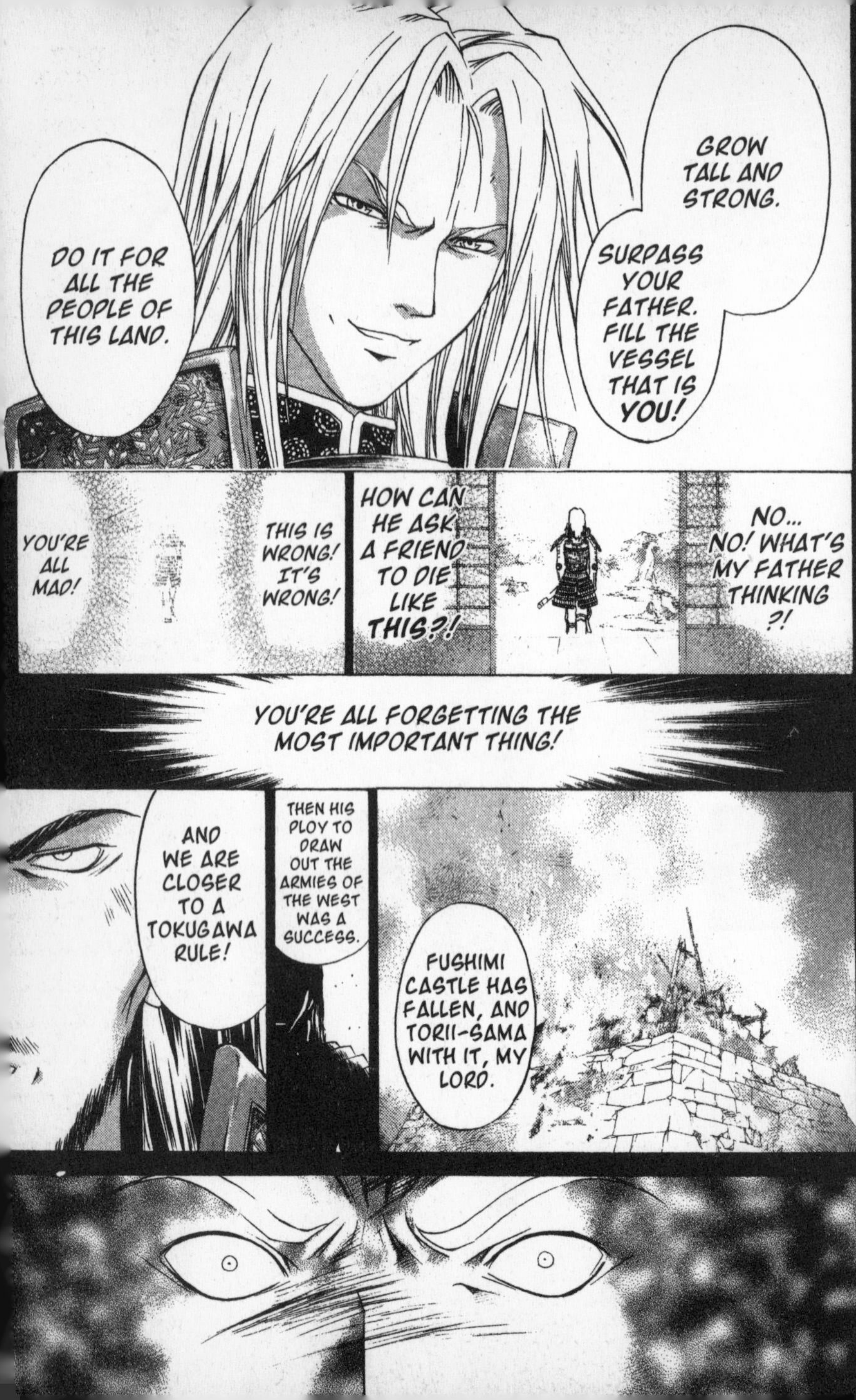
GROW TALL AND STRONG.
SURPASS YOUR FATHER. FILL THE VESSEL THAT IS YOU!
DO IT FOR ALL THE PEOPLE OF THIS LAND.
NO... NO! WHAT'S MY FATHER THINKING?!
HOW CAN HE ASK A FRIEND TO DIE LIKE THIS?!
THIS IS WRONG! IT'S WRONG!
YOU'RE ALL MAD!
YOU'RE ALL FORGETTING THE MOST IMPORTANT THING!
FUSHIMI CASTLE HAS FALLEN, AND TORII-SAMA WITH IT, MY LORD.
THEN HIS PLOY TO DRAW OUT THE ARMIES OF THE WEST WAS A SUCCESS.
AND WE ARE CLOSER TO A TOKUGAWA RULE!

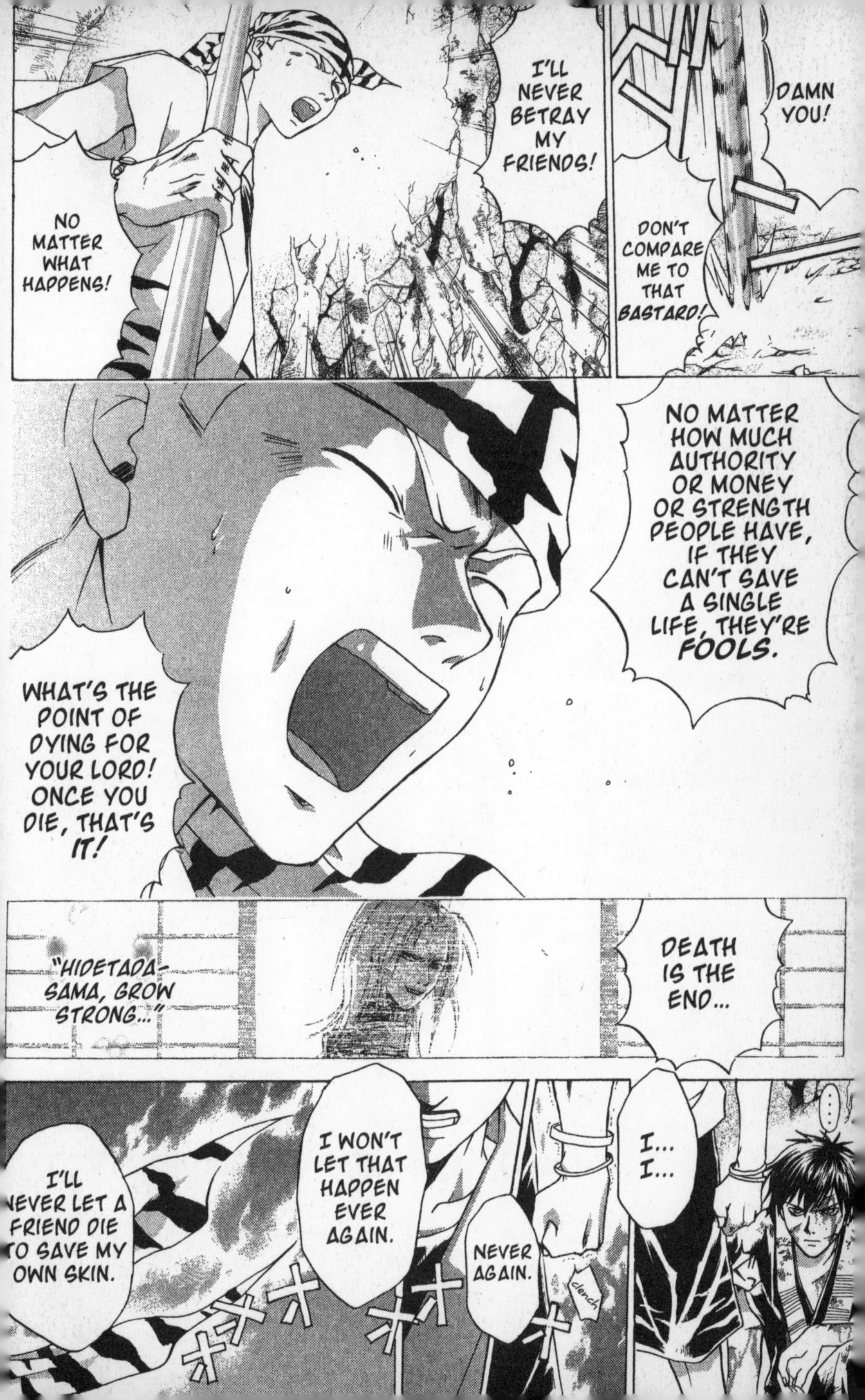
DAMN YOU!
DON'T COMPARE ME TO THAT BASTARD!
I'LL NEVER BETRAY MY FRIENDS!
NO MATTER WHAT HAPPENS!
NO MATTER HOW MUCH AUTHORITY OR MONEY OR STRENGTH PEOPLE HAVE, IF THEY CAN'T SAVE A SINGLE LIFE, THEY'RE FOOLS.
WHAT'S THE POINT OF DYING FOR YOUR LORD! ONCE YOU DIE, THAT'S IT!
DEATH IS THE END...
"HIDETADA-SAMA, GROW STRONG..."
...
I... I...
I WON'T LET THAT HAPPEN EVER AGAIN.
NEVER AGAIN.
clench
I'LL NEVER LET A FRIEND DIE TO SAVE MY OWN SKIN.

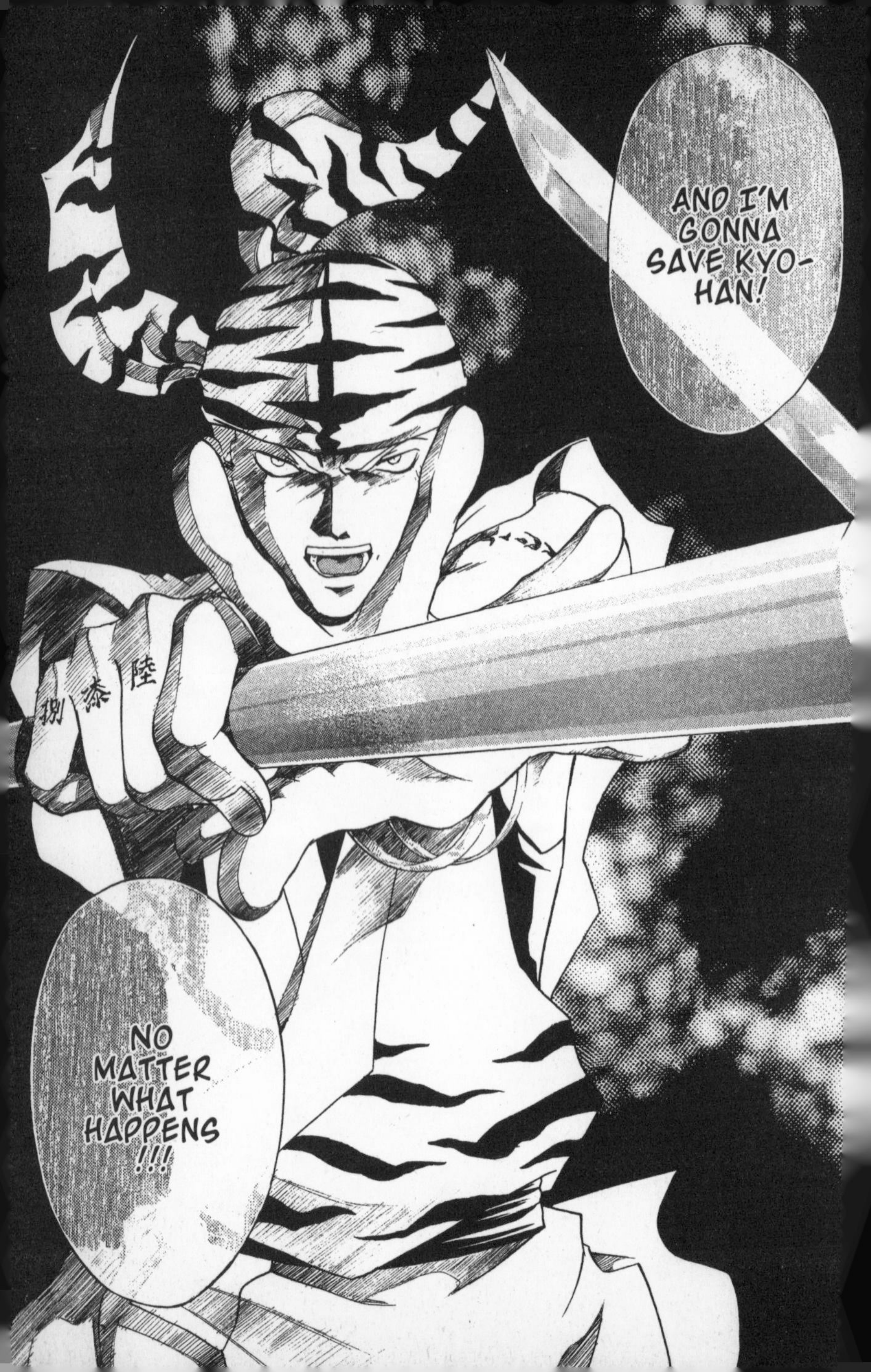
AND I'M GONNA SAVE KYO-HAN!
陸 漆 捌
NO MATTER WHAT HAPPENS!!!

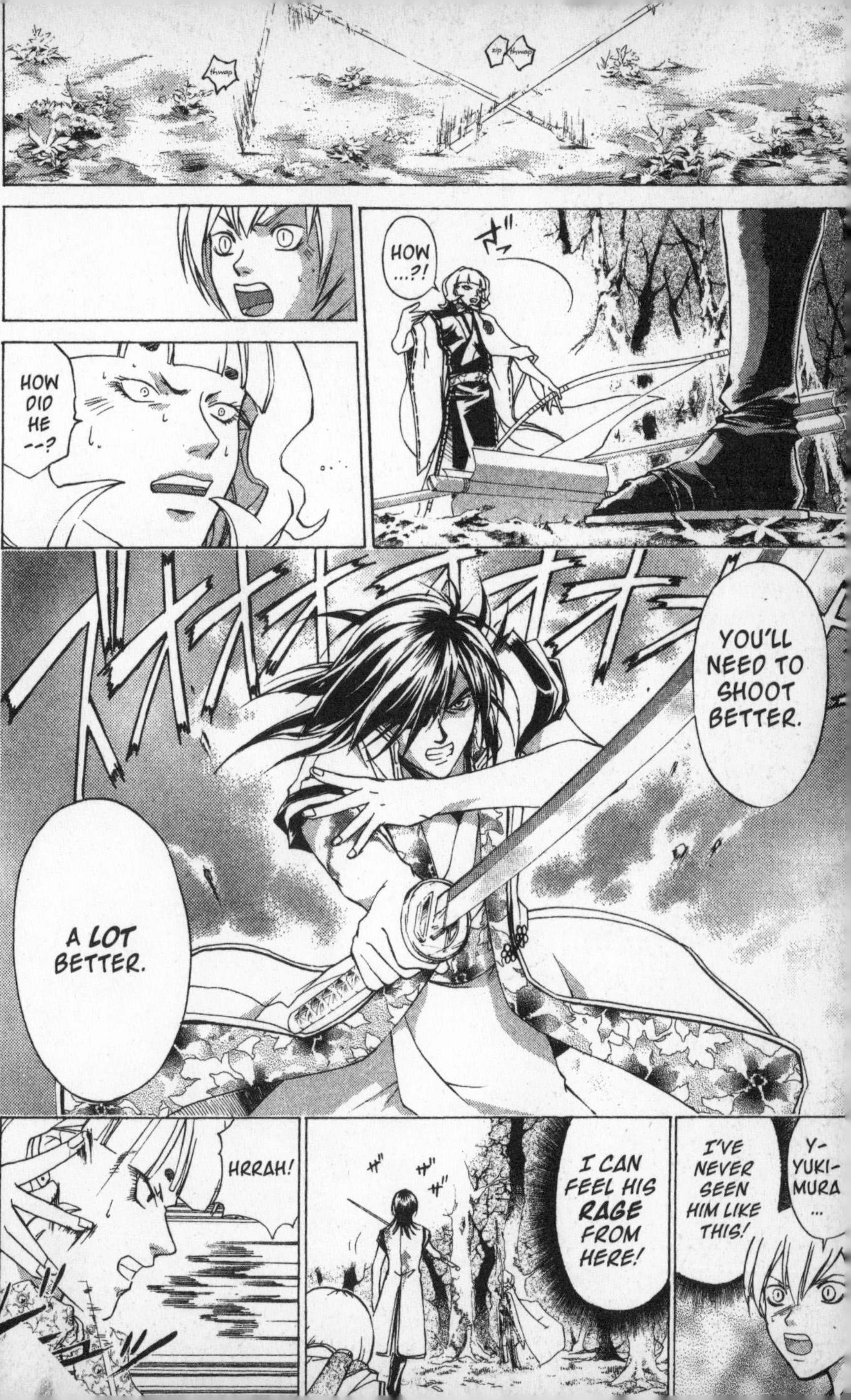
zip
thwap
thwap
HOW ...?!
HOW DID HE --?
YOU'LL NEED TO SHOOT BETTER.
A LOT BETTER.
Y-YUKIMURA ...
I'VE NEVER SEEN HIM LIKE THIS!
I CAN FEEL HIS RAGE FROM HERE!
HRRAH!

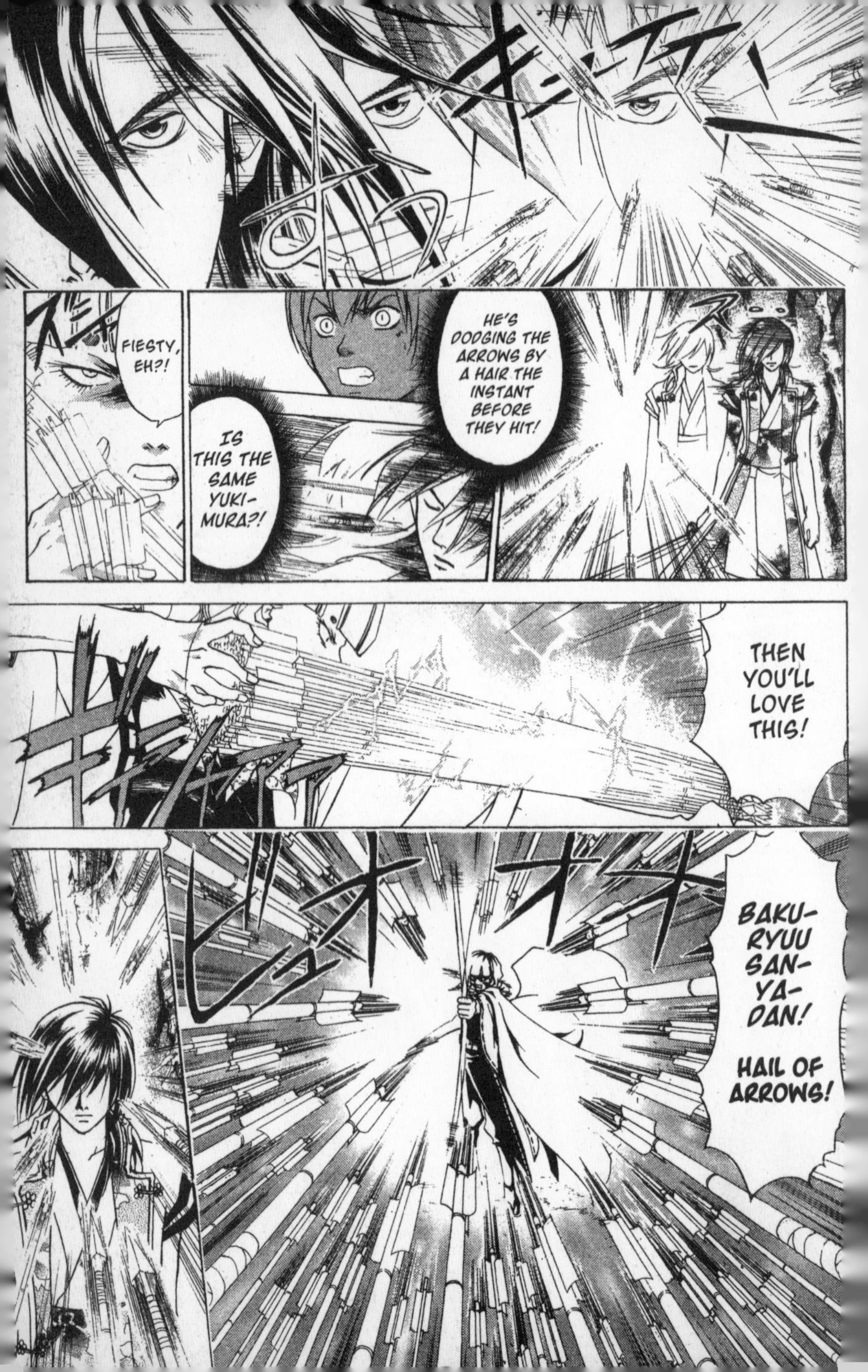
HE'S DODGING THE ARROWS BY A HAIR THE INSTANT BEFORE THEY HIT!
IS THIS THE SAME YUKI-MURA?!
FIESTY, EH?!
THEN YOU'LL LOVE THIS!
BAKU-RYUU SAN-YA-DAN!
HAIL OF ARROWS!

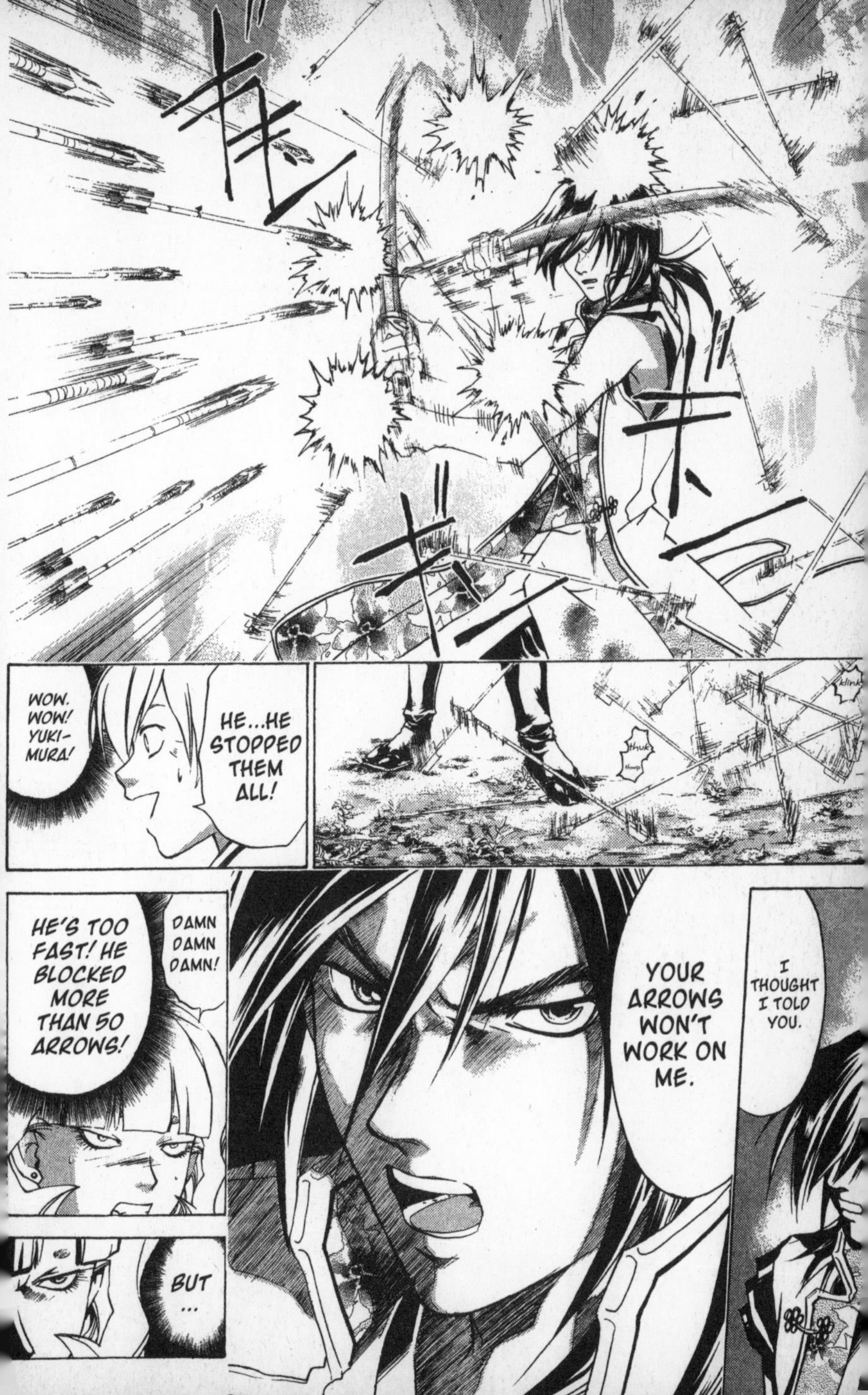
klink
thuk
thwip
HE...HE STOPPED THEM ALL!
WOW. WOW! YUKI-MURA!
I THOUGHT I TOLD YOU.
YOUR ARROWS WON'T WORK ON ME.
DAMN DAMN DAMN!
HE'S TOO FAST! HE BLOCKED MORE THAN 50 ARROWS!
BUT ...

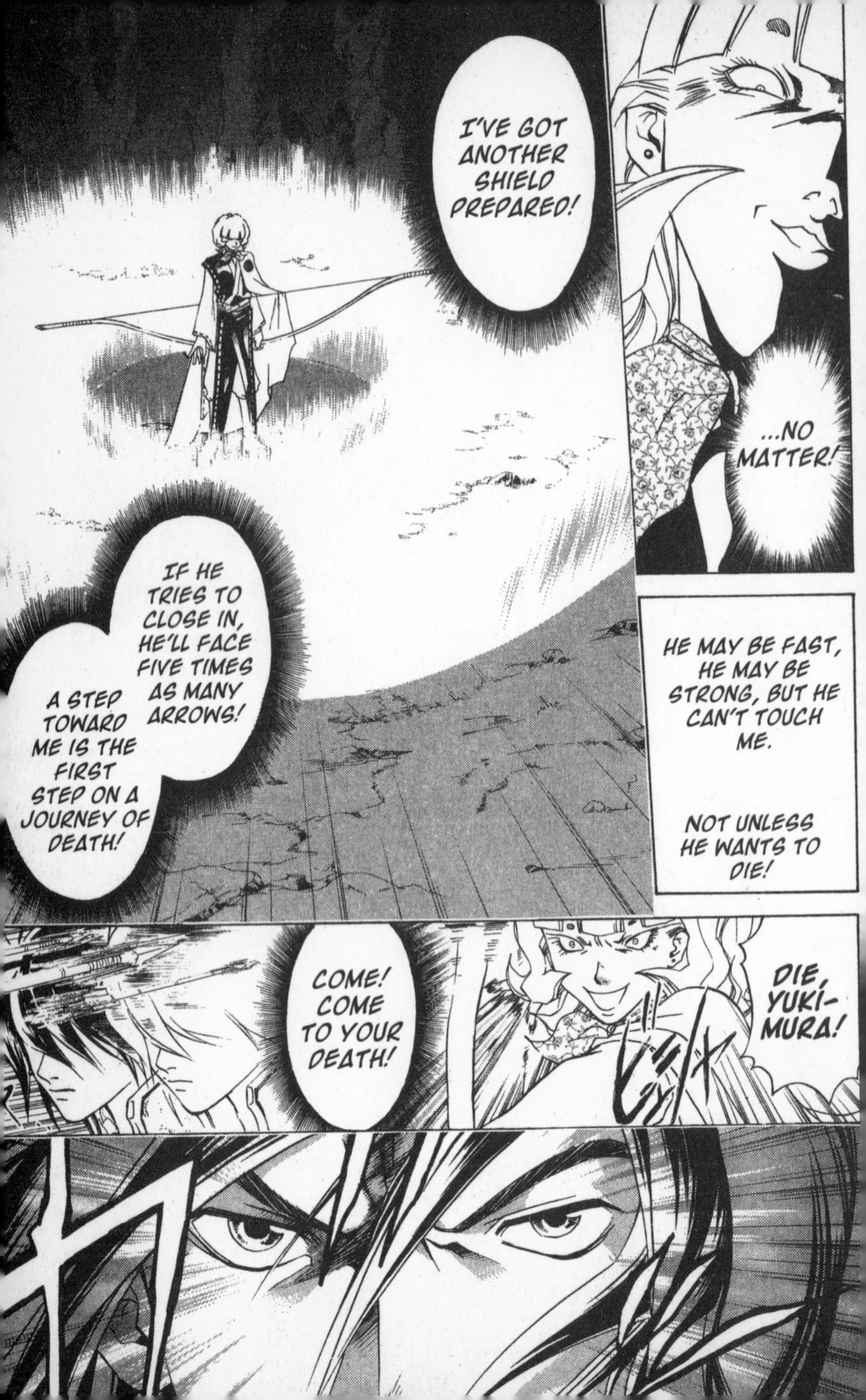
...NO MATTER!
HE MAY BE FAST, HE MAY BE STRONG, BUT HE CAN'T TOUCH ME.
NOT UNLESS HE WANTS TO DIE!
I'VE GOT ANOTHER SHIELD PREPARED!
IF HE TRIES TO CLOSE IN, HE'LL FACE FIVE TIMES AS MANY ARROWS!
A STEP TOWARD ME IS THE FIRST STEP ON A JOURNEY OF DEATH!
DIE, YUKI-MURA!
COME! COME TO YOUR DEATH!

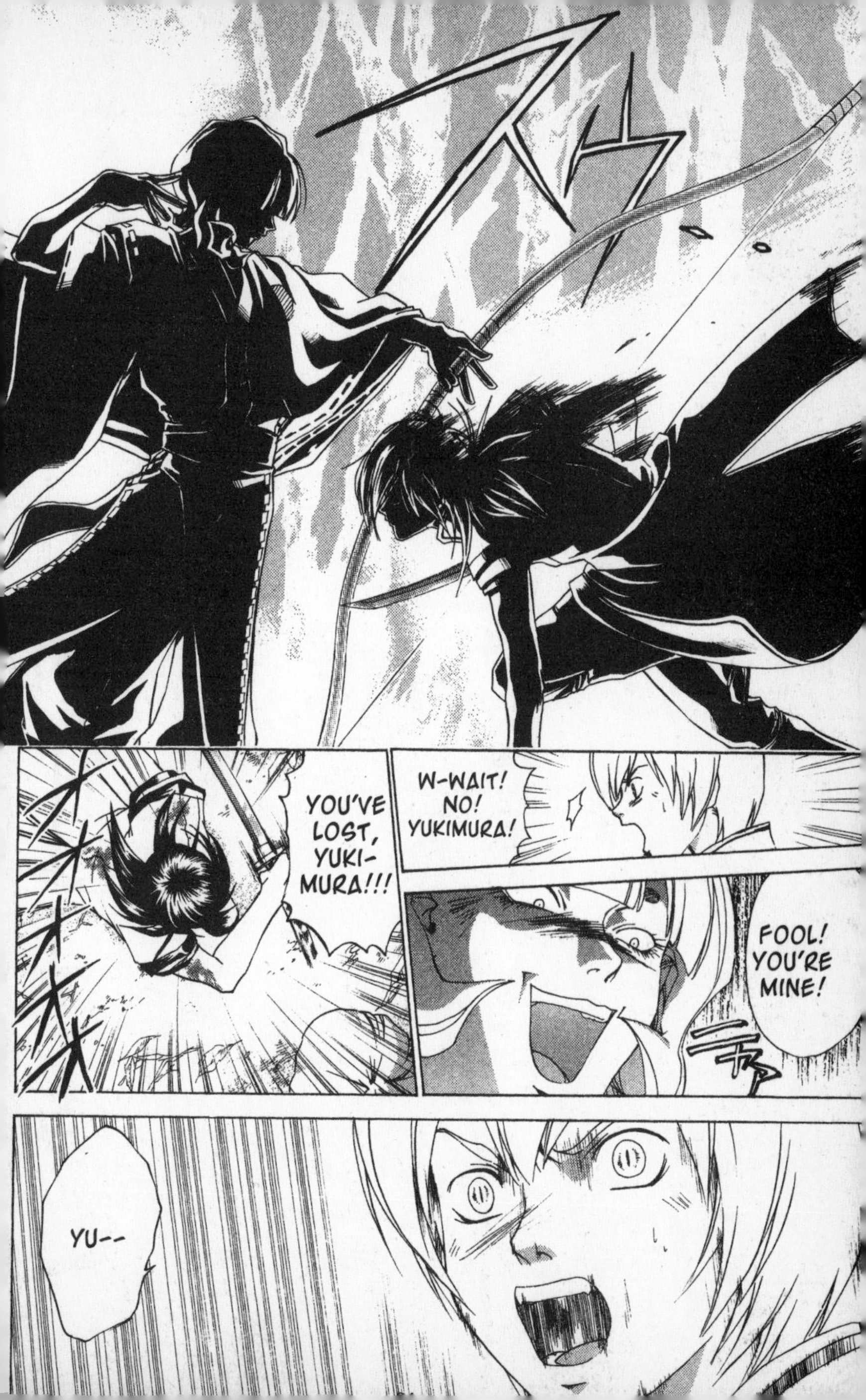
W-WAIT! NO! YUKIMURA!
FOOL! YOU'RE MINE!
YOU'VE LOST, YUKI-MURA!!!
YU--

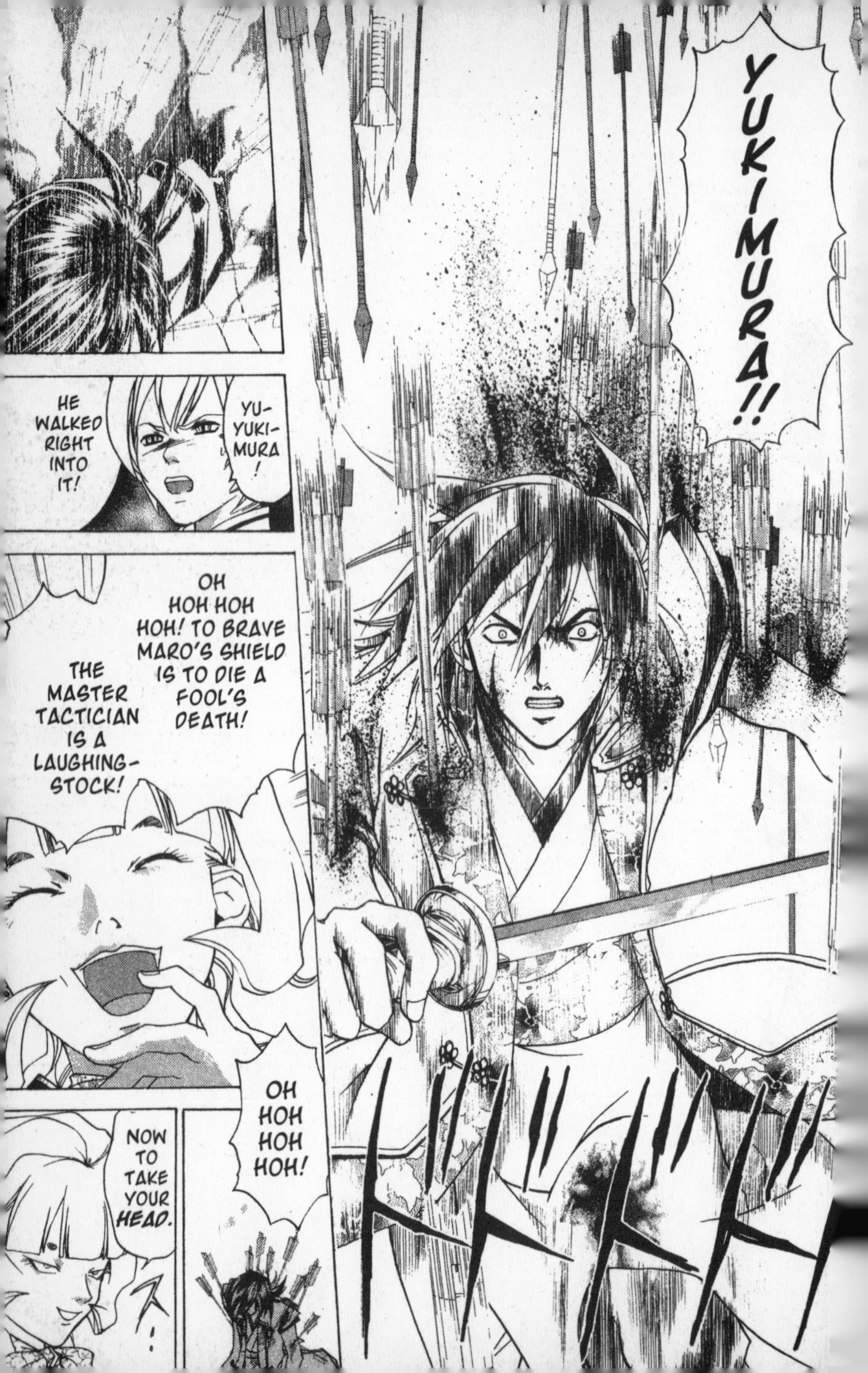
YUKIMURA!!
YU-YUKI-MURA!
HE WALKED RIGHT INTO IT!
OH HOH HOH HOH! TO BRAVE MARO'S SHIELD IS TO DIE A FOOL'S DEATH!
THE MASTER TACTICIAN IS A LAUGHING-STOCK!
OH HOH HOH HOH!
NOW TO TAKE YOUR HEAD.
!

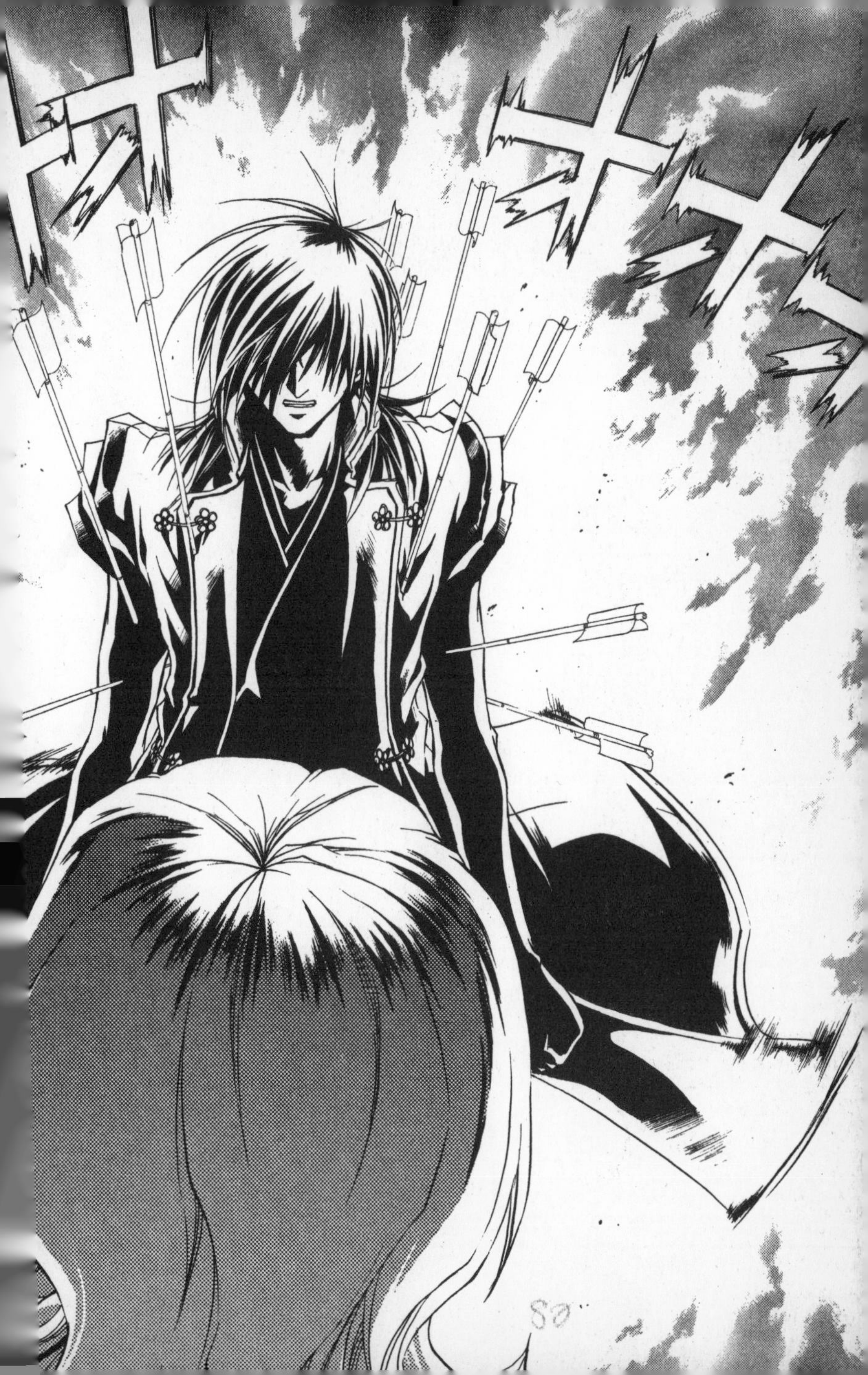

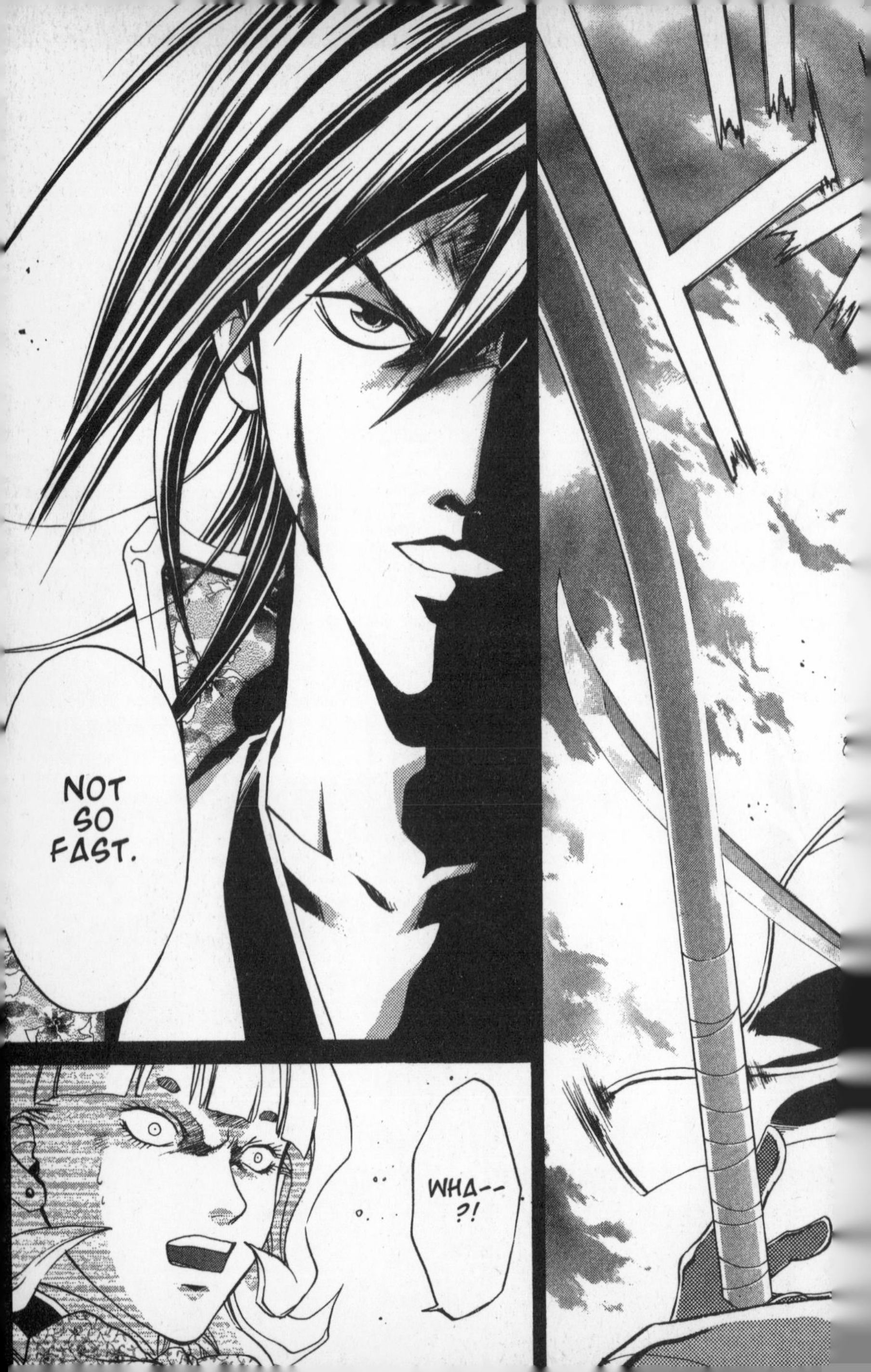
NOT SO FAST.
WHA-- ?!

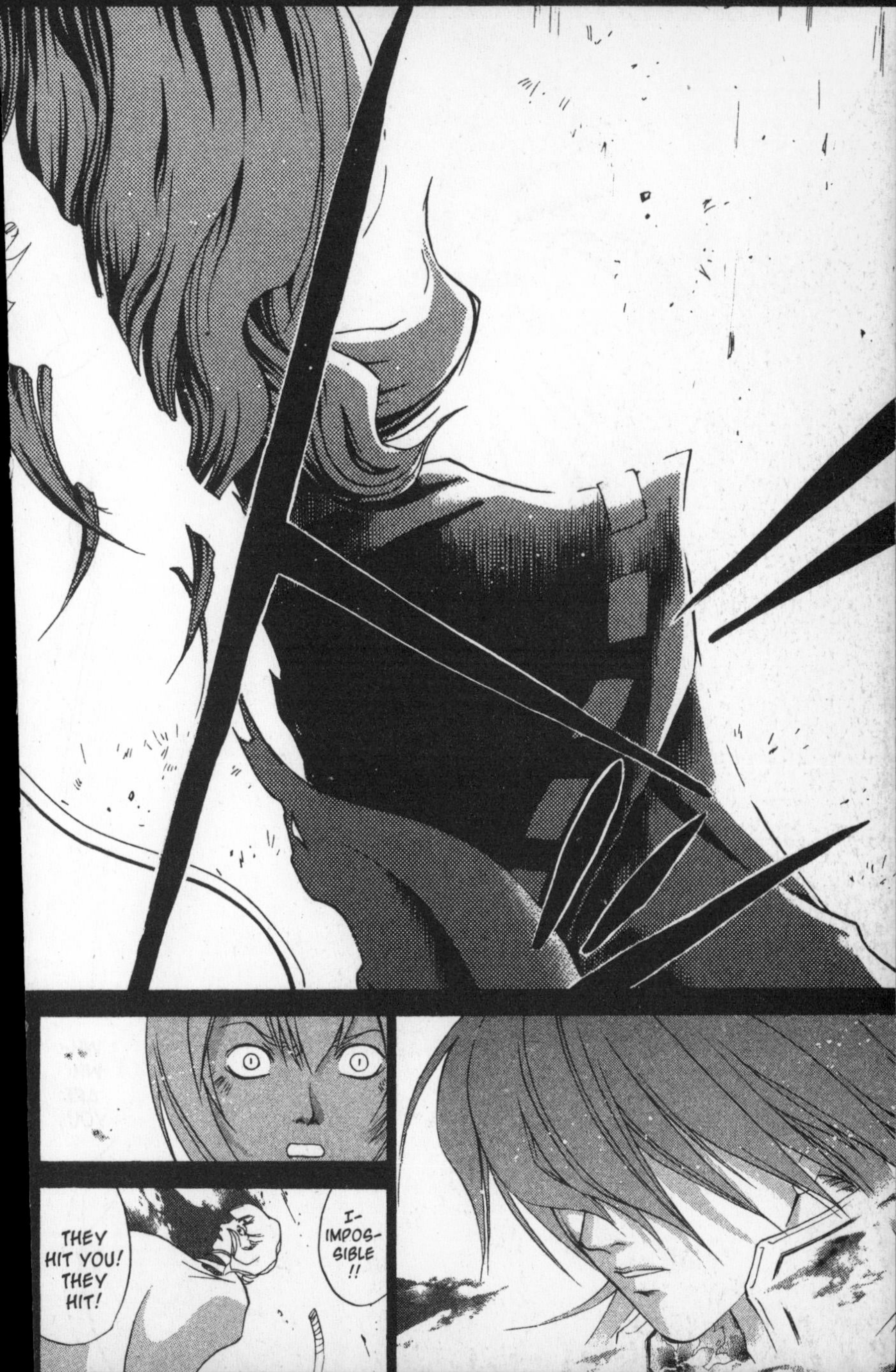
I-IMPOSSIBLE!!
THEY HIT YOU! THEY HIT!

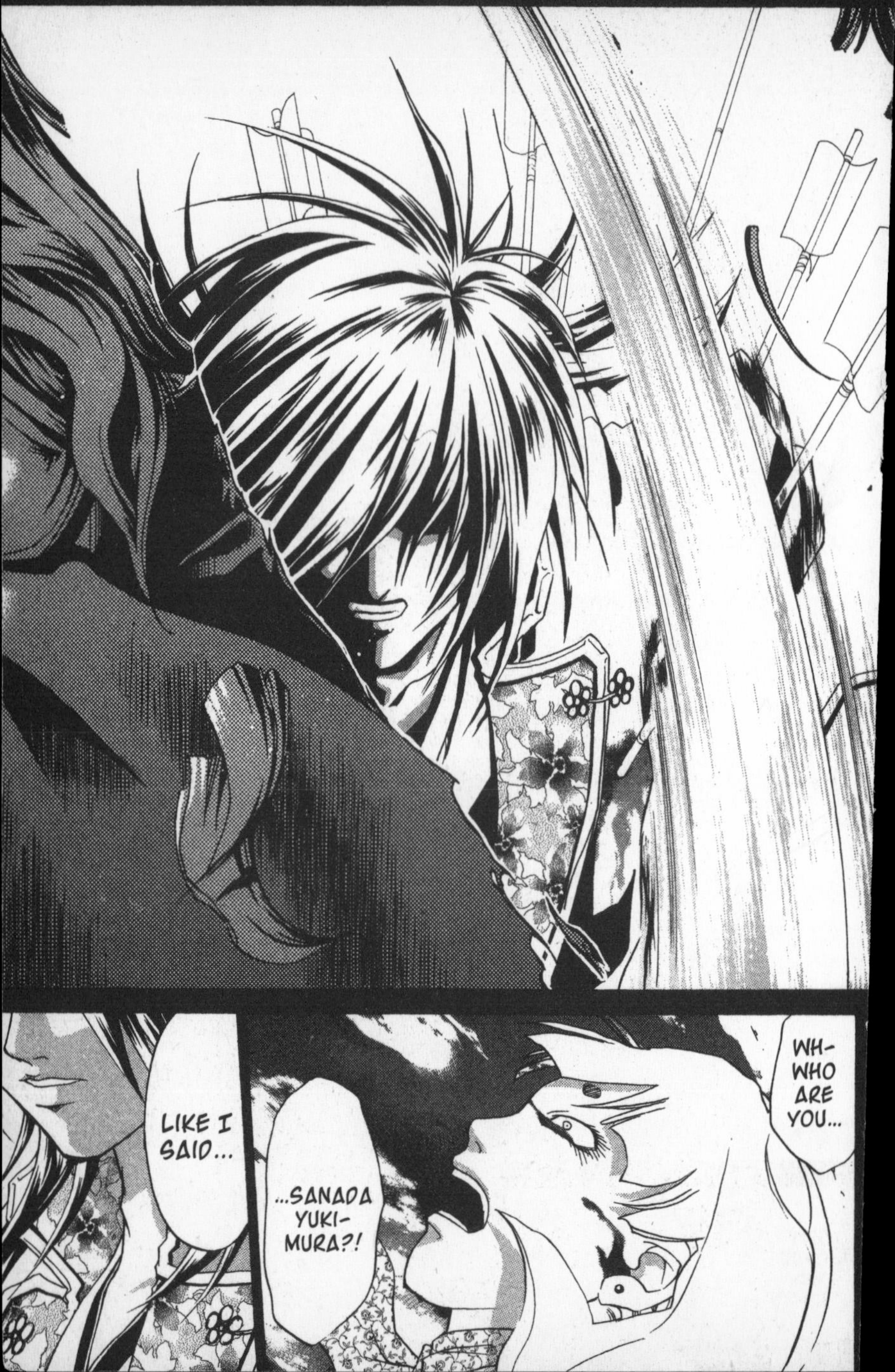
WH-WHO ARE YOU...
...SANADA YUKI-MURA?!
LIKE I SAID...

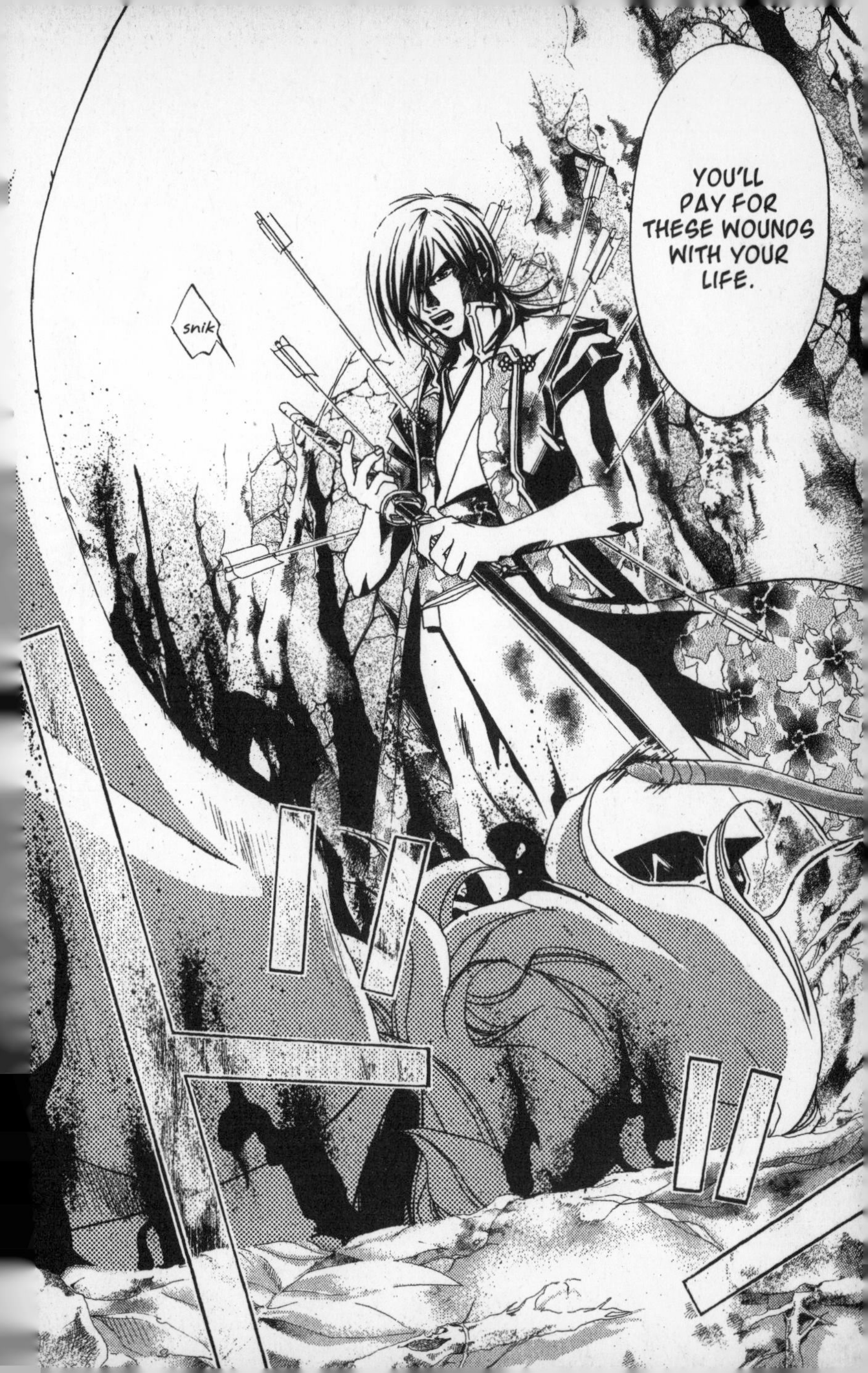
YOU'LL PAY FOR THESE WOUNDS WITH YOUR LIFE.
snik

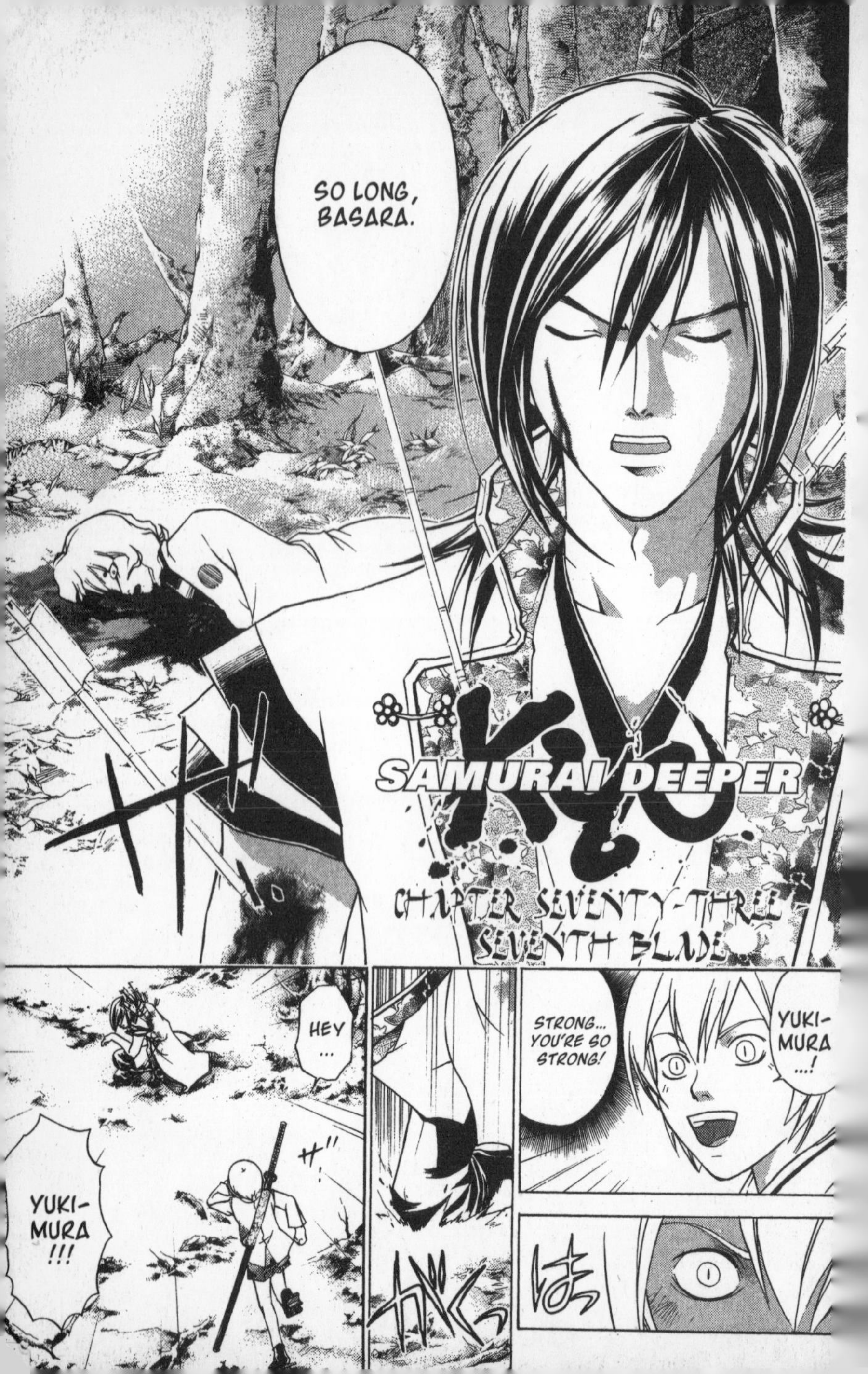
SO LONG, BASARA.
SAMURAI DEEPER KYO
CHAPTER SEVENTY-THREE
SEVENTH BLADE
YUKI-MURA ...!
STRONG... YOU'RE SO STRONG!
はっ
がくっ
HEY ...
YUKI-MURA !!!

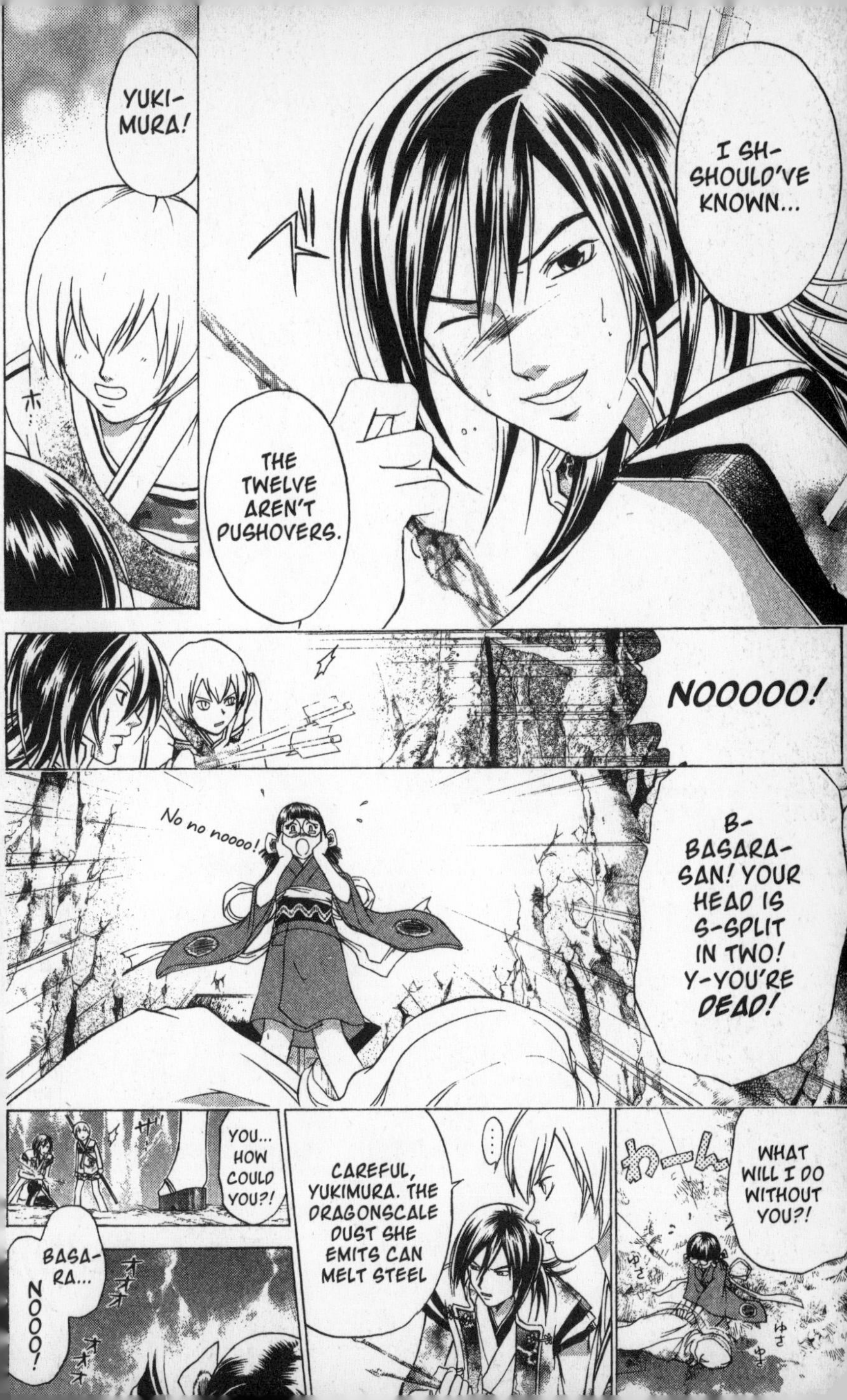
I SH-SHOULD'VE KNOWN...
THE TWELVE AREN'T PUSHOVERS.
YUKI-MURA!
NOOOOO!
B-BASARA-SAN! YOUR HEAD IS S-SPLIT IN TWO! Y-YOU'RE DEAD!
No no noooo!
WHAT WILL I DO WITHOUT YOU?!
...
CAREFUL, YUKIMURA. THE DRAGONSCALE DUST SHE EMITS CAN MELT STEEL
YOU... HOW COULD YOU?!
BASA-RA...
NOOOO!

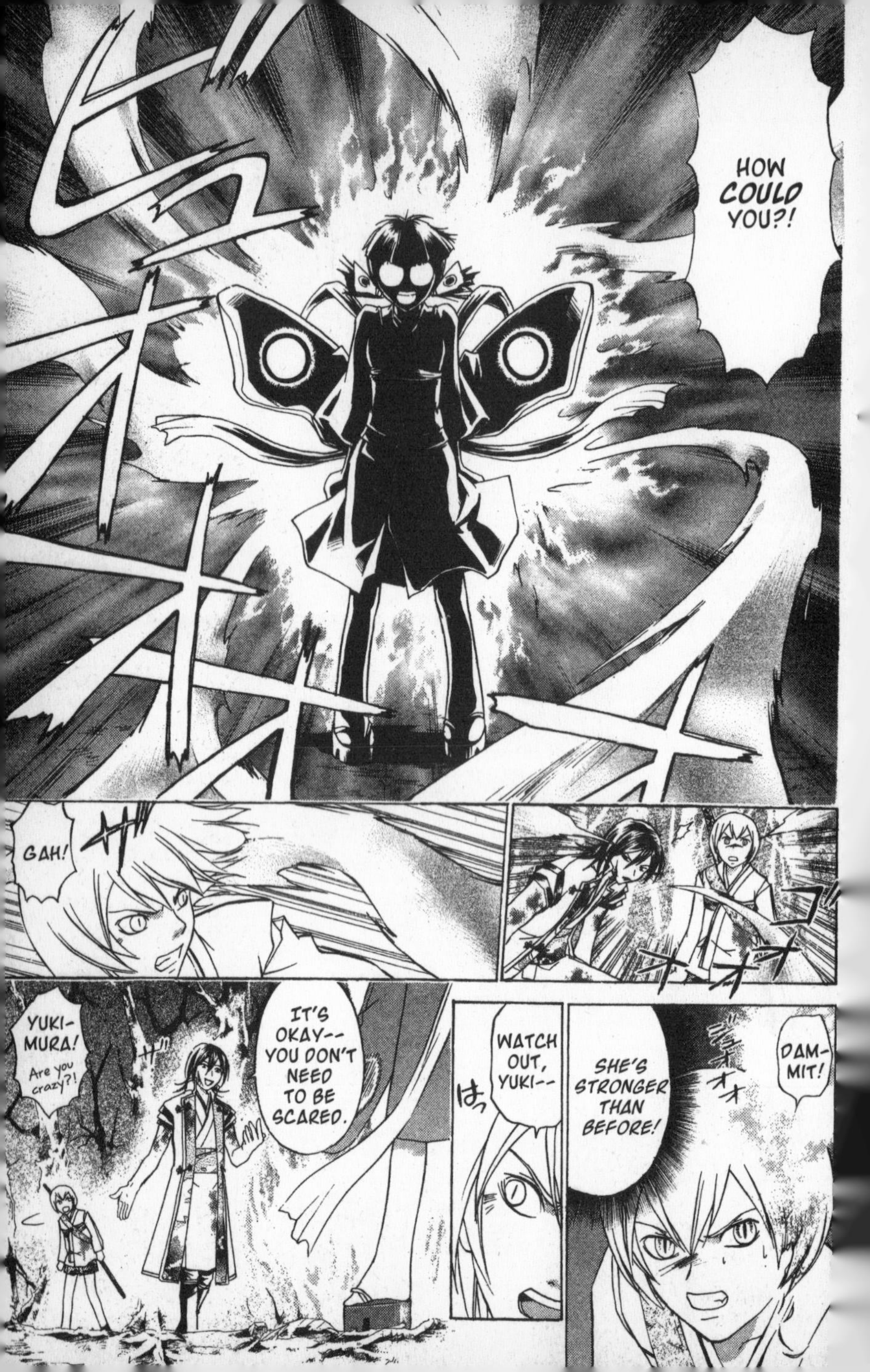

HOW COULD YOU?!
GAH!
DAM-MIT!
SHE'S STRONGER THAN BEFORE!
WATCH OUT, YUKI--
はっ
IT'S OKAY-- YOU DON'T NEED TO BE SCARED.
YUKI-MURA!
Are you crazy?!

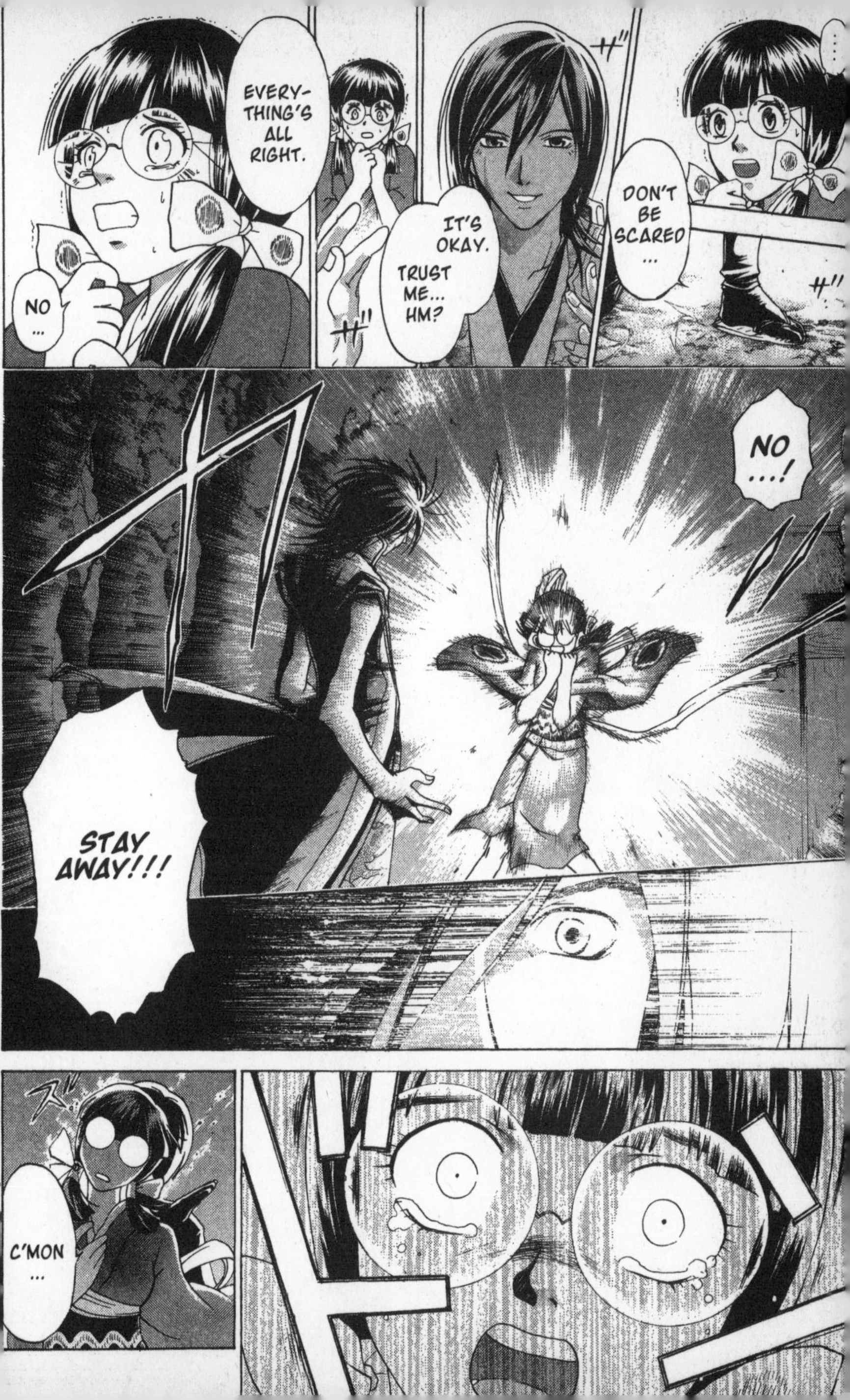
...
DON'T BE SCARED ...
IT'S OKAY.
TRUST ME... HM?
EVERY-THING'S ALL RIGHT.
NO ...
NO ...!
STAY AWAY!!!
C'MON ...

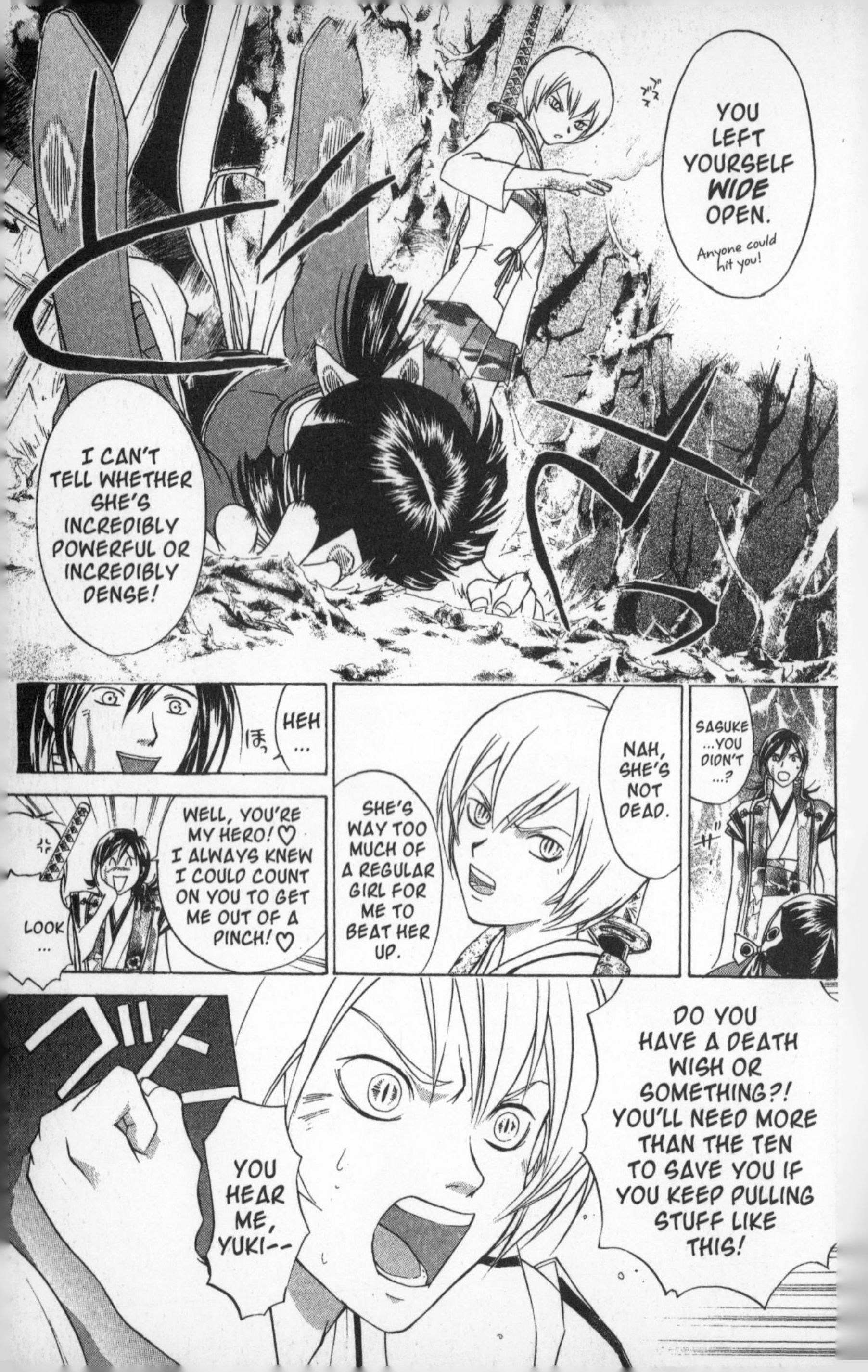
YOU LEFT YOURSELF WIDE OPEN.
Anyone could hit you!
I CAN'T TELL WHETHER SHE'S INCREDIBLY POWERFUL OR INCREDIBLY DENSE!
SASUKE ...YOU DIDN'T ...?
NAH, SHE'S NOT DEAD.
SHE'S WAY TOO MUCH OF A REGULAR GIRL FOR ME TO BEAT HER UP.
HEH ...
WELL, YOU'RE MY HERO! ♡ I ALWAYS KNEW I COULD COUNT ON YOU TO GET ME OUT OF A PINCH! ♡
LOOK ...
DO YOU HAVE A DEATH WISH OR SOMETHING?! YOU'LL NEED MORE THAN THE TEN TO SAVE YOU IF YOU KEEP PULLING STUFF LIKE THIS!
YOU HEAR ME, YUKI--

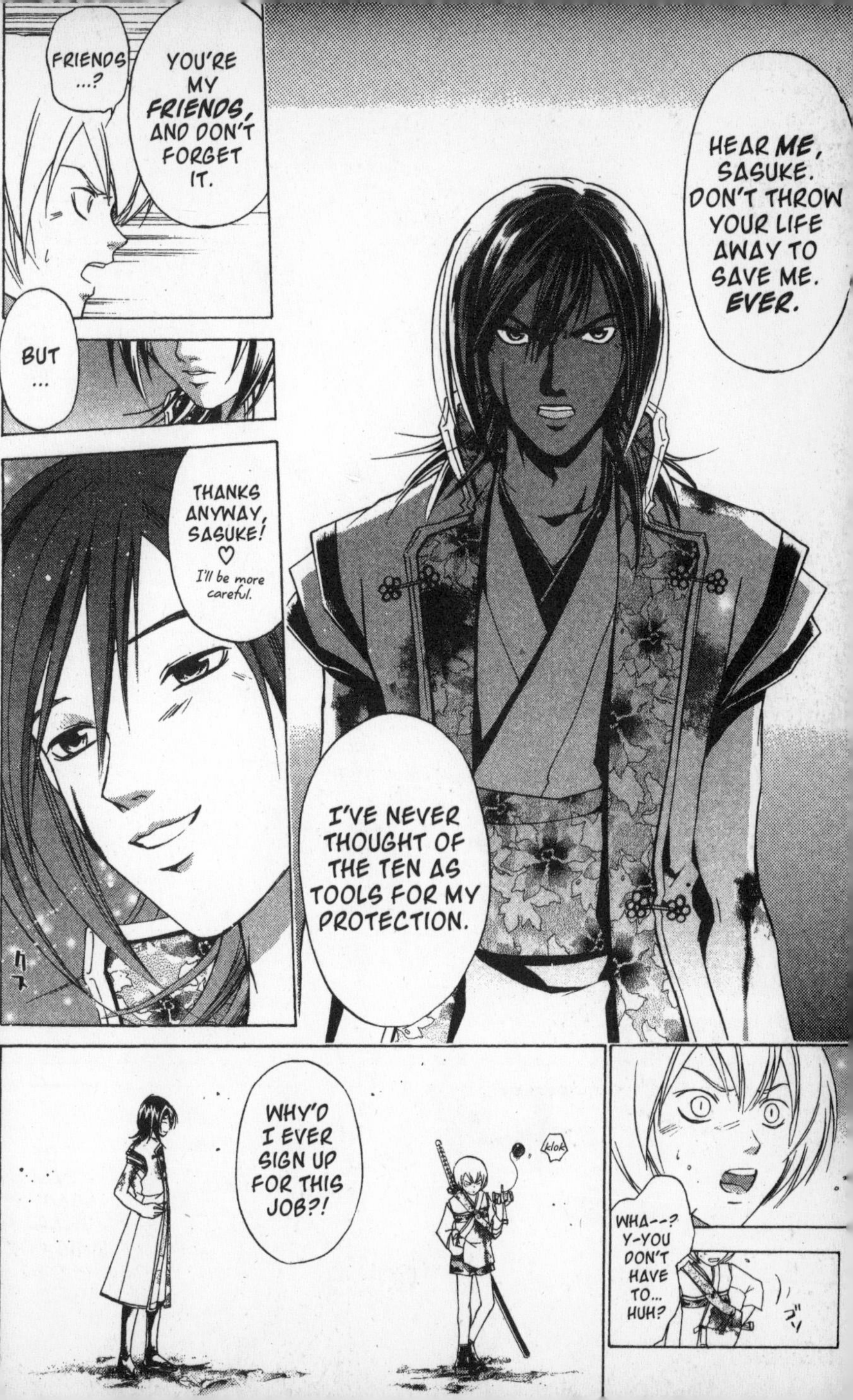
HEAR ME, SASUKE. DON'T THROW YOUR LIFE AWAY TO SAVE ME. EVER.
I'VE NEVER THOUGHT OF THE TEN AS TOOLS FOR MY PROTECTION.
YOU'RE MY FRIENDS, AND DON'T FORGET IT.
FRIENDS ...?
BUT ...
THANKS ANYWAY, SASUKE! ♡
I'll be more careful.
WHA--? Y-YOU DON'T HAVE TO... HUH?
klok
WHY'D I EVER SIGN UP FOR THIS JOB?!

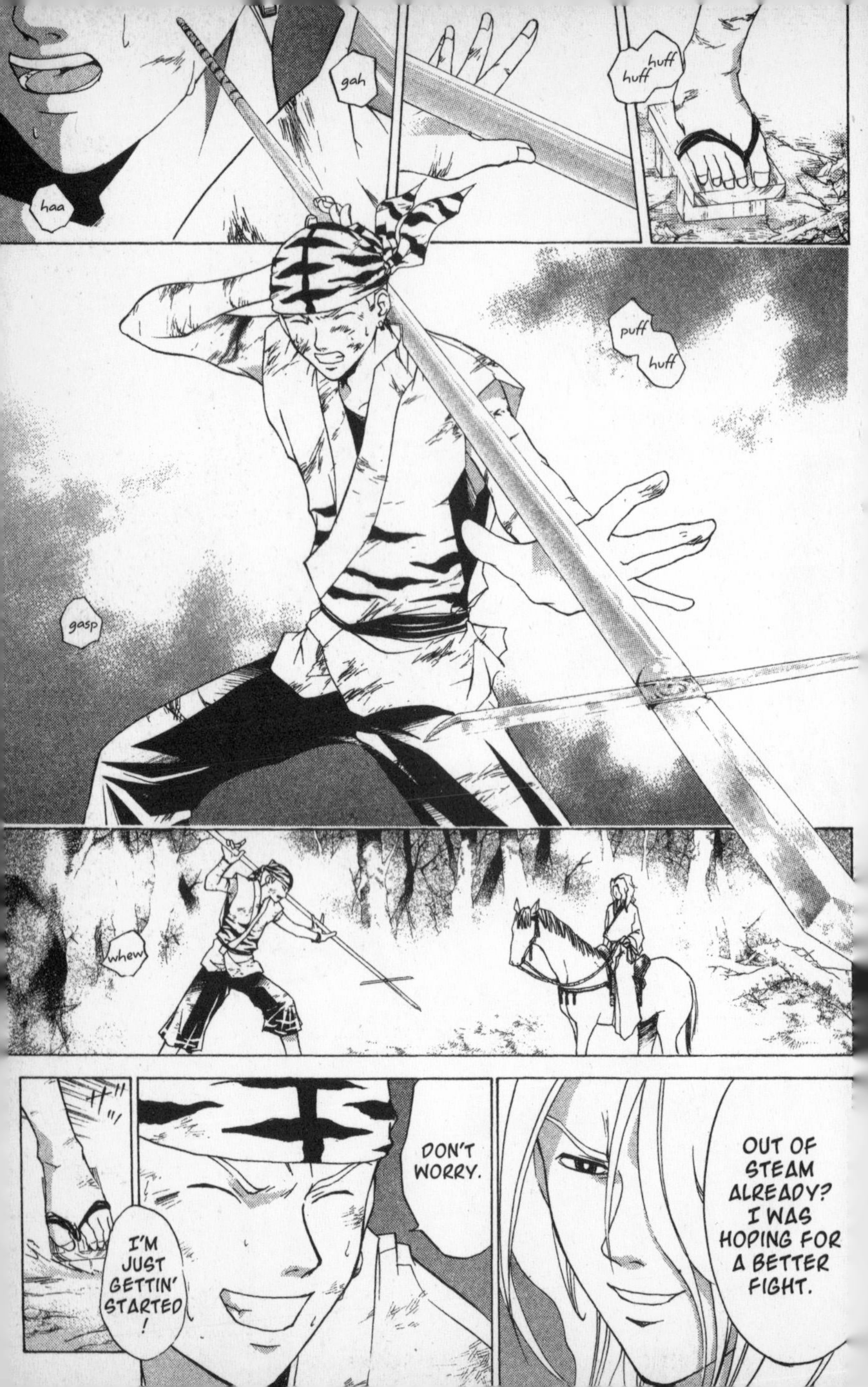
huff huff
gah
haa
puff huff
gasp
whew
OUT OF STEAM ALREADY? I WAS HOPING FOR A BETTER FIGHT.
DON'T WORRY.
I'M JUST GETTIN' STARTED!

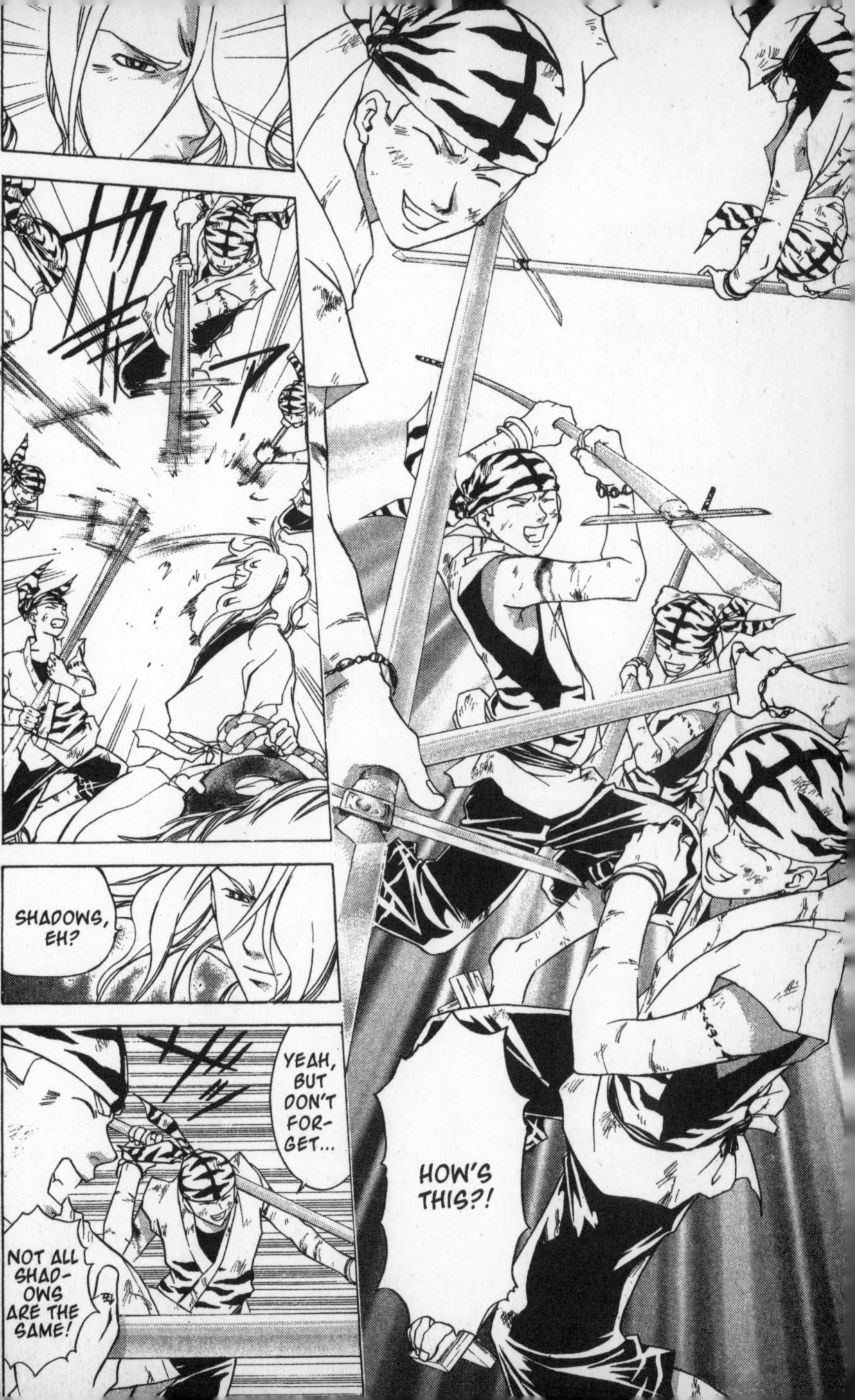
HOW'S THIS?!
SHADOWS, EH?
YEAH, BUT DON'T FOR-GET...
NOT ALL SHAD-OWS ARE THE SAME!

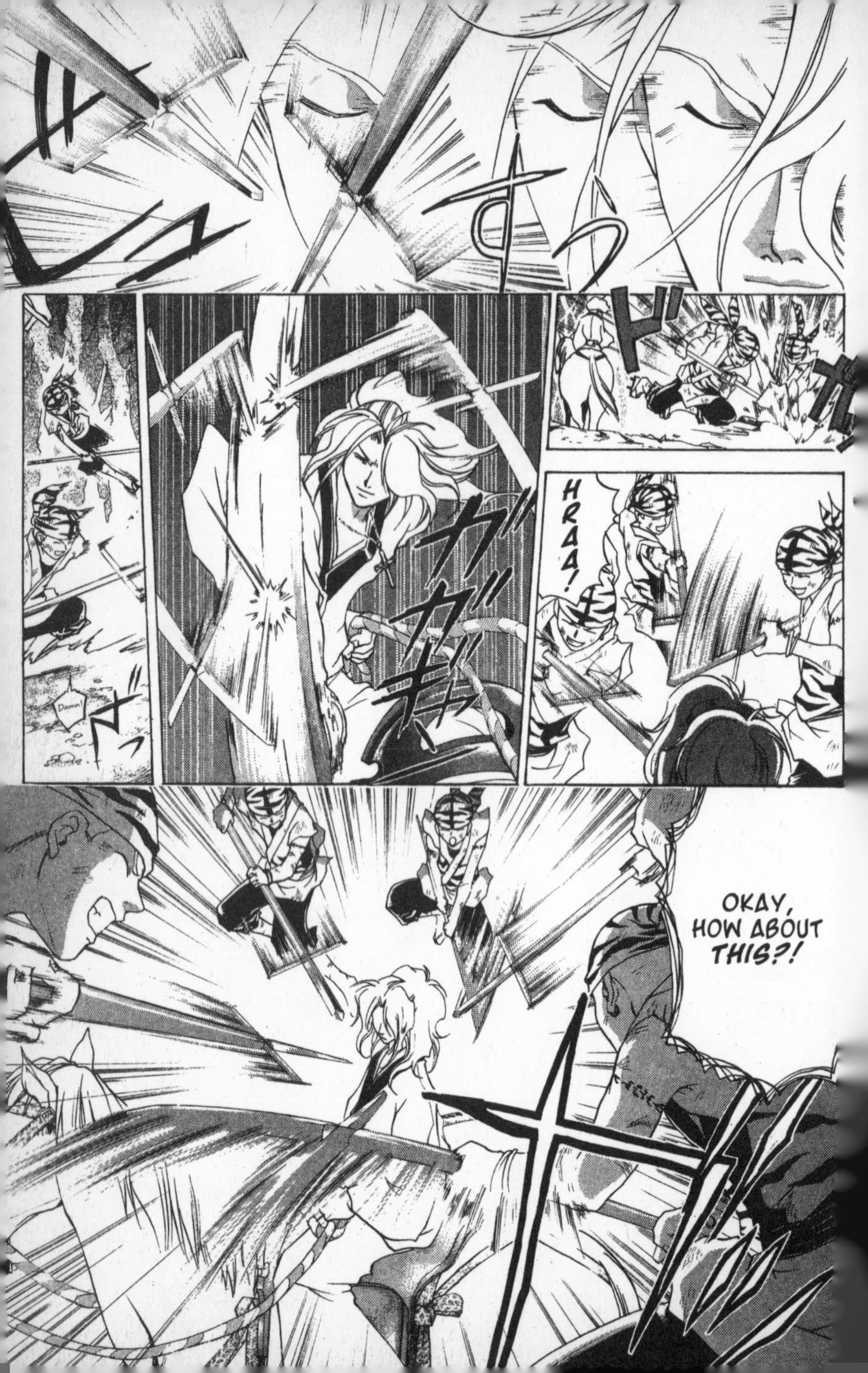
HRAA!
Damn!
OKAY, HOW ABOUT THIS?!

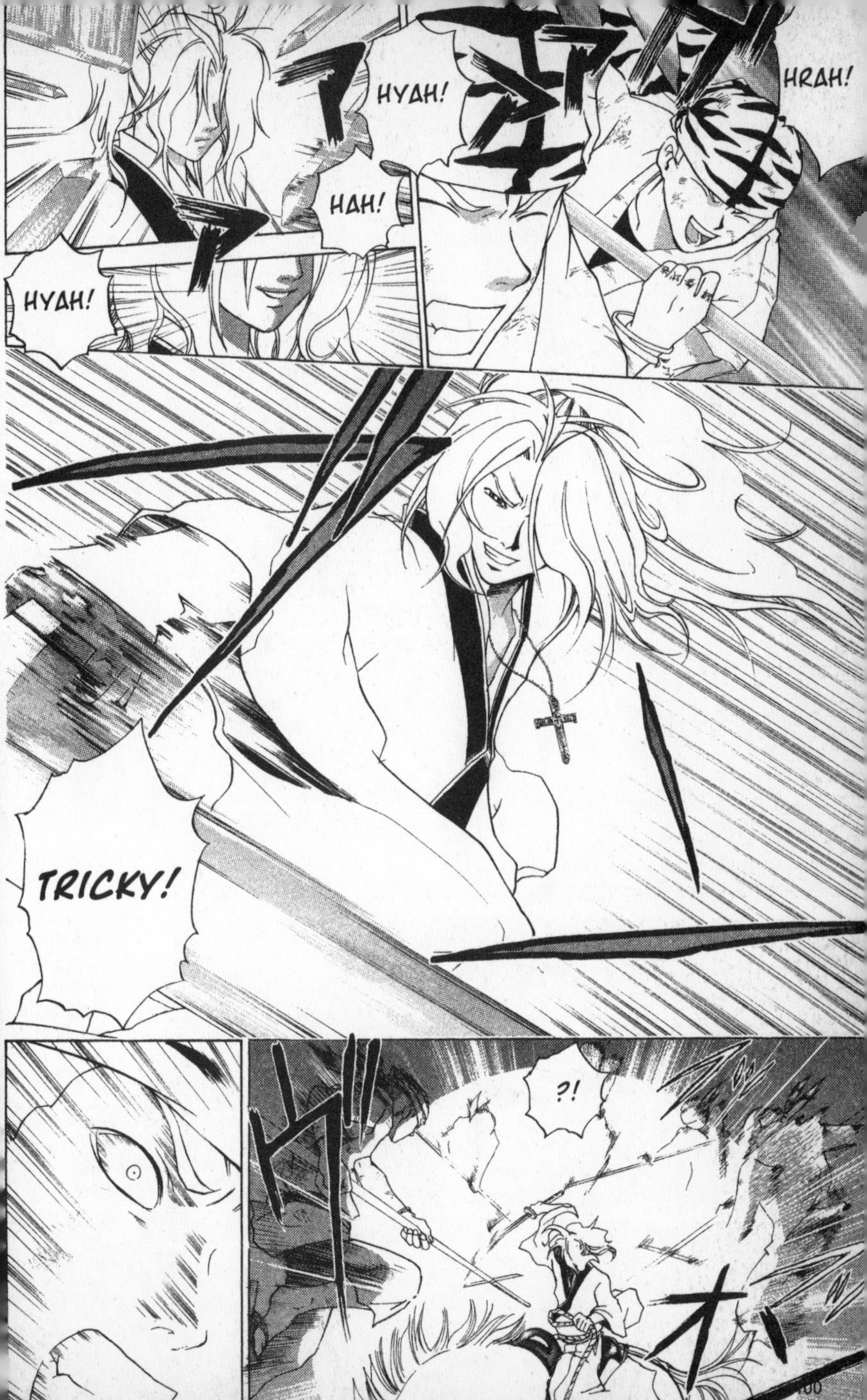
HRAH!
HYAH!
HAH!
HYAH!
TRICKY!
?!

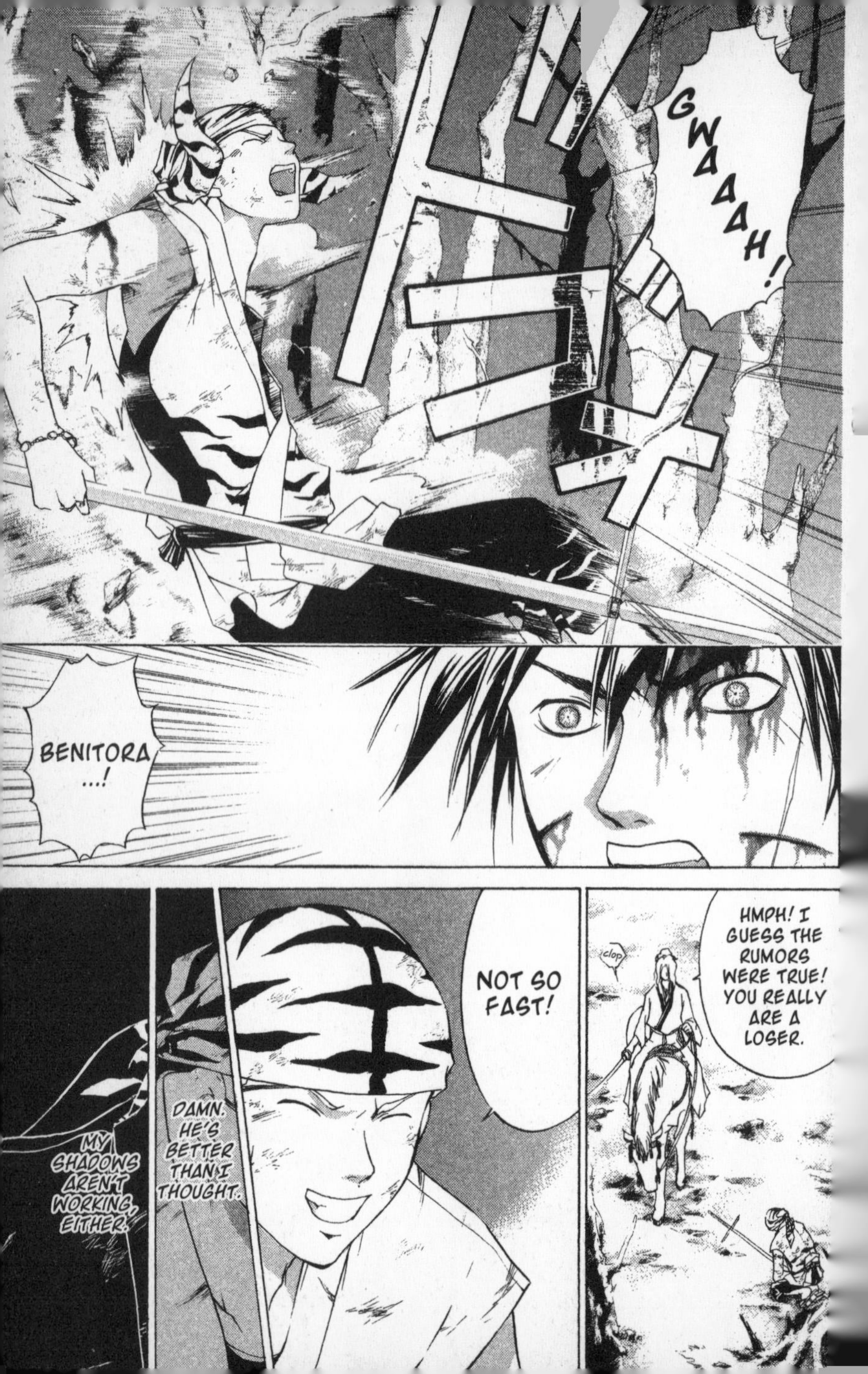
GWAAAH!
BENITORA ...!
clop
HMPH! I GUESS THE RUMORS WERE TRUE! YOU REALLY ARE A LOSER.
NOT SO FAST!
DAMN. HE'S BETTER THAN I THOUGHT.
MY SHADOWS AREN'T WORKING, EITHER.

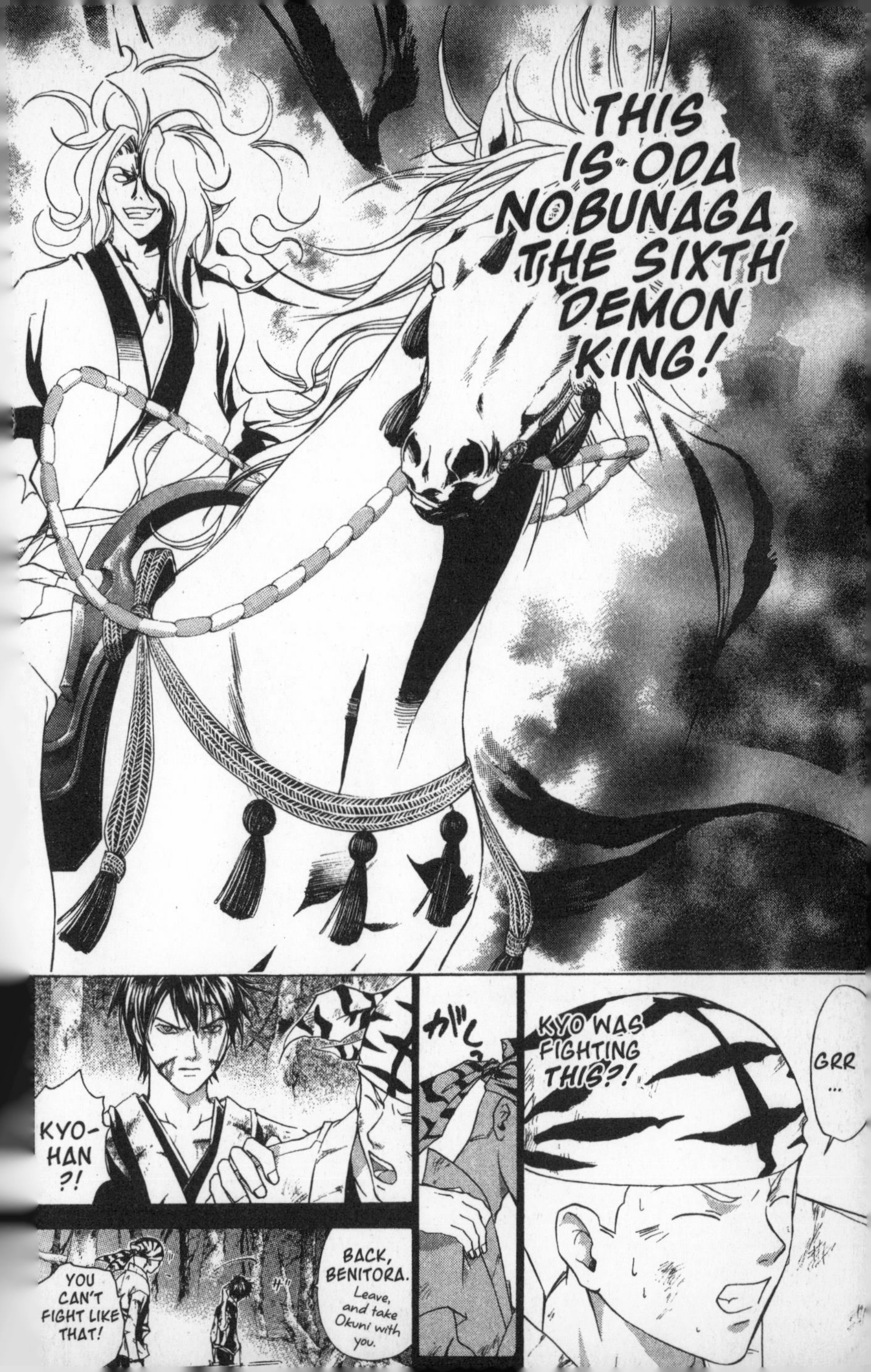
THIS IS ODA NOBUNAGA, THE SIXTH DEMON KING!
GRR ...
KYO WAS FIGHTING THIS?!
がしっ
KYO-HAN ?!
BACK, BENITORA. Leave, and take Okuni with you.
YOU CAN'T FIGHT LIKE THAT!

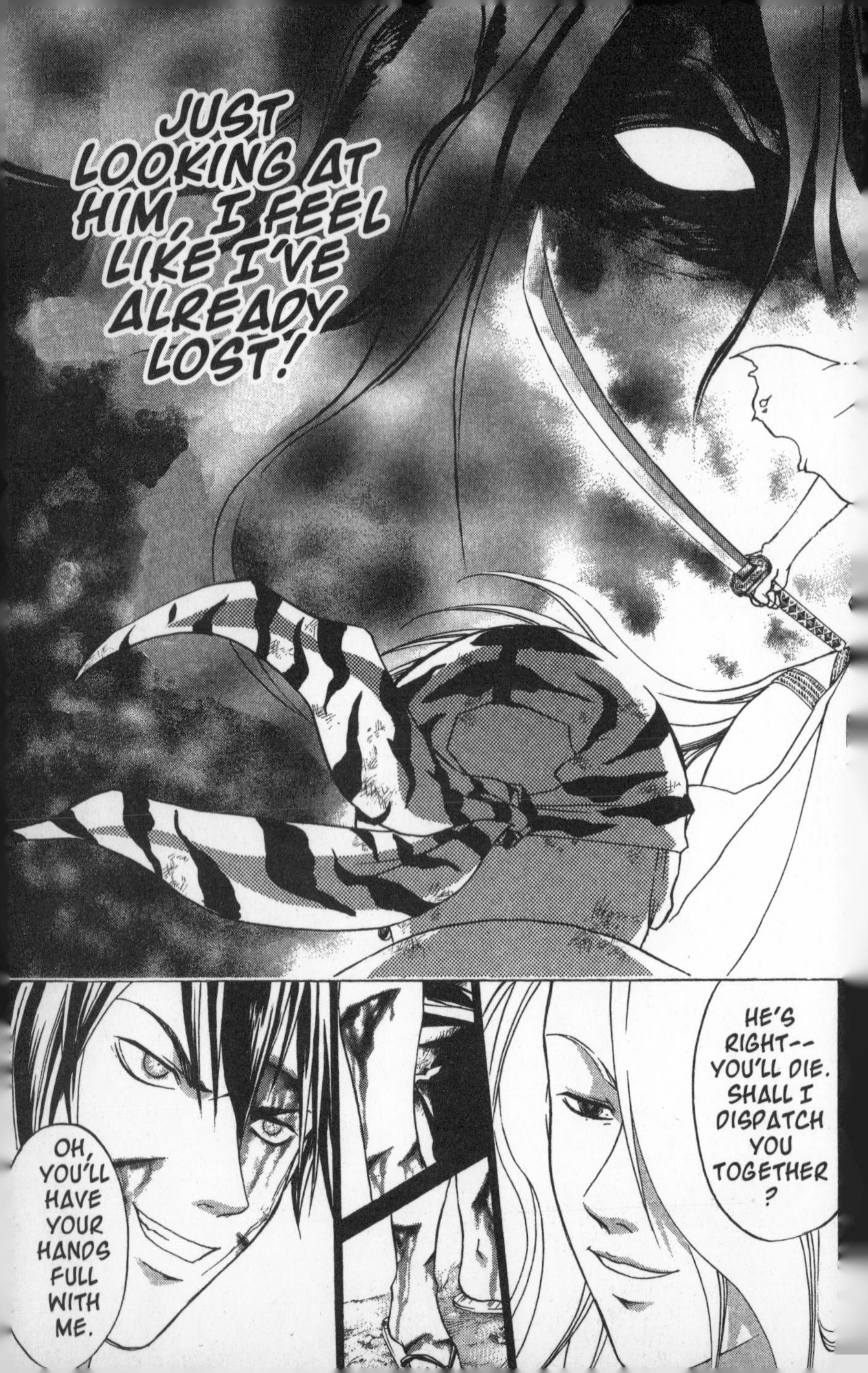
JUST LOOKING AT HIM, I FEEL LIKE I'VE ALREADY LOST!
HE'S RIGHT-- YOU'LL DIE. SHALL I DISPATCH YOU TOGETHER?
OH, YOU'LL HAVE YOUR HANDS FULL WITH ME.

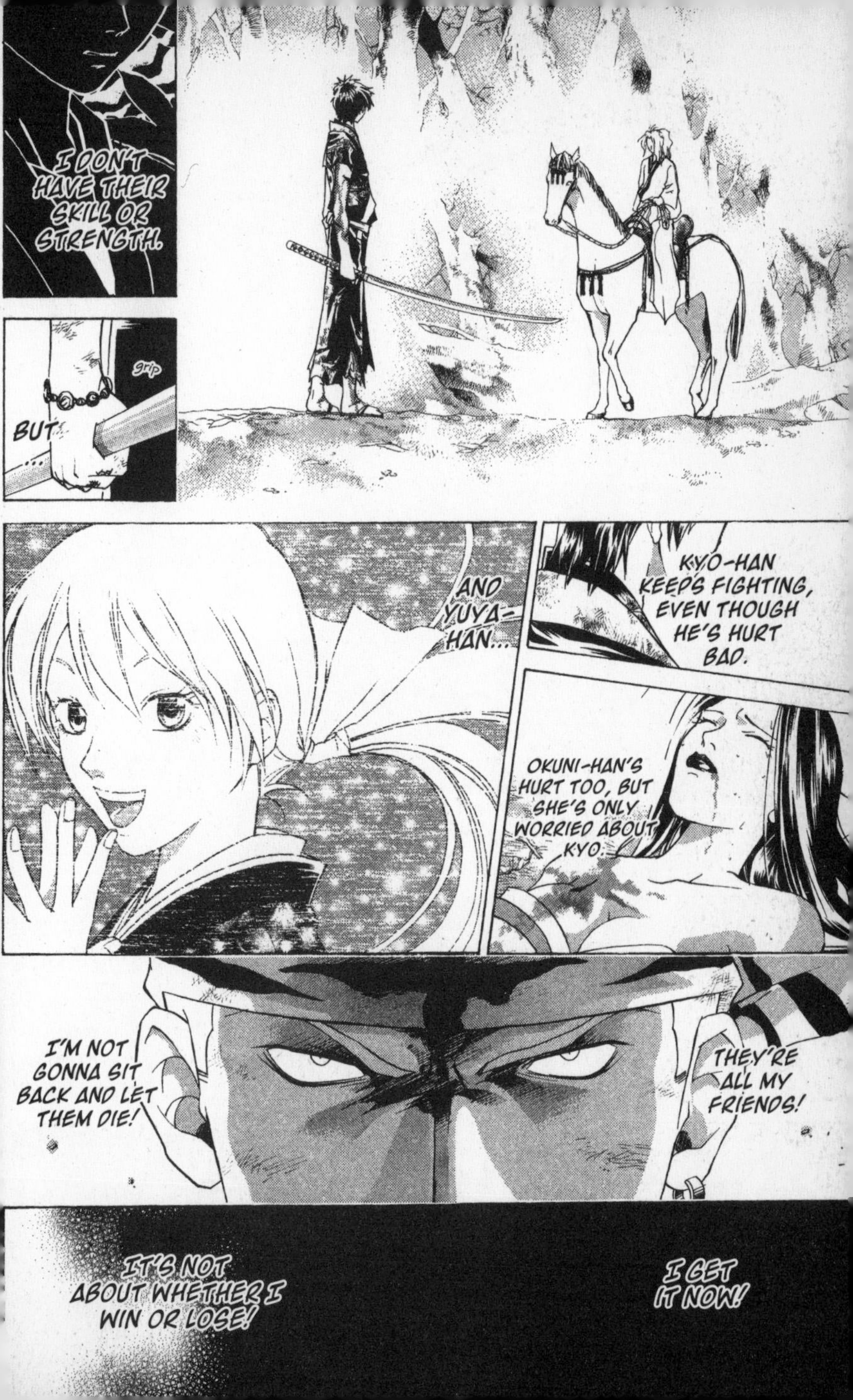
I DON'T HAVE THEIR SKILL OR STRENGTH.
grip
BUT...
KYO-HAN KEEPS FIGHTING, EVEN THOUGH HE'S HURT BAD.
OKUNI-HAN'S HURT TOO, BUT SHE'S ONLY WORRIED ABOUT KYO.
AND YUYA-HAN...
THEY'RE ALL MY FRIENDS!
I'M NOT GONNA SIT BACK AND LET THEM DIE!
I GET IT NOW!
IT'S NOT ABOUT WHETHER I WIN OR LOSE!

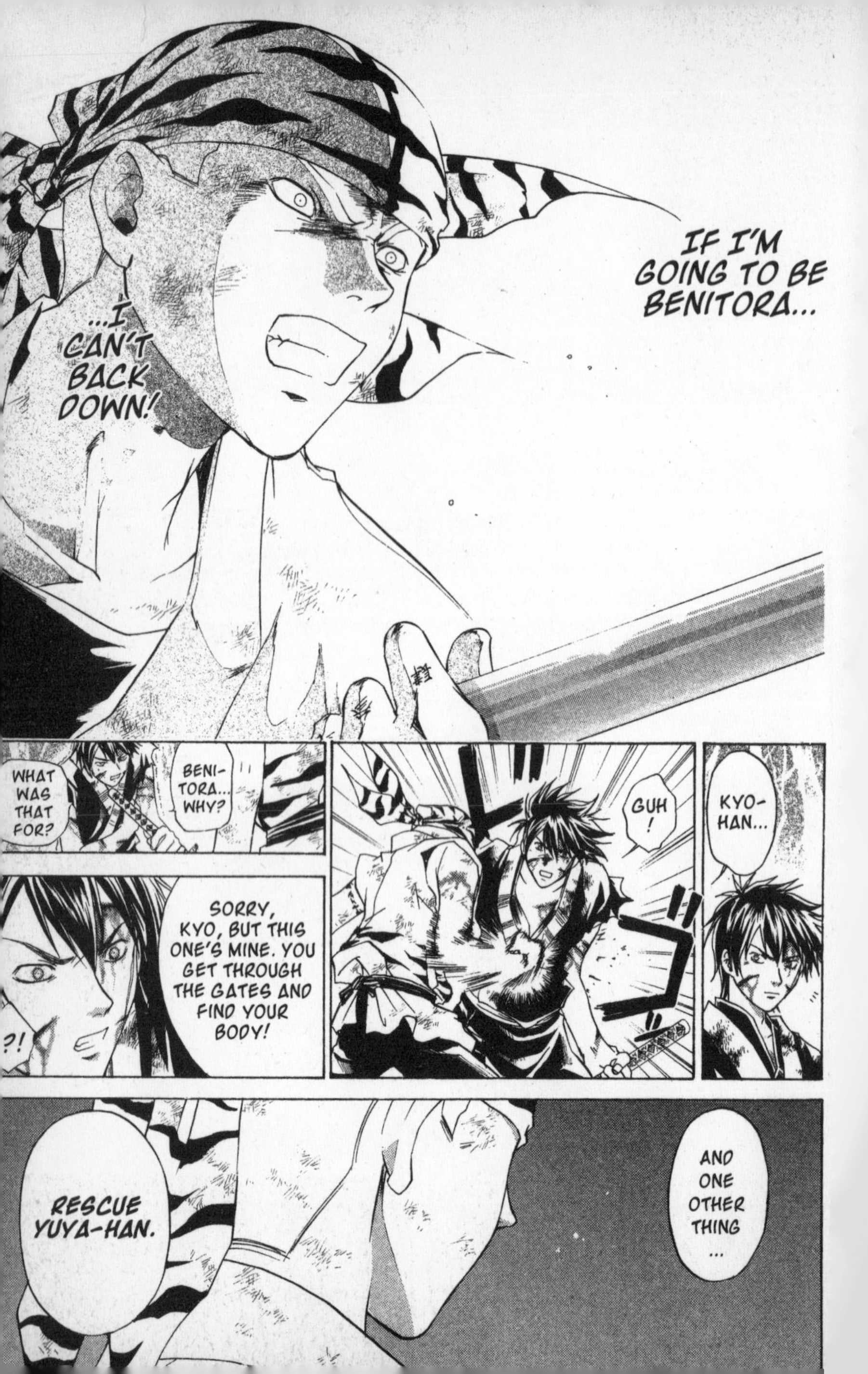
IF I'M GOING TO BE BENITORA...
...I CAN'T BACK DOWN!
KYO-HAN...
GUH!
BENI-TORA... WHY?
WHAT WAS THAT FOR?
SORRY, KYO, BUT THIS ONE'S MINE. YOU GET THROUGH THE GATES AND FIND YOUR BODY!
?!
AND ONE OTHER THING...
RESCUE YUYA-HAN.

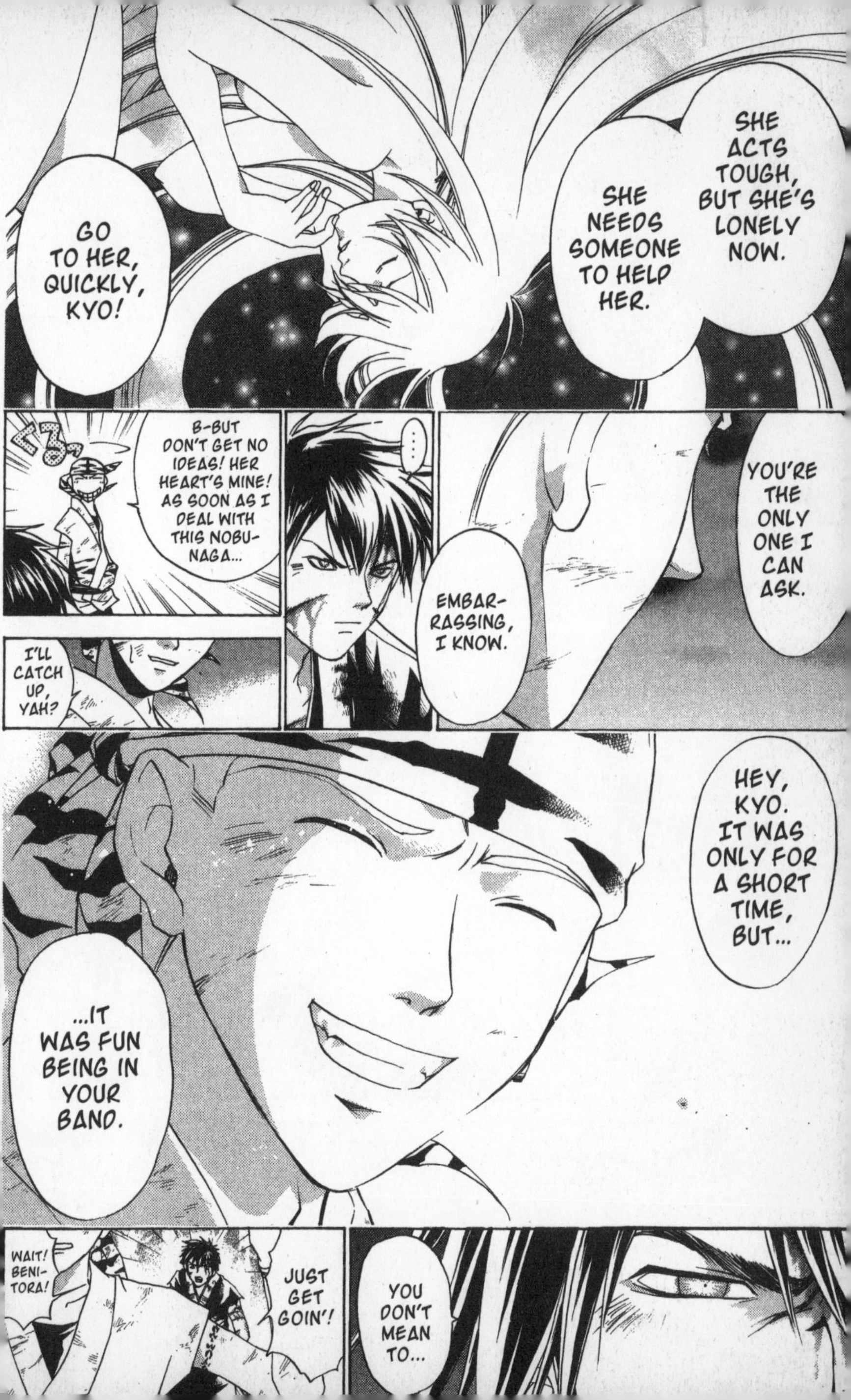

SHE ACTS TOUGH, BUT SHE'S LONELY NOW.
SHE NEEDS SOMEONE TO HELP HER.
GO TO HER, QUICKLY, KYO!
YOU'RE THE ONLY ONE I CAN ASK.
...
EMBAR-RASSING, I KNOW.
B-BUT DON'T GET NO IDEAS! HER HEART'S MINE! AS SOON AS I DEAL WITH THIS NOBU-NAGA...
I'LL CATCH UP, YAH?
HEY, KYO. IT WAS ONLY FOR A SHORT TIME, BUT...
...IT WAS FUN BEING IN YOUR BAND.
YOU DON'T MEAN TO...
JUST GET GOIN'!
WAIT! BENI-TORA!

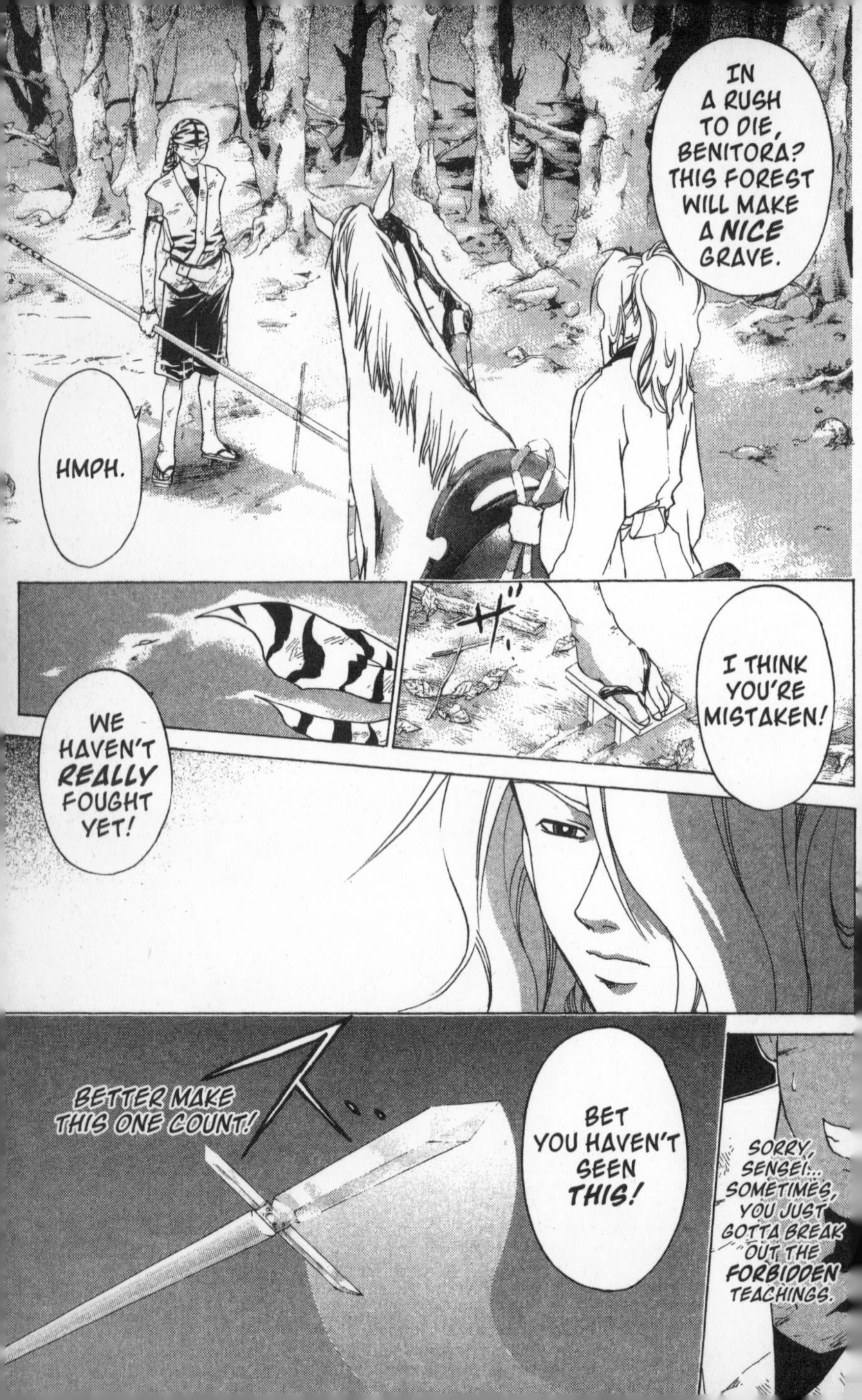
IN A RUSH TO DIE, BENITORA? THIS FOREST WILL MAKE A NICE GRAVE.
HMPH.
I THINK YOU'RE MISTAKEN!
WE HAVEN'T REALLY FOUGHT YET!
SORRY, SENSEI... SOMETIMES, YOU JUST GOTTA BREAK OUT THE FORBIDDEN TEACHINGS.
BET YOU HAVEN'T SEEN THIS!
BETTER MAKE THIS ONE COUNT!

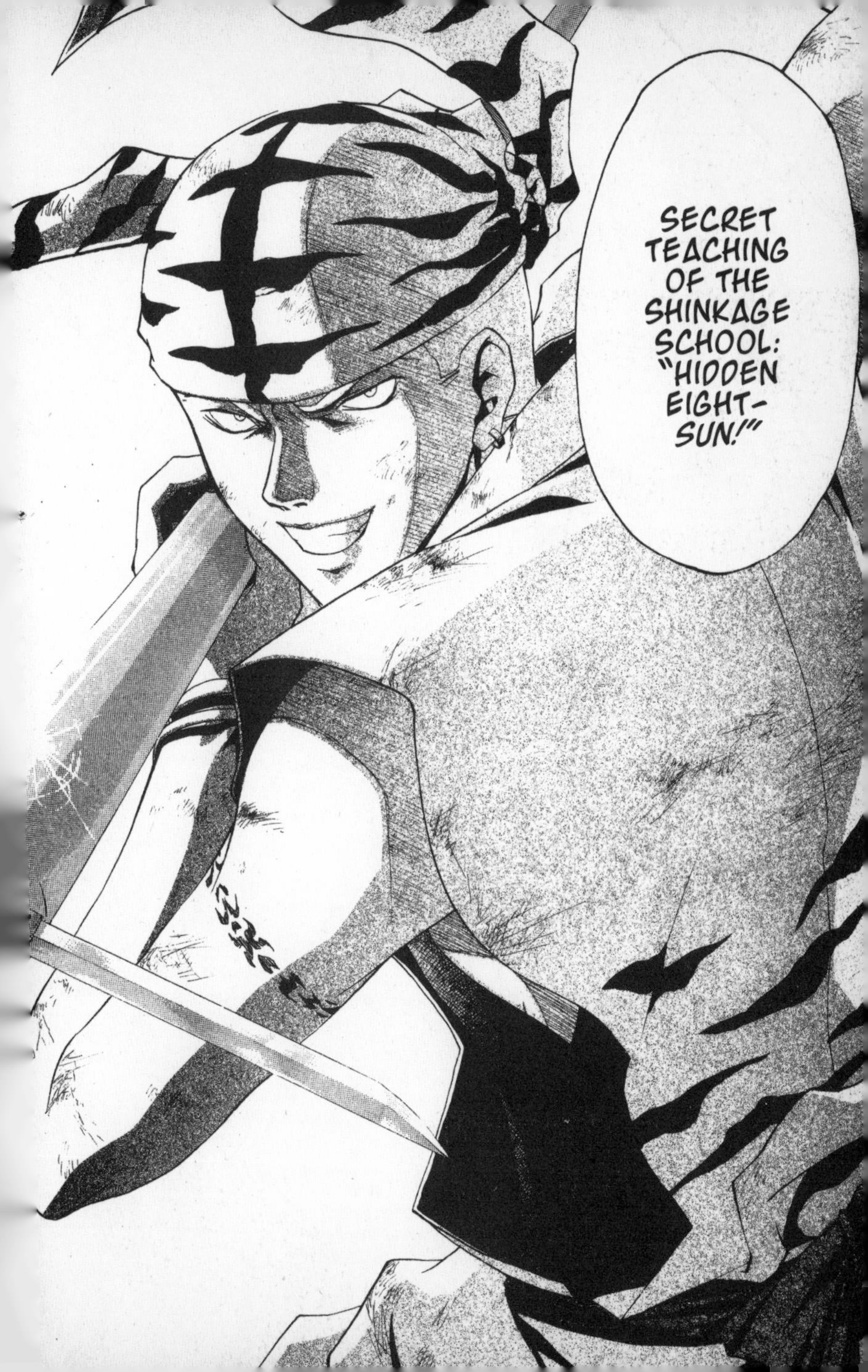
SECRET TEACHING OF THE SHINKAGE SCHOOL: "HIDDEN EIGHT-SUN!"

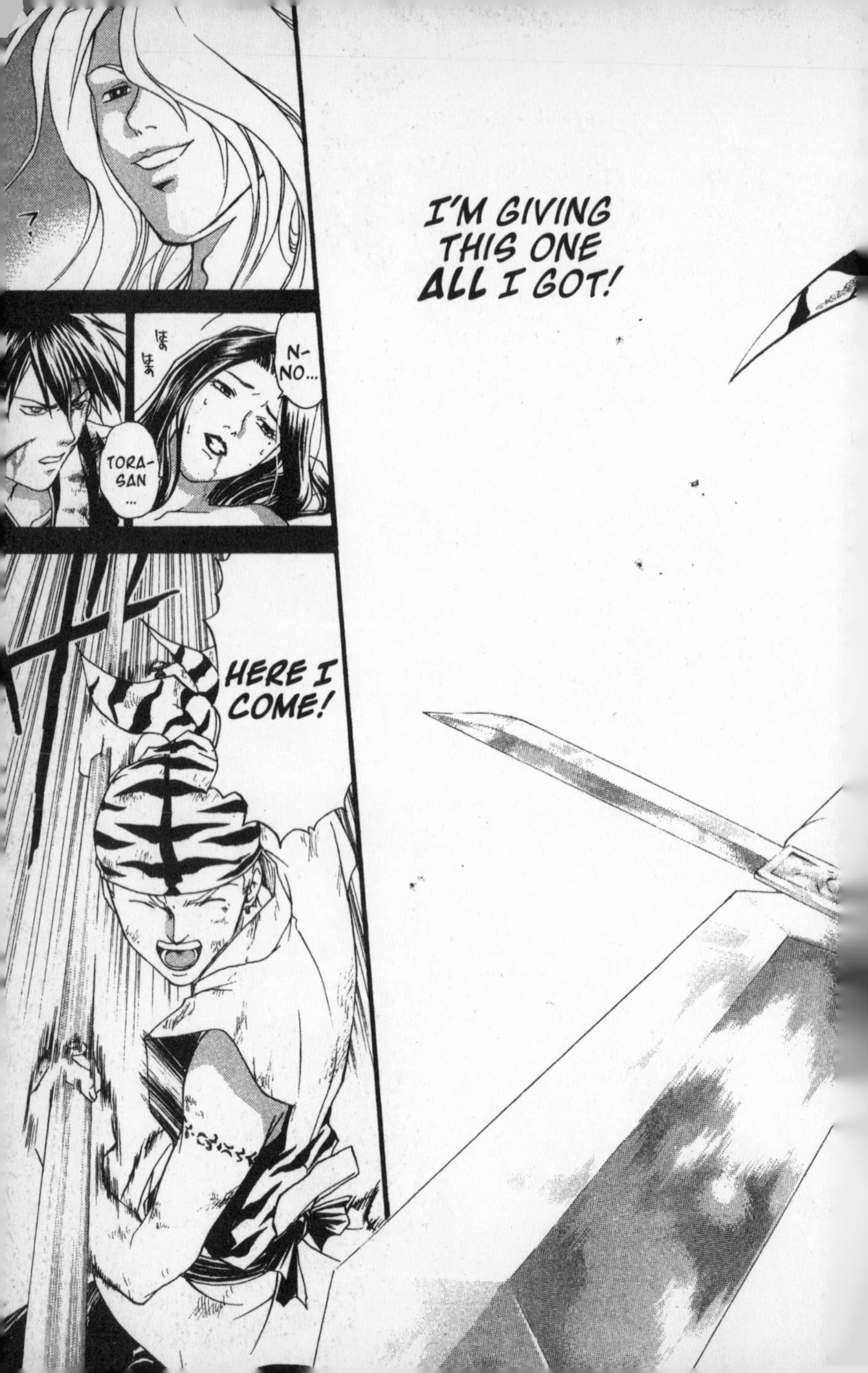
I'M GIVING THIS ONE ALL I GOT!
はぁ はぁ
N-NO...
TORA-SAN...
HERE I COME!

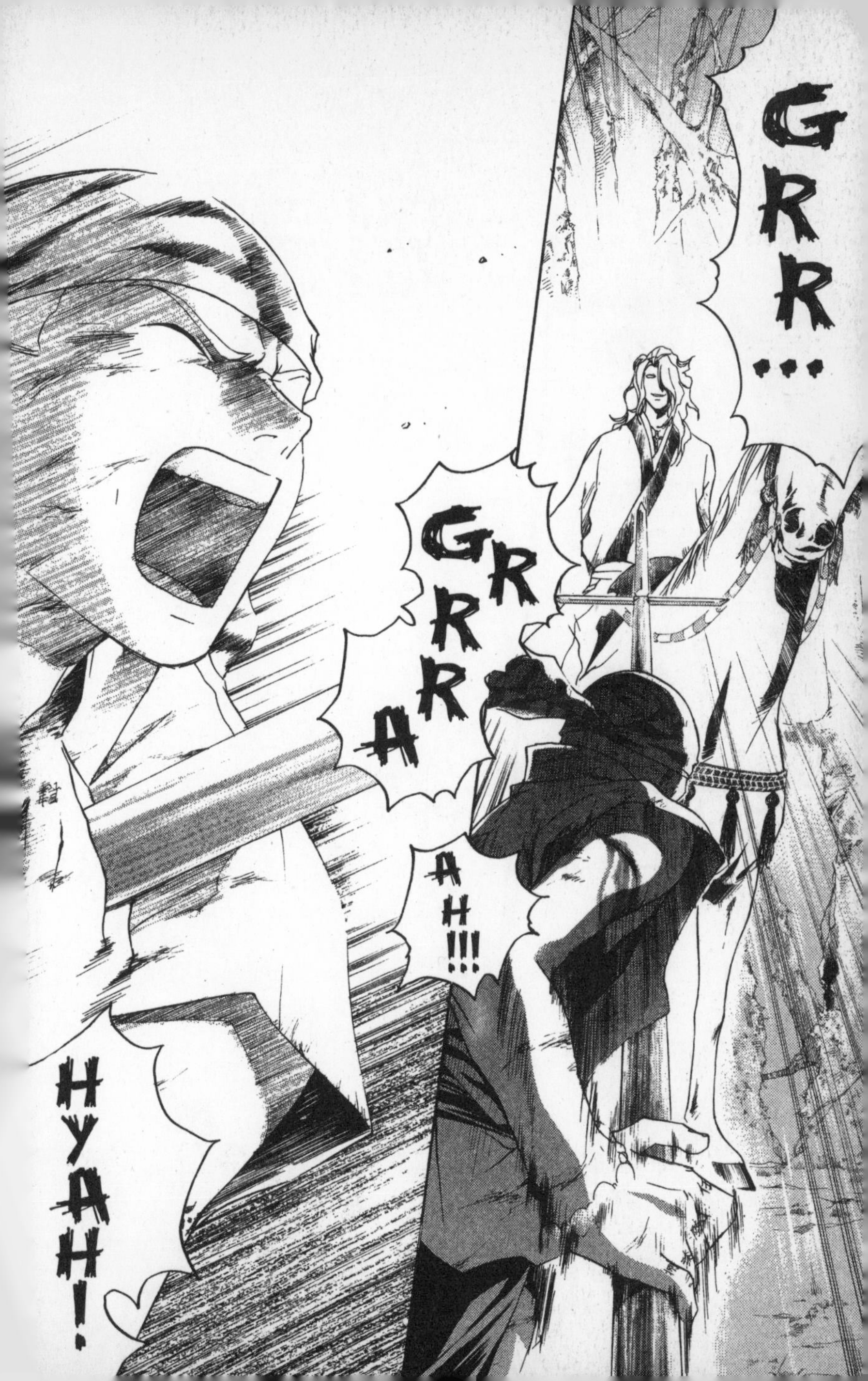
GRR...
GRRRA
AH!!!
HYAH!

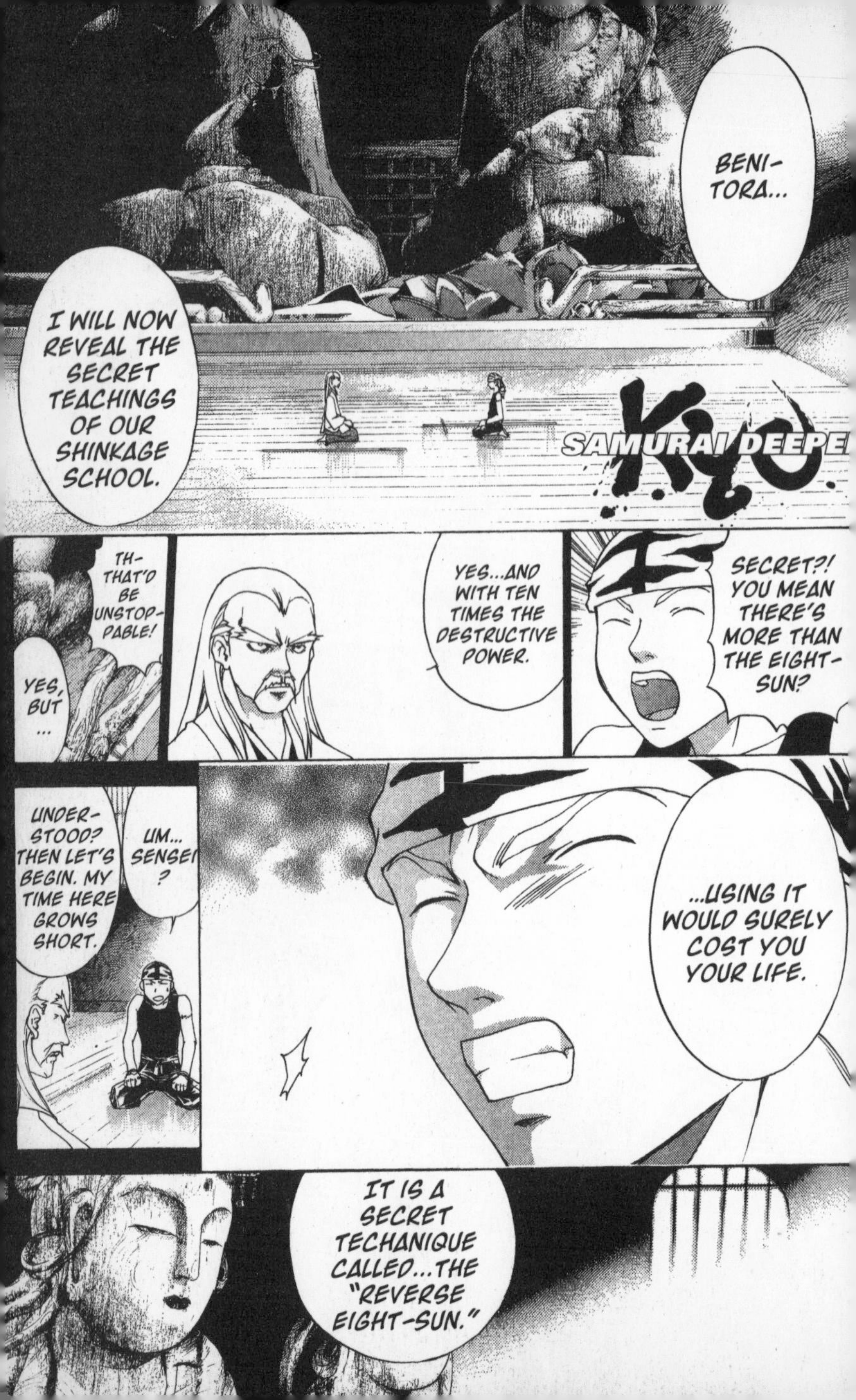
BENI-TORA...
I WILL NOW REVEAL THE SECRET TEACHINGS OF OUR SHINKAGE SCHOOL.
SECRET?! YOU MEAN THERE'S MORE THAN THE EIGHT-SUN?
YES...AND WITH TEN TIMES THE DESTRUCTIVE POWER.
TH-THAT'D BE UNSTOPPABLE!
YES, BUT ...
...USING IT WOULD SURELY COST YOU YOUR LIFE.
UM... SENSEI?
UNDERSTOOD? THEN LET'S BEGIN. MY TIME HERE GROWS SHORT.
IT IS A SECRET TECHANIQUE CALLED...THE "REVERSE EIGHT-SUN."

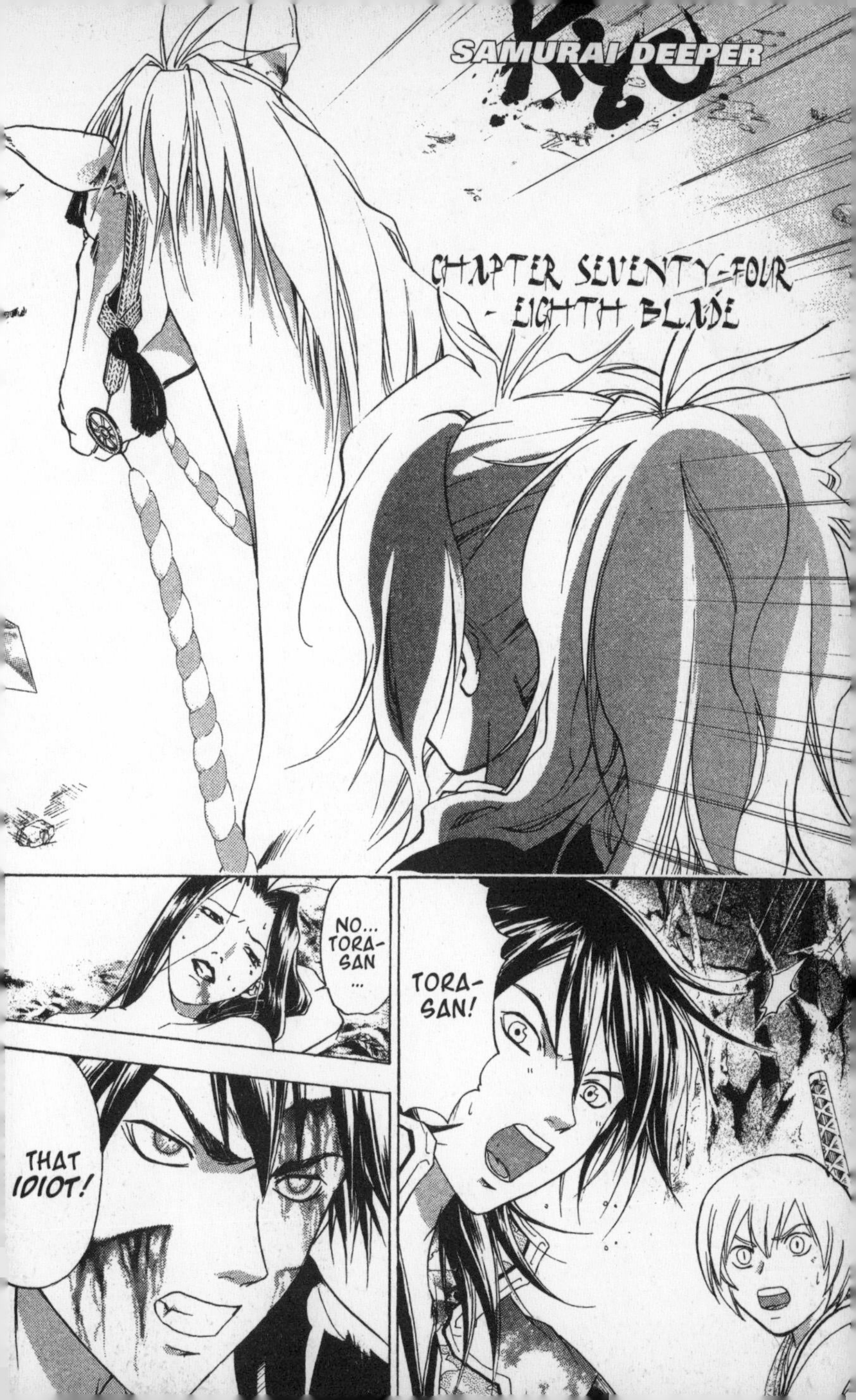
SAMURAI DEEPER KYO
CHAPTER SEVENTY-FOUR - EIGHTH BLADE
TORA-SAN!
NO... TORA-SAN ...
THAT IDIOT!

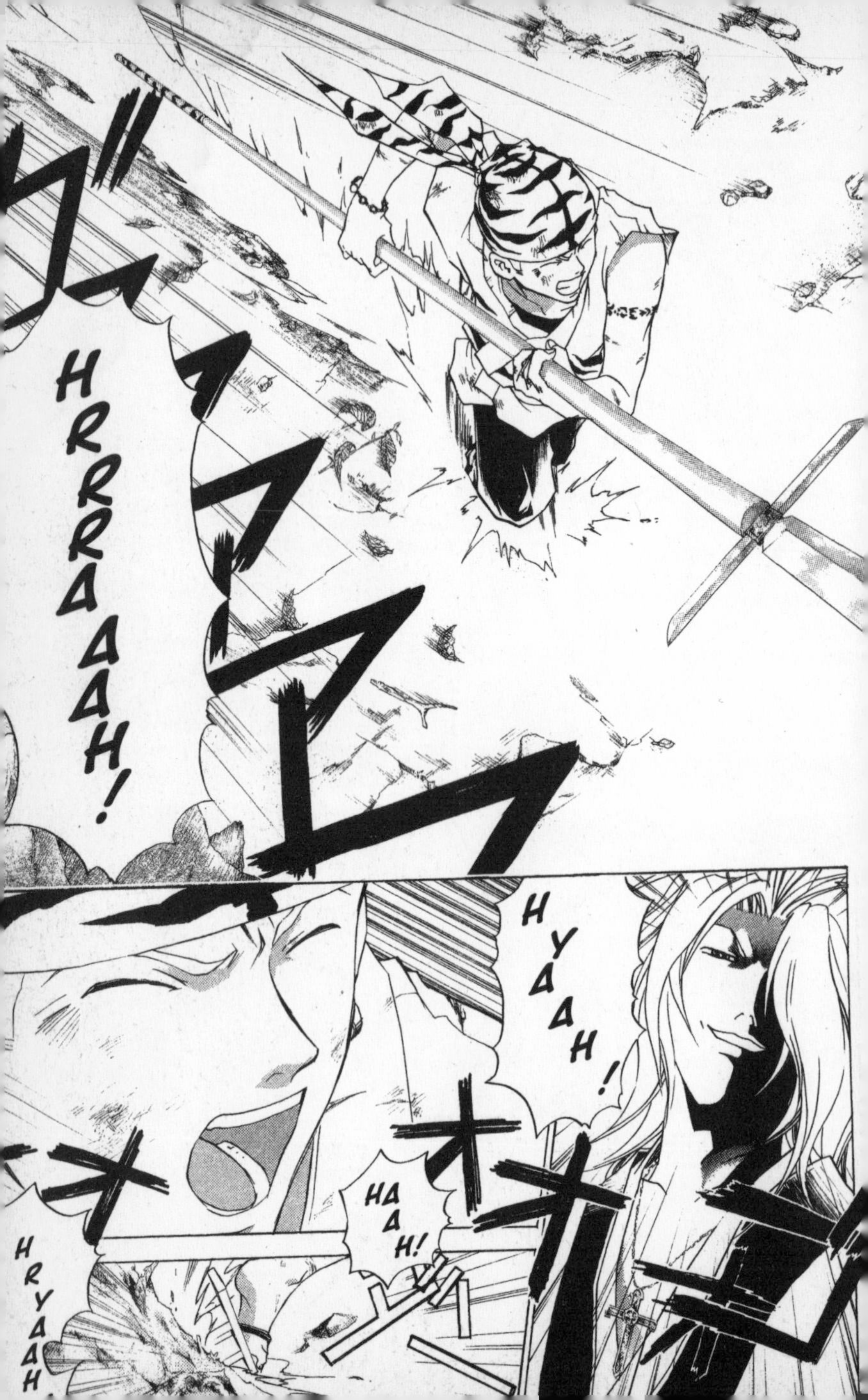
HRRRAAAH!
HYAAAH!
HAAAH!
HRYAAAH

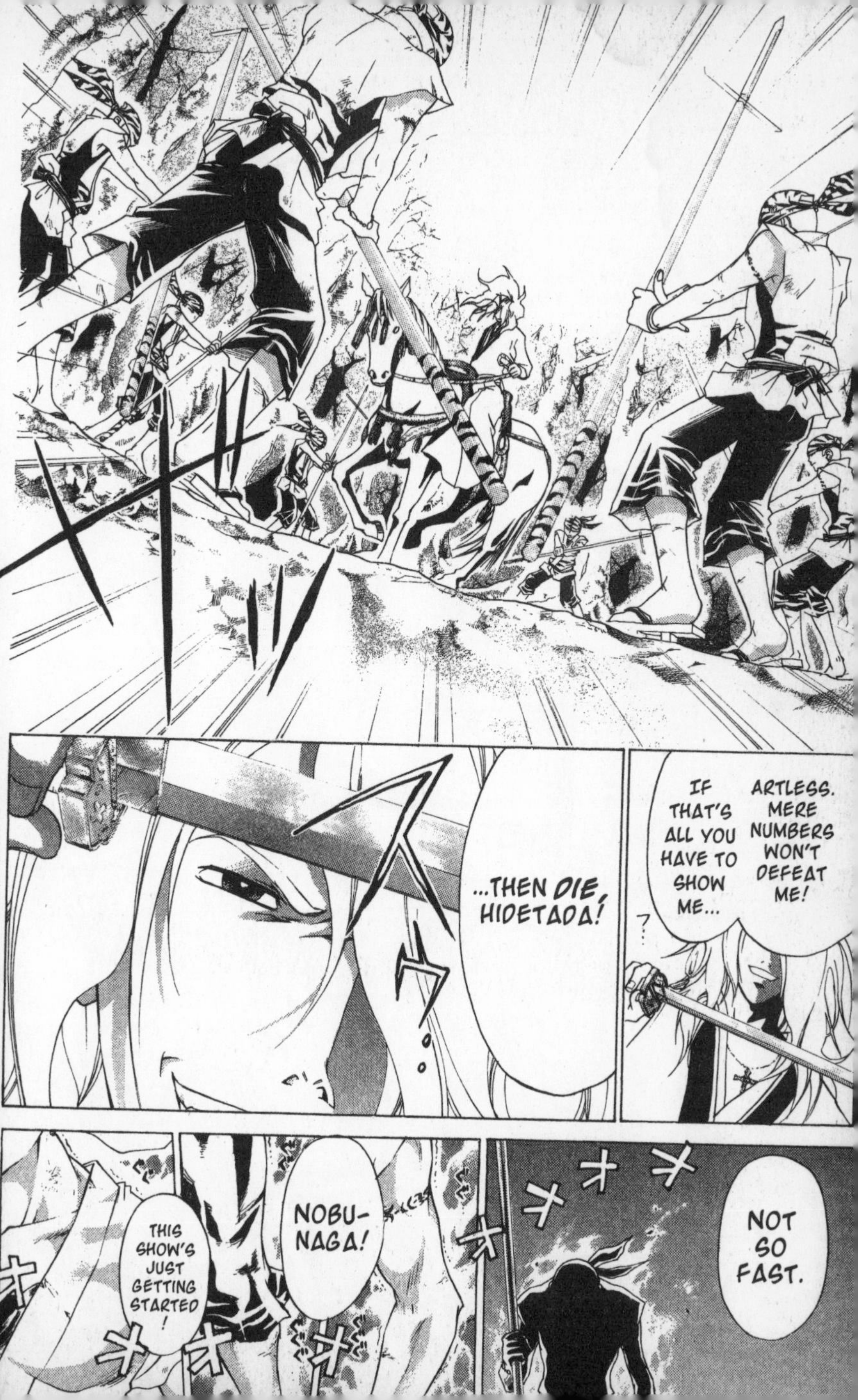

ARTLESS. MERE NUMBERS WON'T DEFEAT ME!
IF THAT'S ALL YOU HAVE TO SHOW ME...
?...
...THEN DIE, HIDETADA!
NOT SO FAST.
NOBU-NAGA!
THIS SHOW'S JUST GETTING STARTED!

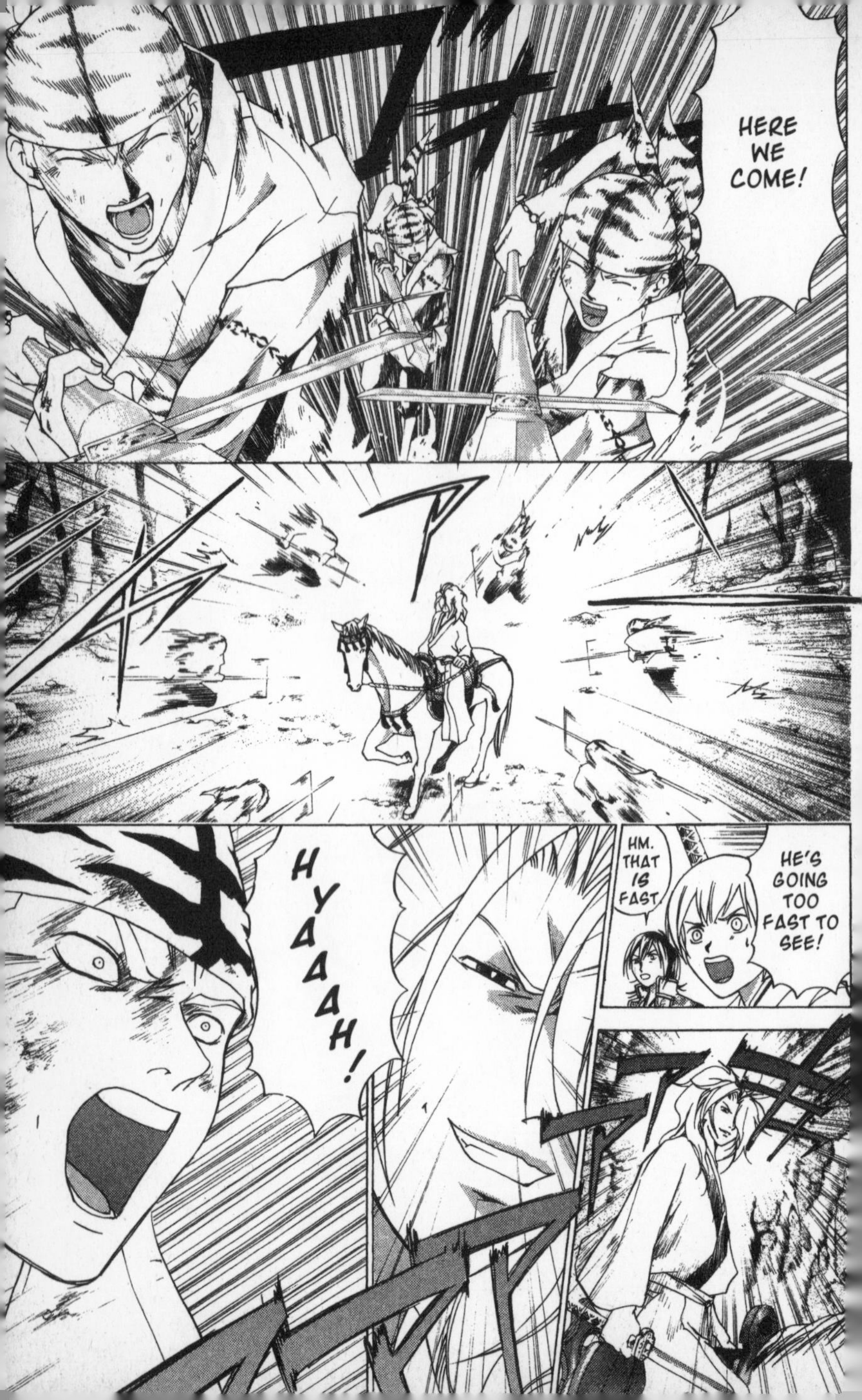
HERE WE COME!
HE'S GOING TOO FAST TO SEE!
HM. THAT IS FAST.
HYAAAH!

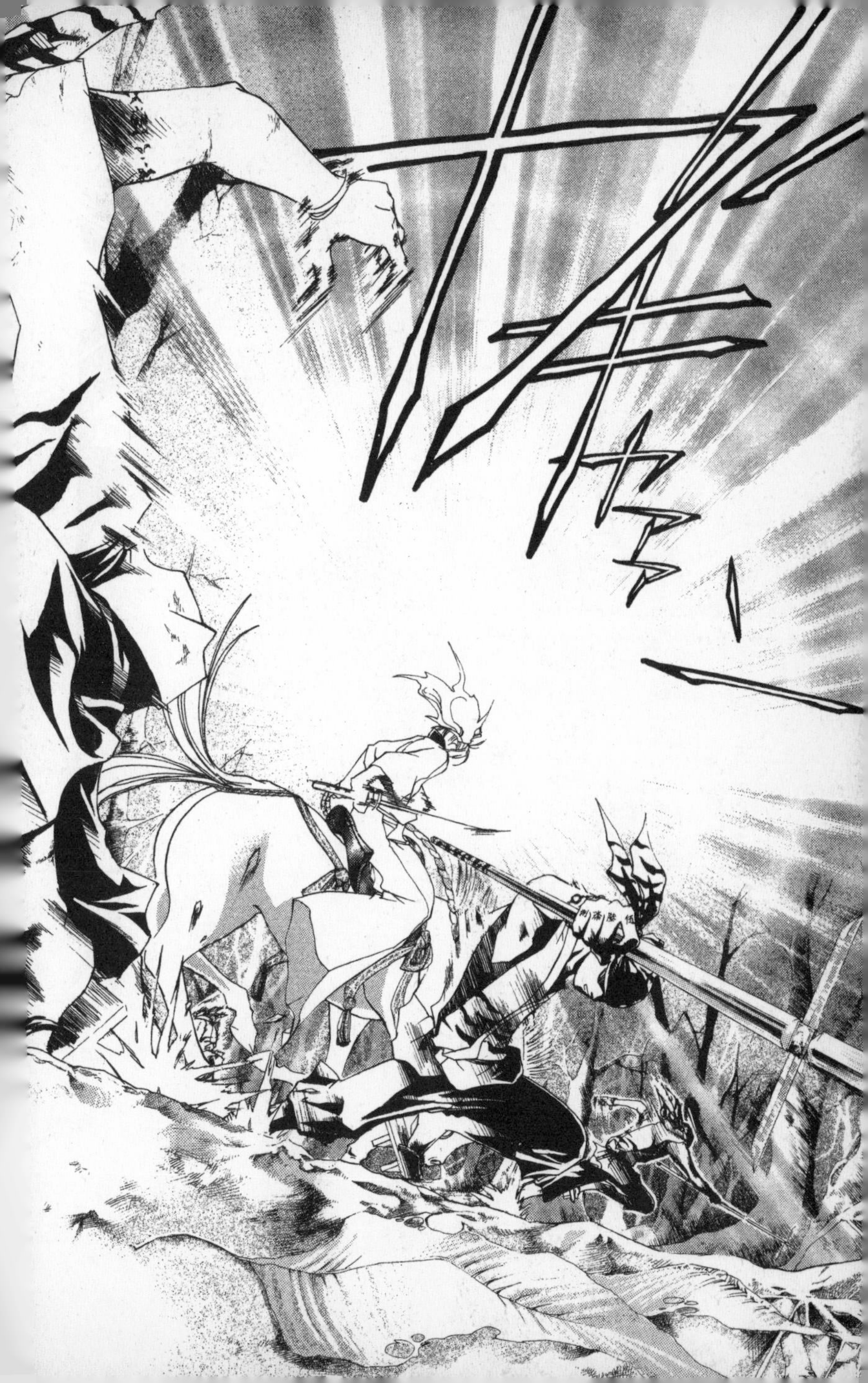
ズギャアーー

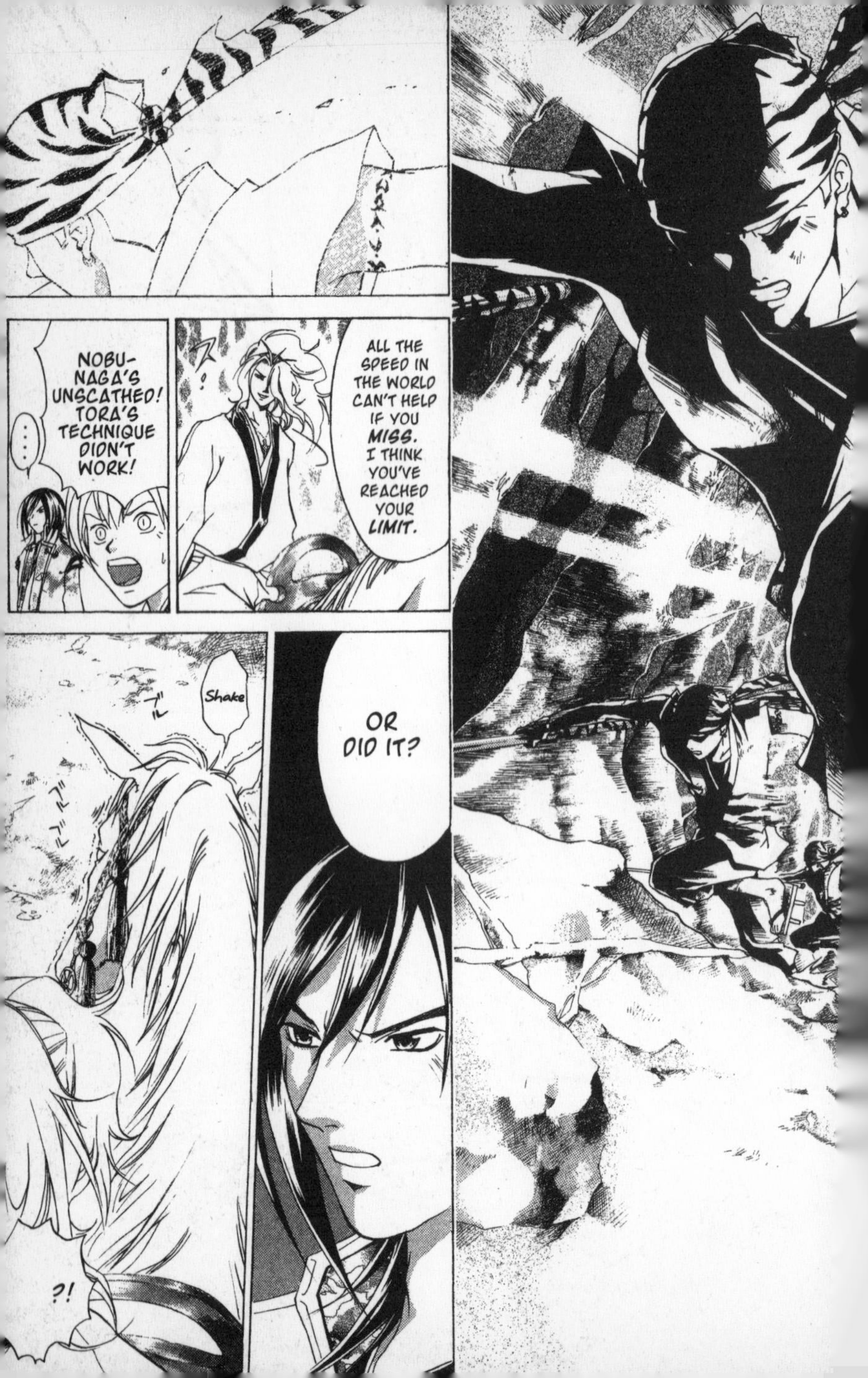
ALL THE SPEED IN THE WORLD CAN'T HELP IF YOU **MISS.** I THINK YOU'VE REACHED YOUR **LIMIT.**
NOBU-NAGA'S UNSCATHED! TORA'S TECHNIQUE DIDN'T WORK!
...
OR DID IT?
Shake
?!

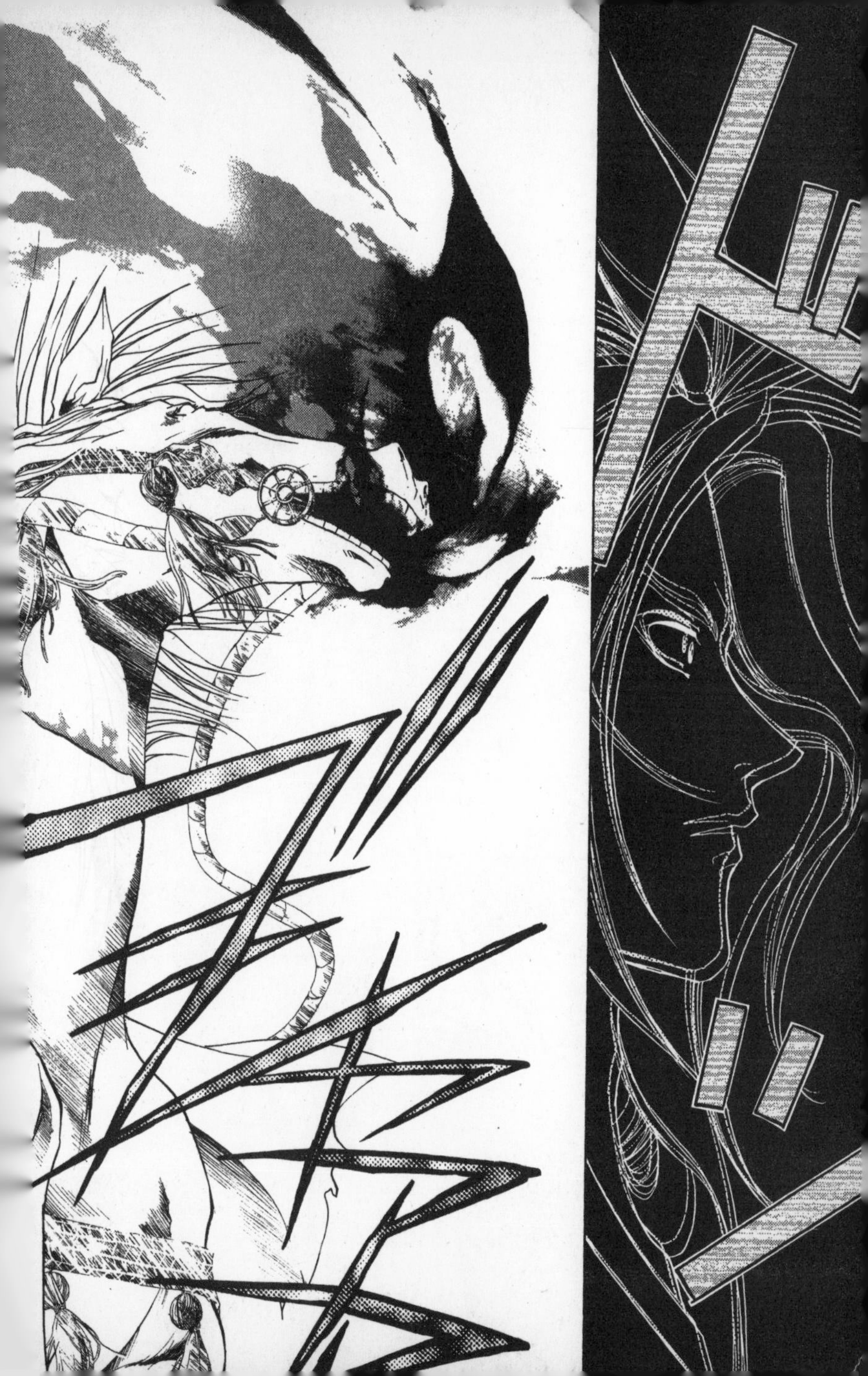

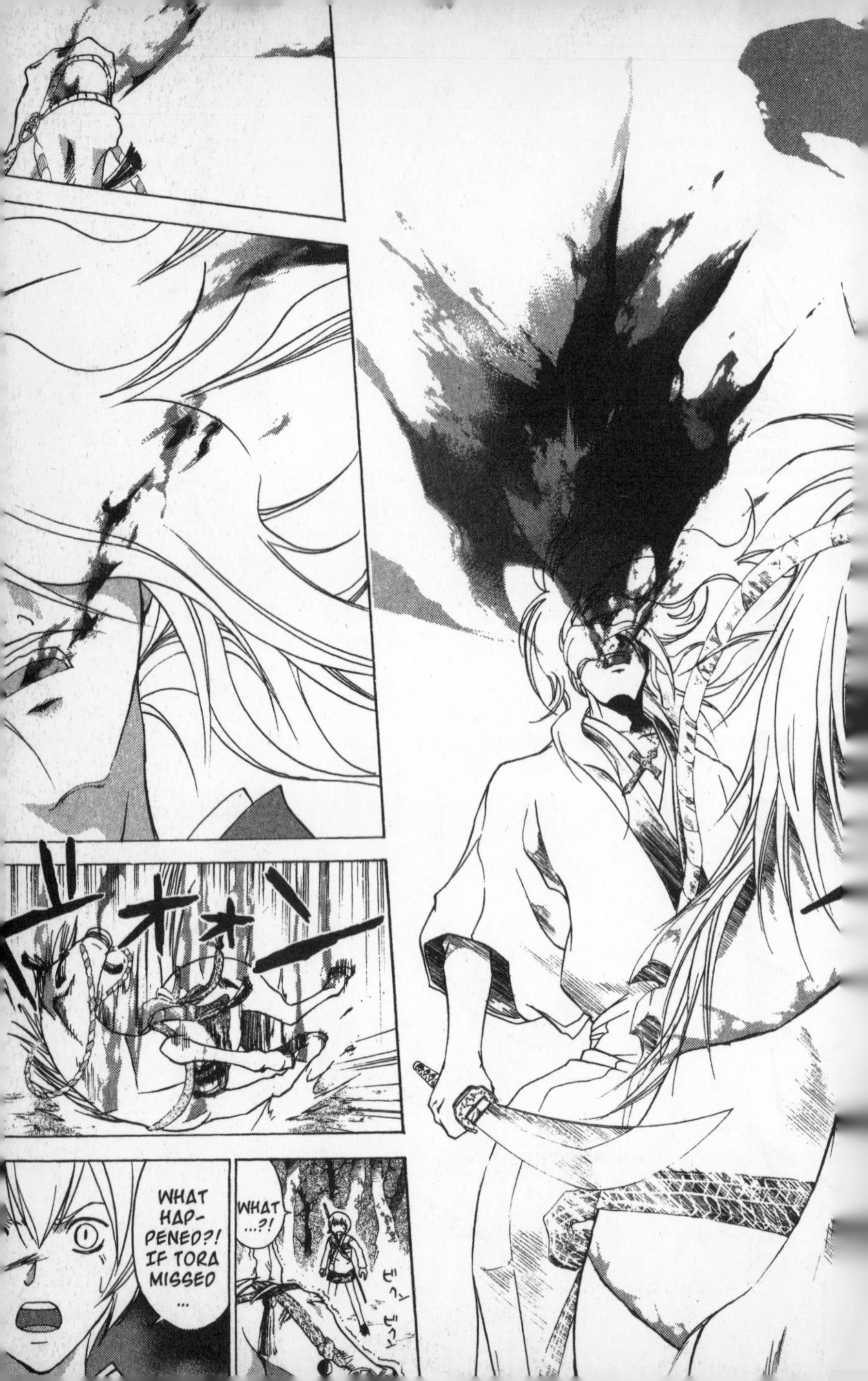
WHAT ...?!
WHAT HAP-PENED?! IF TORA MISSED ...

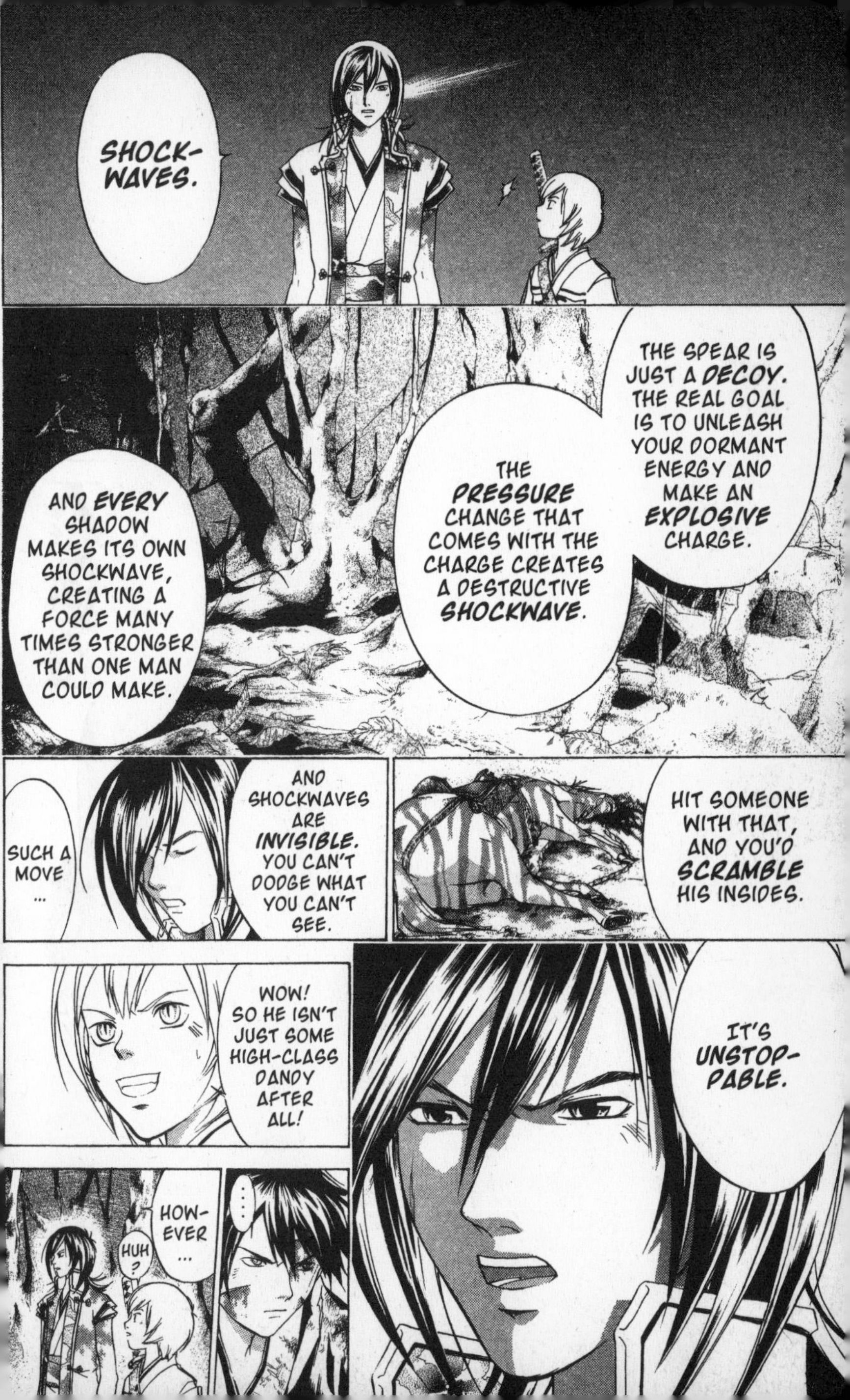
SHOCK-WAVES.
THE SPEAR IS JUST A DECOY. THE REAL GOAL IS TO UNLEASH YOUR DORMANT ENERGY AND MAKE AN EXPLOSIVE CHARGE.
THE PRESSURE CHANGE THAT COMES WITH THE CHARGE CREATES A DESTRUCTIVE SHOCKWAVE.
AND EVERY SHADOW MAKES ITS OWN SHOCKWAVE, CREATING A FORCE MANY TIMES STRONGER THAN ONE MAN COULD MAKE.
HIT SOMEONE WITH THAT, AND YOU'D SCRAMBLE HIS INSIDES.
AND SHOCKWAVES ARE INVISIBLE. YOU CAN'T DODGE WHAT YOU CAN'T SEE.
SUCH A MOVE ...
IT'S UNSTOP-PABLE.
WOW! SO HE ISN'T JUST SOME HIGH-CLASS DANDY AFTER ALL!
...
HOW-EVER ...
HUH ?

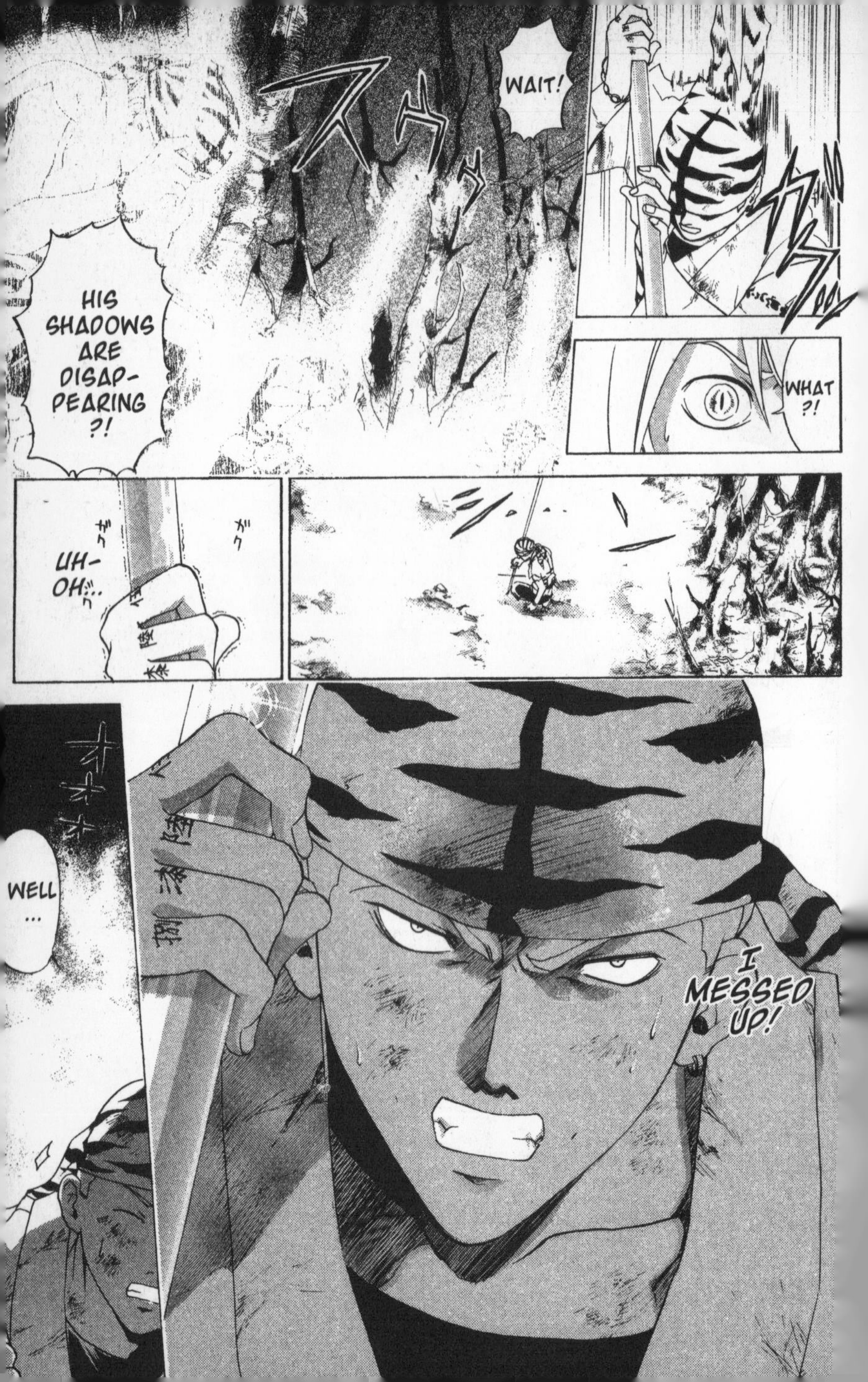
WHAT?!
WAIT!
HIS SHADOWS ARE DISAP-PEARING?!
UH-OH...
WELL...
I MESSED UP!

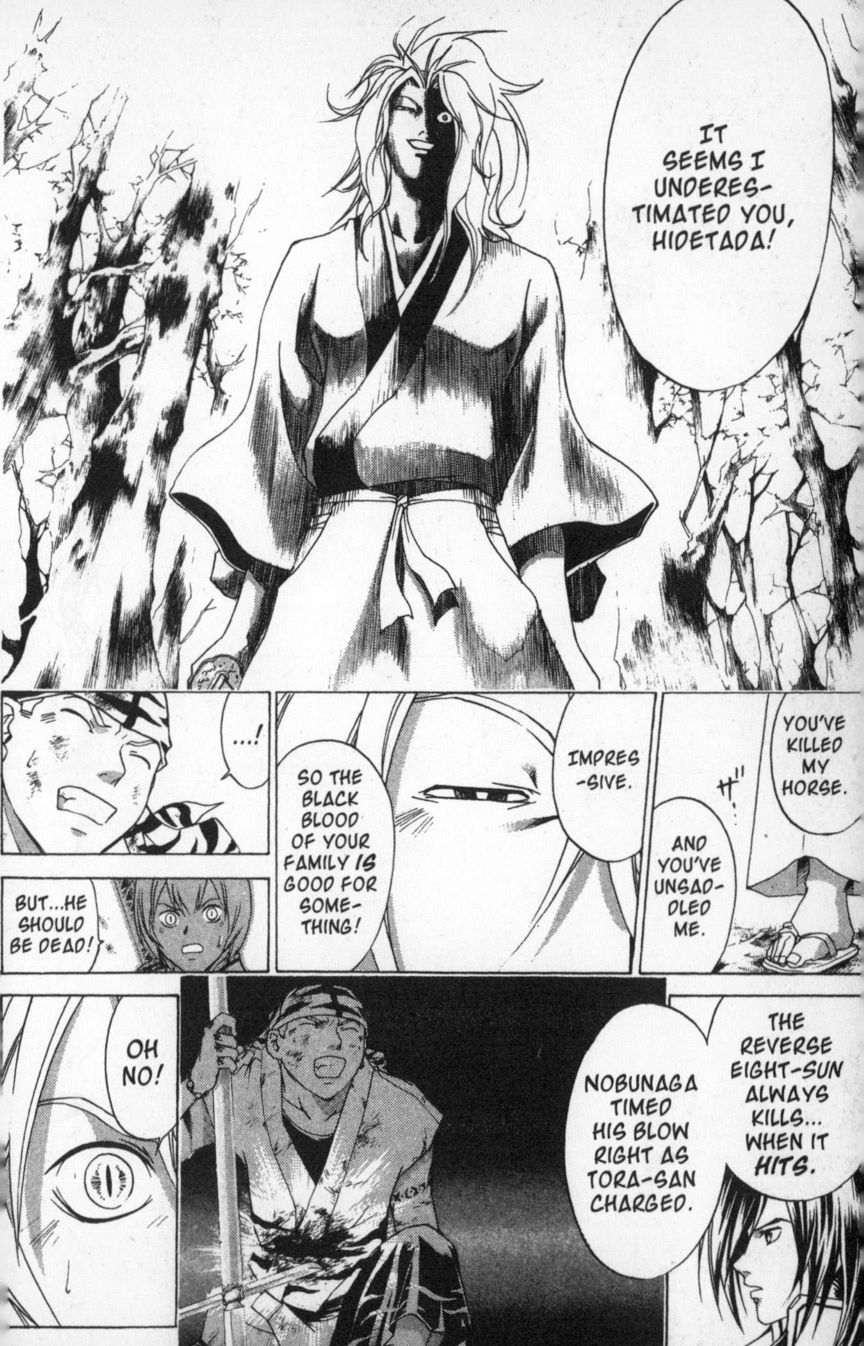
IT SEEMS I UNDERES-TIMATED YOU, HIDETADA!
YOU'VE KILLED MY HORSE.
AND YOU'VE UNSADDLED ME.
IMPRES-SIVE.
SO THE BLACK BLOOD OF YOUR FAMILY *IS* GOOD FOR SOMETHING!
...!
BUT...HE SHOULD BE DEAD!
THE REVERSE EIGHT-SUN ALWAYS KILLS... WHEN IT *HITS*.
NOBUNAGA TIMED HIS BLOW RIGHT AS TORA-SAN CHARGED.
OH NO!

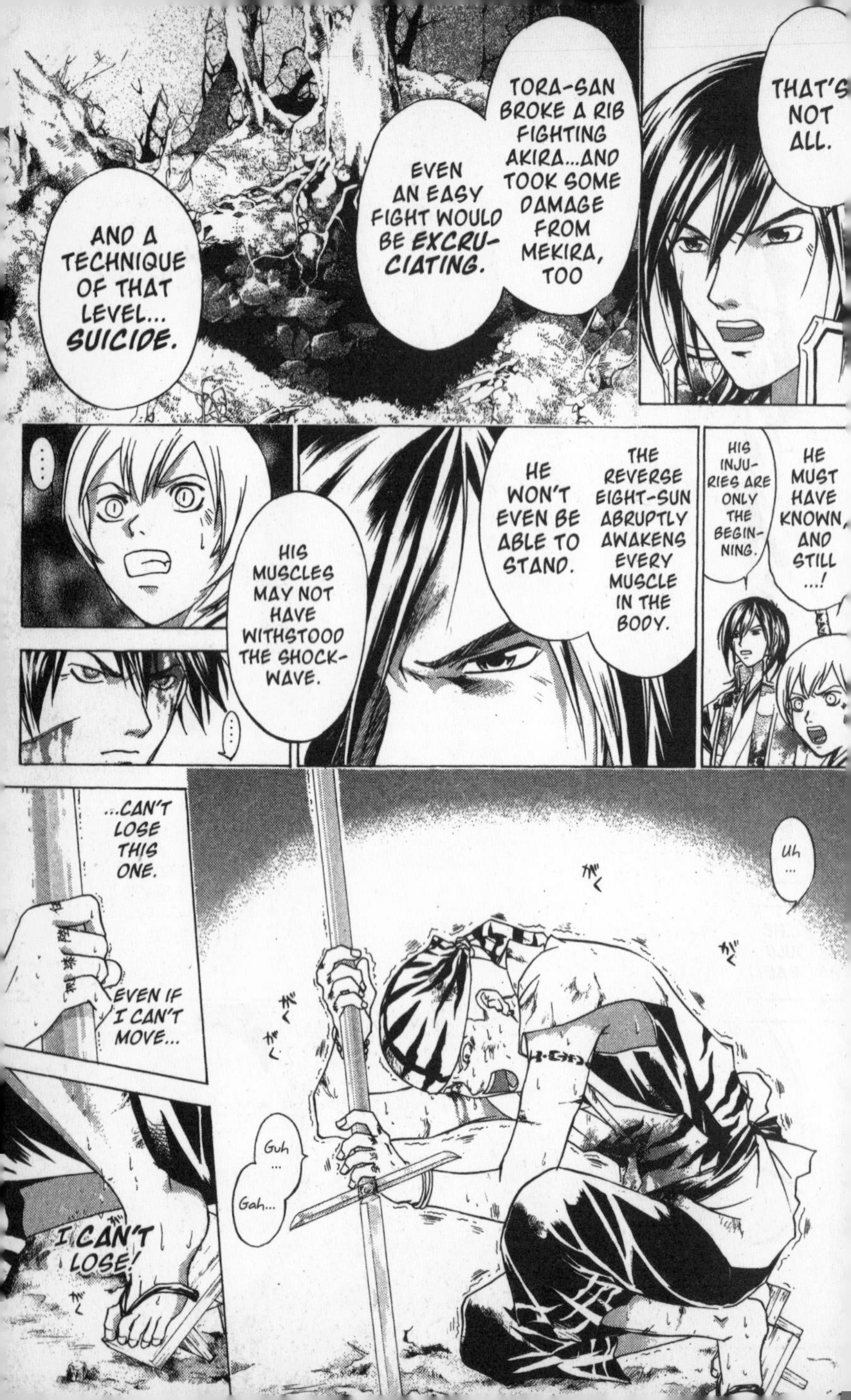
THAT'S NOT ALL.
TORA-SAN BROKE A RIB FIGHTING AKIRA...AND TOOK SOME DAMAGE FROM MEKIRA, TOO
EVEN AN EASY FIGHT WOULD BE EXCRUCIATING.
AND A TECHNIQUE OF THAT LEVEL... SUICIDE.
HE MUST HAVE KNOWN, AND STILL ...!
HIS INJURIES ARE ONLY THE BEGINNING.
THE REVERSE EIGHT-SUN ABRUPTLY AWAKENS EVERY MUSCLE IN THE BODY.
HE WON'T EVEN BE ABLE TO STAND.
HIS MUSCLES MAY NOT HAVE WITHSTOOD THE SHOCKWAVE.
......
...
Uh ...
...CAN'T LOSE THIS ONE.
Guh ...
Gah...
EVEN IF I CAN'T MOVE...
I CAN'T LOSE!

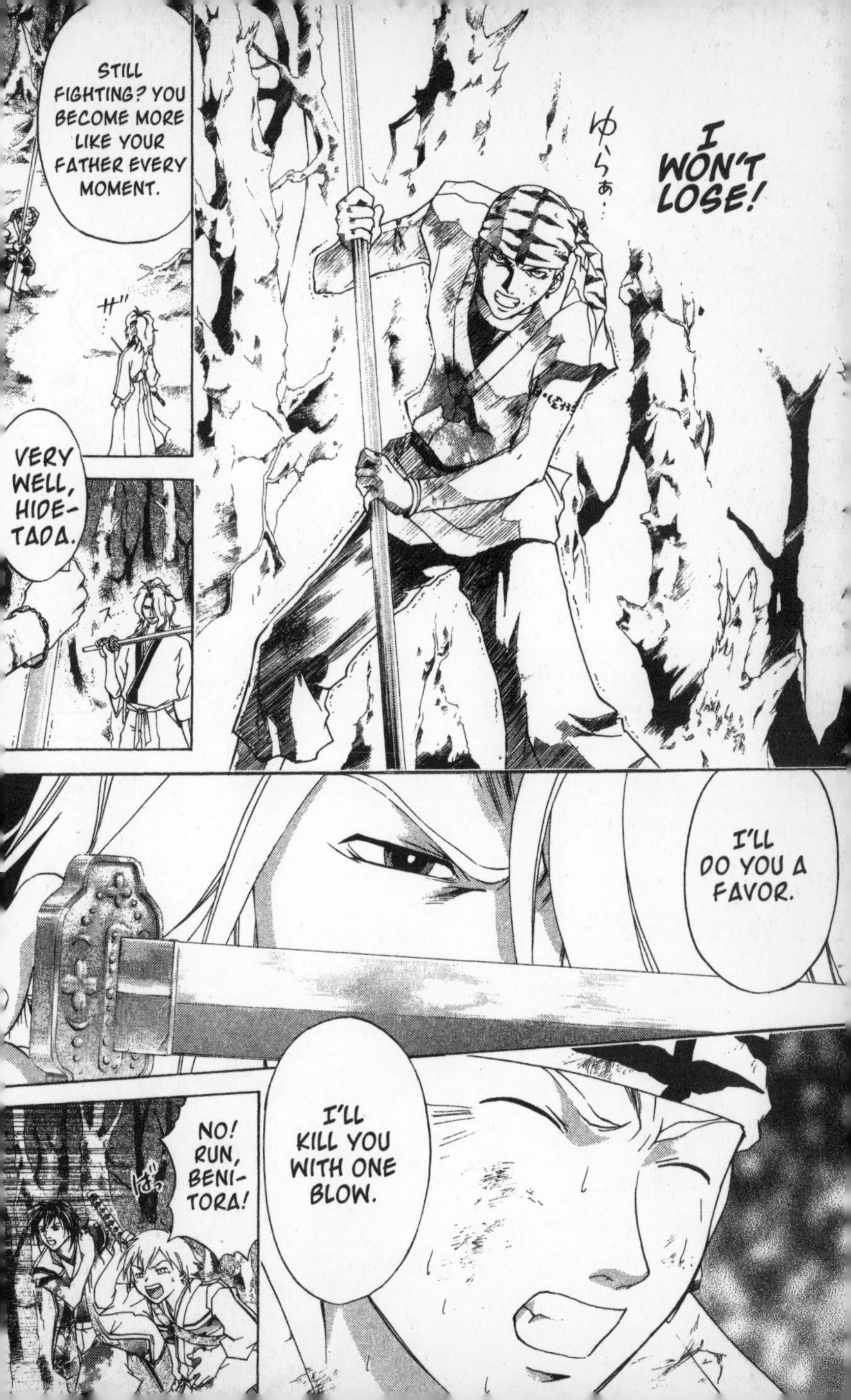
ゆらぁ…
I WON'T LOSE!
STILL FIGHTING? YOU BECOME MORE LIKE YOUR FATHER EVERY MOMENT.
VERY WELL, HIDE-TADA.
I'LL DO YOU A FAVOR.
I'LL KILL YOU WITH ONE BLOW.
NO! RUN, BENI-TORA!

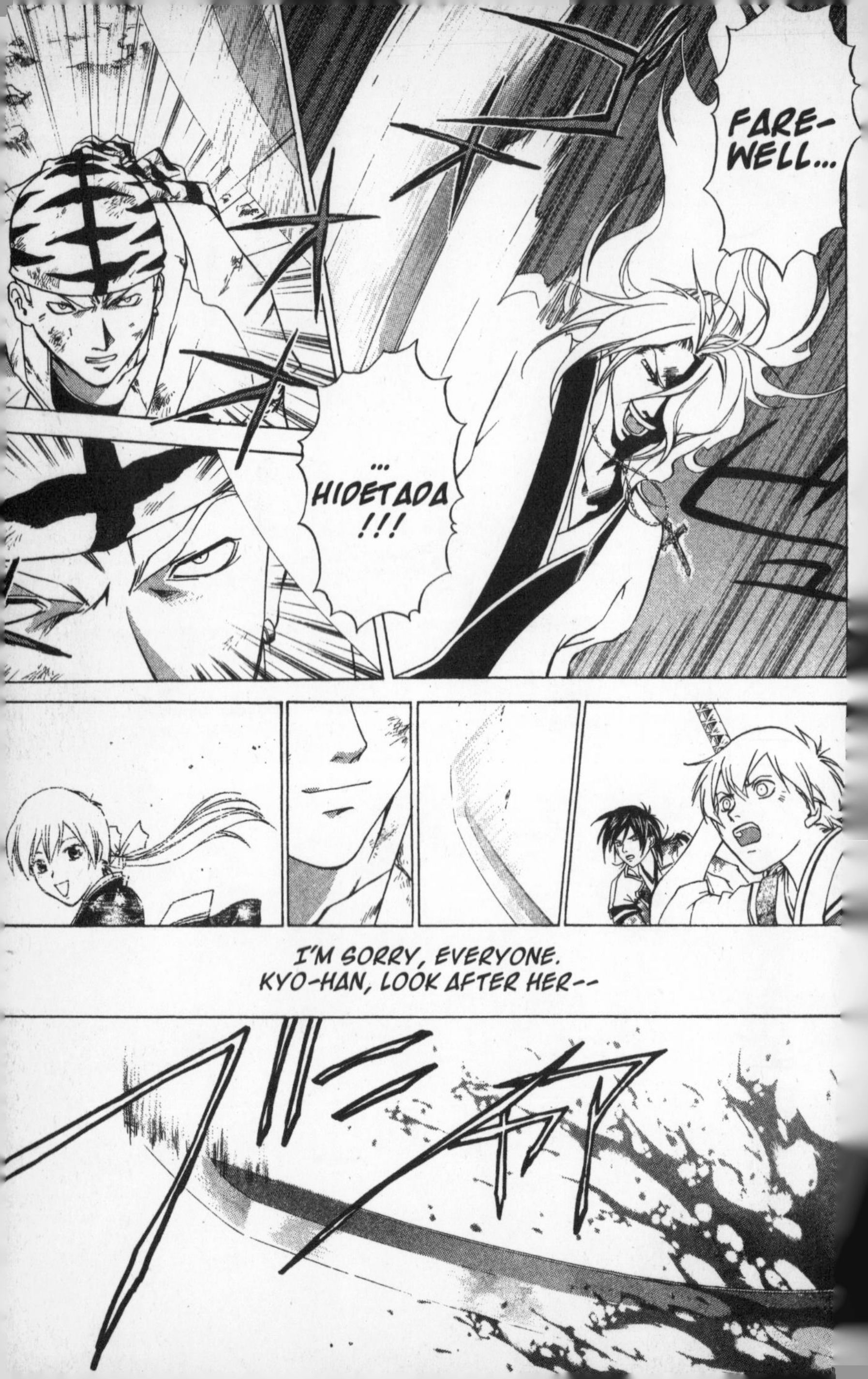
FARE-WELL...
...HIDETADA!!!
I'M SORRY, EVERYONE. KYO-HAN, LOOK AFTER HER--

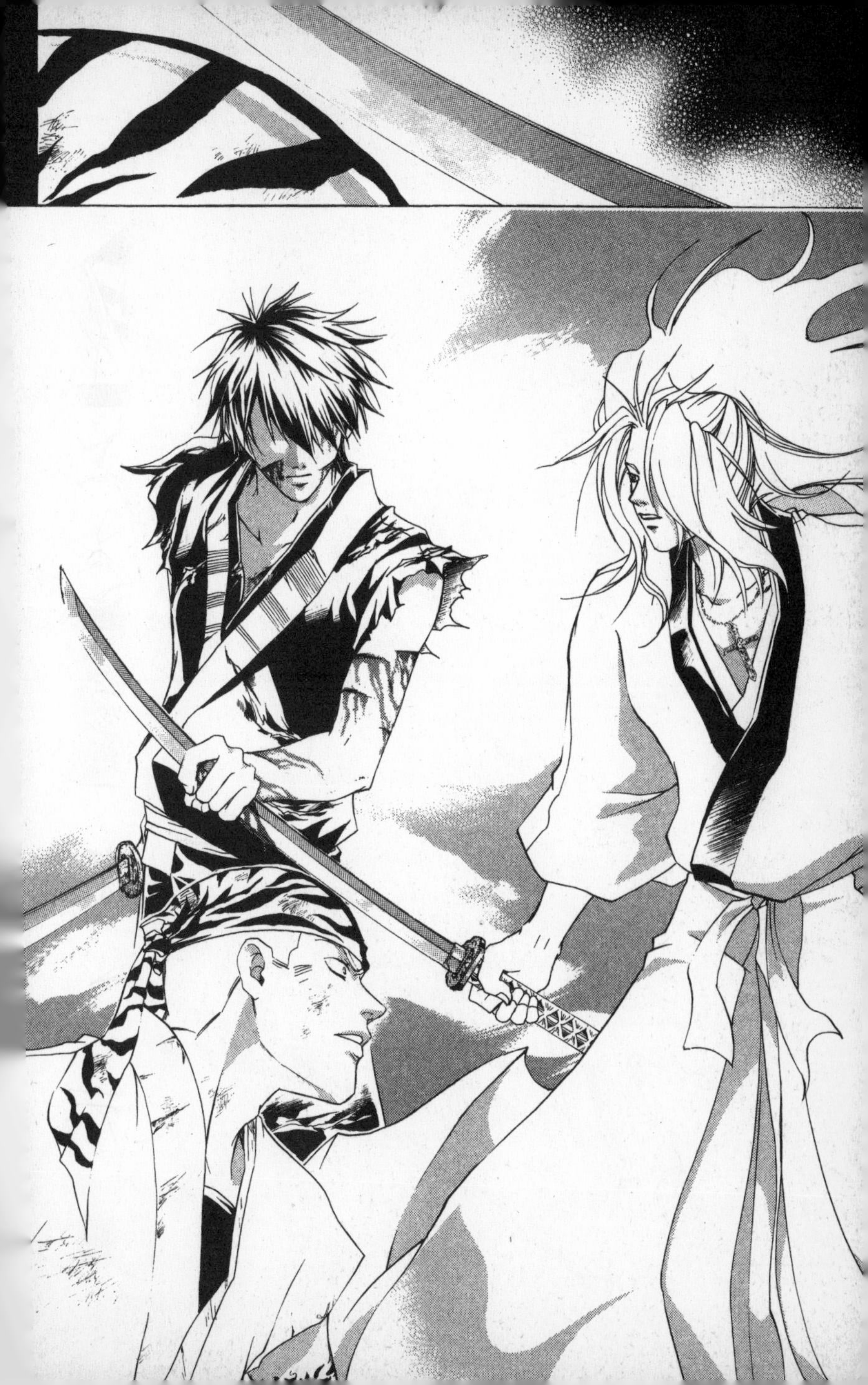

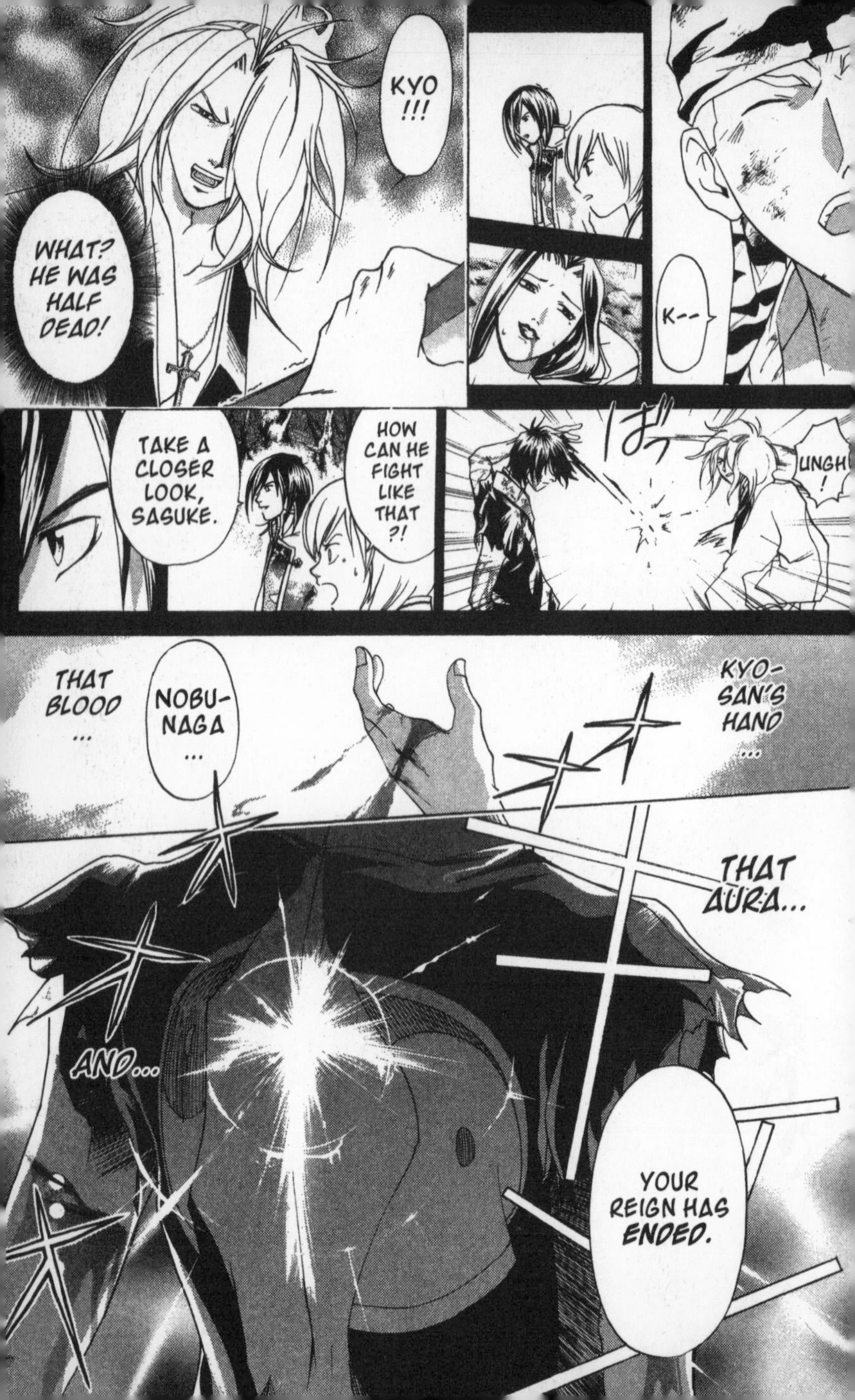
K--
KYO !!!
WHAT? HE WAS HALF DEAD!
UNGH !
HOW CAN HE FIGHT LIKE THAT ?!
TAKE A CLOSER LOOK, SASUKE.
KYO-SAN'S HAND ...
NOBUNAGA ...
THAT BLOOD ...
THAT AURA...
AND...
YOUR REIGN HAS ENDED.

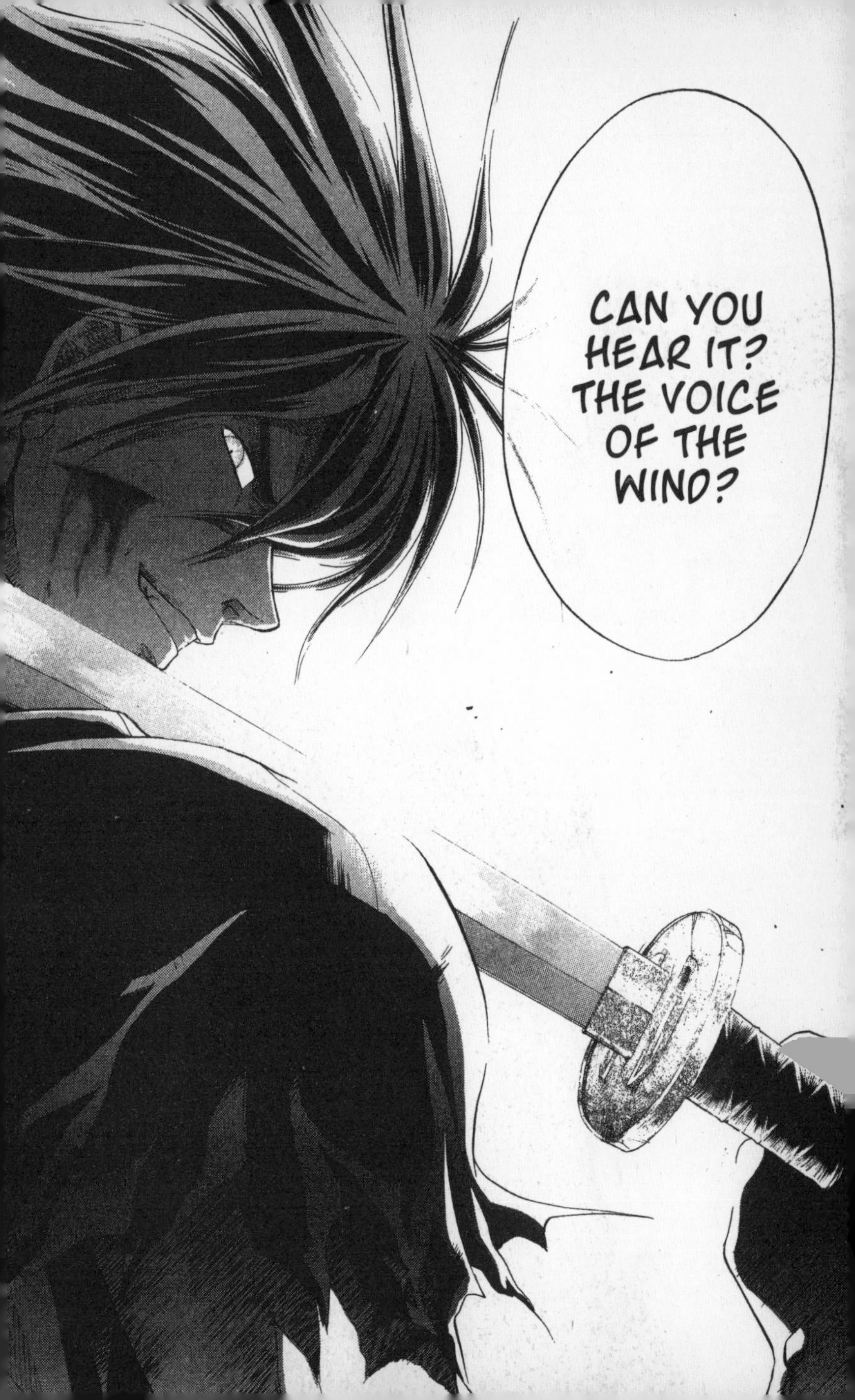
CAN YOU HEAR IT? THE VOICE OF THE WIND?

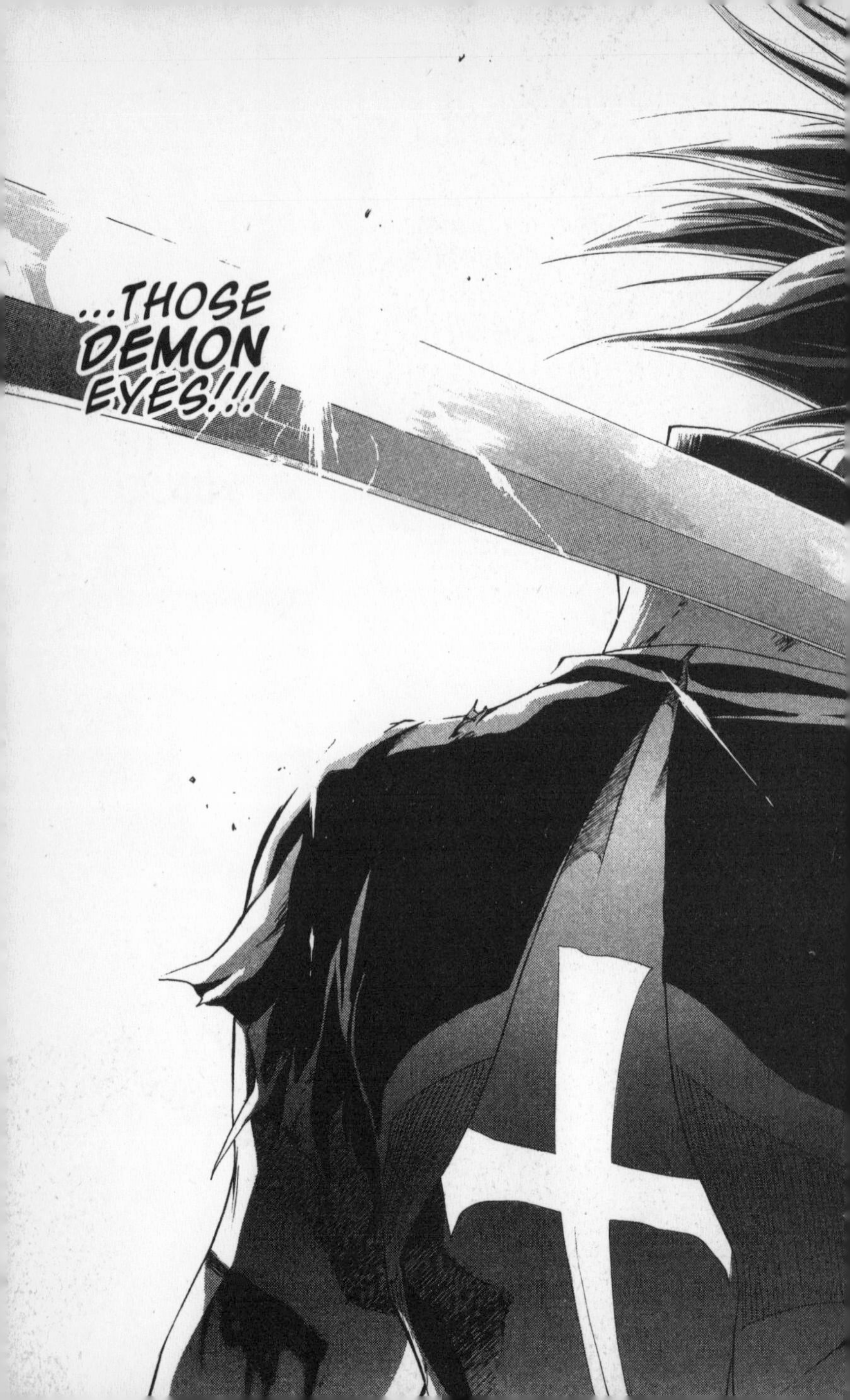
...THOSE DEMON EYES!!!

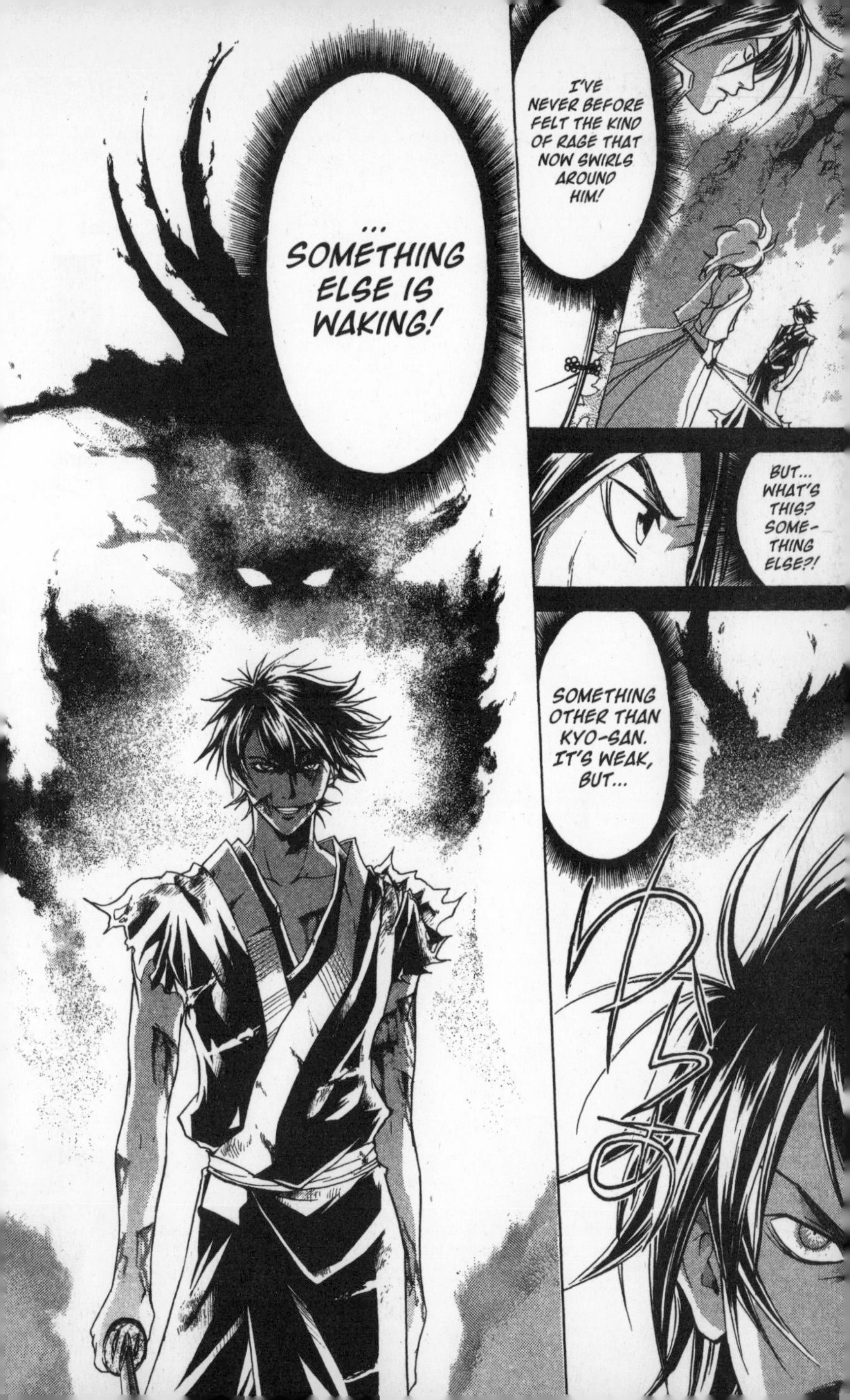
I'VE NEVER BEFORE FELT THE KIND OF RAGE THAT NOW SWIRLS AROUND HIM!
BUT... WHAT'S THIS? SOME-THING ELSE?!
SOMETHING OTHER THAN KYO-SAN. IT'S WEAK, BUT...
... SOMETHING ELSE IS WAKING!

The battles for Kyo's body-- a recap!

The battles rage in the forest at Mt. Fuji's feet. Here are the ones that will go down in history!

No. 1 The Rivals Collide!

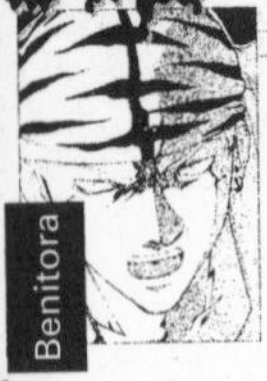
Benitora

Winning Blow

Shinkage School Eight-Sun. His former colleague, Gihyo, tricks him, but Benitora prevails!

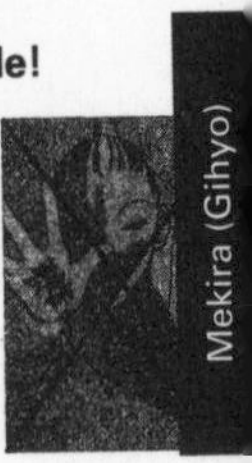
Mekira (Gihyo)

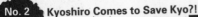

No. 2 Kyoshiro Comes to Save Kyo?!

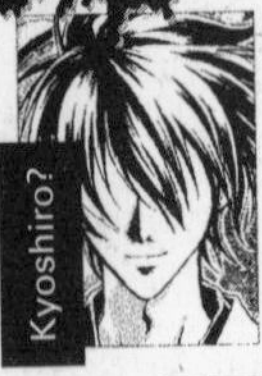
Kyoshiro?

Winning Blow

Strength of the Demon? All was calculated, but Kyo's power was greater than Kubira knew.

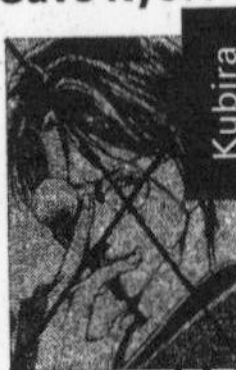
Kubira

No. 3 Four Years After Sekigahara...

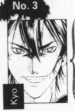

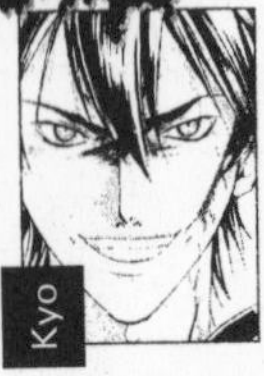
Kyo

Winning Blow

The Demon Eyes open! Kyo has Bikara on the ropes, but Shindara comes to his rescue. To be continued...

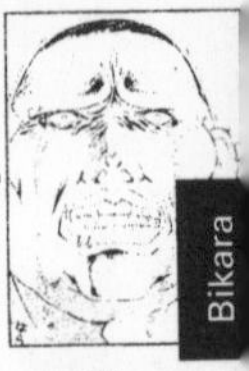
Bikara

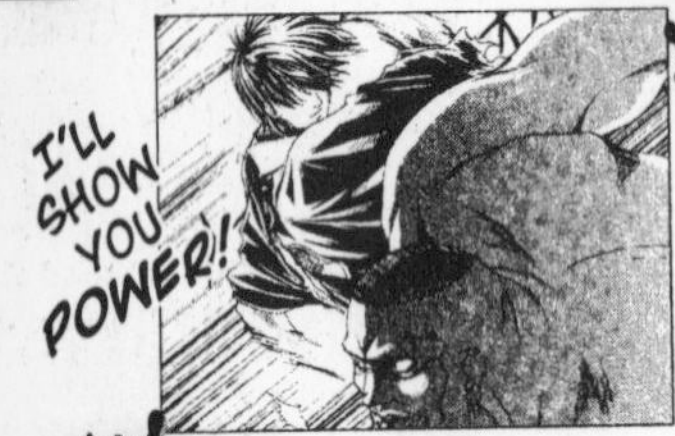
I'LL SHOW YOU POWER!

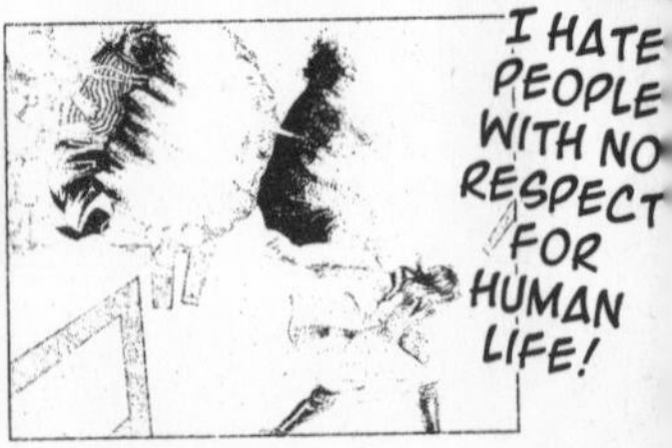
I HATE PEOPLE WITH NO RESPECT FOR HUMAN LIFE!

No. 4 The Wrath of Yukimura!

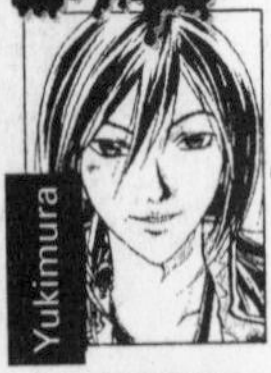
Yukimura

Winning Blow

Splitting rocks in two! Seeing Haira use people like pawns incites Yukimura's anger!

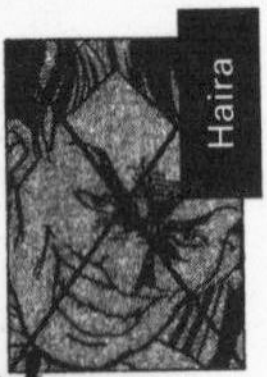
Haira

No. 5 The Great Battle: Kyo vs. the Red Giant!

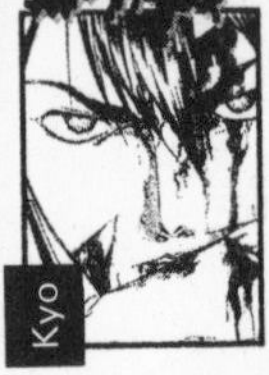
Kyo

Winning Blow

???
Kyo's friends drop like flies before the Sixth Demon King, Nobunaga's might--and the Tenma Mukurode takes down Kyo! But wait!

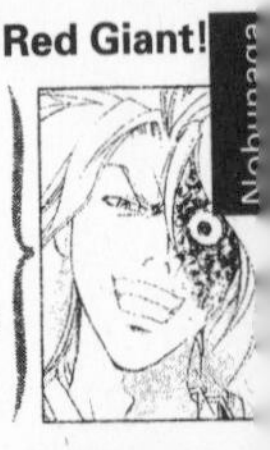
Nobunaga

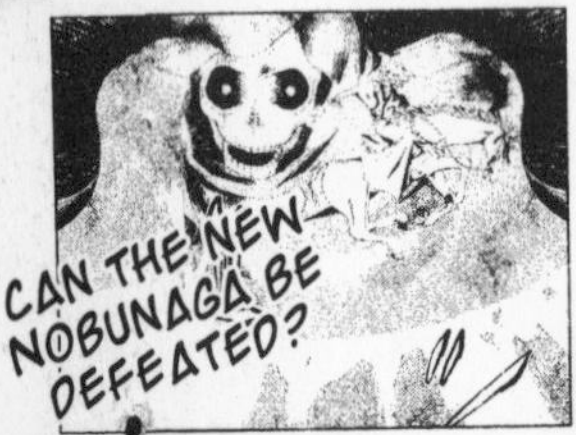
CAN THE NEW NOBUNAGA BE DEFEATED?

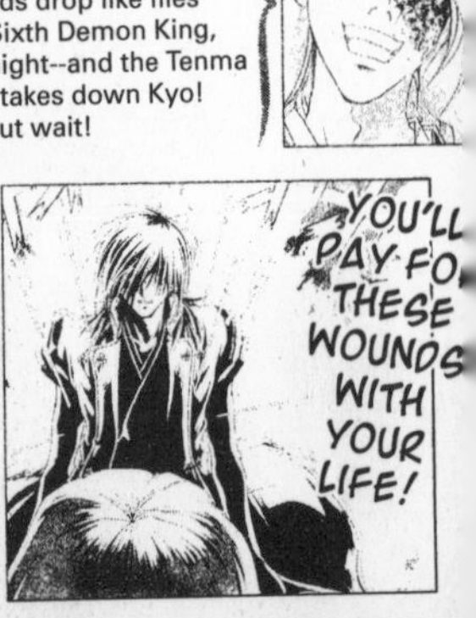
YOU'LL PAY FOR THESE WOUNDS WITH YOUR LIFE!

No. 6 Yukimura's Sword vs. Basara's "Shield"!

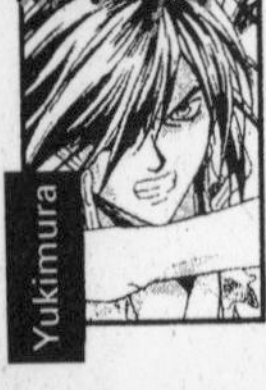
Yukimura

Winning Blow

Cut in Two!
Yukimura charges willfully into Basara's shield of arrows! He's hit, but it doesn't stop him from cutting Basara in two!

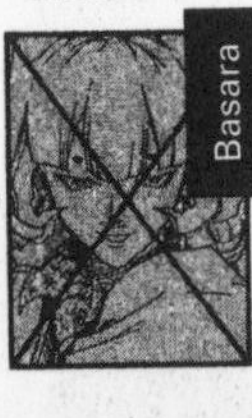
Basara

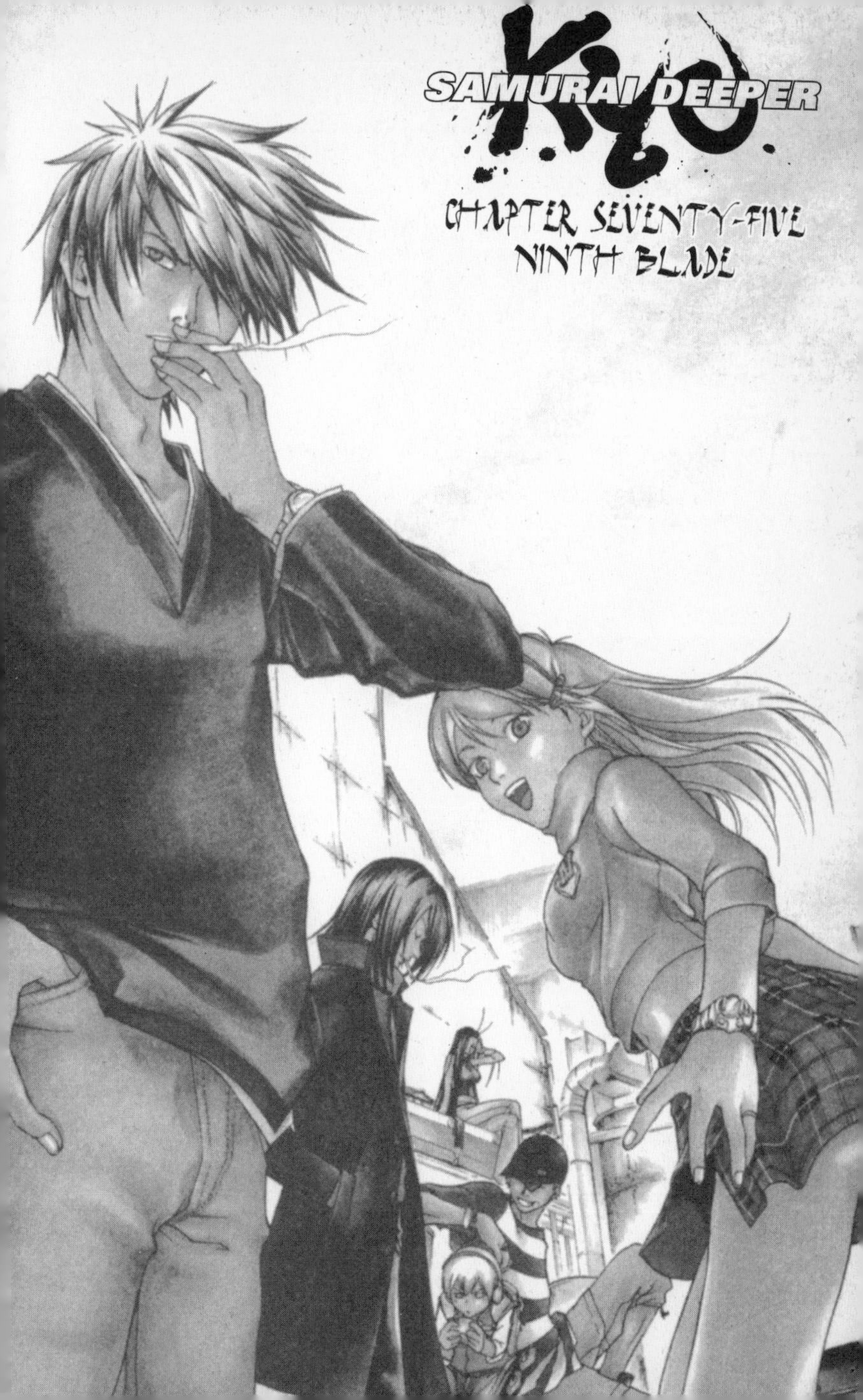
SAMURAI DEEPER KYO
CHAPTER SEVENTY-FIVE
NINTH BLADE

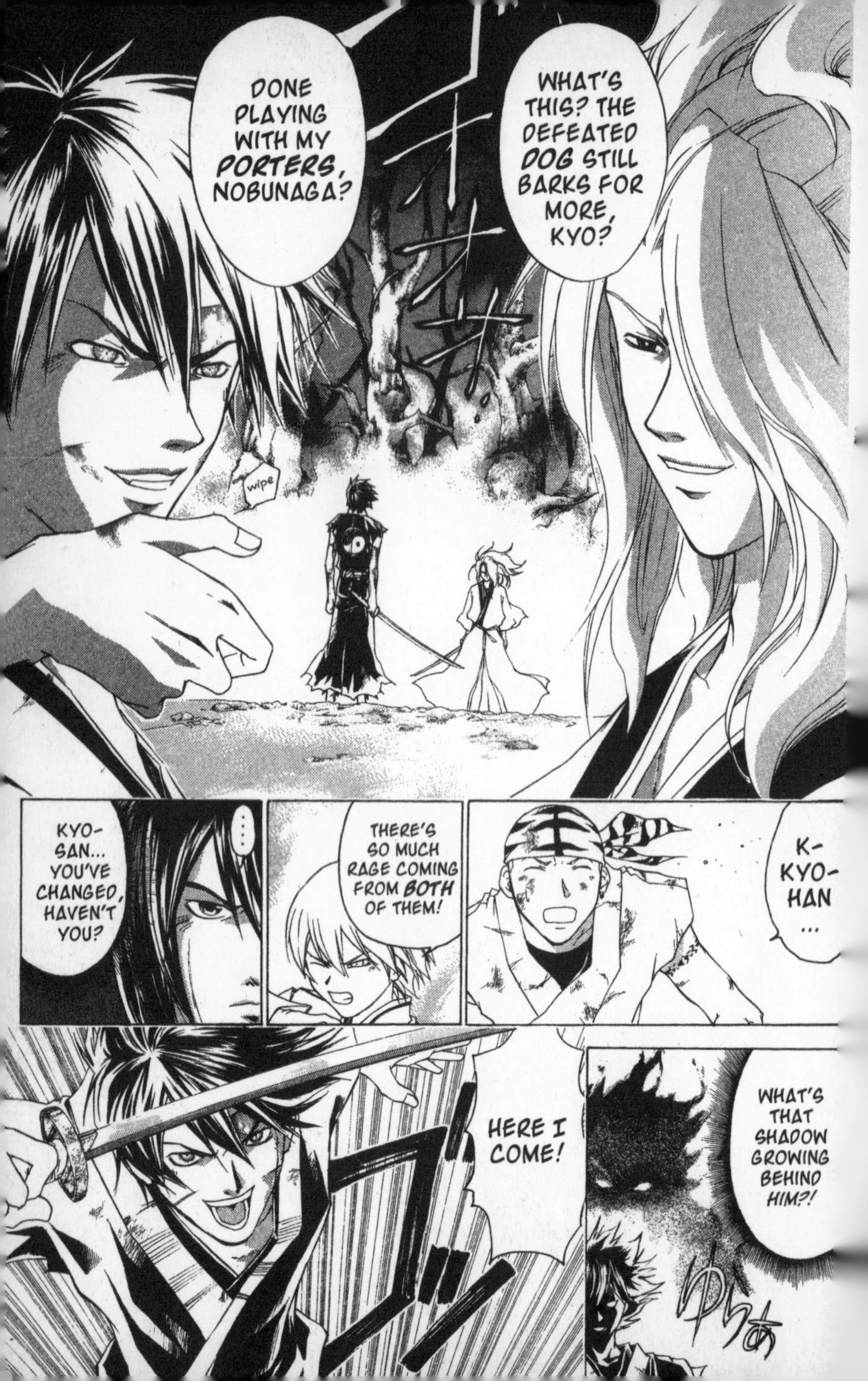
WHAT'S THIS? THE DEFEATED *DOG* STILL BARKS FOR MORE, KYO?
DONE PLAYING WITH MY *PORTERS*, NOBUNAGA?
wipe
K-KYO-HAN...
THERE'S SO MUCH RAGE COMING FROM *BOTH* OF THEM!
...
KYO-SAN... YOU'VE CHANGED, HAVEN'T YOU?
WHAT'S THAT SHADOW GROWING BEHIND HIM?!
HERE I COME!

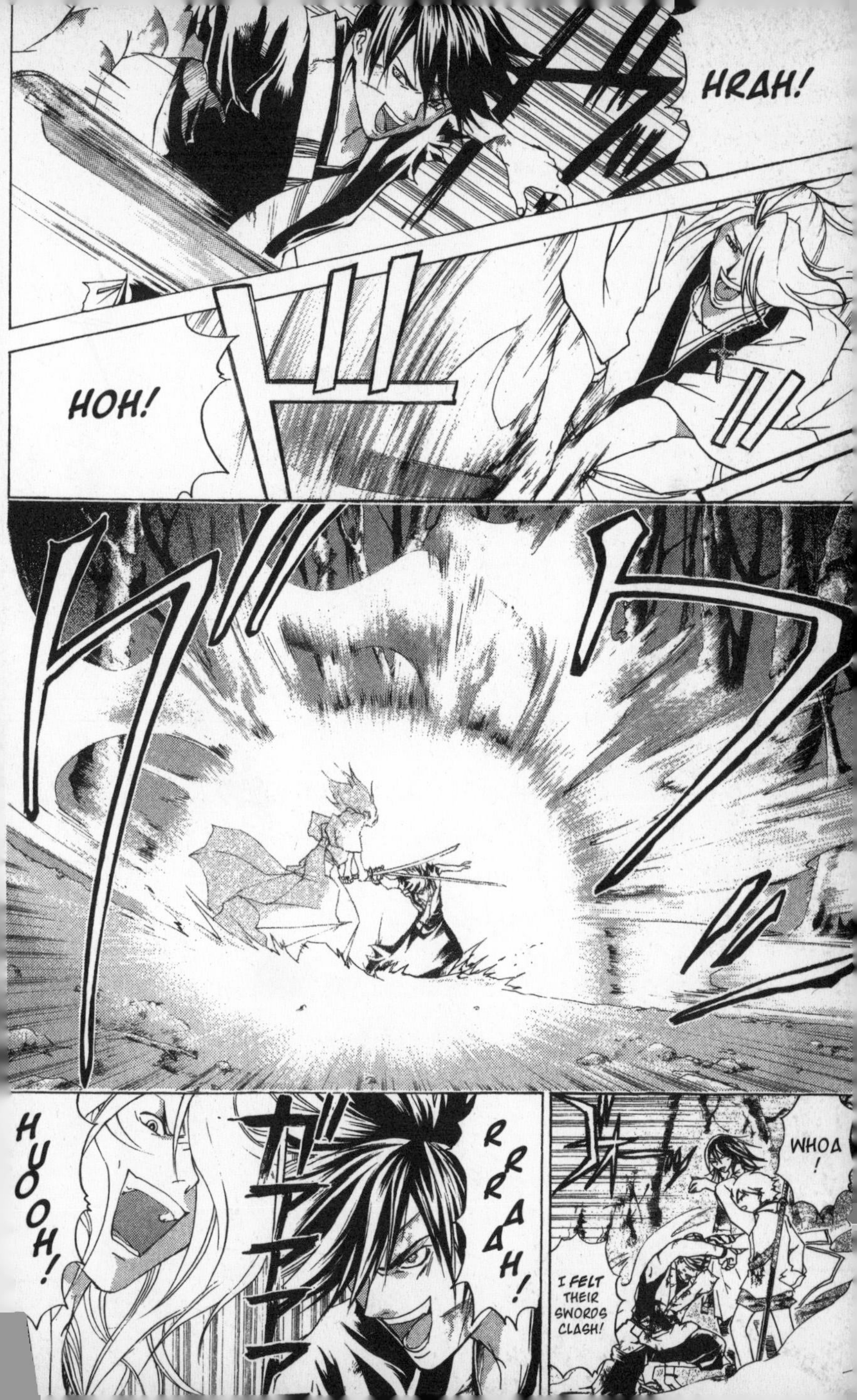
HRAH!
HOH!
WHOA!
I FELT THEIR SWORDS CLASH!
RRRAAH!
HUOOOH!

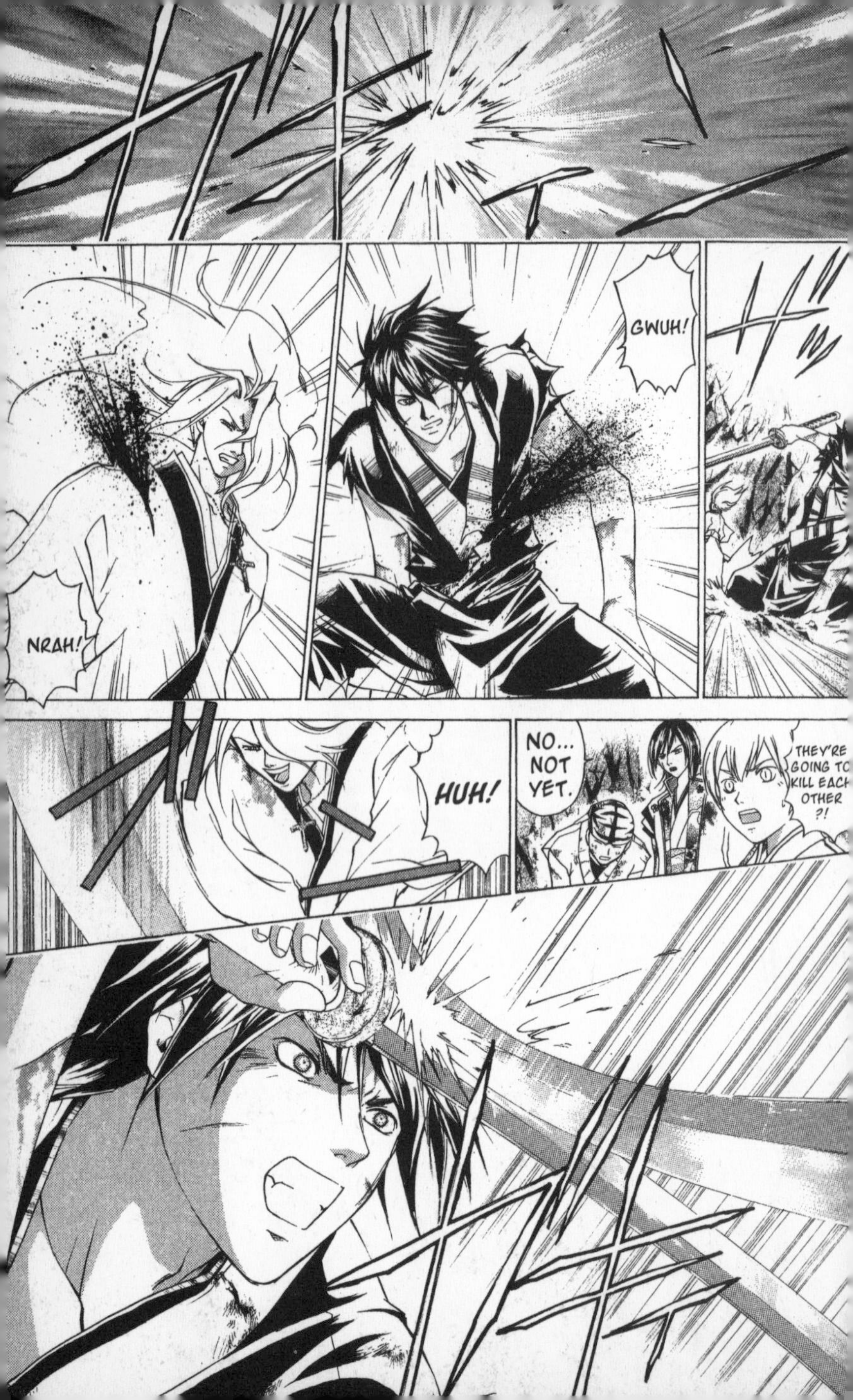
GWUH!
NRAH!
THEY'RE GOING TO KILL EACH OTHER ?!
NO... NOT YET.
HUH!

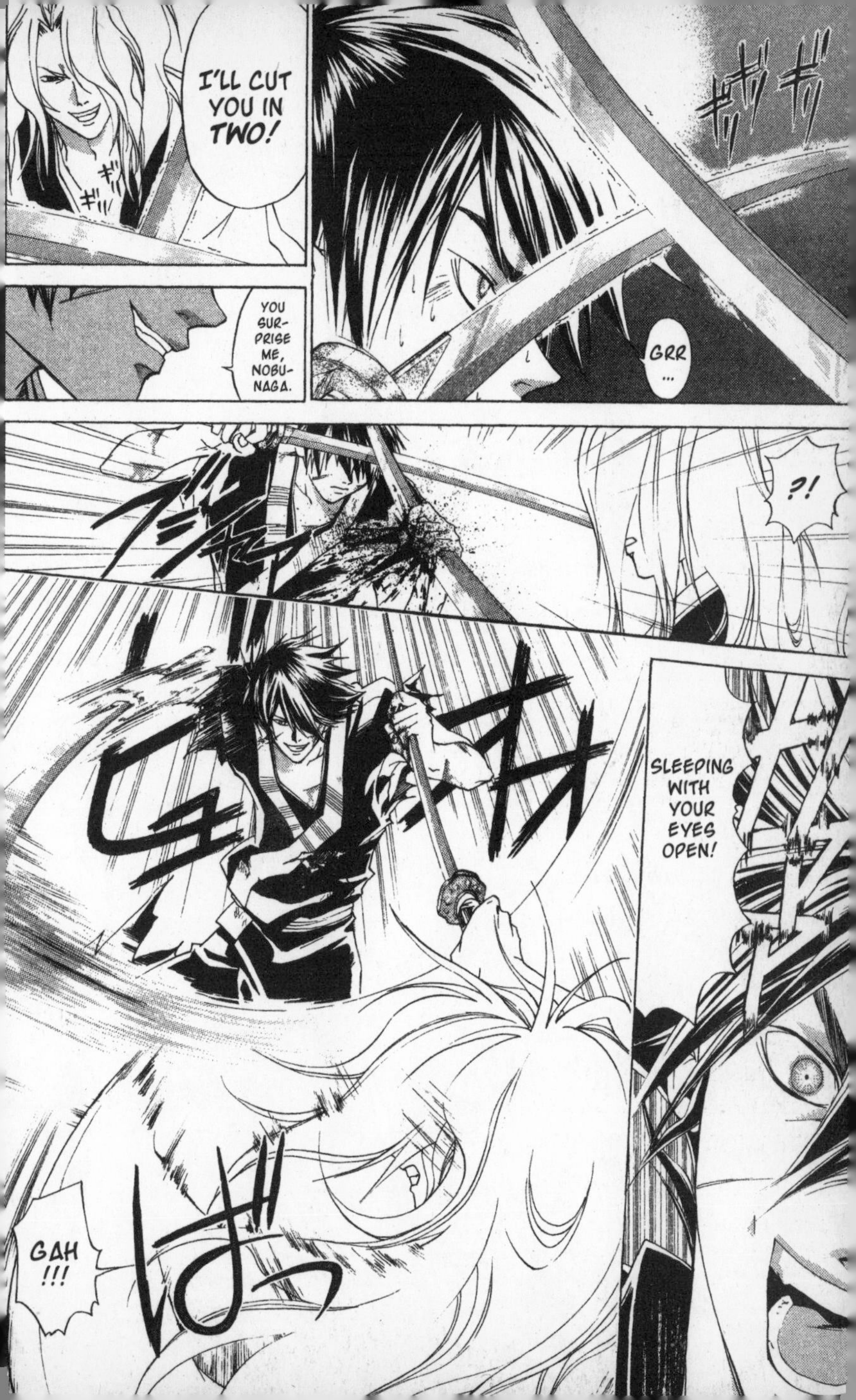
GRR ...
I'LL CUT YOU IN TWO!
YOU SUR-PRISE ME, NOBU-NAGA.
?!
SLEEPING WITH YOUR EYES OPEN!
GAH !!!

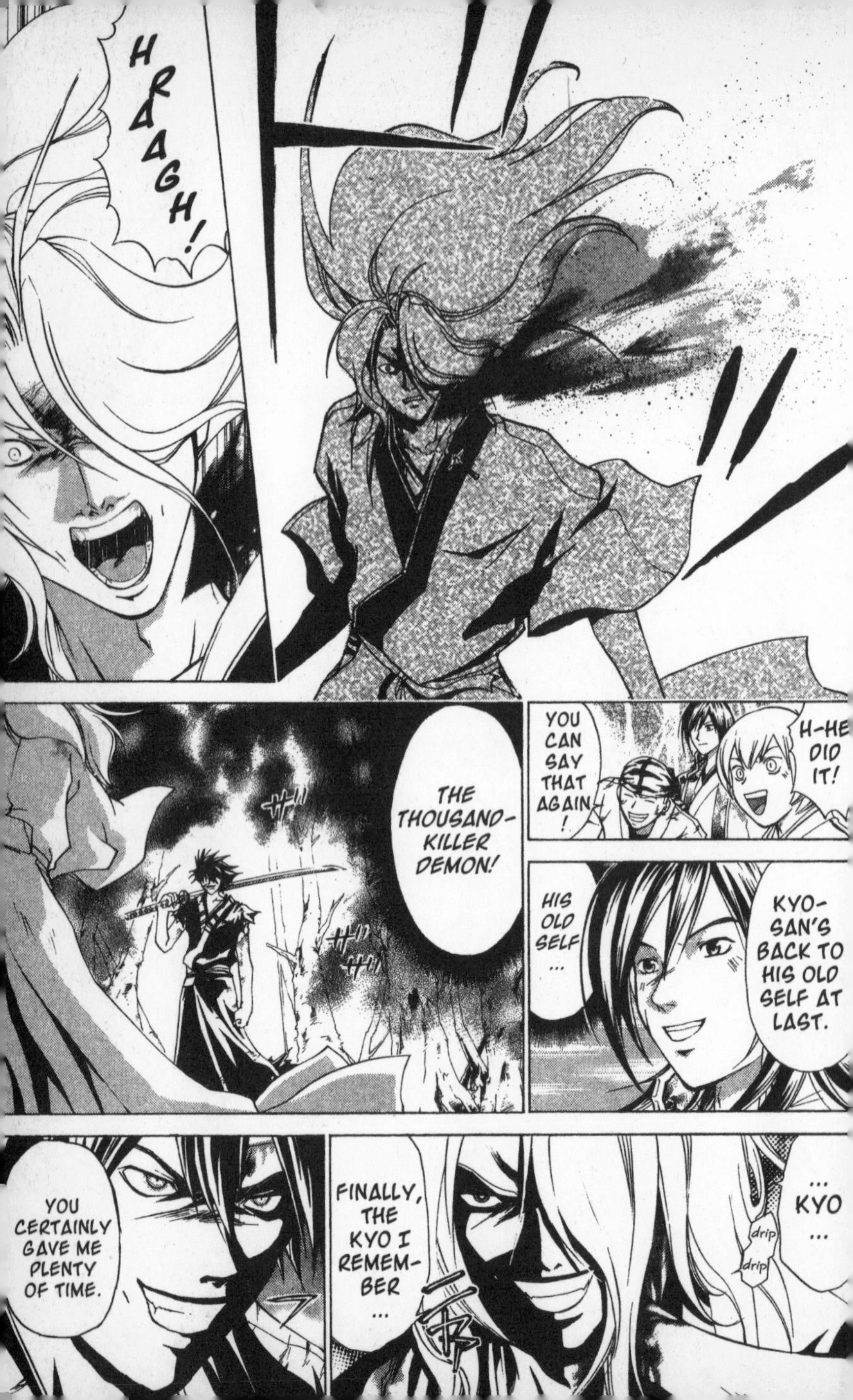
HRAAGH!
H-HE DID IT!
YOU CAN SAY THAT AGAIN!
KYO-SAN'S BACK TO HIS OLD SELF AT LAST.
HIS OLD SELF...
THE THOUSAND-KILLER DEMON!
...KYO...
drip
drip
FINALLY, THE KYO I REMEMBER...
YOU CERTAINLY GAVE ME PLENTY OF TIME.

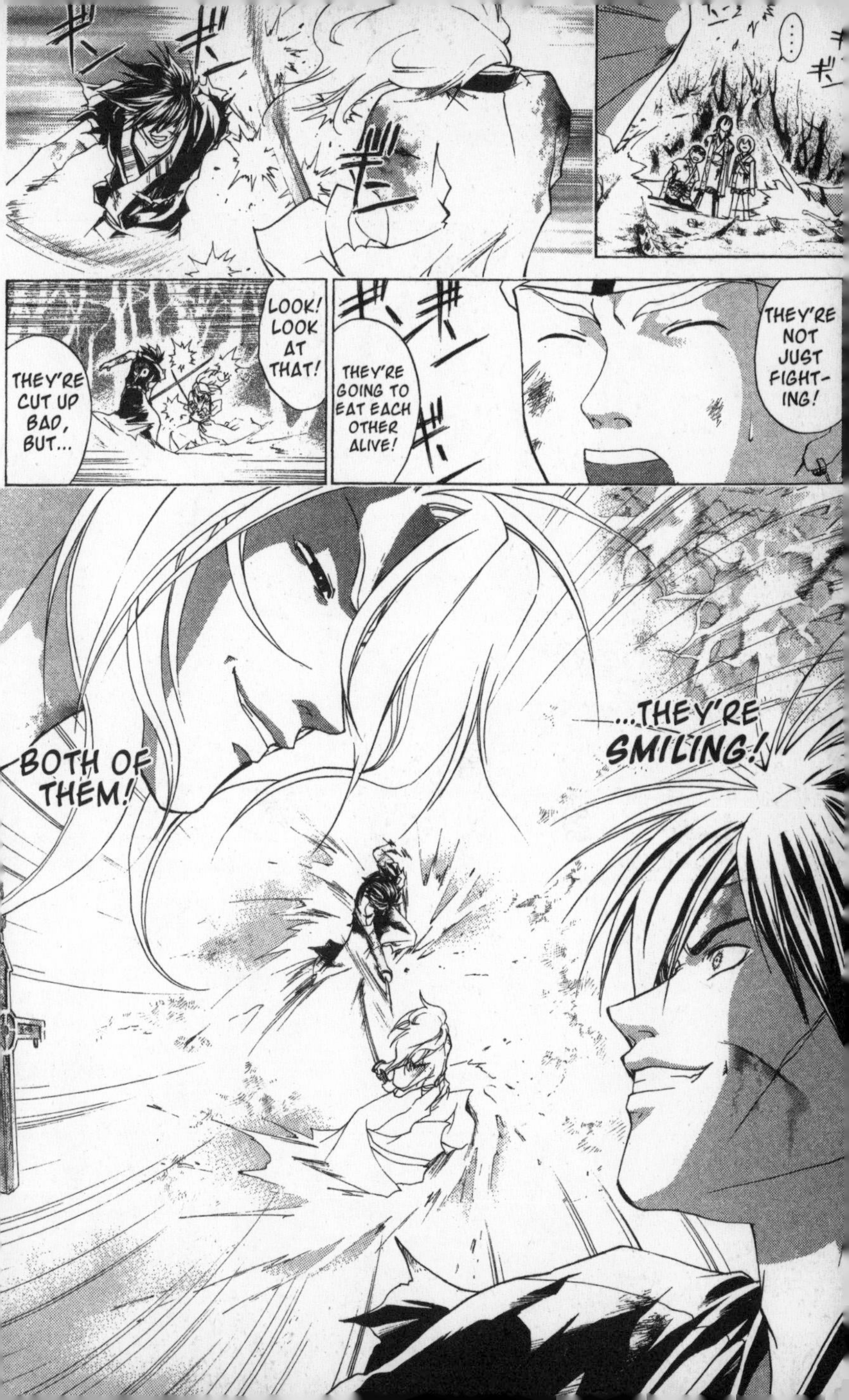
...
THEY'RE NOT JUST FIGHTING!
THEY'RE GOING TO EAT EACH OTHER ALIVE!
LOOK! LOOK AT THAT!
THEY'RE CUT UP BAD, BUT...
...THEY'RE SMILING!
BOTH OF THEM!

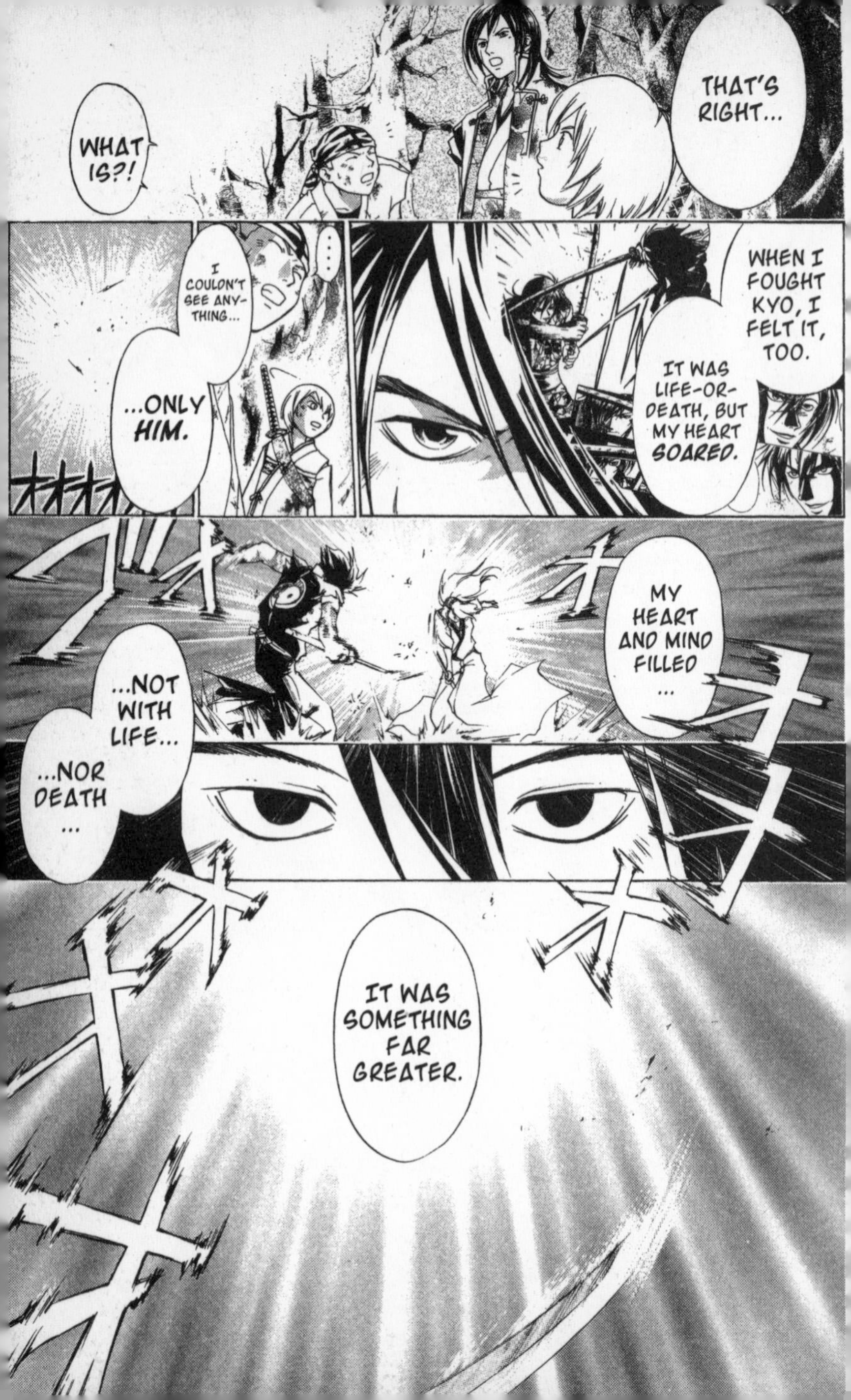
THAT'S RIGHT...
WHAT IS?!
WHEN I FOUGHT KYO, I FELT IT, TOO.
IT WAS LIFE-OR-DEATH, BUT MY HEART SOARED.
...
I COULDN'T SEE ANYTHING...
...ONLY HIM.
MY HEART AND MIND FILLED ...
...NOT WITH LIFE...
...NOR DEATH ...
IT WAS SOMETHING FAR GREATER.

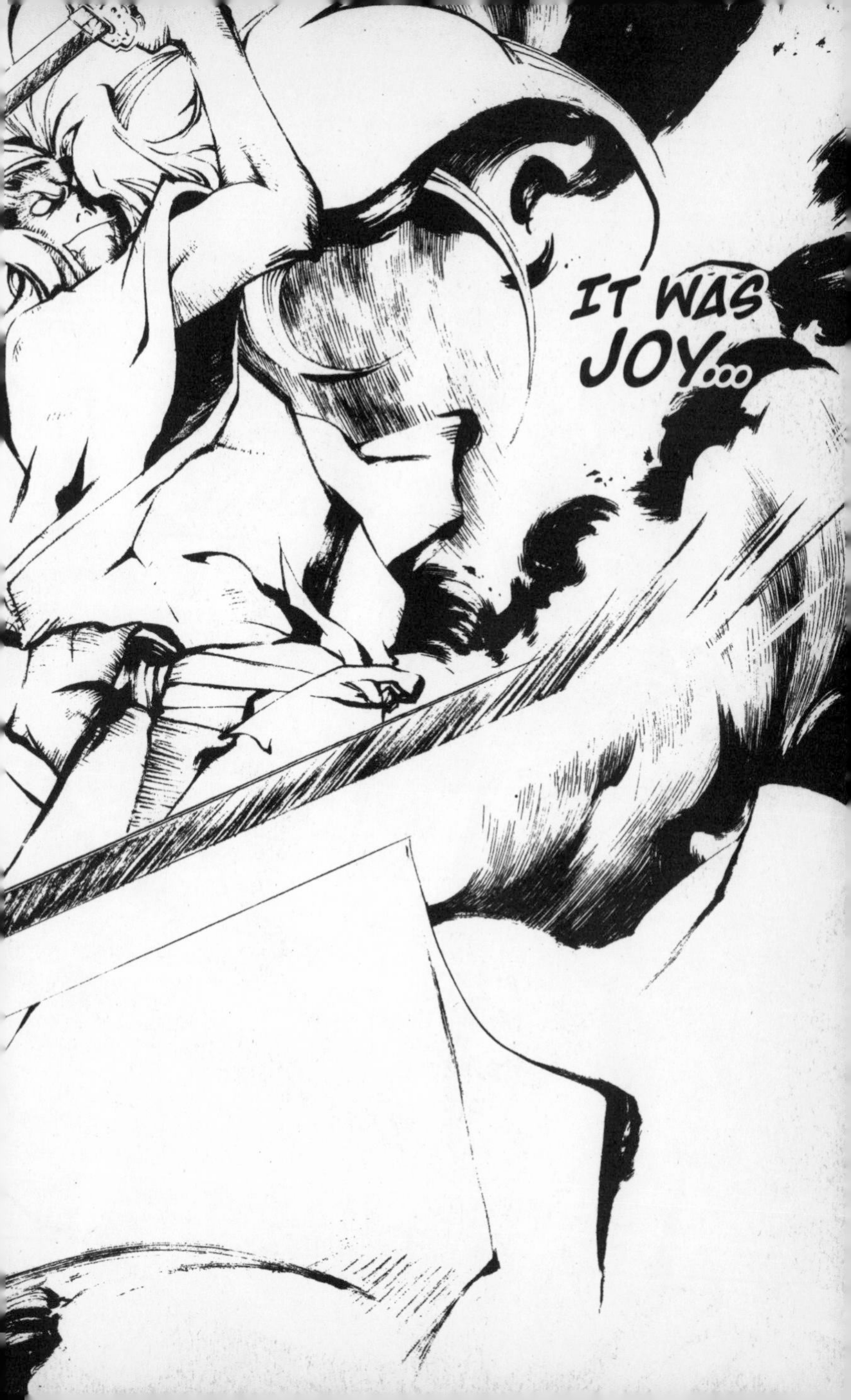
IT WAS JOY...

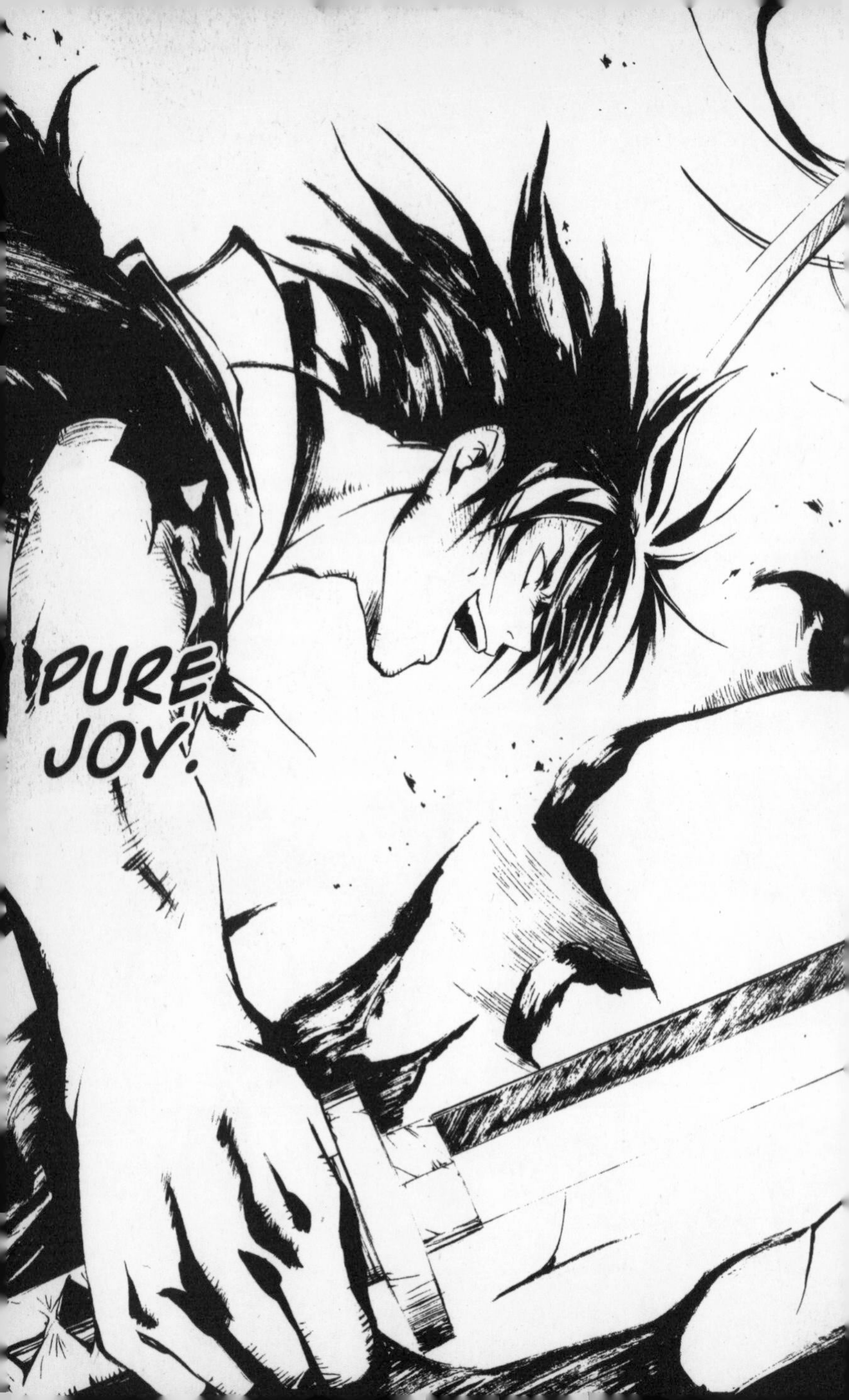
PURE JOY!

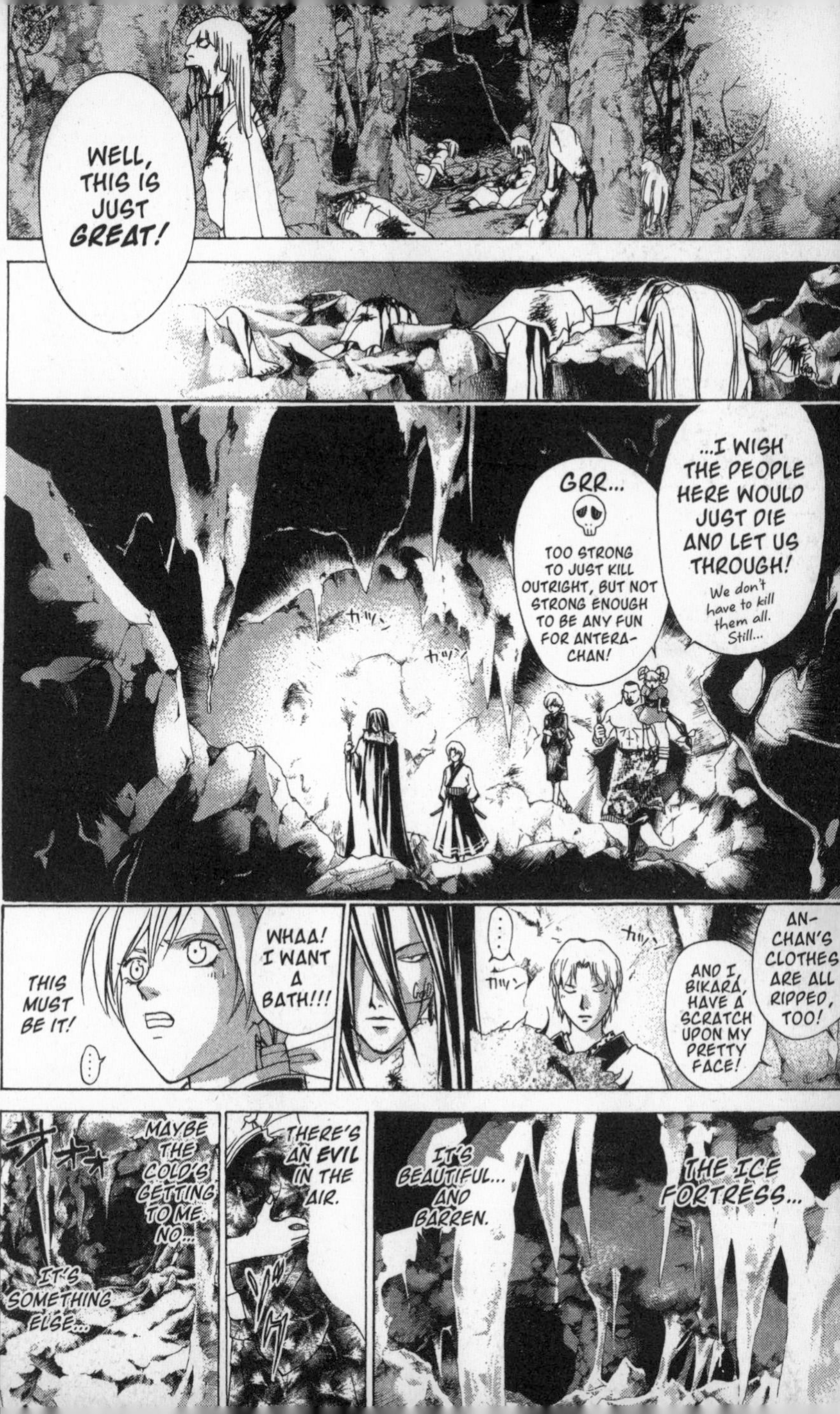
WELL, THIS IS JUST GREAT!
...I WISH THE PEOPLE HERE WOULD JUST DIE AND LET US THROUGH!
We don't have to kill them all. Still...
GRR...
TOO STRONG TO JUST KILL OUTRIGHT, BUT NOT STRONG ENOUGH TO BE ANY FUN FOR ANTERA-CHAN!
AN-CHAN'S CLOTHES ARE ALL RIPPED, TOO!
AND I, BIKARA, HAVE A SCRATCH UPON MY PRETTY FACE!
...
WHAA! I WANT A BATH!!!
THIS MUST BE IT!
...
THE ICE FORTRESS...
IT'S BEAUTIFUL... AND BARREN.
THERE'S AN EVIL IN THE AIR.
MAYBE THE COLD'S GETTING TO ME. NO...
IT'S SOMETHING ELSE...

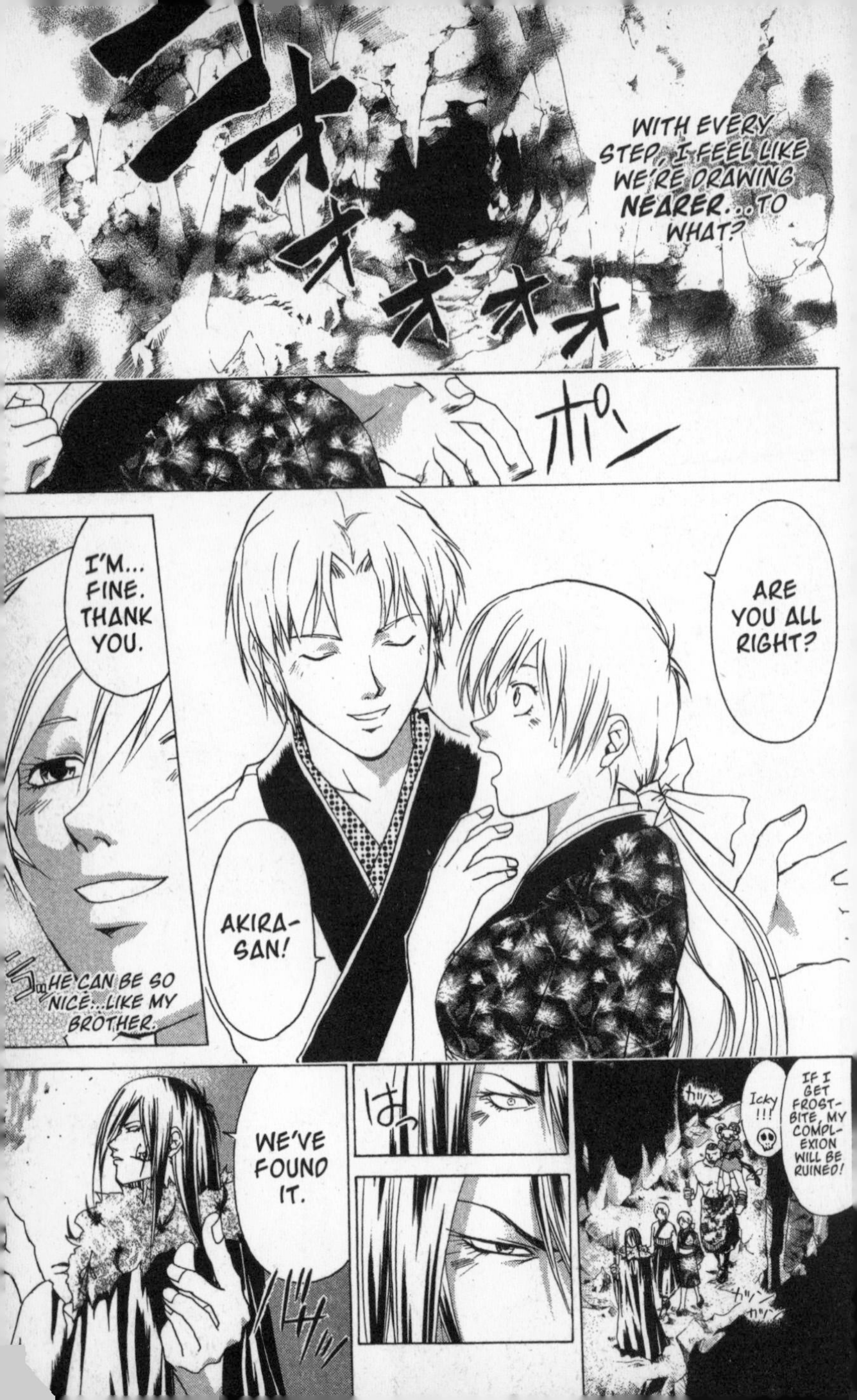

WITH EVERY STEP, I FEEL LIKE WE'RE DRAWING NEARER... TO WHAT?
ARE YOU ALL RIGHT?
AKIRA-SAN!
I'M... FINE. THANK YOU.
HE CAN BE SO NICE... LIKE MY BROTHER.
IF I GET FROST-BITE, MY COMPLEXION WILL BE RUINED!
Icky!!!
はっ
WE'VE FOUND IT.

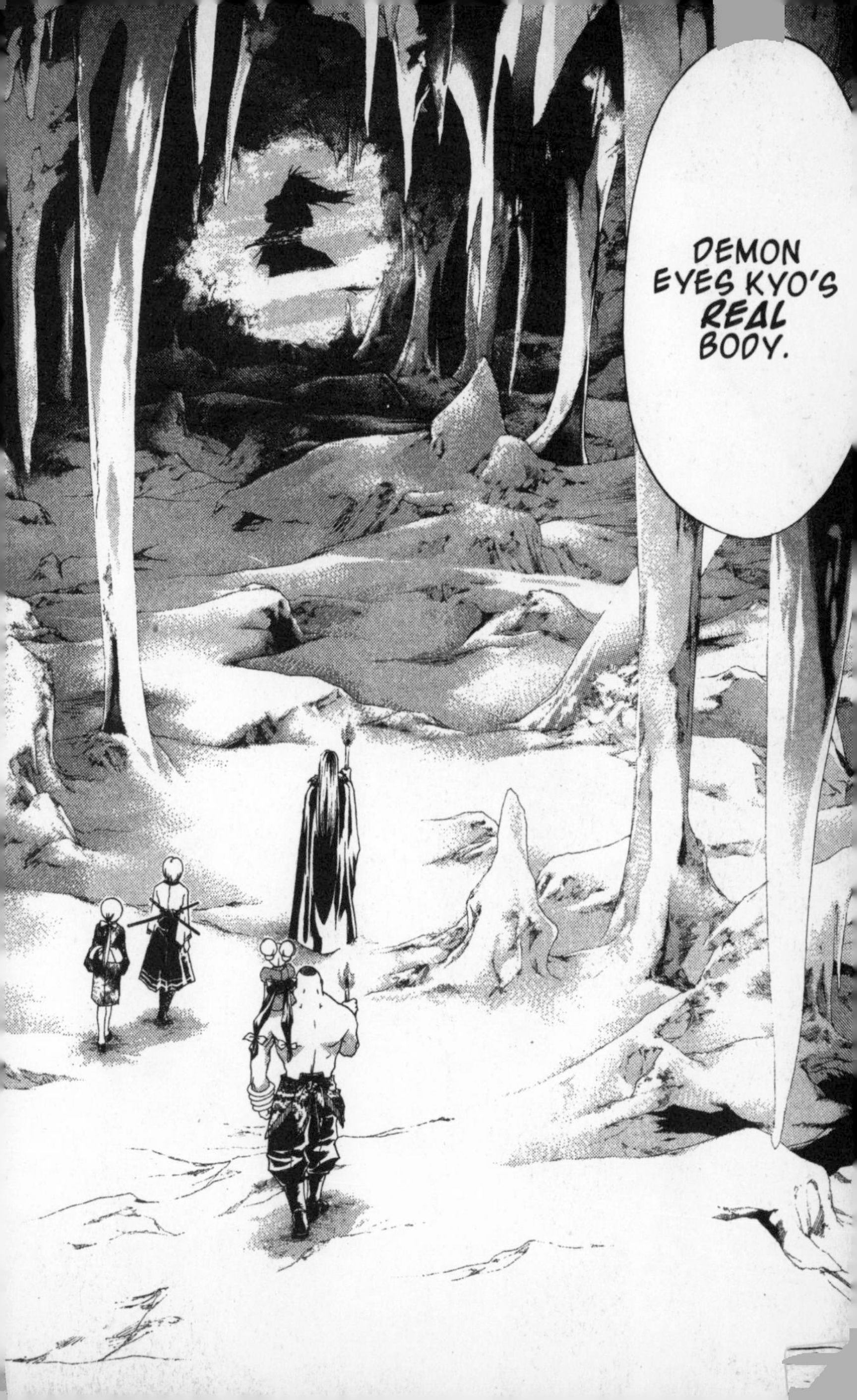
DEMON EYES KYO'S REAL BODY.

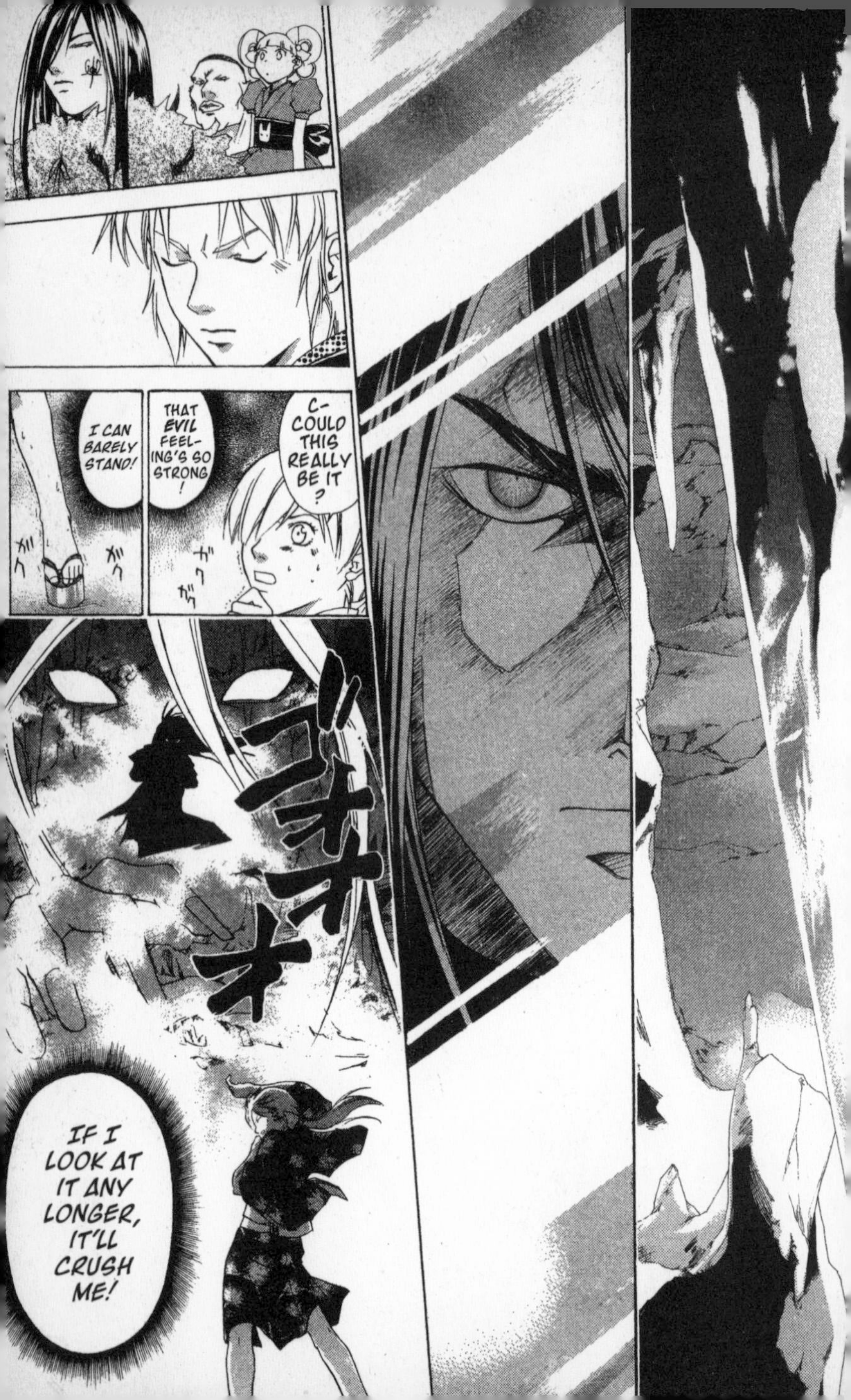
C-COULD THIS REALLY BE IT?
THAT EVIL FEELING'S SO STRONG!
I CAN BARELY STAND!
IF I LOOK AT IT ANY LONGER, IT'LL CRUSH ME!

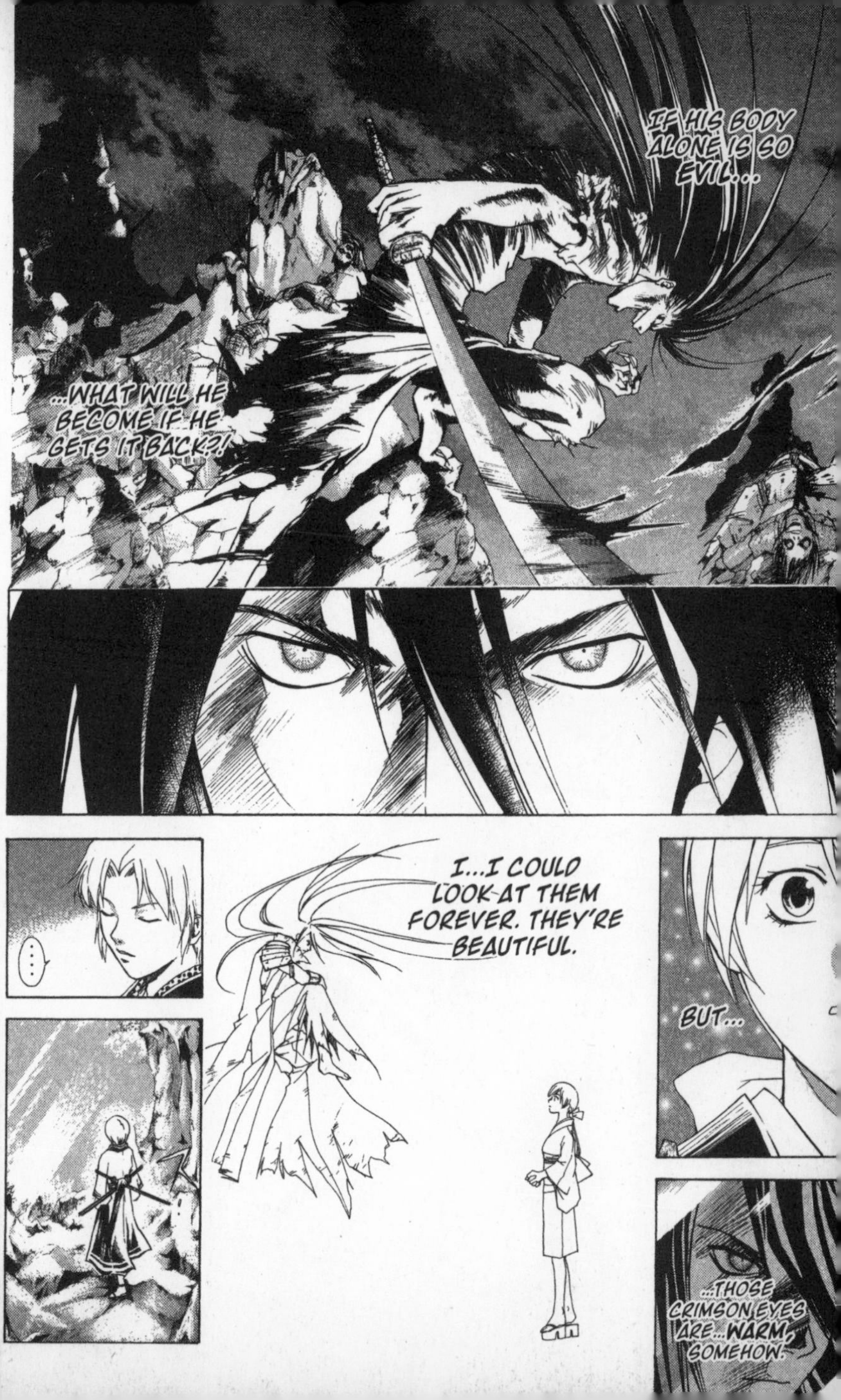
IF HIS BODY ALONE IS SO EVIL...
...WHAT WILL HE BECOME IF HE GETS IT BACK?!
BUT...
...THOSE CRIMSON EYES ARE...WARM, SOMEHOW.
I...I COULD LOOK AT THEM FOREVER. THEY'RE BEAUTIFUL.
....

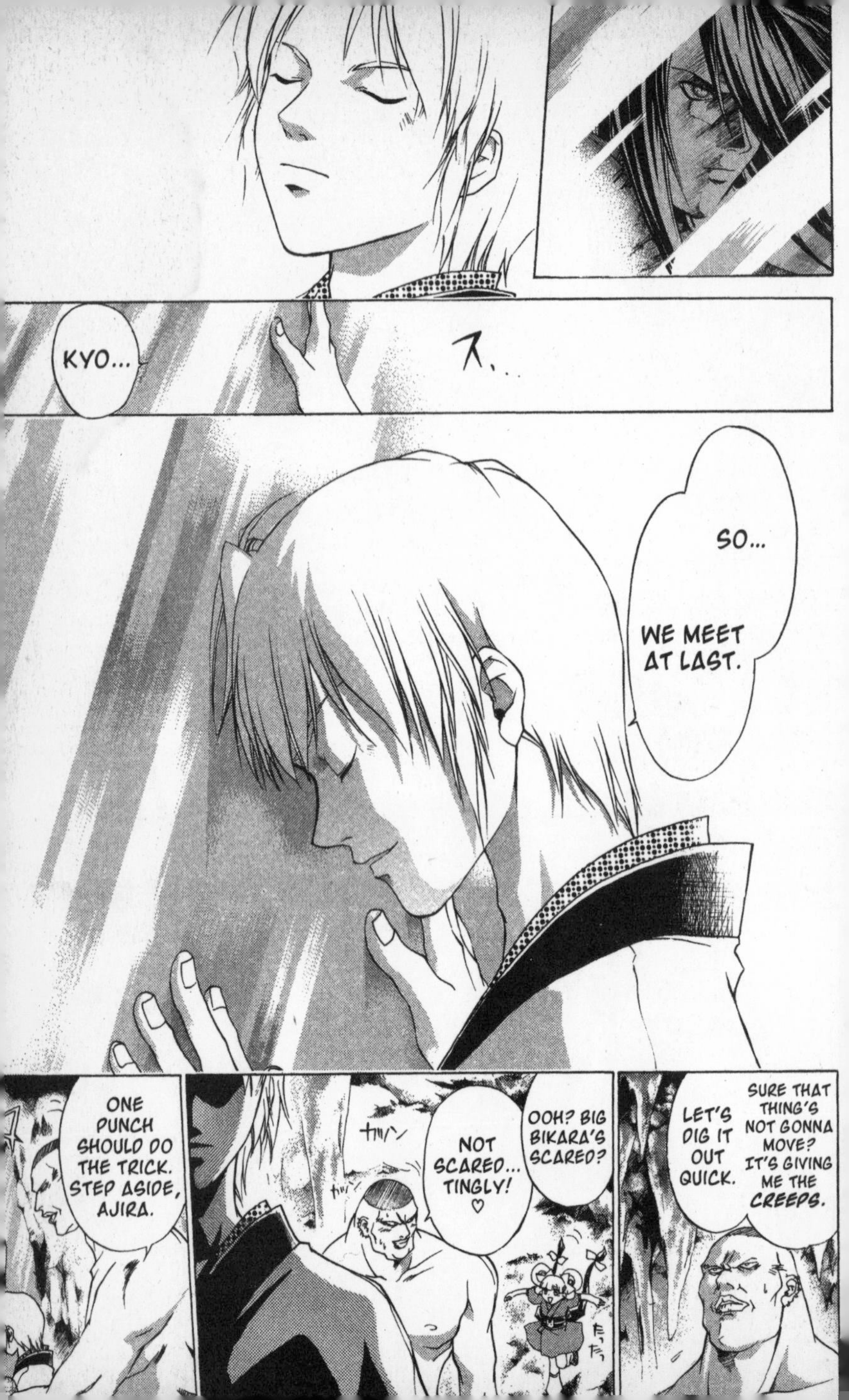
KYO...
ス...
SO...
WE MEET AT LAST.
SURE THAT THING'S NOT GONNA MOVE? IT'S GIVING ME THE CREEPS.
LET'S DIG IT OUT QUICK.
OOH? BIG BIKARA'S SCARED?
NOT SCARED... TINGLY! ♡
ONE PUNCH SHOULD DO THE TRICK. STEP ASIDE, AJIRA.

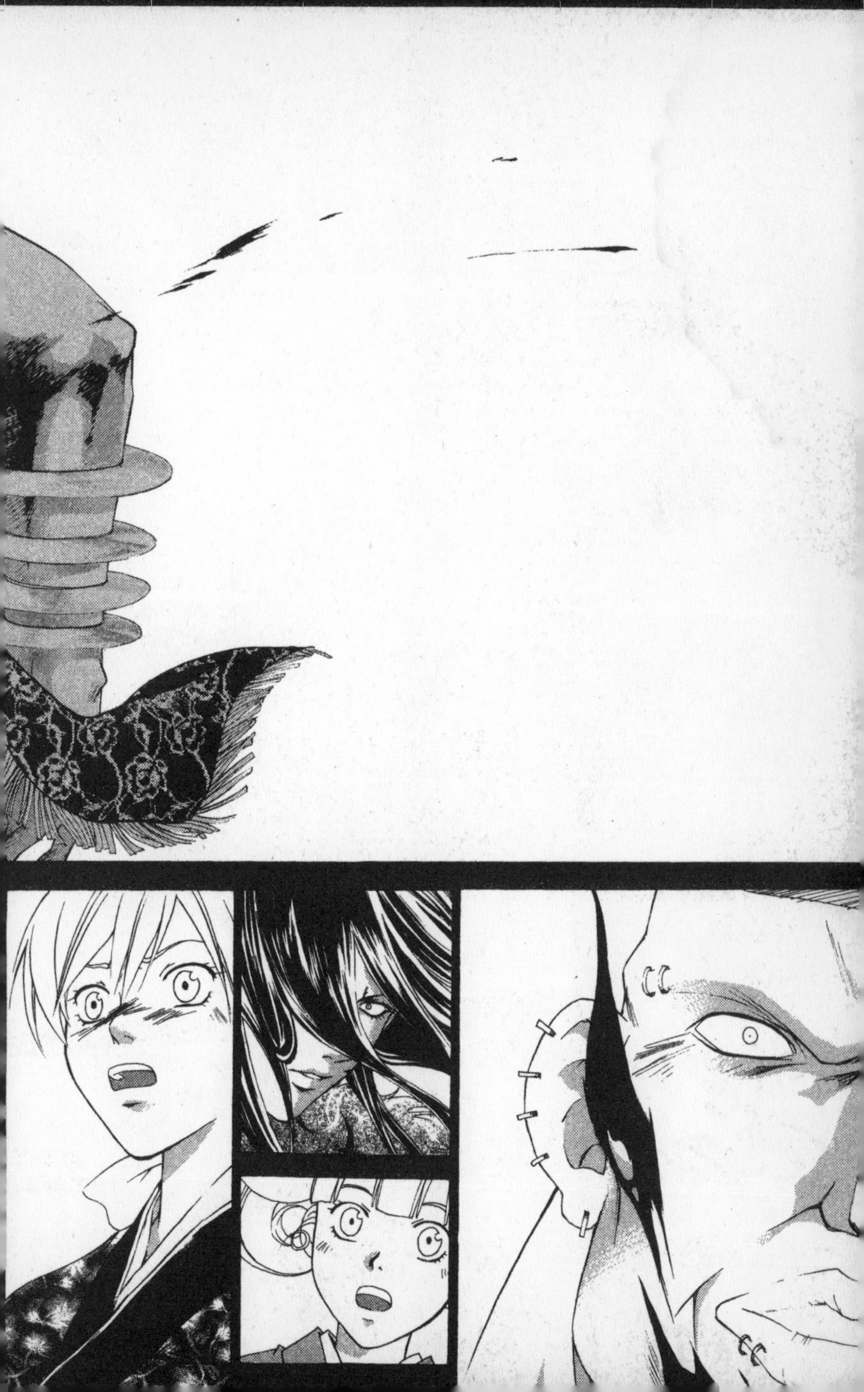

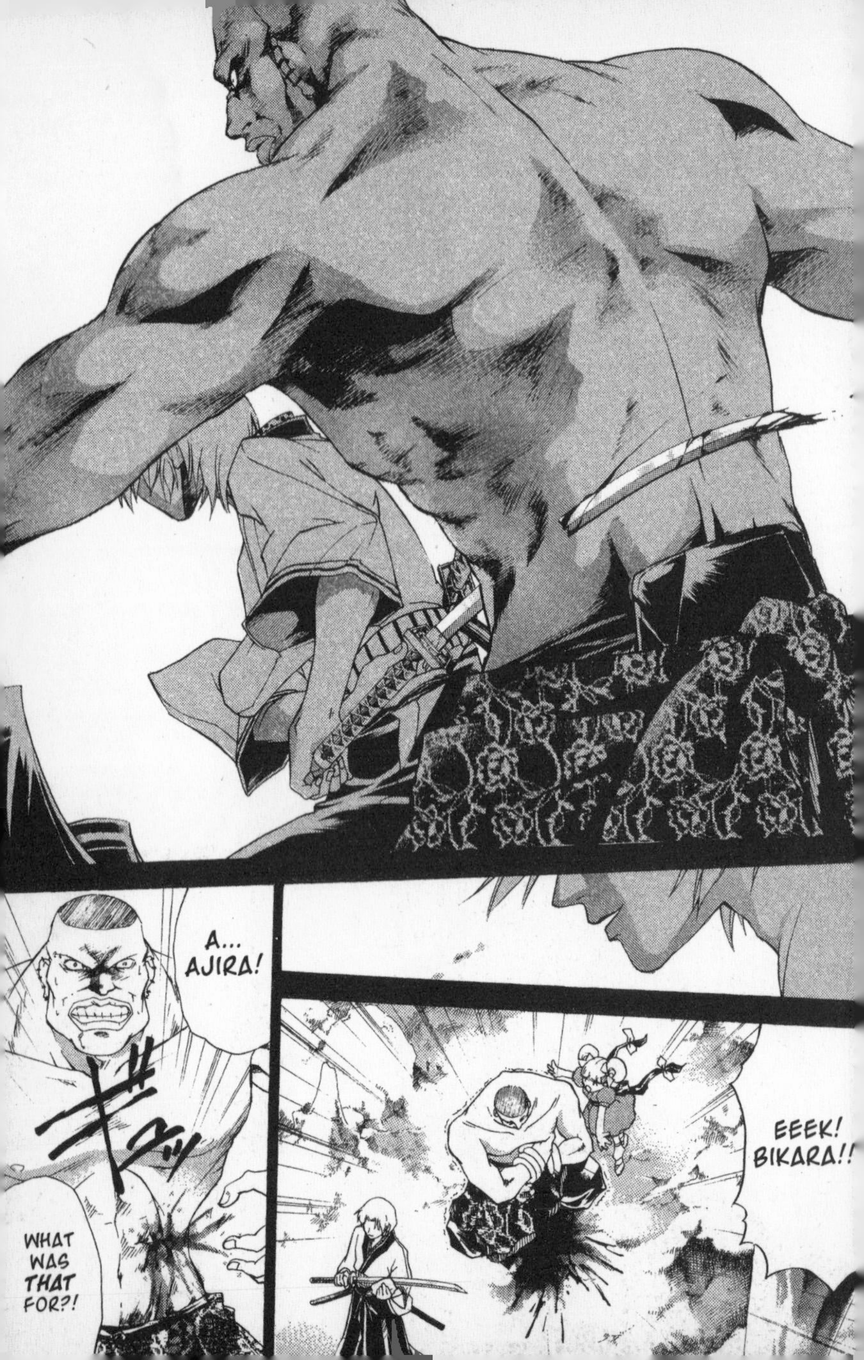
EEEK! BIKARA!!
A... AJIRA!
WHAT WAS THAT FOR?!

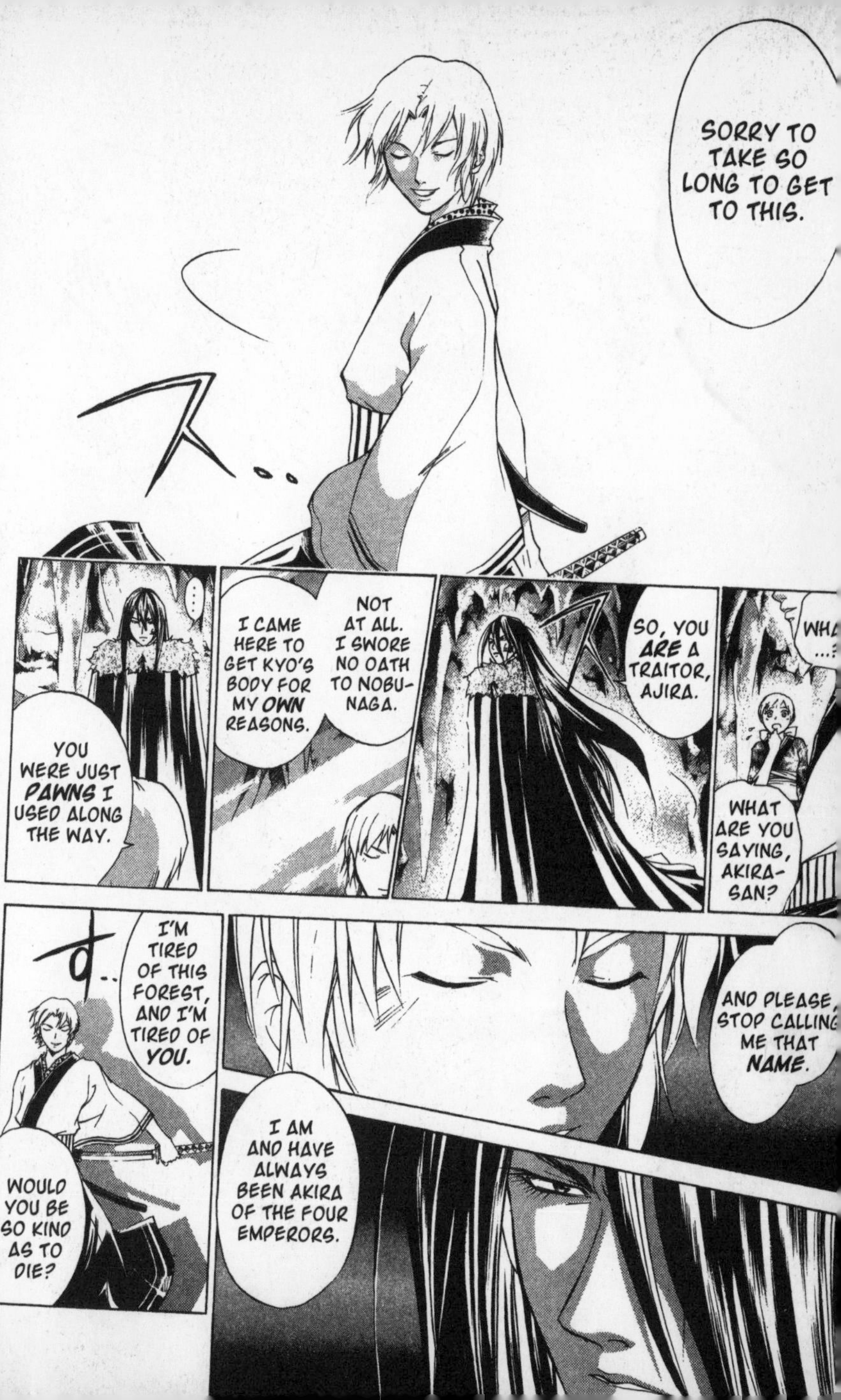
SORRY TO TAKE SO LONG TO GET TO THIS.
ス..
WHA ...?
WHAT ARE YOU SAYING, AKIRA-SAN?
SO, YOU ARE A TRAITOR, AJIRA.
NOT AT ALL. I SWORE NO OATH TO NOBU-NAGA.
I CAME HERE TO GET KYO'S BODY FOR MY OWN REASONS.
...
YOU WERE JUST PAWNS I USED ALONG THE WAY.
AND PLEASE, STOP CALLING ME THAT NAME.
I AM AND HAVE ALWAYS BEEN AKIRA OF THE FOUR EMPERORS.
す..
I'M TIRED OF THIS FOREST, AND I'M TIRED OF YOU.
WOULD YOU BE SO KIND AS TO DIE?

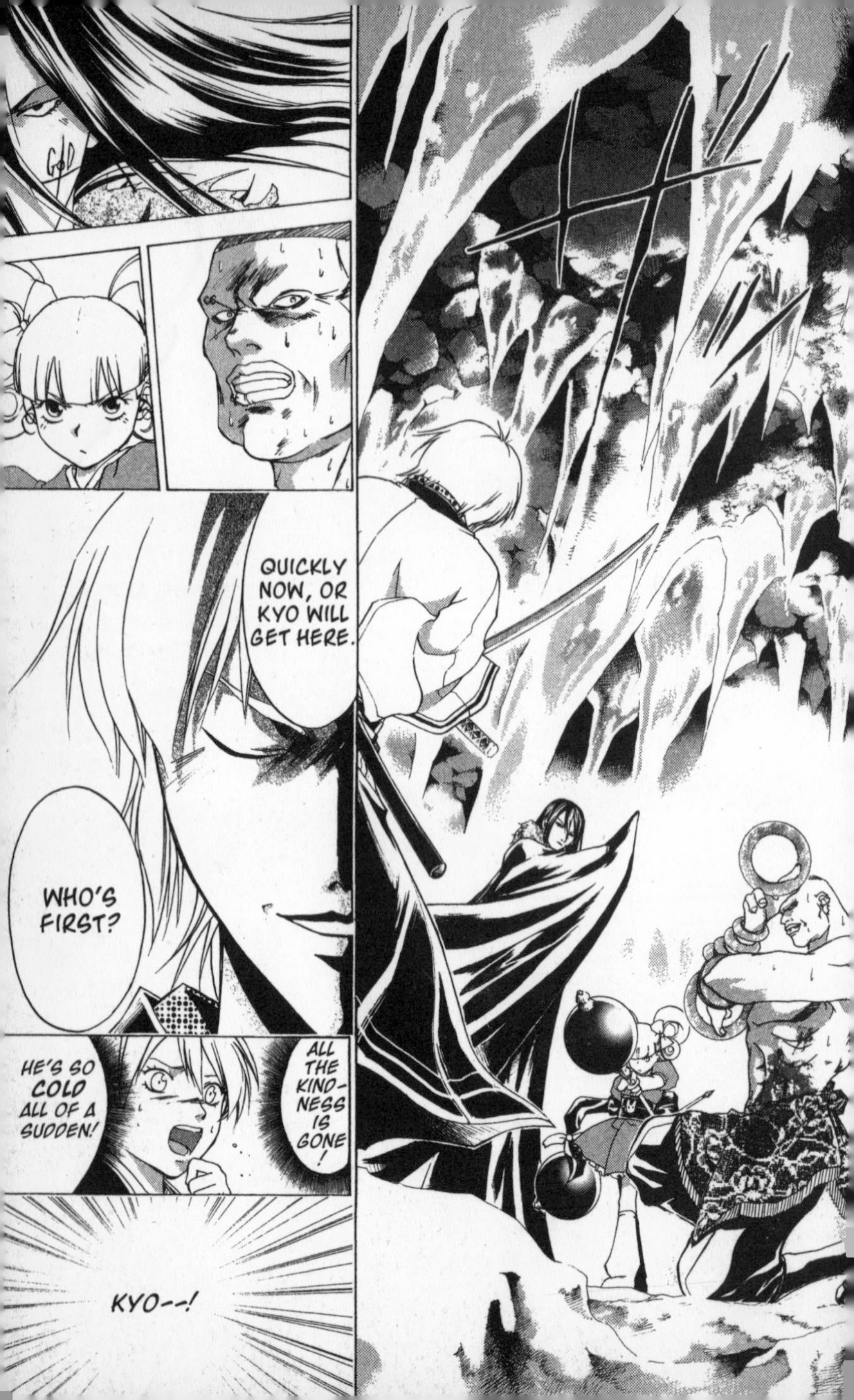
QUICKLY NOW, OR KYO WILL GET HERE.
WHO'S FIRST?
ALL THE KIND-NESS IS GONE!
HE'S SO COLD ALL OF A SUDDEN!
KYO--!

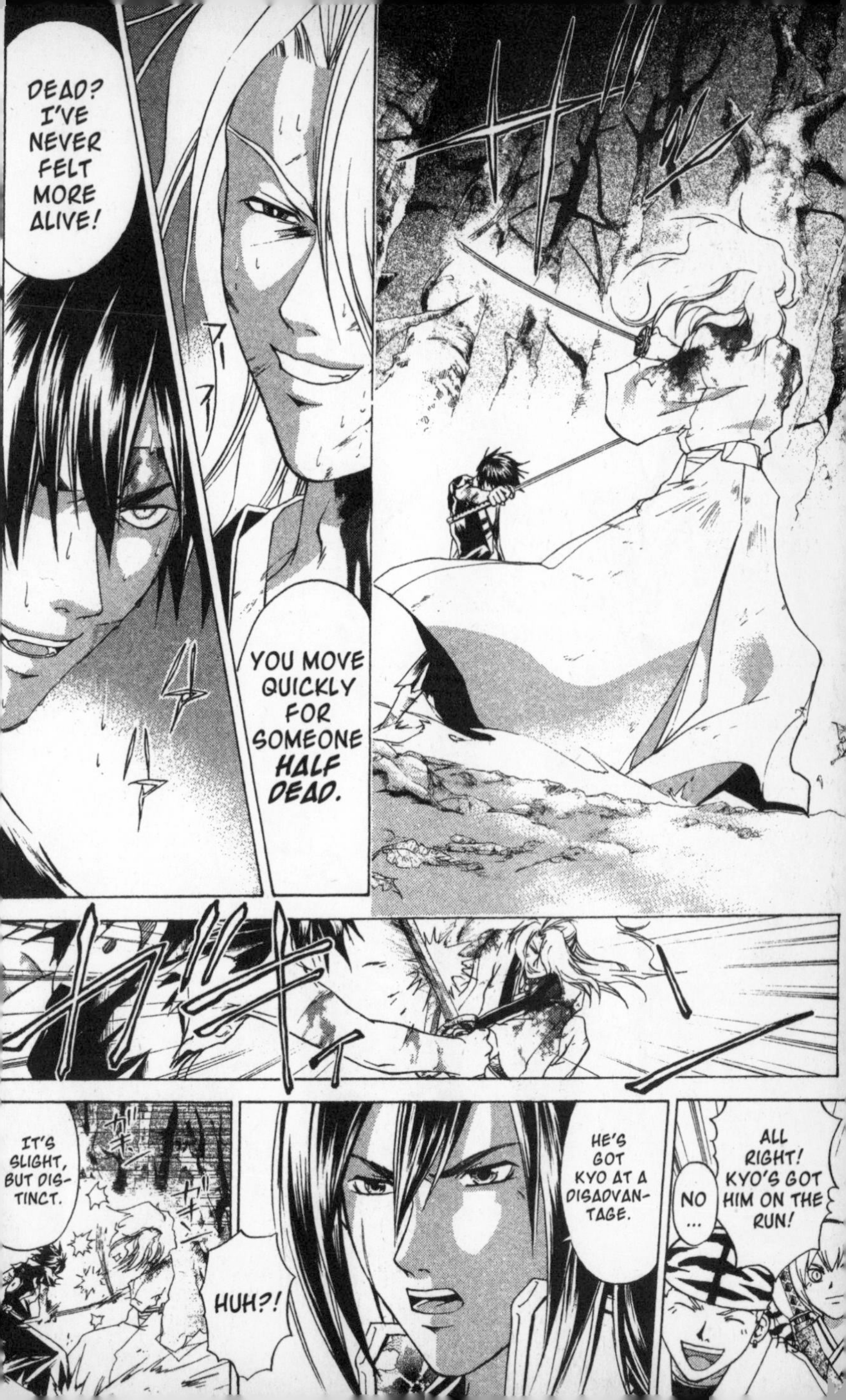
YOU MOVE QUICKLY FOR SOMEONE HALF DEAD.
DEAD? I'VE NEVER FELT MORE ALIVE!
ALL RIGHT! KYO'S GOT HIM ON THE RUN!
NO ...
HE'S GOT KYO AT A DISADVAN-TAGE.
HUH?!
IT'S SLIGHT, BUT DIS-TINCT.

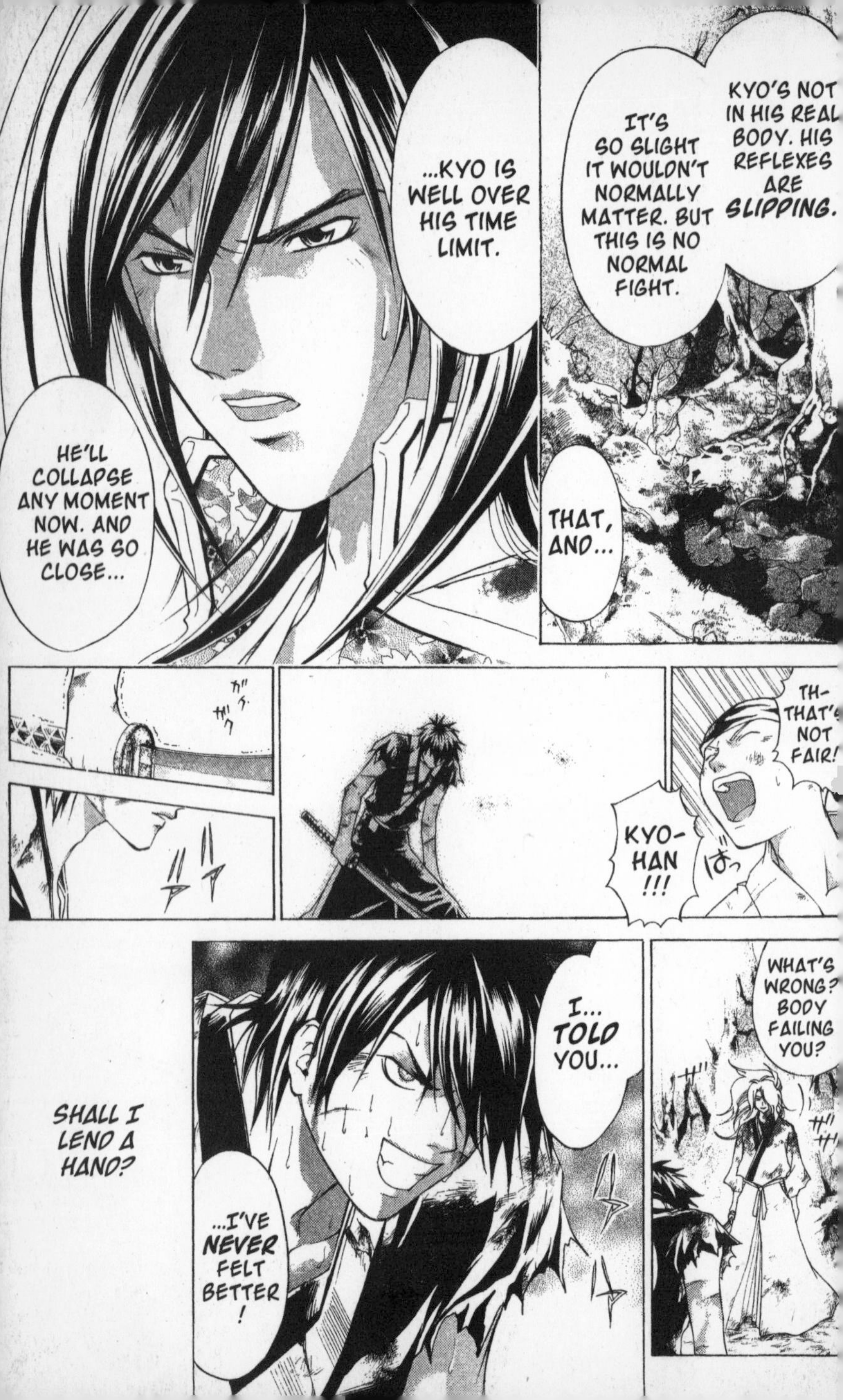
KYO'S NOT IN HIS REAL BODY. HIS REFLEXES ARE SLIPPING.
IT'S SO SLIGHT IT WOULDN'T NORMALLY MATTER. BUT THIS IS NO NORMAL FIGHT.
THAT, AND...
...KYO IS WELL OVER HIS TIME LIMIT.
HE'LL COLLAPSE ANY MOMENT NOW. AND HE WAS SO CLOSE...
TH-THAT'S NOT FAIR!
KYO-HAN!!!
ばっ
WHAT'S WRONG? BODY FAILING YOU?
I... TOLD YOU...
...I'VE NEVER FELT BETTER!
SHALL I LEND A HAND?

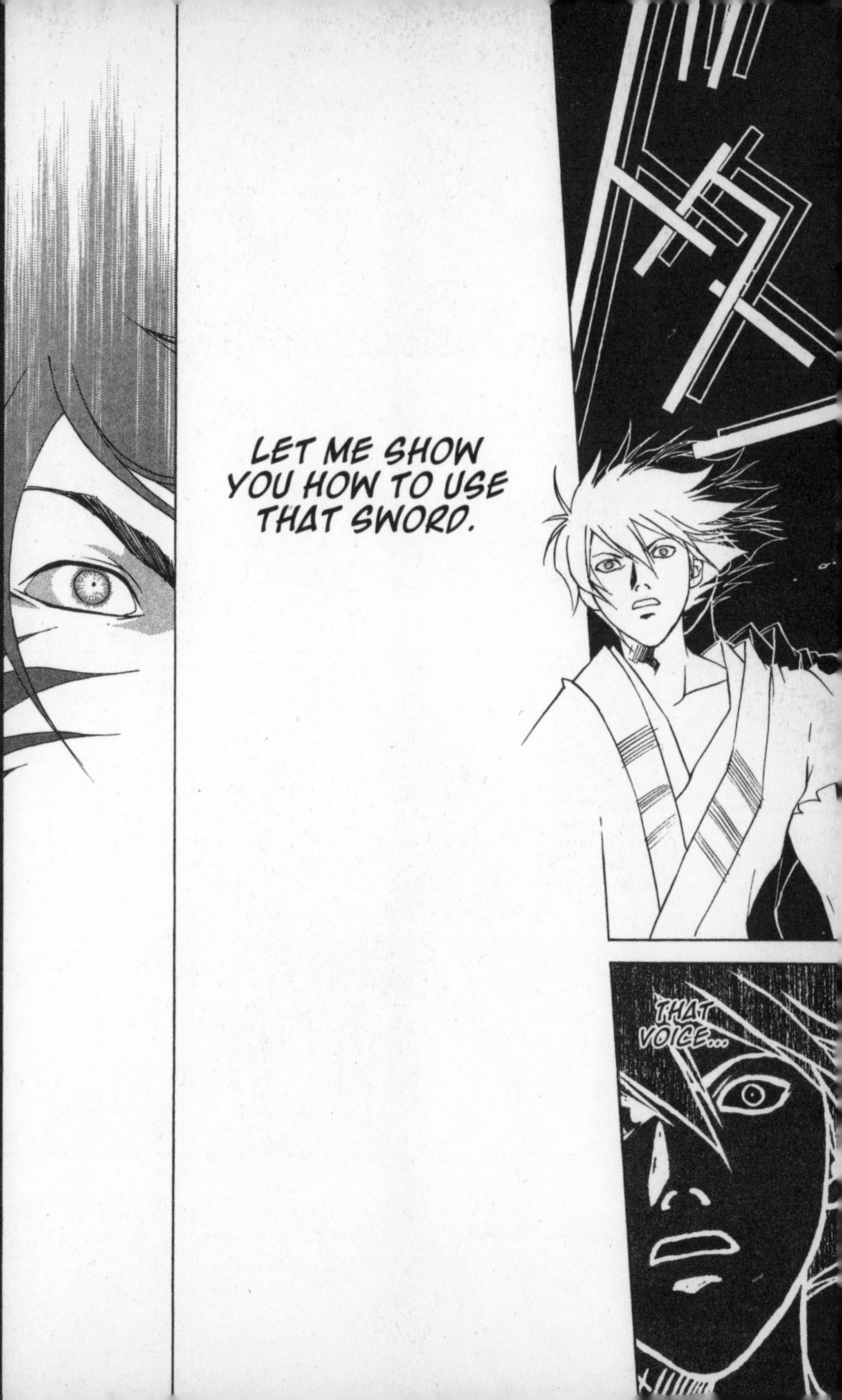
LET ME SHOW YOU HOW TO USE THAT SWORD.
THAT VOICE...

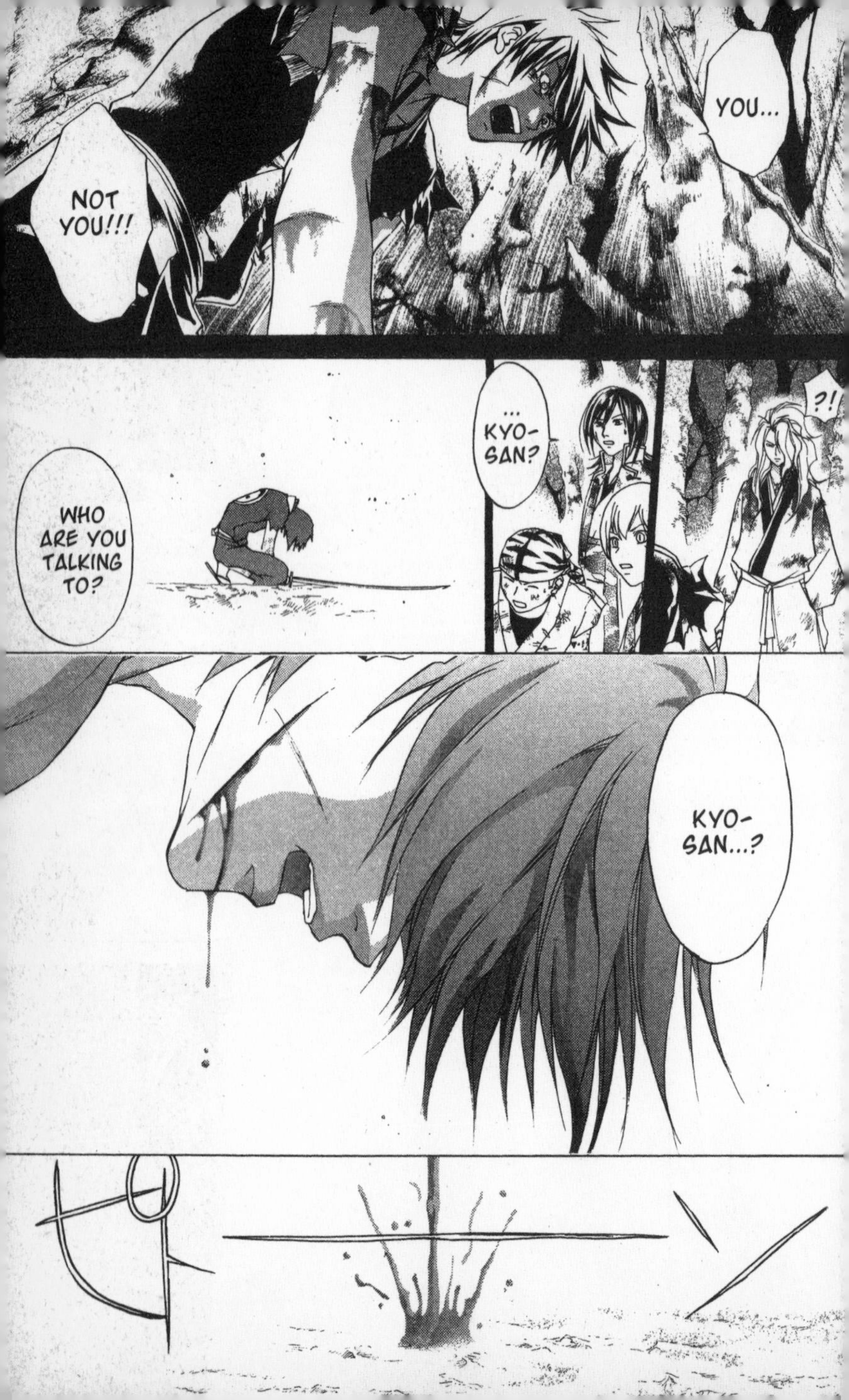
YOU...
NOT YOU!!!
?!
...KYO-SAN?
WHO ARE YOU TALKING TO?
KYO-SAN...?

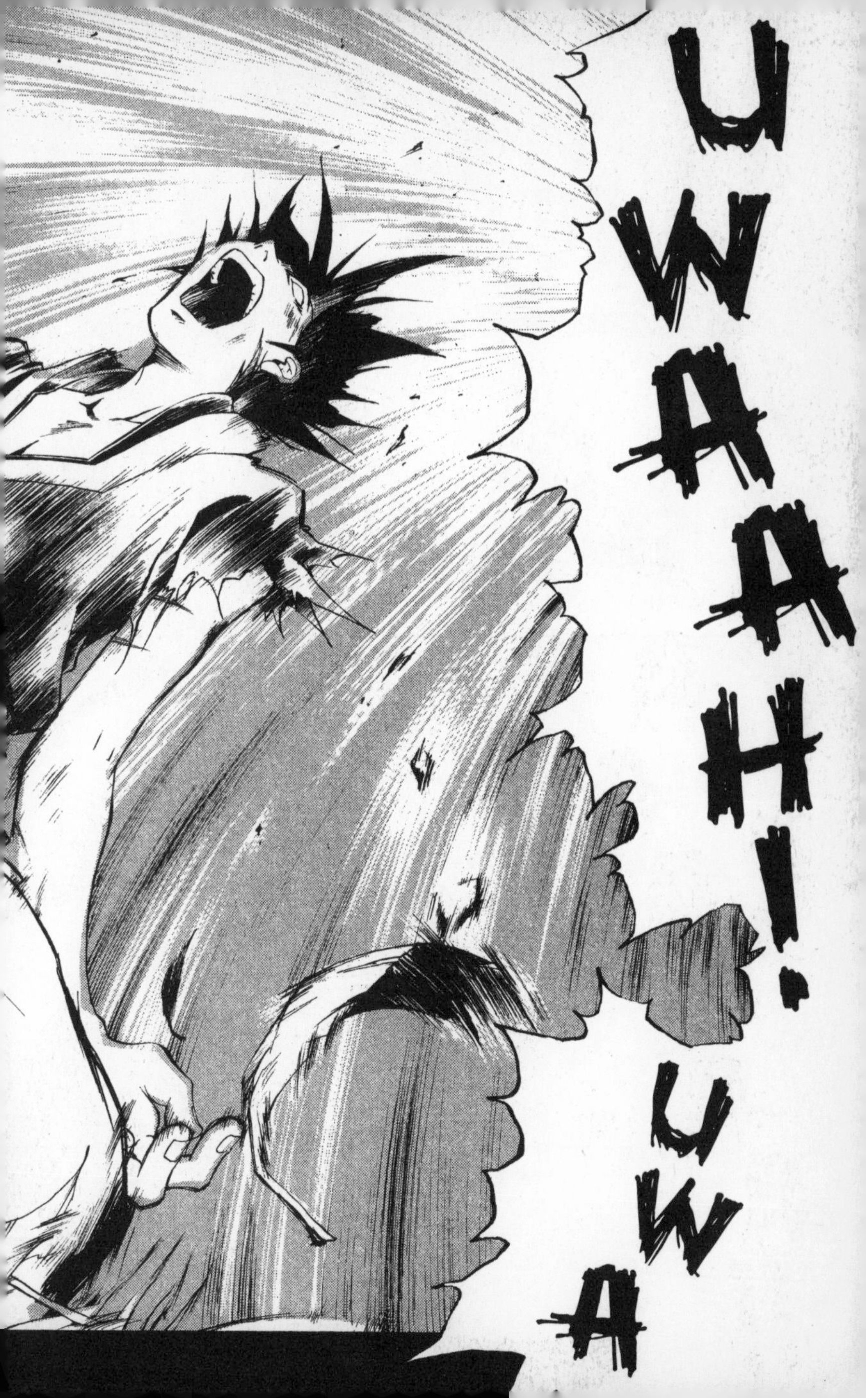
UWAAAH!! UWA

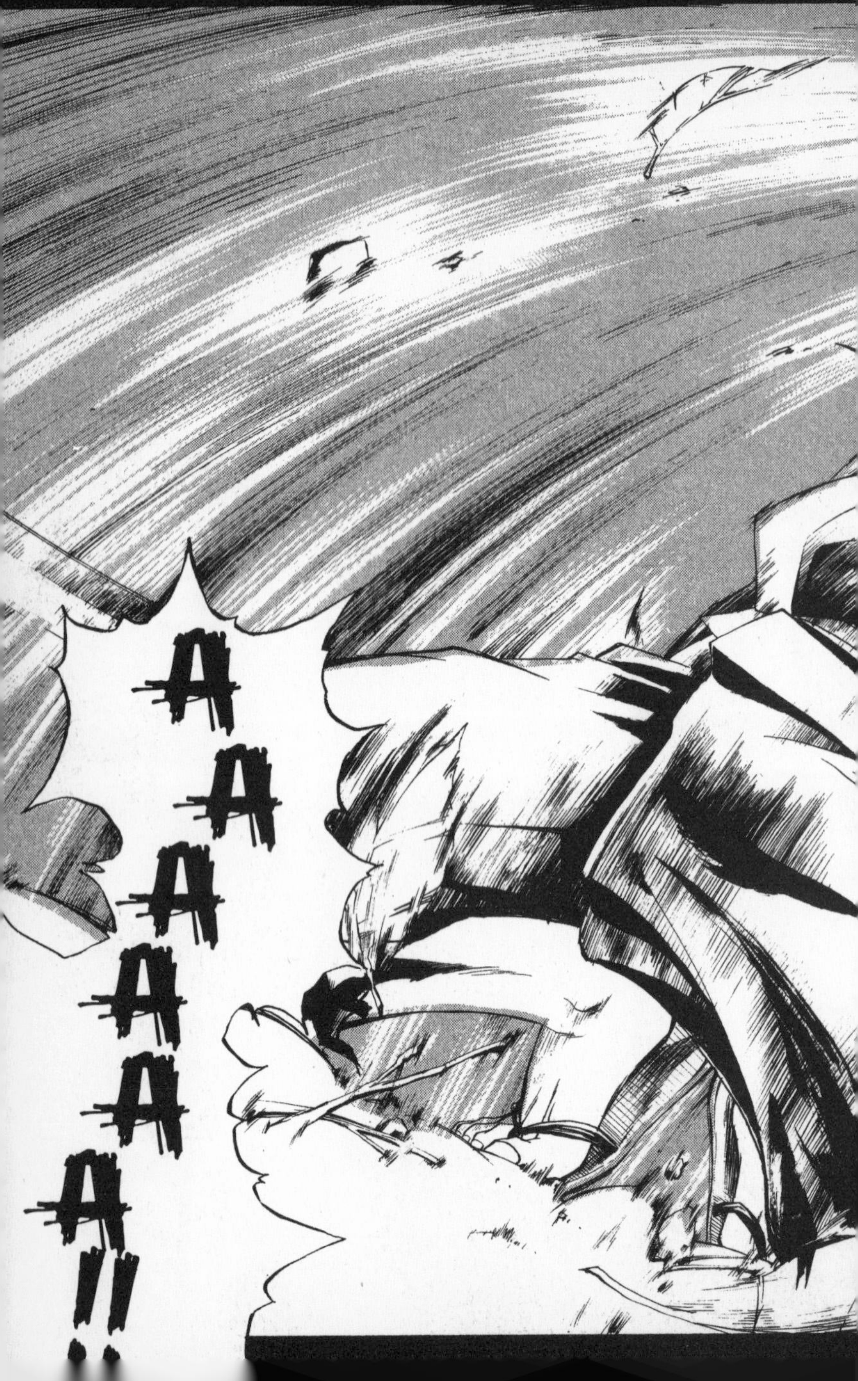
AAAAAA!!

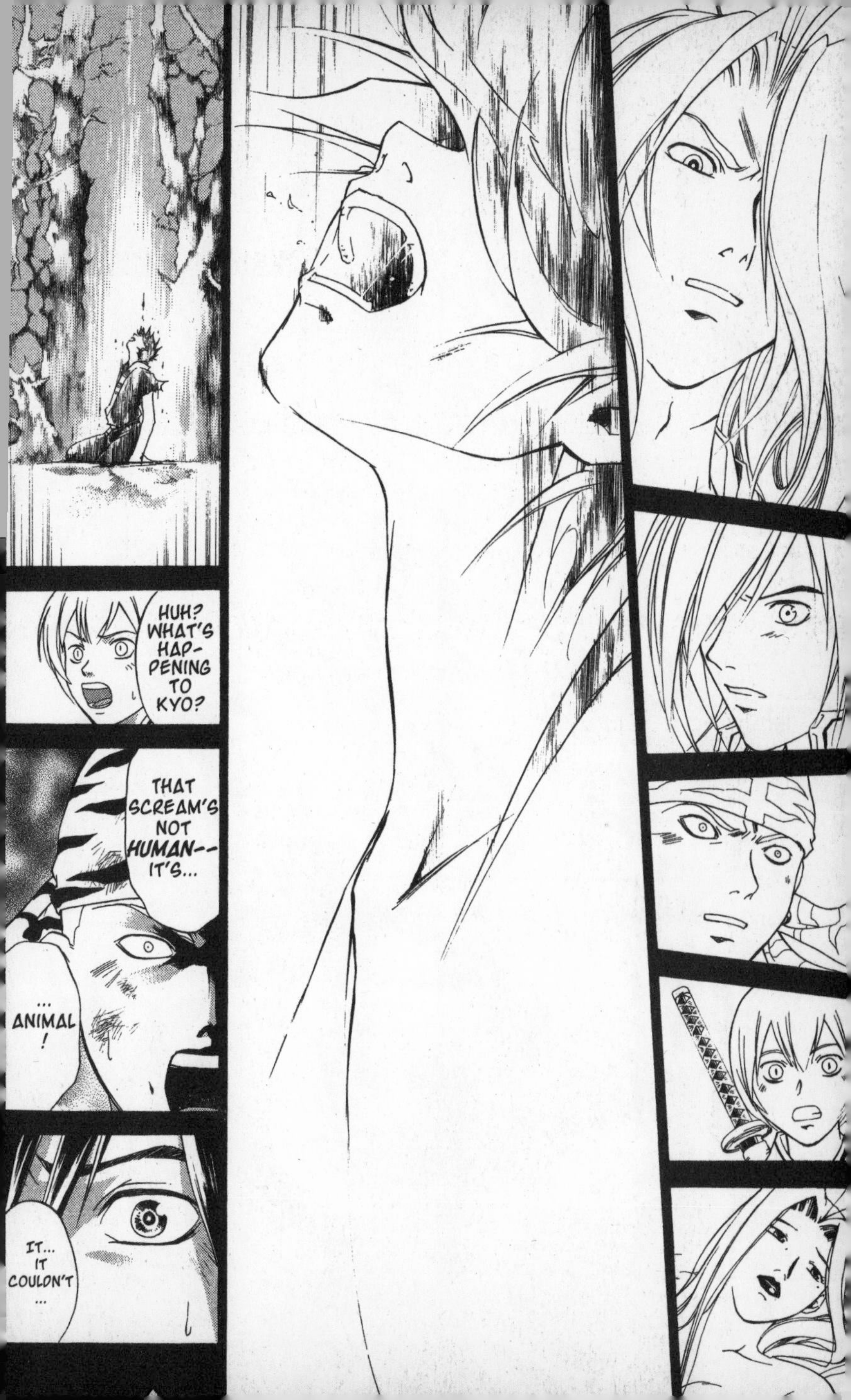
HUH? WHAT'S HAPPENING TO KYO?
THAT SCREAM'S NOT HUMAN--IT'S...
...ANIMAL!
IT... IT COULDN'T ...

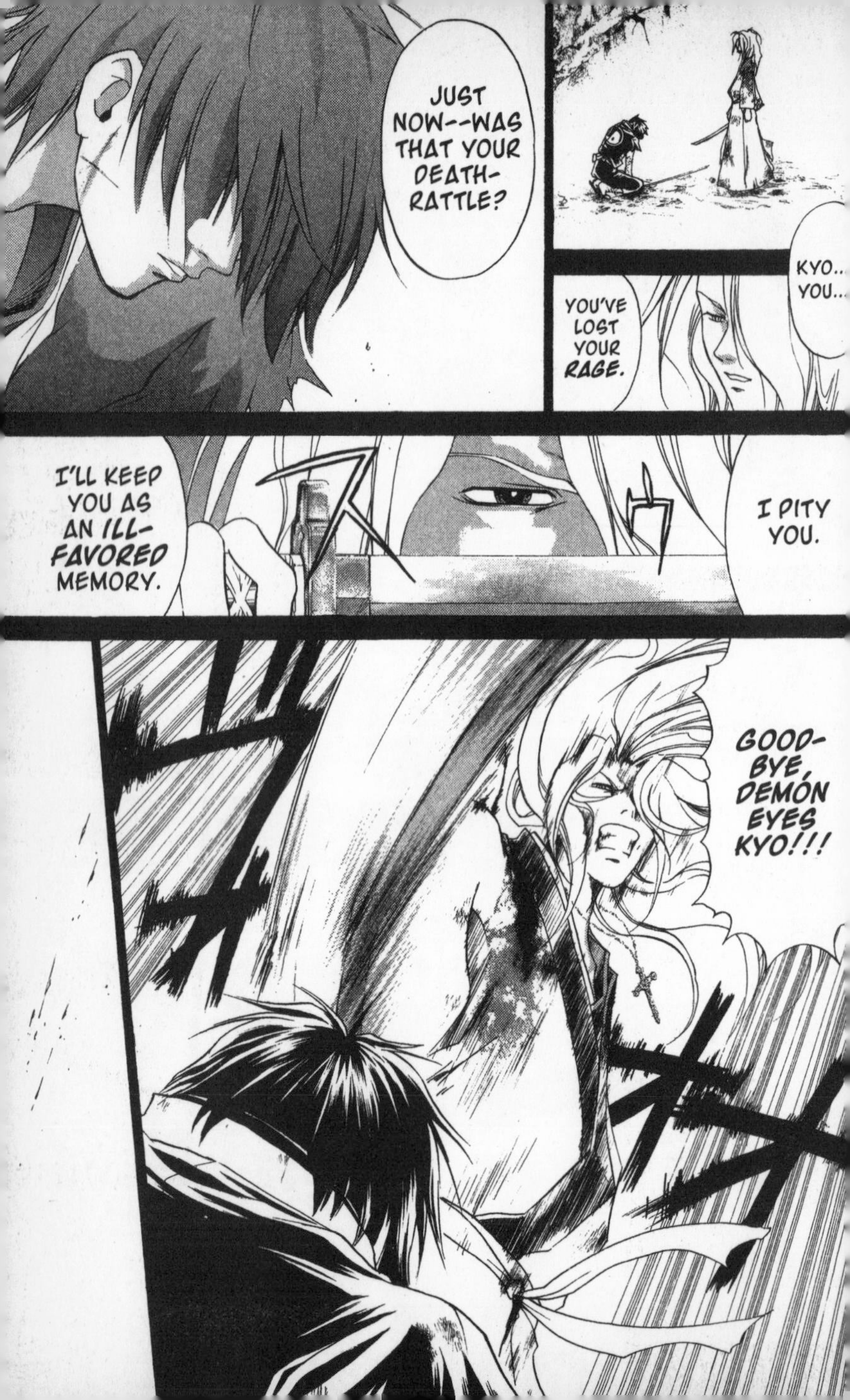
KYO... YOU...
YOU'VE LOST YOUR *RAGE*.
JUST NOW--WAS THAT YOUR DEATH-RATTLE?
I PITY YOU.
I'LL KEEP YOU AS AN *ILL-FAVORED* MEMORY.
GOOD-BYE, DEMON EYES KYO!!!

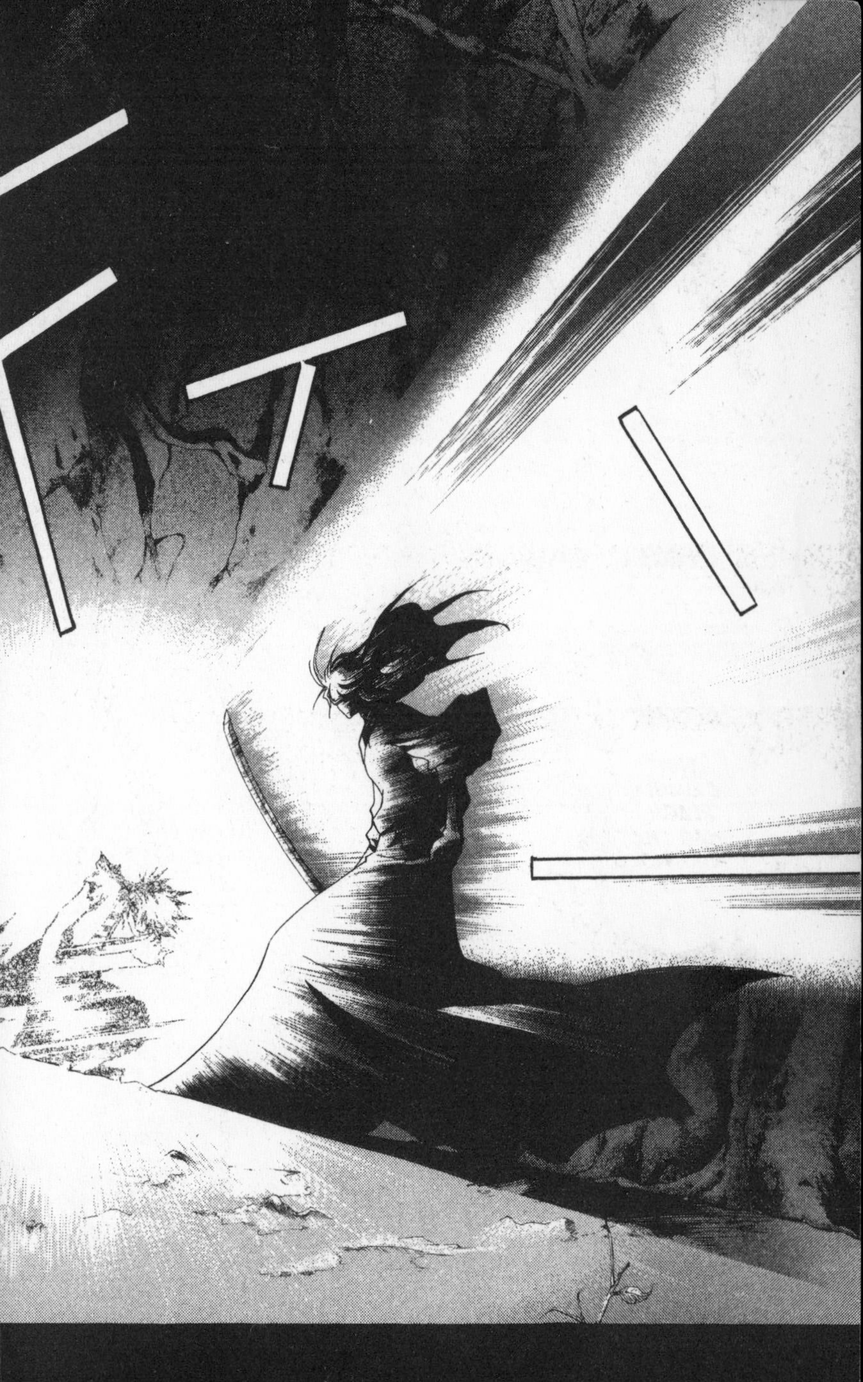

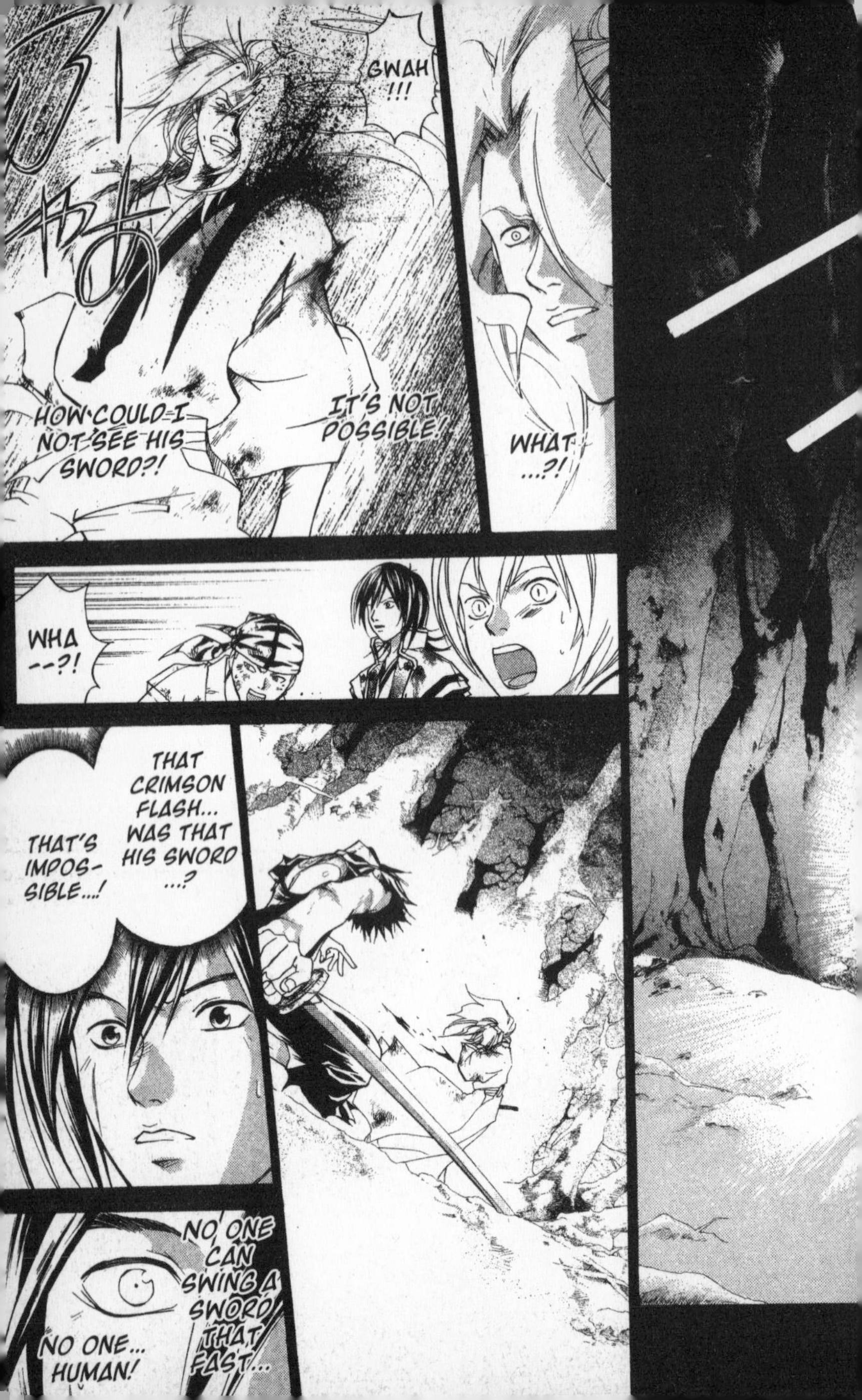
WHAT ...?!
GWAH !!!
IT'S NOT POSSIBLE!
HOW COULD I NOT SEE HIS SWORD?!
WHA --?!
THAT CRIMSON FLASH... WAS THAT HIS SWORD ...?
THAT'S IMPOS-SIBLE...!
NO ONE CAN SWING A SWORD THAT FAST...
NO ONE... HUMAN!

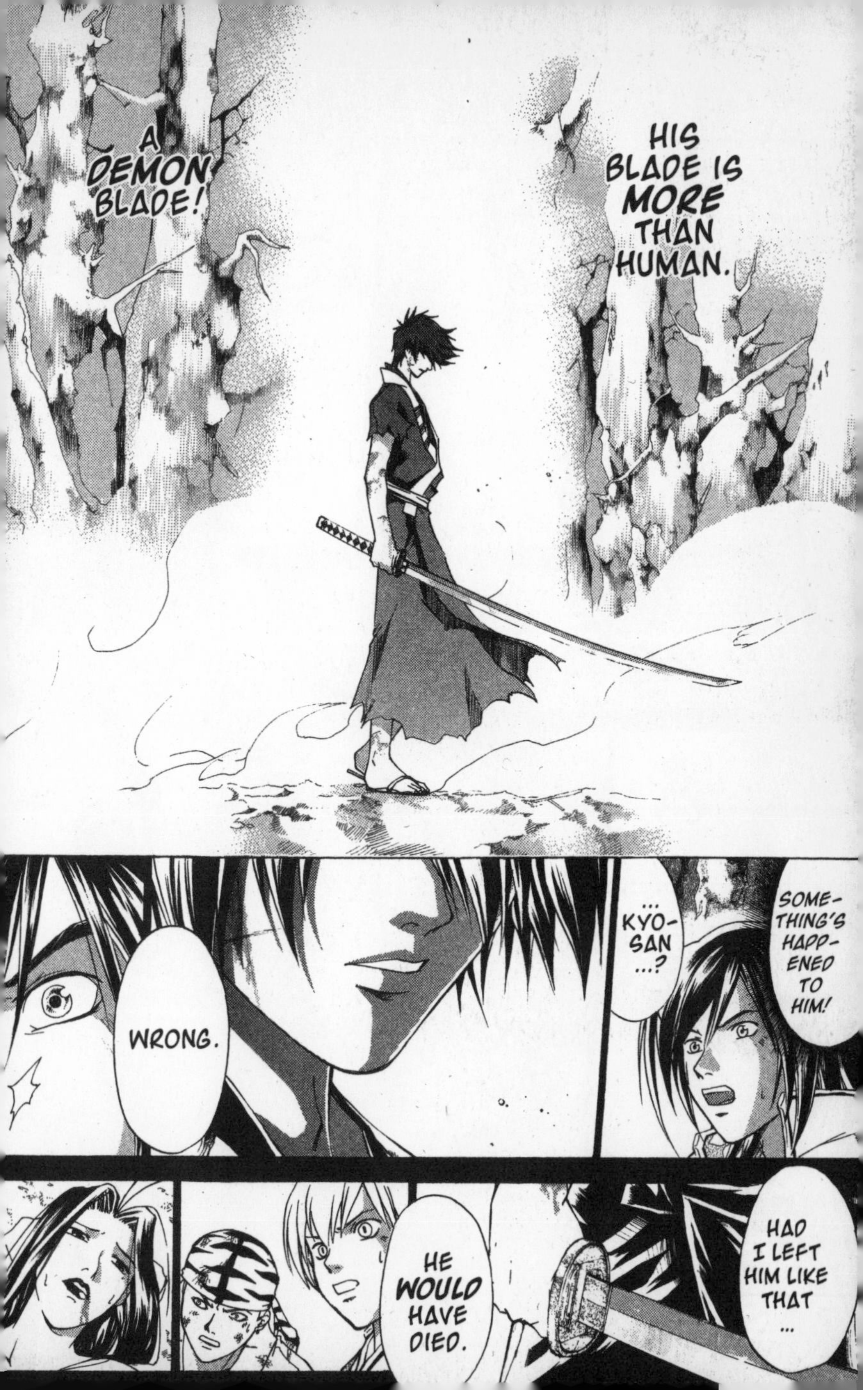

HIS BLADE IS MORE THAN HUMAN.
A DEMON BLADE!
SOME-THING'S HAPP-ENED TO HIM!
... KYO-SAN ...?
WRONG.
HAD I LEFT HIM LIKE THAT ...
HE WOULD HAVE DIED.

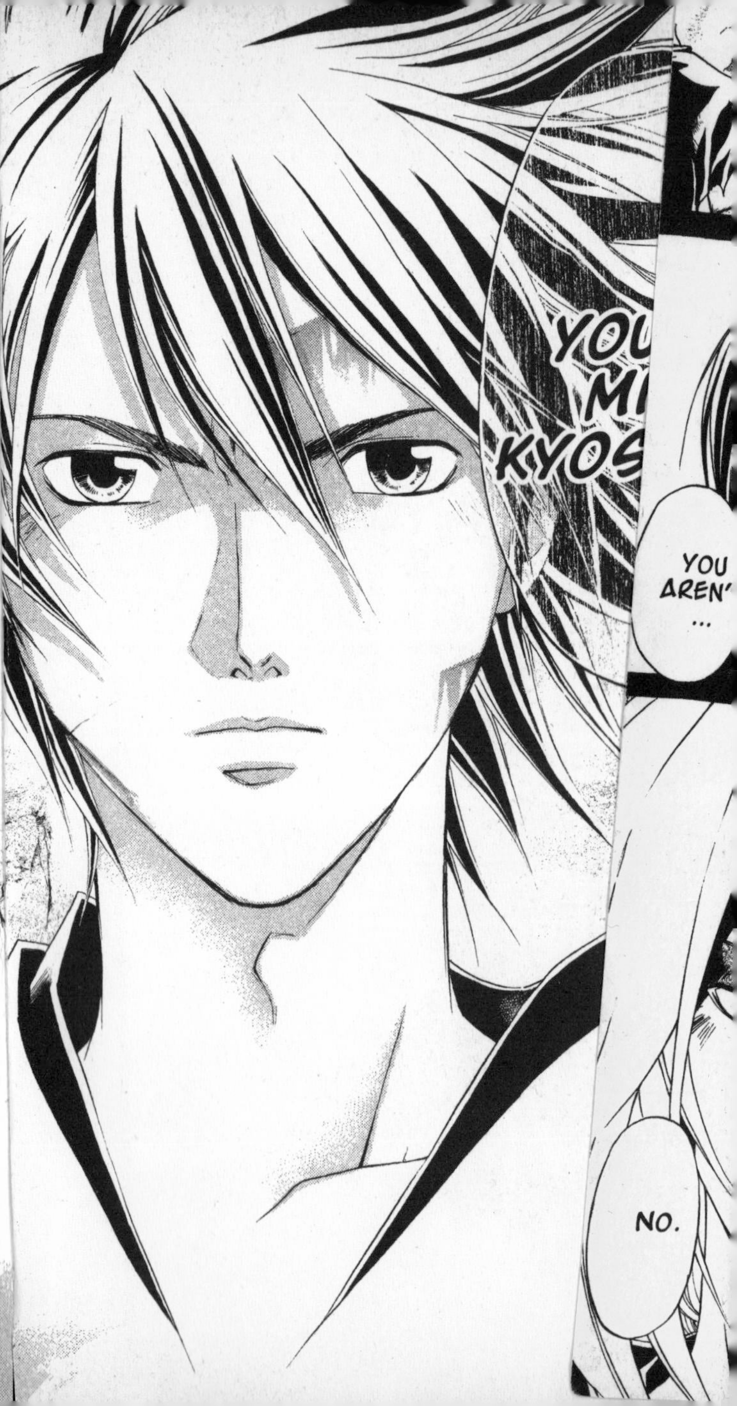
YOU AREN' ...
NO.
YOU
MI
KYOS

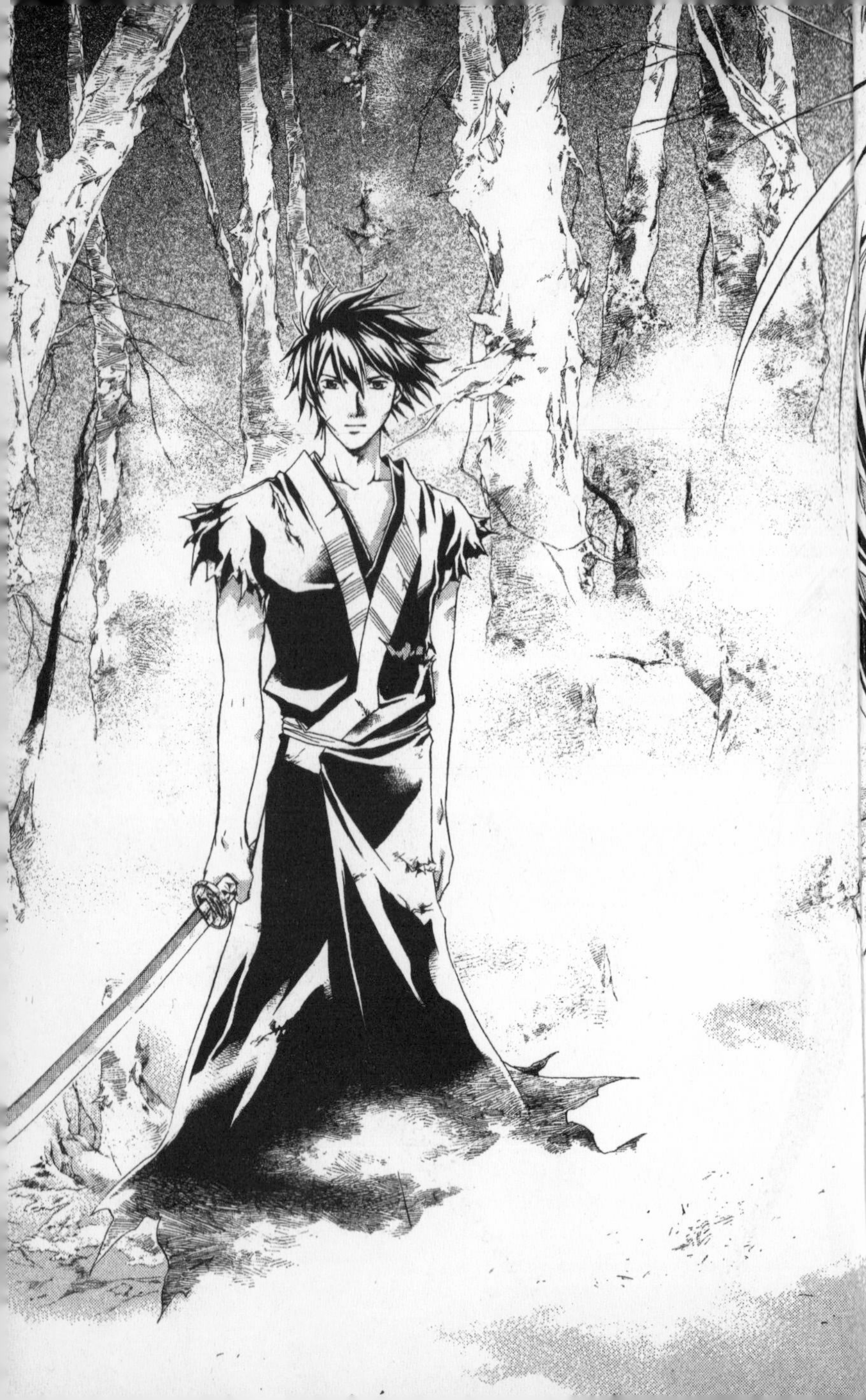

Kamijyo Circumstances

Yo, Kamijyo here. I was able to put a lot of extra pages into this volume, so I hope that all of you reading me weekly (and those of you who aren't, too) will enjoy this!*

I had one color page in the weekly (p. 126 in vol. 9), so I decided to do SDK modern-style... Typical, I know, but I figure we deserved to bust out after two years. Normally they don't reprint these pages in these collections, but since it was SO cool...
We have someone on staff (or people from Editing) in charge of these pages, so usually I don't even know about it until the first draft check. You should see how happy I am when I get a surprise like this. Heh heh.
Manga work isn't all fun and games, but seeing these pages reminds me that manga aren't made by one person alone, and that gives me the boost I need to draw more.

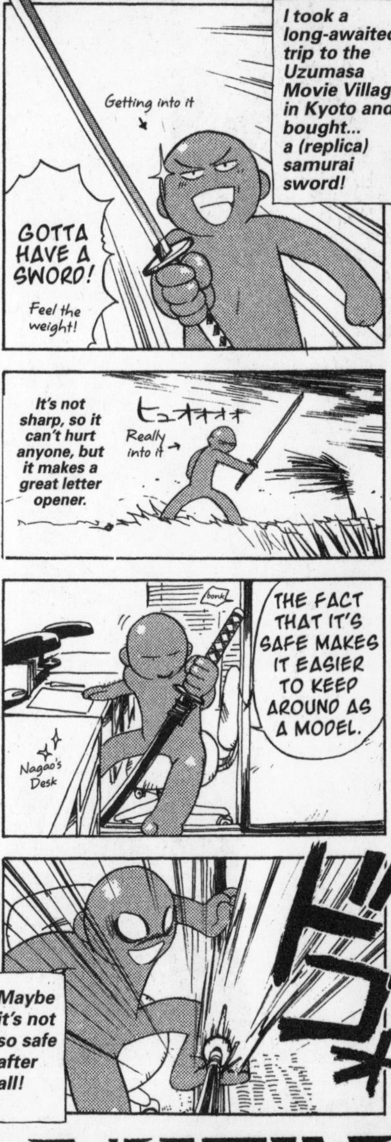

I'm a Samurai!
I took a long-awaited trip to the Uzumasa Movie Village in Kyoto and bought... a (replica) samurai sword!
Getting into it
GOTTA HAVE A SWORD!
Feel the weight!
It's not sharp, so it can't hurt anyone, but it makes a great letter opener.
ヒュオオオオ
Really into it
THE FACT THAT IT'S SAFE MAKES IT EASIER TO KEEP AROUND AS A MODEL.
bonk
Nagao's Desk
ドゴォ
Maybe it's not so safe after all!

*In Japan, *SDK* is serialized in weekly Shonen magazine.

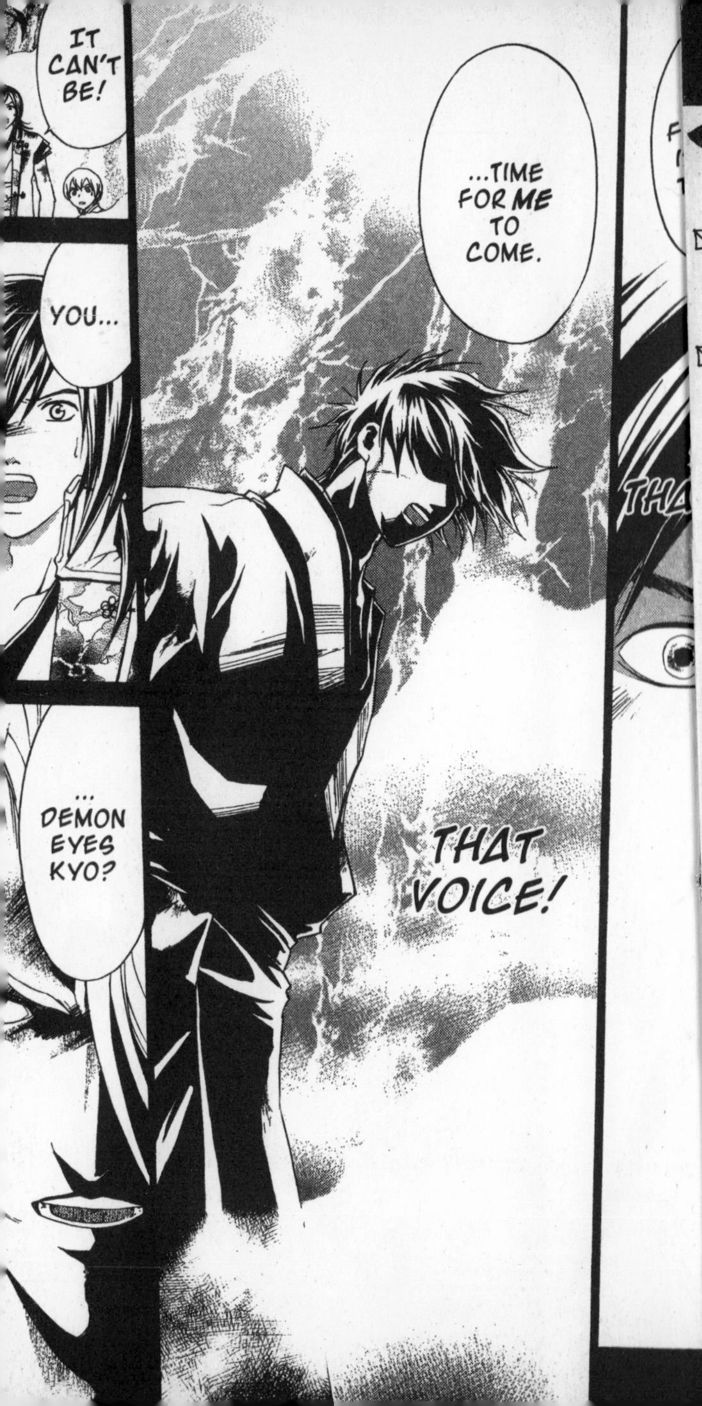

...TIME FOR ME TO COME.
IT CAN'T BE!
YOU...
THAT VOICE!
...DEMON EYES KYO?

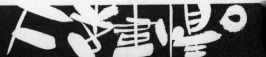

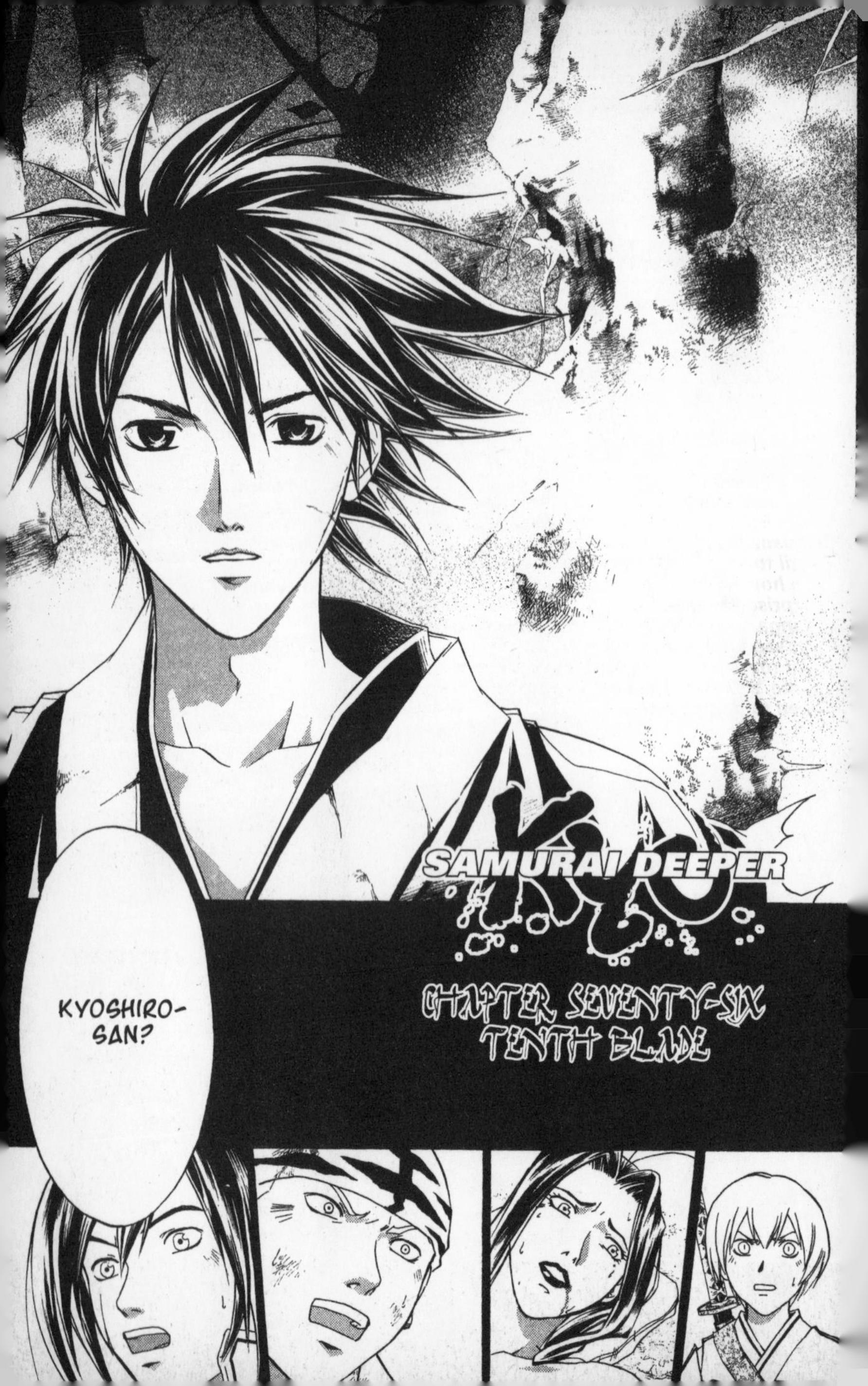
SAMURAI DEEPER KYO
CHAPTER SEVENTY-SIX
TENTH BLADE
KYOSHIRO-SAN?

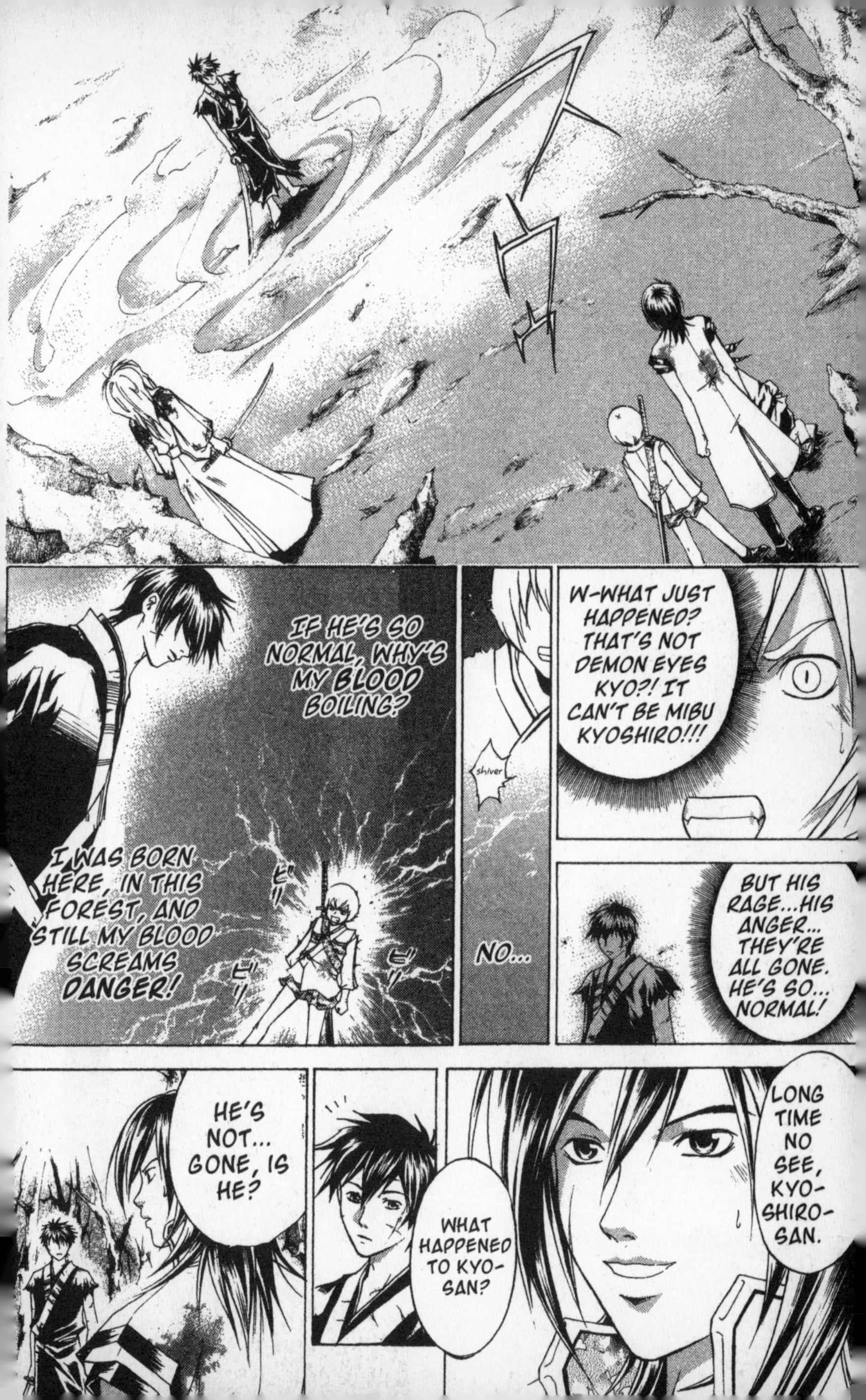
W-WHAT JUST HAPPENED? THAT'S NOT DEMON EYES KYO?! IT CAN'T BE MIBU KYOSHIRO!!!
shiver
BUT HIS RAGE...HIS ANGER... THEY'RE ALL GONE. HE'S SO... NORMAL!
NO...
IF HE'S SO NORMAL, WHY'S MY BLOOD BOILING?
I WAS BORN HERE, IN THIS FOREST, AND STILL MY BLOOD SCREAMS DANGER!
LONG TIME NO SEE, KYO-SHIRO-SAN.
WHAT HAPPENED TO KYO-SAN?
HE'S NOT... GONE, IS HE?

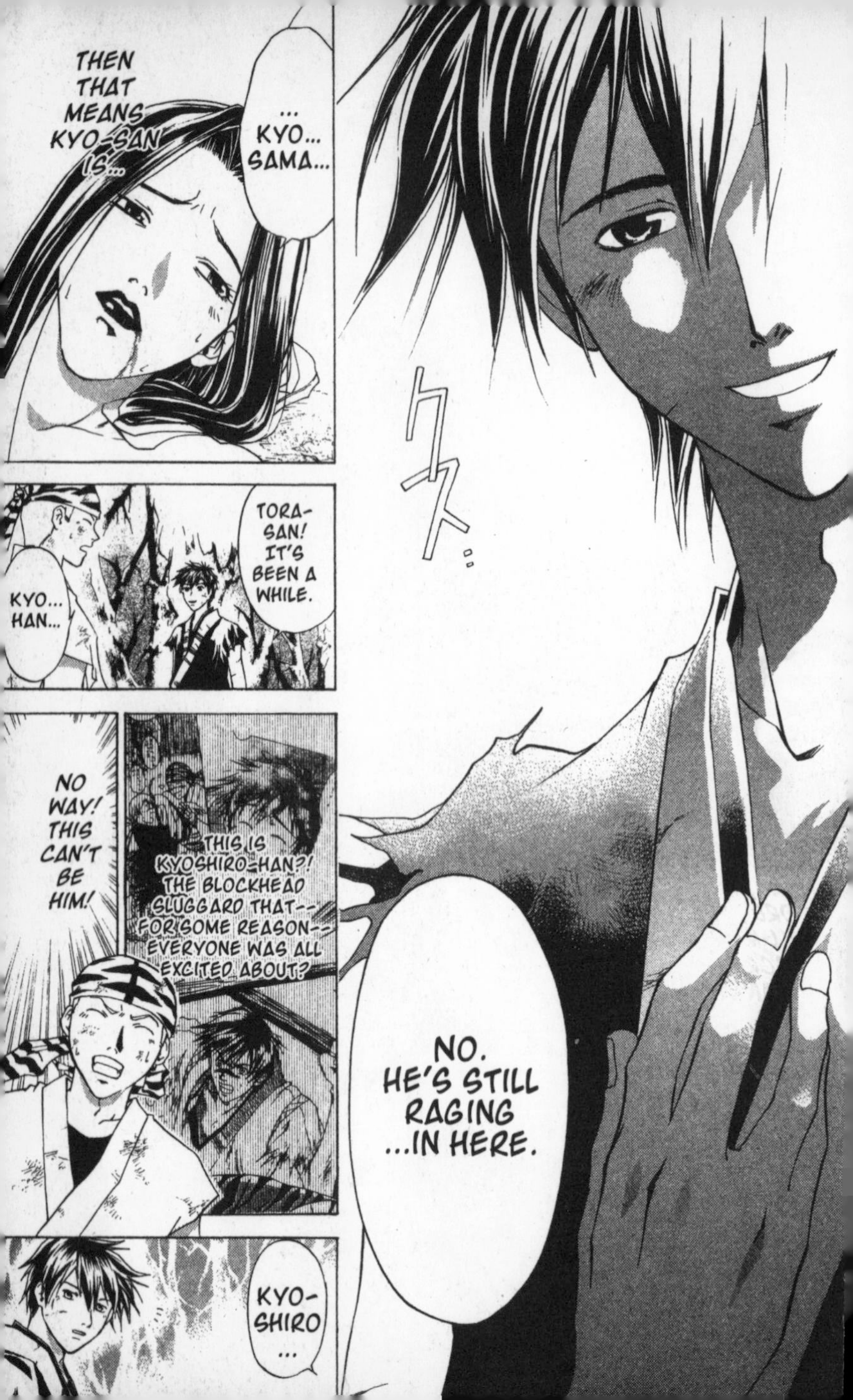
クスッ
NO. HE'S STILL RAGING ...IN HERE.
... KYO... SAMA...
THEN THAT MEANS KYO-SAN IS...
TORA-SAN! IT'S BEEN A WHILE.
KYO... HAN...
THIS IS KYOSHIRO-HAN?! THE BLOCKHEAD SLUGGARD THAT--FOR SOME REASON--EVERYONE WAS ALL EXCITED ABOUT?
NO WAY! THIS CAN'T BE HIM!
KYO-SHIRO ...

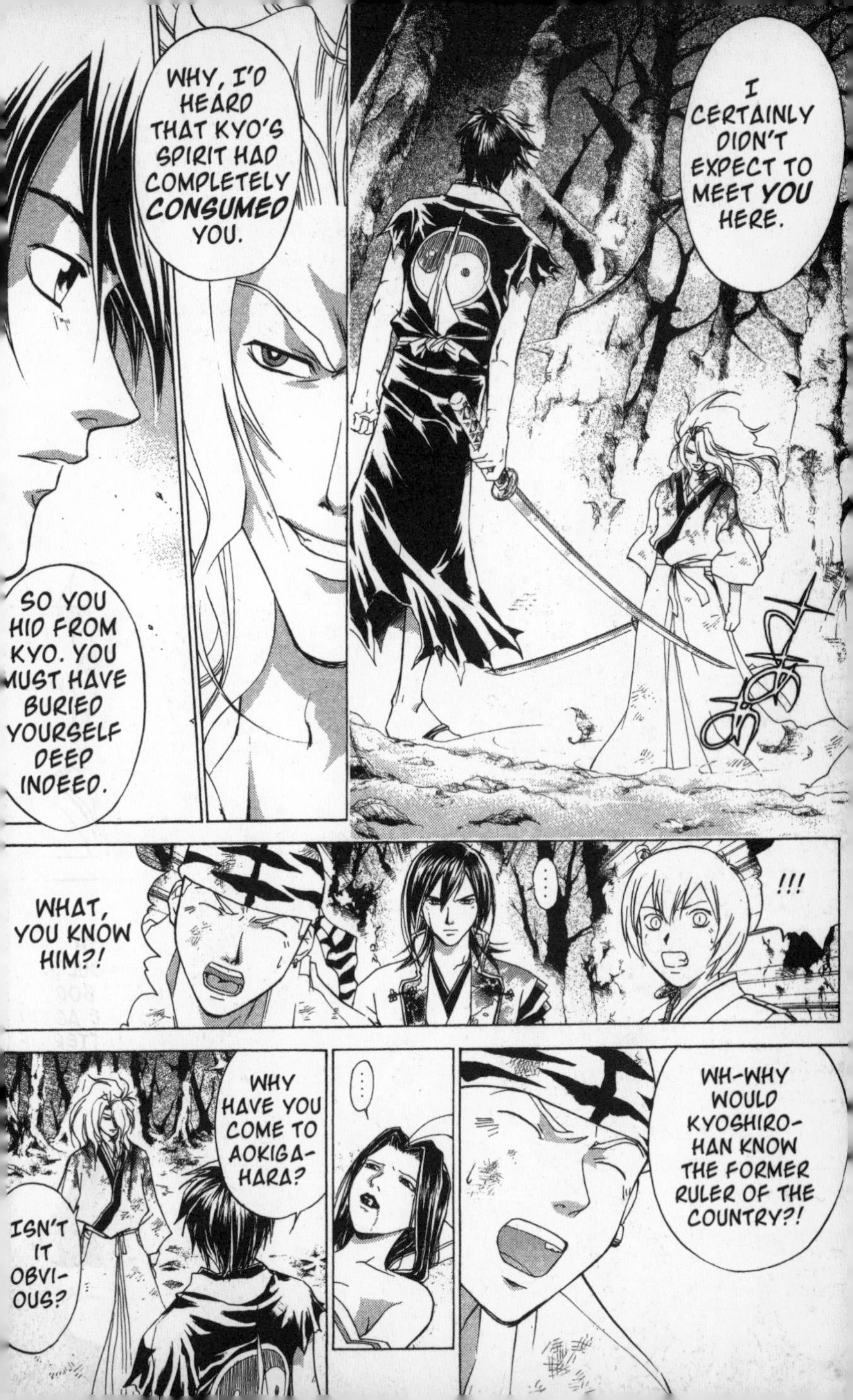
I CERTAINLY DIDN'T EXPECT TO MEET YOU HERE.
WHY, I'D HEARD THAT KYO'S SPIRIT HAD COMPLETELY CONSUMED YOU.
SO YOU HID FROM KYO. YOU MUST HAVE BURIED YOURSELF DEEP INDEED.
!!!
...
WHAT, YOU KNOW HIM?!
WH-WHY WOULD KYOSHIRO-HAN KNOW THE FORMER RULER OF THE COUNTRY?!
...
WHY HAVE YOU COME TO AOKIGA-HARA?
ISN'T IT OBVI-OUS?

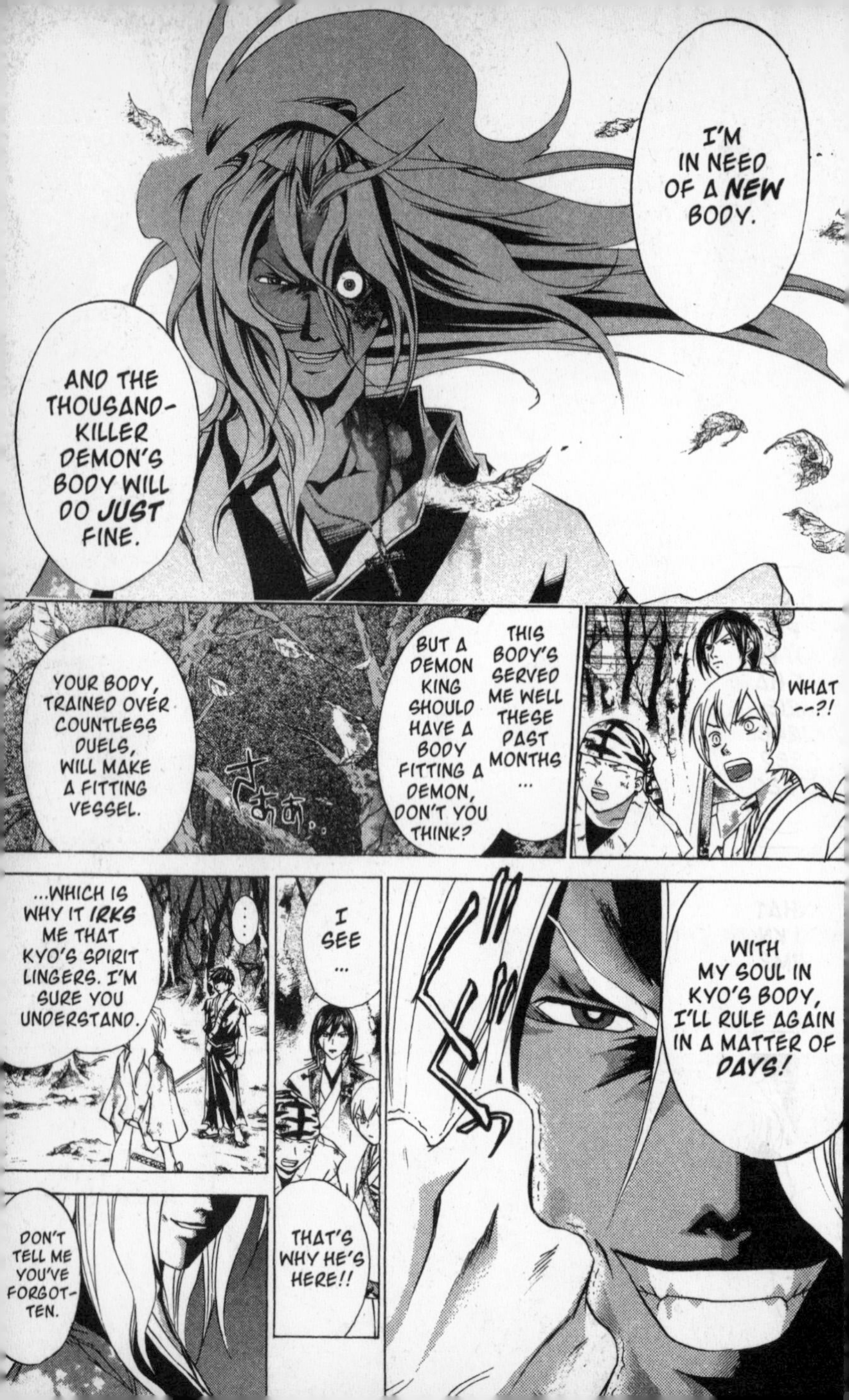
I'M IN NEED OF A NEW BODY.
AND THE THOUSAND-KILLER DEMON'S BODY WILL DO JUST FINE.
WHAT--?!
THIS BODY'S SERVED ME WELL THESE PAST MONTHS...
BUT A DEMON KING SHOULD HAVE A BODY FITTING A DEMON, DON'T YOU THINK?
YOUR BODY, TRAINED OVER COUNTLESS DUELS, WILL MAKE A FITTING VESSEL.
WITH MY SOUL IN KYO'S BODY, I'LL RULE AGAIN IN A MATTER OF DAYS!
I SEE...
THAT'S WHY HE'S HERE!!
...
...WHICH IS WHY IT IRKS ME THAT KYO'S SPIRIT LINGERS. I'M SURE YOU UNDERSTAND.
DON'T TELL ME YOU'VE FORGOTTEN.

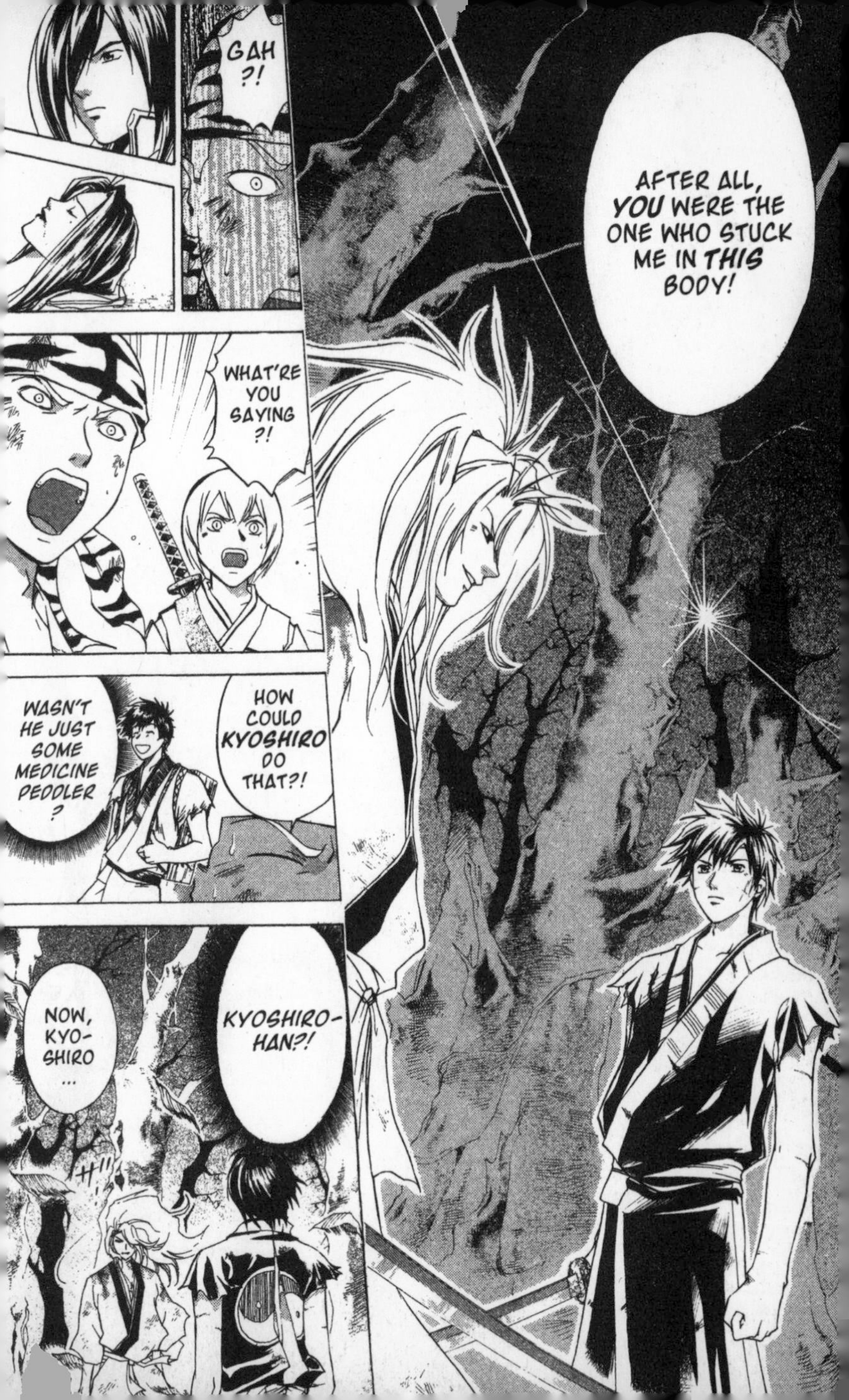
AFTER ALL, YOU WERE THE ONE WHO STUCK ME IN THIS BODY!
GAH ?!
WHAT'RE YOU SAYING ?!
HOW COULD KYOSHIRO DO THAT?!
WASN'T HE JUST SOME MEDICINE PEDDLER ?
KYOSHIRO-HAN?!
NOW, KYO-SHIRO ...

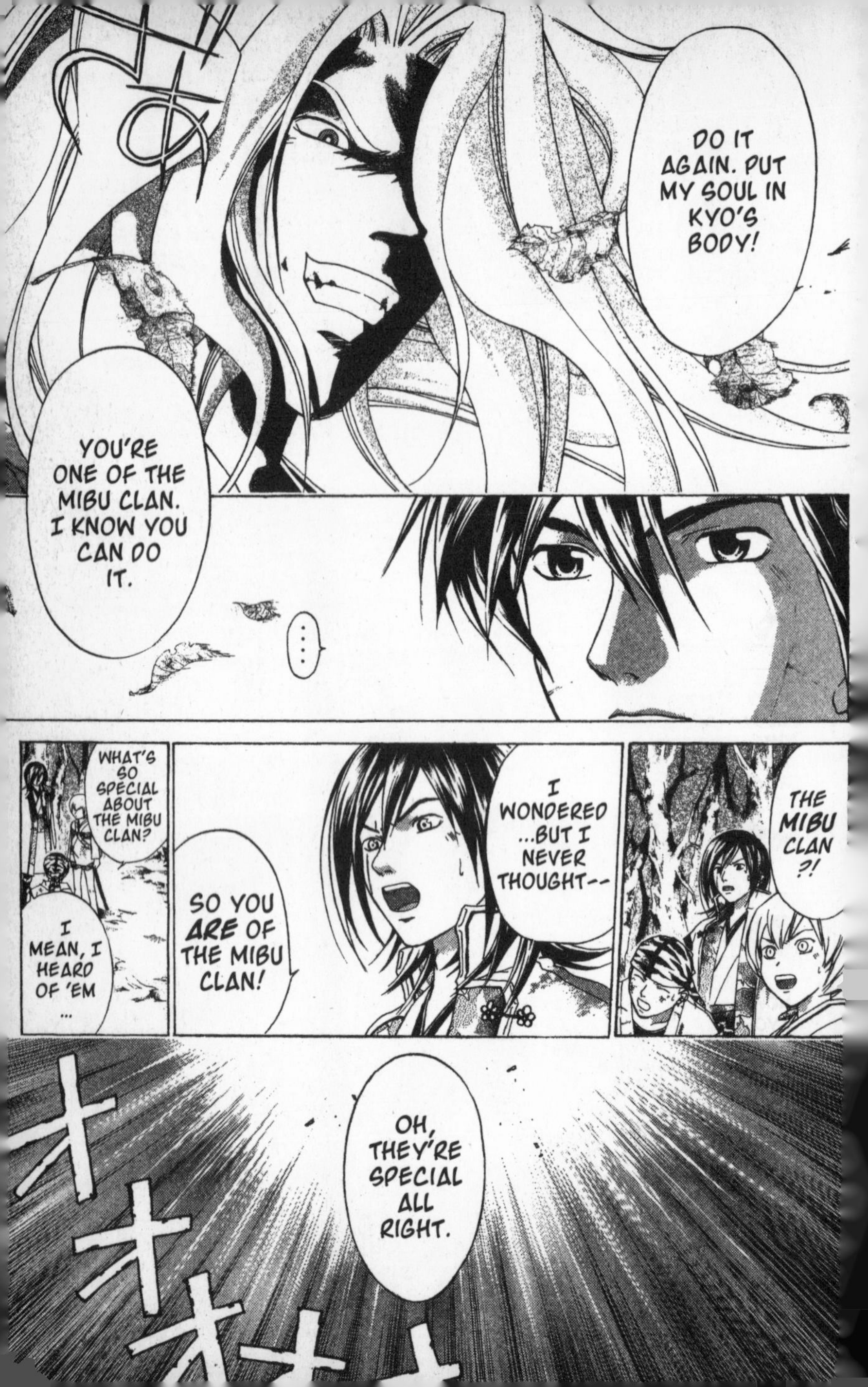
DO IT AGAIN. PUT MY SOUL IN KYO'S BODY!
YOU'RE ONE OF THE MIBU CLAN. I KNOW YOU CAN DO IT.
....
THE MIBU CLAN?!
I WONDERED ...BUT I NEVER THOUGHT--
SO YOU *ARE* OF THE MIBU CLAN!
WHAT'S SO SPECIAL ABOUT THE MIBU CLAN?
I MEAN, I HEARD OF 'EM ...
OH, THEY'RE SPECIAL ALL RIGHT.

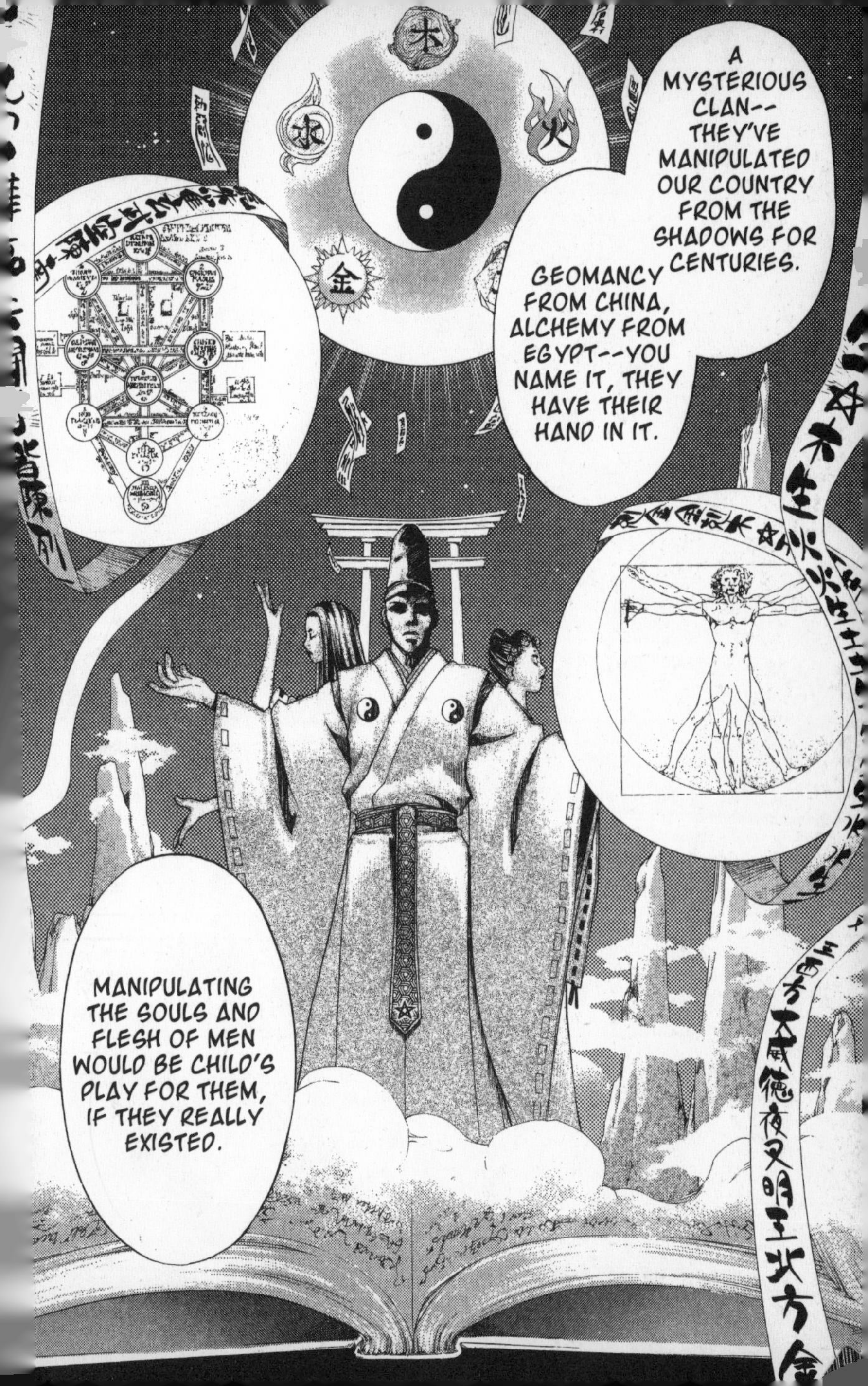
A MYSTERIOUS CLAN-- THEY'VE MANIPULATED OUR COUNTRY FROM THE SHADOWS FOR CENTURIES.
GEOMANCY FROM CHINA, ALCHEMY FROM EGYPT--YOU NAME IT, THEY HAVE THEIR HAND IN IT.
MANIPULATING THE SOULS AND FLESH OF MEN WOULD BE CHILD'S PLAY FOR THEM, IF THEY REALLY EXISTED.

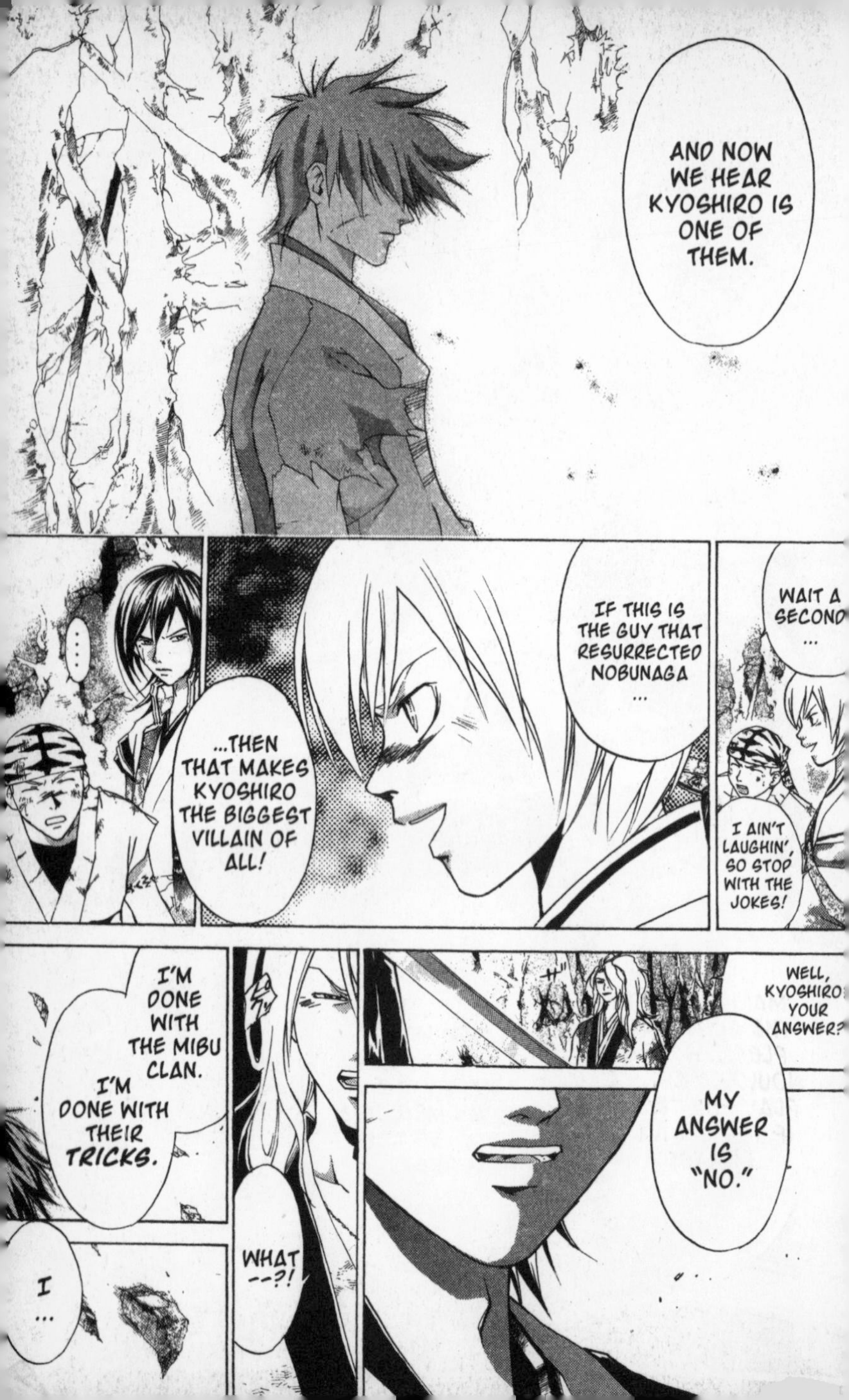
AND NOW WE HEAR KYOSHIRO IS ONE OF THEM.
WAIT A SECOND ...
I AIN'T LAUGHIN', SO STOP WITH THE JOKES!
IF THIS IS THE GUY THAT RESURRECTED NOBUNAGA ...
...THEN THAT MAKES KYOSHIRO THE BIGGEST VILLAIN OF ALL!
...
WELL, KYOSHIRO: YOUR ANSWER?
MY ANSWER IS "NO."
WHAT--?!
I'M DONE WITH THE MIBU CLAN. I'M DONE WITH THEIR TRICKS.
I ...

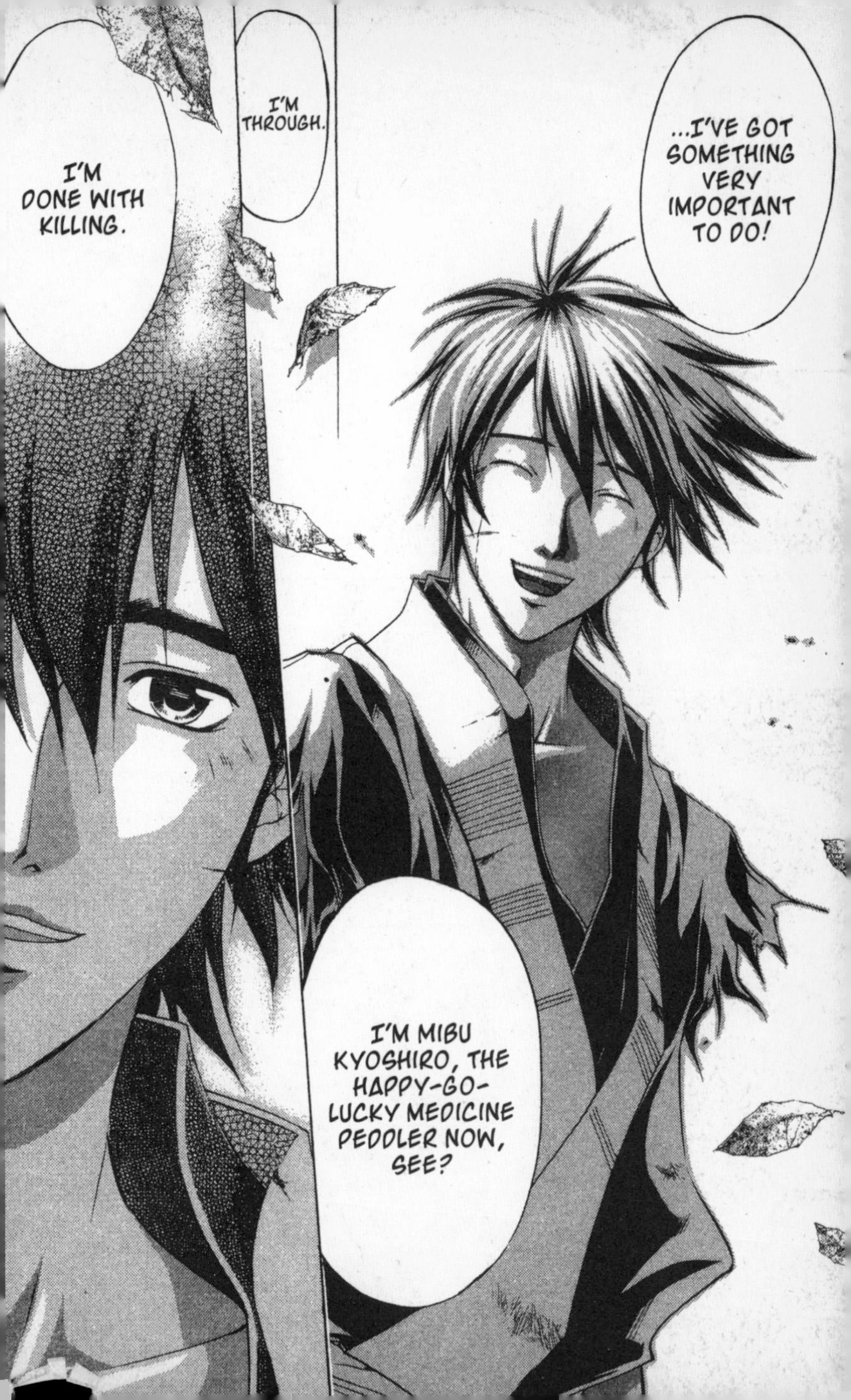
...I'VE GOT SOMETHING VERY IMPORTANT TO DO!
I'M THROUGH.
I'M DONE WITH KILLING.
I'M MIBU KYOSHIRO, THE HAPPY-GO-LUCKY MEDICINE PEDDLER NOW, SEE?

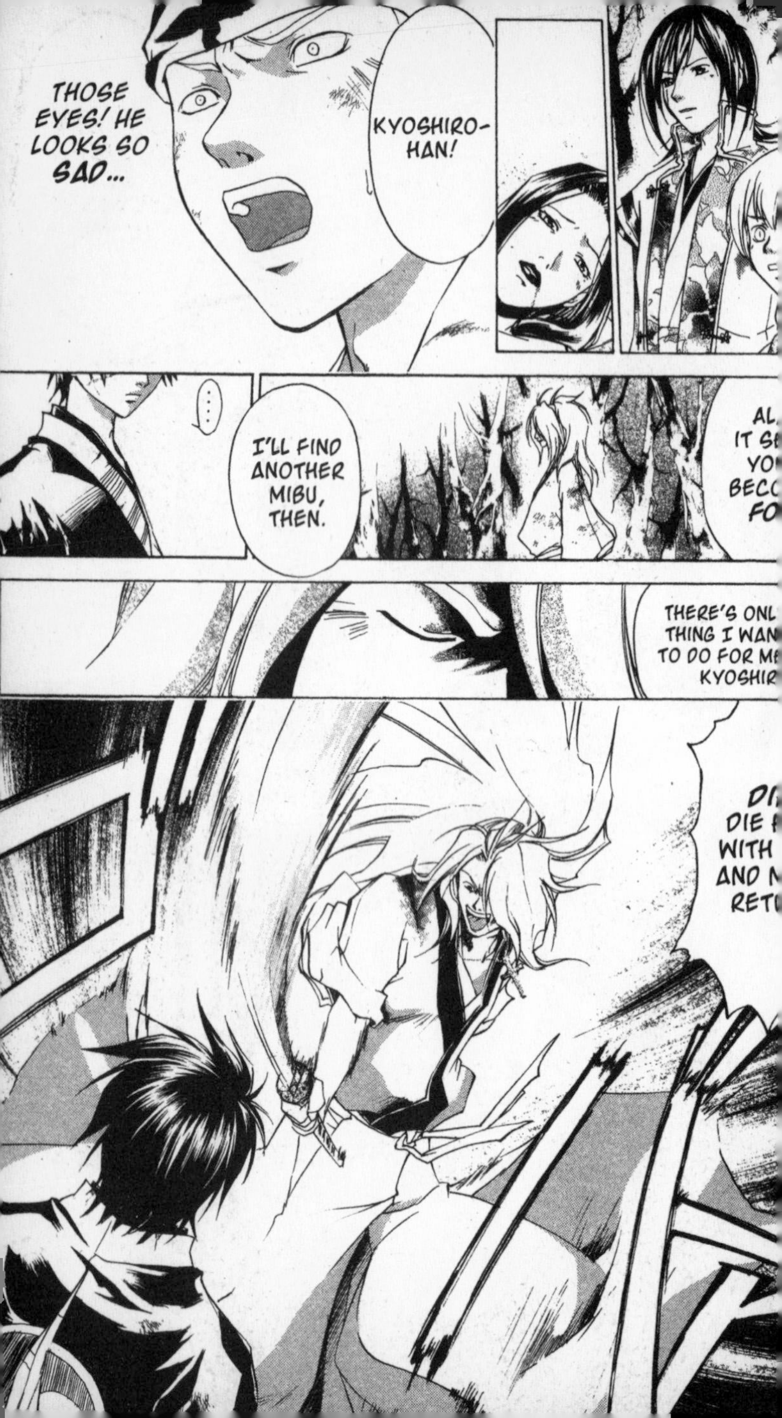
KYOSHIRO-HAN!
THOSE EYES! HE LOOKS SO SAD...
AL IT SE YO BECO FO
I'LL FIND ANOTHER MIBU, THEN.
...
THERE'S ONL THING I WAN TO DO FOR ME KYOSHIR
DI DIE WITH AND M RET

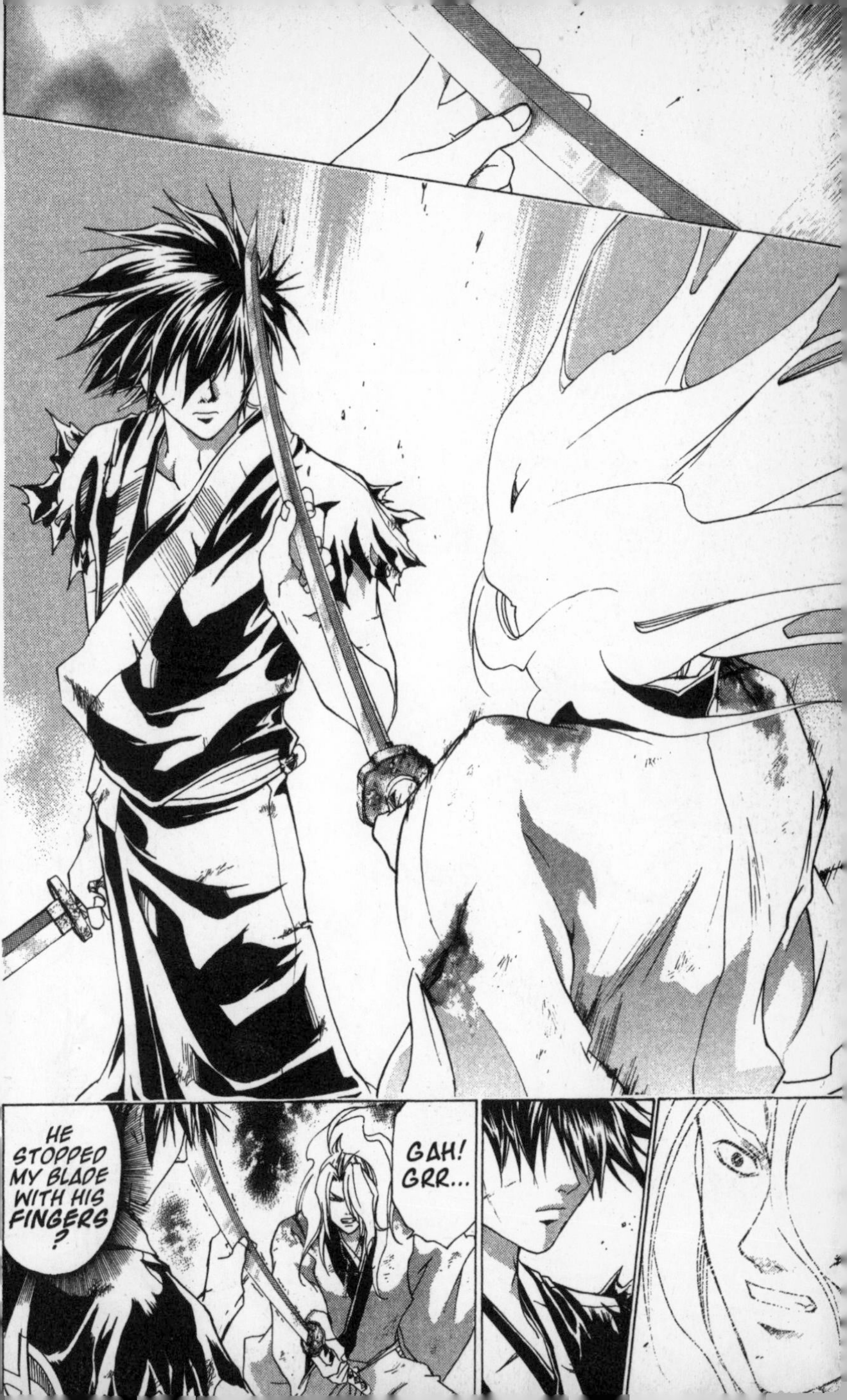
GAH! GRR...
HE STOPPED MY BLADE WITH HIS FINGERS?

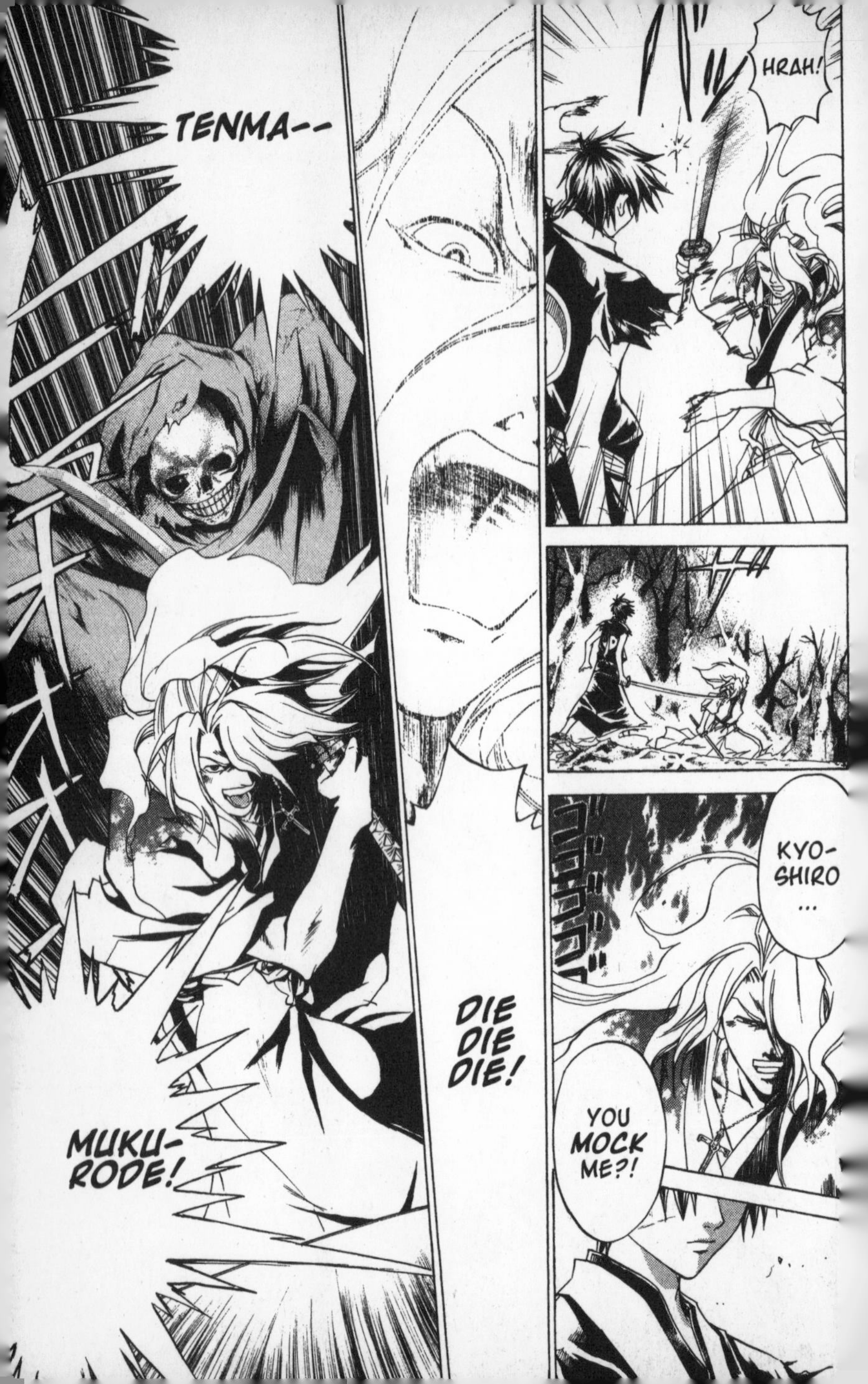
HRAH!
KYO-SHIRO...
YOU MOCK ME?!
DIE DIE DIE!
TENMA--
MUKU-RODE!

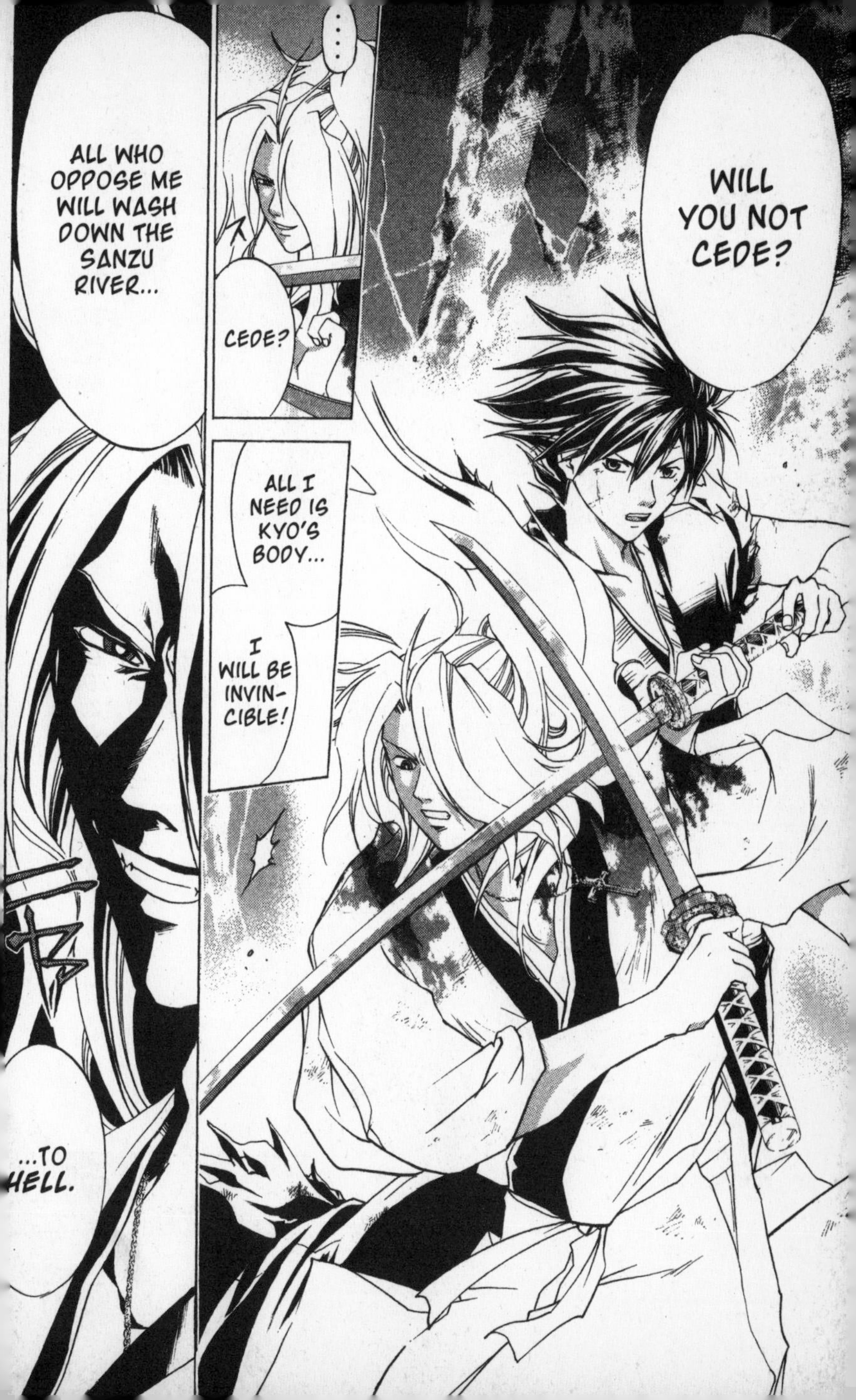
WILL YOU NOT CEDE?
....
CEDE?
ALL I NEED IS KYO'S BODY...
I WILL BE INVINCIBLE!
ALL WHO OPPOSE ME WILL WASH DOWN THE SANZU RIVER...
...TO HELL.

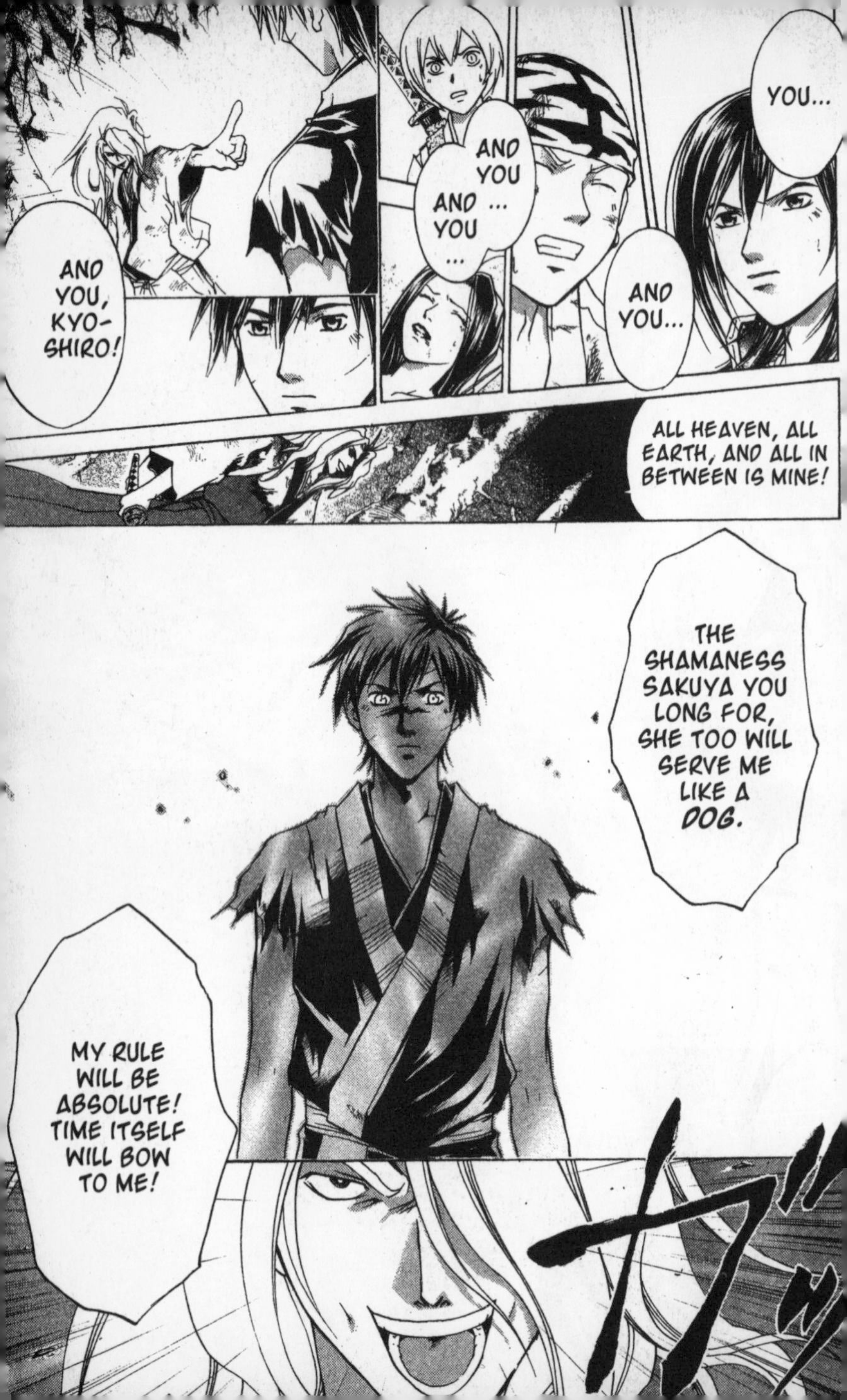
YOU...
AND YOU...
AND YOU ...
AND YOU ...
AND YOU, KYO-SHIRO!
ALL HEAVEN, ALL EARTH, AND ALL IN BETWEEN IS MINE!
THE SHAMANESS SAKUYA YOU LONG FOR, SHE TOO WILL SERVE ME LIKE A DOG.
MY RULE WILL BE ABSOLUTE! TIME ITSELF WILL BOW TO ME!

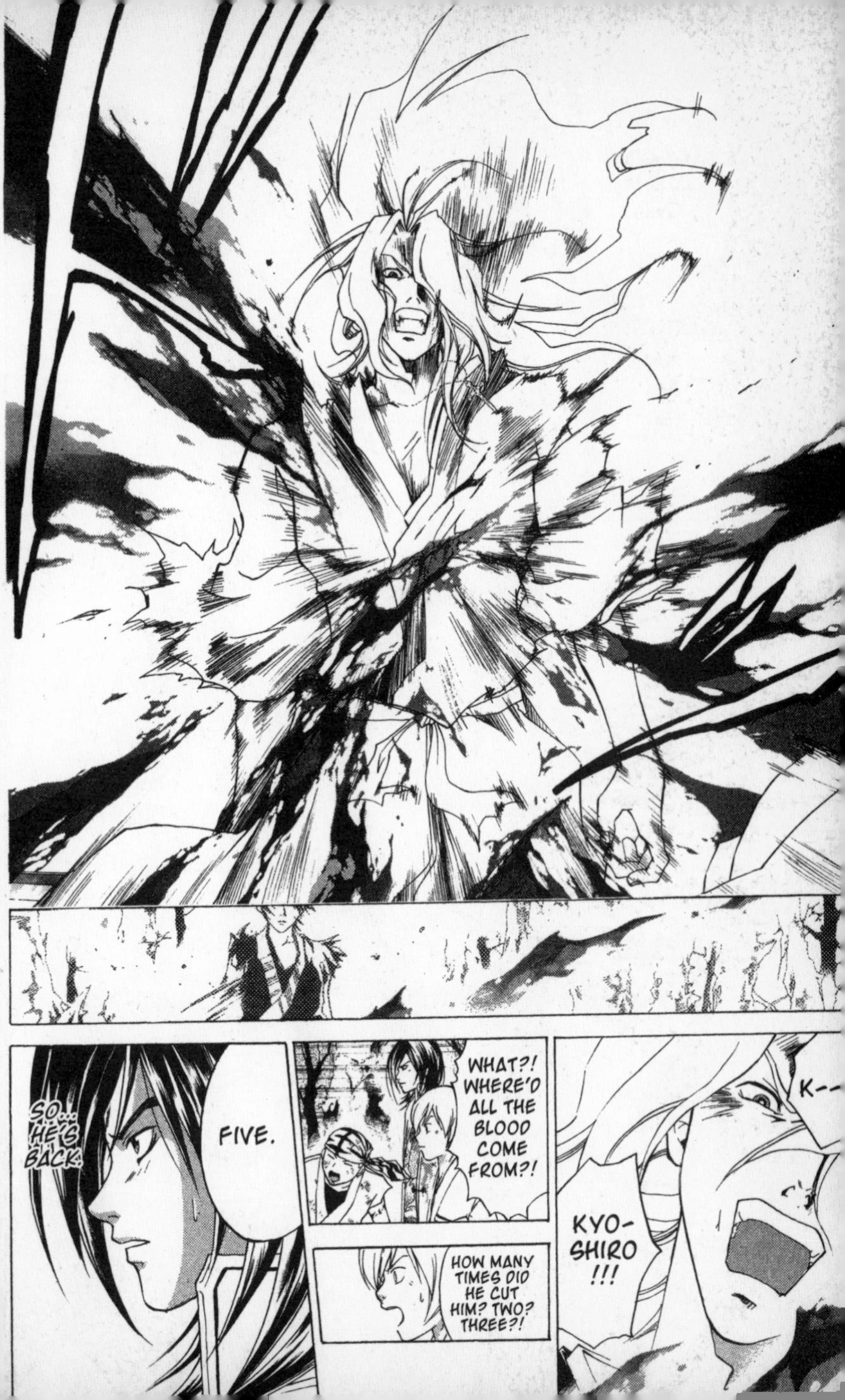
K--
KYO-SHIRO!!!
WHAT?! WHERE'D ALL THE BLOOD COME FROM?!
HOW MANY TIMES DID HE CUT HIM? TWO? THREE?!
FIVE.
SO... HE'S BACK.

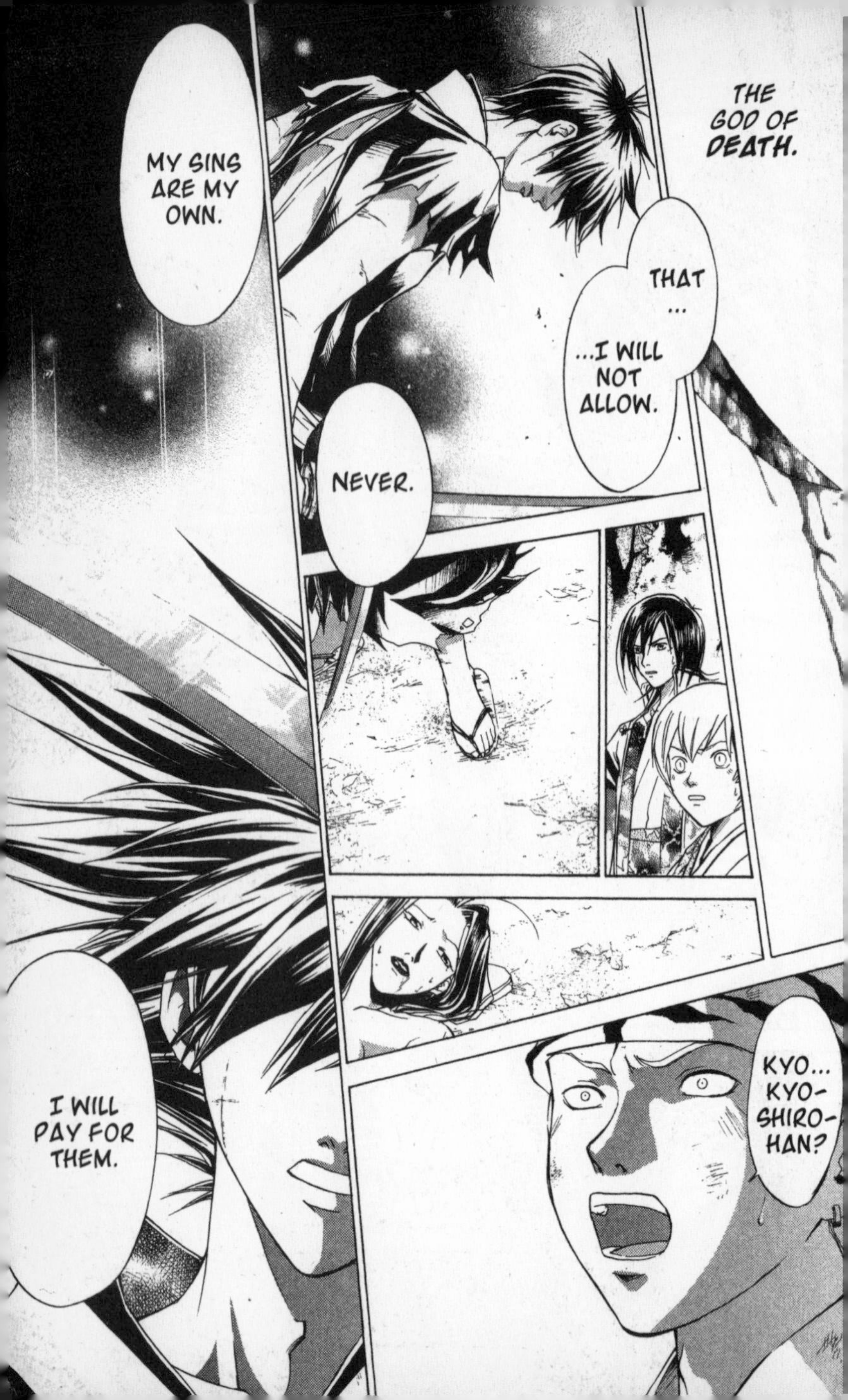
THE GOD OF DEATH.
THAT ... ...I WILL NOT ALLOW.
NEVER.
MY SINS ARE MY OWN.
KYO... KYO-SHIRO-HAN?
I WILL PAY FOR THEM.

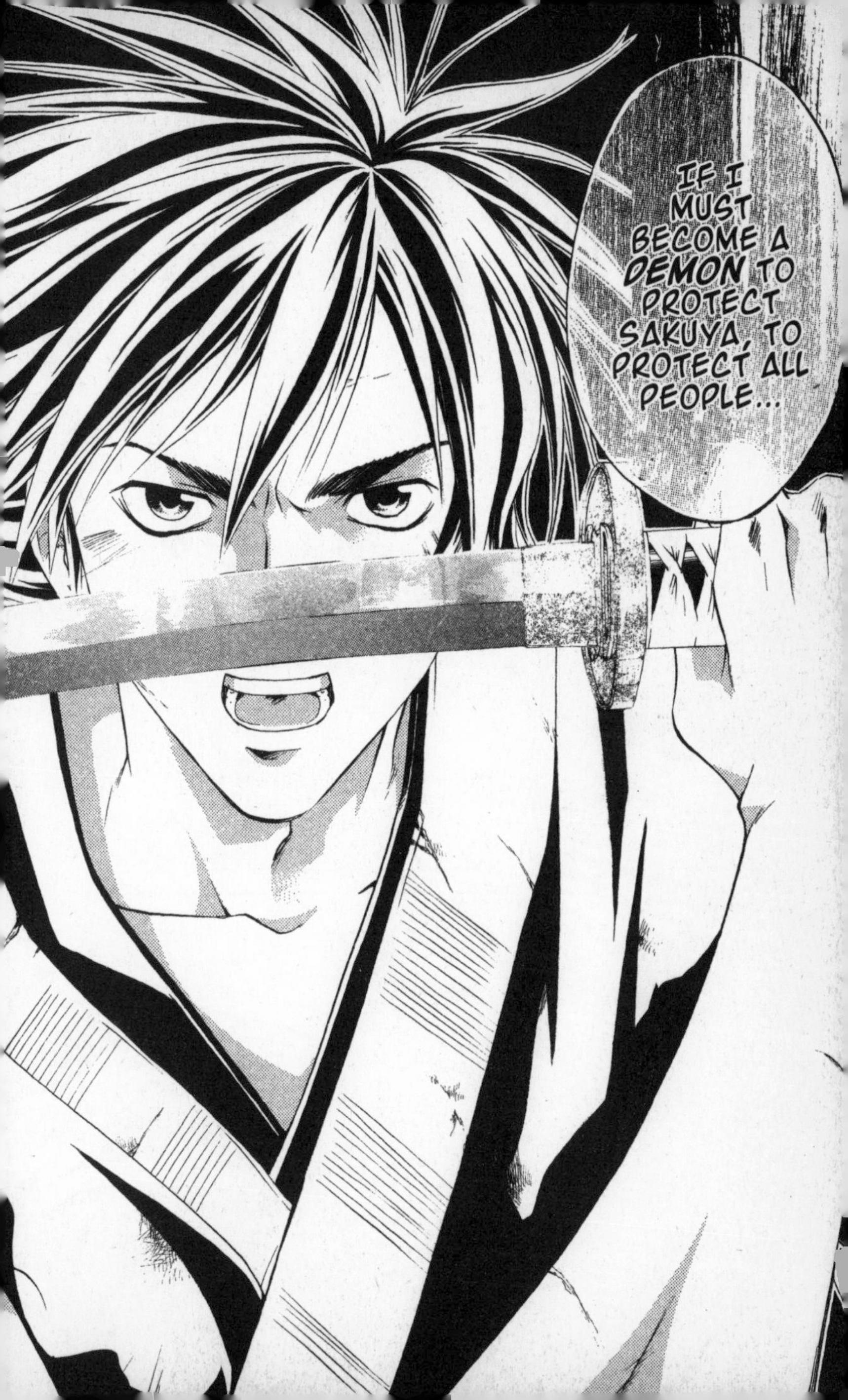
IF I MUST BECOME A **DEMON** TO PROTECT SAKUYA, TO PROTECT ALL PEOPLE...

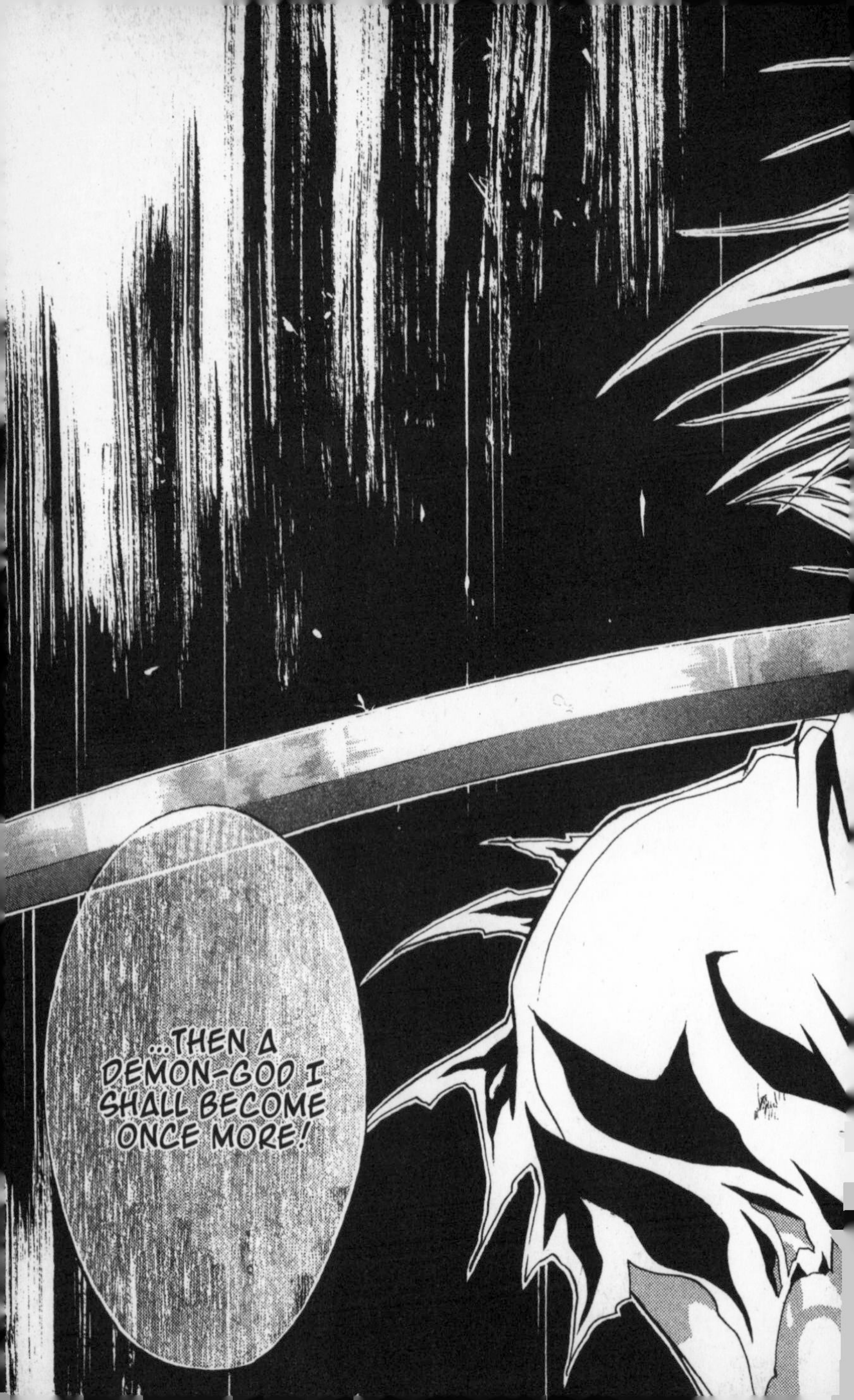
...THEN A DEMON-GOD I SHALL BECOME ONCE MORE!

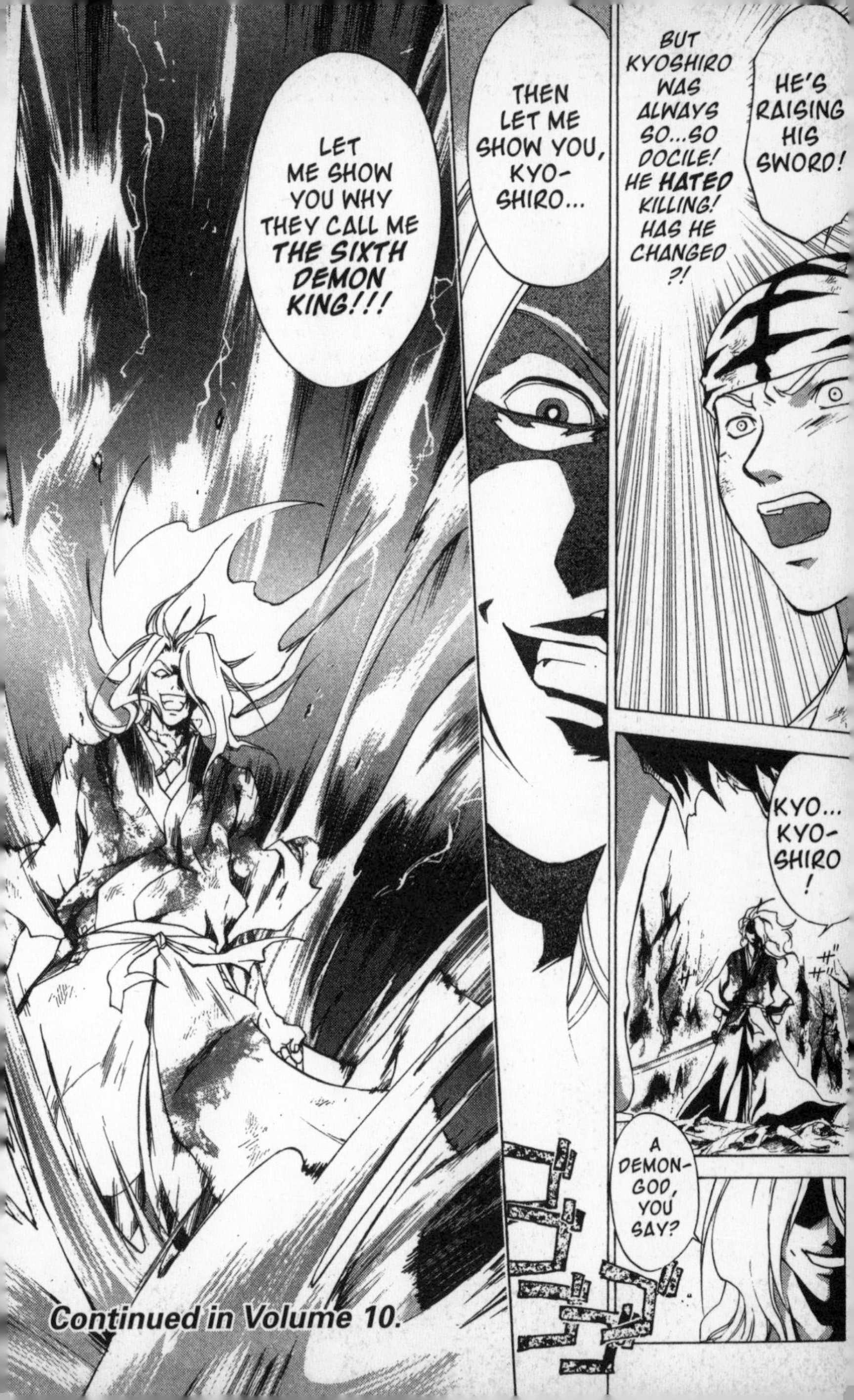
HE'S RAISING HIS SWORD!
BUT KYOSHIRO WAS ALWAYS SO...SO DOCILE! HE **HATED** KILLING! HAS HE CHANGED ?!
KYO... KYO-SHIRO !
A DEMON-GOD, YOU SAY?
THEN LET ME SHOW YOU, KYO-SHIRO...
LET ME SHOW YOU WHY THEY CALL ME **THE SIXTH DEMON KING!!!**

Continued in Volume 10.

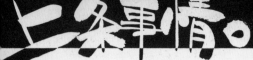

Kamijyo, Demon-auteur

OKAY! EDITORIAL THANKS YOU FOR TURNING IT IN EARLY.
MR. H
THANK YOU!
THE ONE BEFORE HAD SO MANY FIXES THAT EDITORIAL WAS REALLY PRESSED FOR TIME, YOU KNOW.
Eh heh...
Straight face
MR. H
BUT I'M SURE THE READERS APPRECIATE ALL THE EXTRA WORK, SO THANKS...
UMMM ... CAN I FIX THIS UP A BIT?
J-just a little...
SO, YOU SAY THIS REPLICA CAN'T CUT, KAMIJYO?
Care to test it, hmm?
MR. H
J-JUST TWO HOURS! ONE! I'LL DO IT IN ONE!

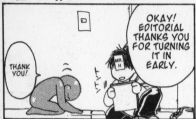

I was honored to work with "GetBackers" author Ayamine-sensei and "Rave" author Mashima-sensei on a collaborative piece a while back. Unfortunately, we couldn't reprint it in this book (makes you want to read the weekly magazine, eh?) but it was a great experience for me.
Sorry I couldn't keep up with you on the namings, Ayamine-sensei! And sorry for yelling at you all the time, Mashima-sensei!

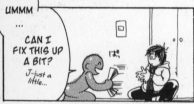

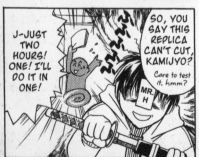

CHARACTER PROFILE

Saizo : First, a declaration! I am a ninja, and it is against my nature to speak of personal matters before others! Especially when Yukimura-sama isn't around

Kamijyo : But Yukimura and Sasuke were very forthcoming...

S: Wha--?! It just shows you how lax Sasuke is. He's one of the Ten for crying out loud! Eh?! Yukimura-sama, too?! How bold, with so many people after his life! ...But I'm sure he gave it deep consideration...

K: He told me his sizes, too.

S: ...Yukimura-sama...*sob*

K: But he did say he loves his Ten!

S: ...Yukimura-sama...*weep*

K: ...Okay, I think we understand you're a serious fellow who honors Yukimura and Sasuke and the Ten quite highly. Maybe you could tell me your profile so that the world might better known the glory of the Ten? Hmm?

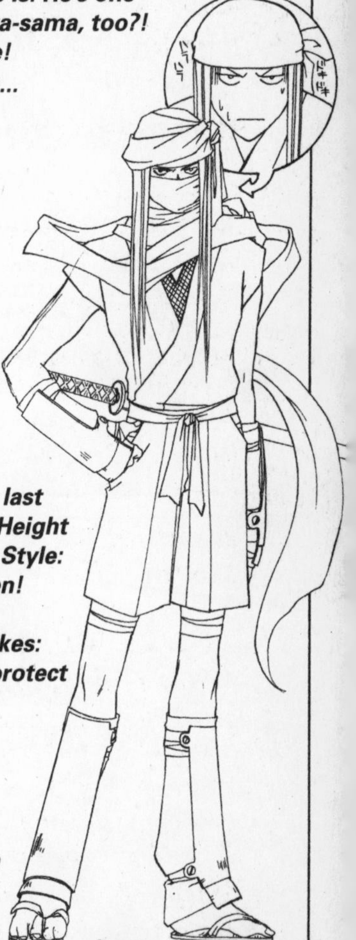

S: Well, if you put it that way, of course! My last name is Kirigakure, first name, Saizo. Male, Height 175cm, Weight 60kg, Blood Type A, Combat Style: Iga School, Profession: one of the Sanada Ten! I protect the Sanada Clan, which is to say, Yukimura-sama. Likes: Yukimura-sama, Dislikes: Yukimura's enemies. My life's mission is to protect Yukimura-sama, and nothing else! Okay! Ask me anything! Go ahead!

K: Um, uh...we've heard quite a lot already. Any parting words?

S: Don't you want to ask me more about the glory of the Ten?!

K: Noooo! Enough of that! Thank you very much.

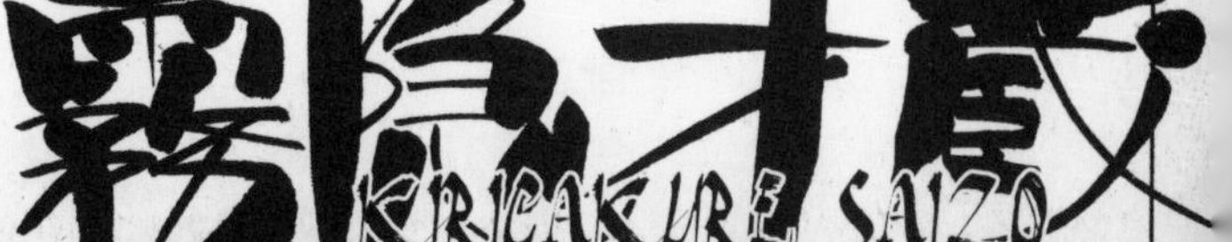

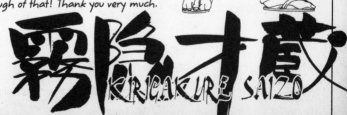

霧隠才蔵
KIRIGAKURE SAIZO

Q&A CORNER

AT LAST, THE SDK Q&A YOU'VE ALL BEEN WAITING FOR!

Why did you start writing SDK?

I've always liked heroes who change from one form to another, and I've always wanted to do a character with multiple personalities. One day, I discussed it with Mr. H and Mr. S, and the rest is history!

Which character do you like best in SDK?

There's no character I dislike. But saying I like them all best is lame, so if I had to choose, I'd say maybe...Benitora or Saizo? Right now, at least.

Which of the characters in SDK resembles you the most?

It's hard to pick just one--I think they all reflect things I've noticed in other people, and things I've felt myself over the years: Kyo's shyness, Kyoshiro's self-abusive nature, Yuya's strength, Benitora's identity complex, Okuni's clumsiness, Yukimura's by-the-seat-of-his-pants attitude, Sasuke's childishness--everything I've seen in me and around me. It's kind of embarrassing, being a manga writer...

When Yuya-san's naked, why do you always hide the good parts? Please draw more clearly.

Peek-a-boo! Work that imagination! (laugh) (Oh, if only they'd let me...eh heh heh...)

I HOPE I ANSWERED YOUR QUESTIONS. SEND MORE! THANKS!

STAFF

Yuzu Haruno (The Chief)

Haruno-san had work this month, so his page is taking a break. Check out this seal he gave me as a present, though!

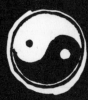

Haruno-san is currently writing under the pen name "Hayato Ayase." Check it out!

Hazuki Asami

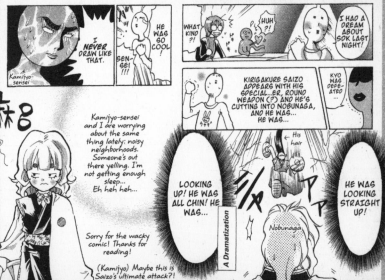

The Chief (Haruno-san)'s Dream.
I HAD A DREAM ABOUT SDK LAST NIGHT!
HUH?!
WHAT KIND?!
KYO WAS DEFEATED...
KIRIGAKURE SAIZO APPEARS WITH HIS SPECIAL...ER, ROUND WEAPON (?) AND HE'S CUTTING INTO NOBUNAGA, AND HE WAS... HE WAS...
HE WAS LOOKING STRAIGHT UP!
His hair
Nobunaga
LOOKING UP! HE WAS ALL CHIN! HE WAS...
A Dramatization
HE WAS SO COOL!
SENSEI!!!
I NEVER DRAW LIKE THAT.
Kamijyo-sensei
Kamijyo-sensei and I are worrying about the same thing lately: noisy neighborhoods. Someone's out there yelling. I'm not getting enough sleep... Eh heh heh...
Sorry for the wacky comic! Thanks for reading!
(Kamijyo) Maybe this is Saizo's ultimate attack?! (laugh)

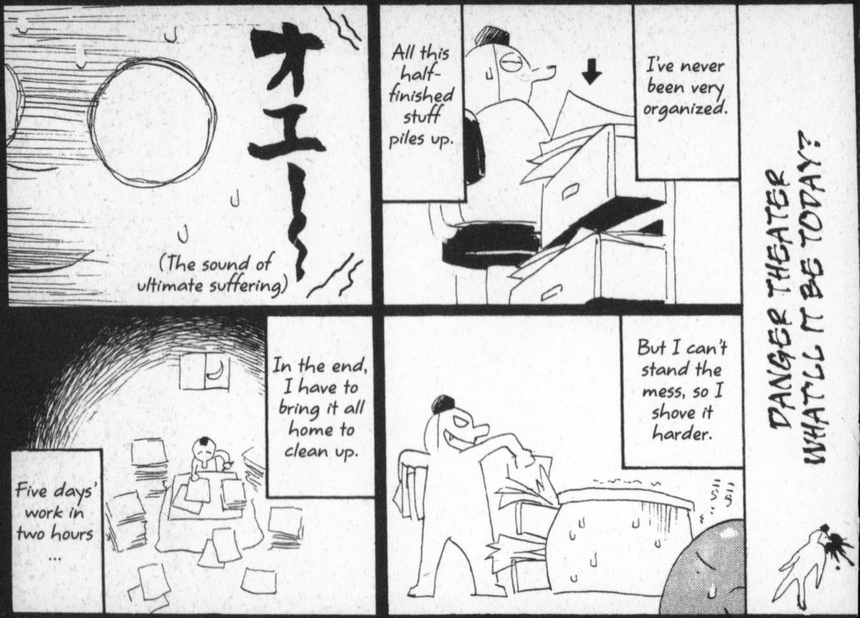
DANGER THEATER
WHAT'LL IT BE TODAY?
I've never been very organized.
All this half-finished stuff piles up.
オエー
(The sound of ultimate suffering)
But I can't stand the mess, so I shove it harder.
In the end, I have to bring it all home to clean up.
Five days' work in two hours ...

⬆ **Ken'ichi Suetake**

Takaya Nagao ⬇

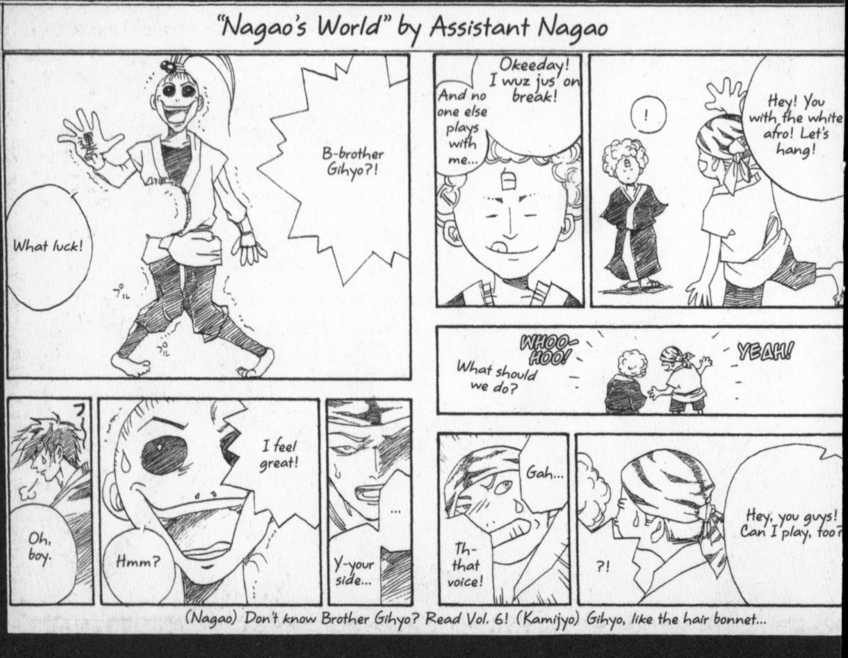
"Nagao's World" by Assistant Nagao
Hey! You with the white afro! Let's hang!
!
Okeeday! I wuz jus' on break!
And no one else plays with me...
WHOO-HOO!
YEAH!
What should we do?
B-brother Gihyo?!
What luck!
Hey, you guys! Can I play, too?
?!
Gah...
Th-that voice!
...
Y-your side...
I feel great!
Hmm?
Oh, boy.

(Nagao) Don't know Brother Gihyo? Read Vol. 6! (Kamijyo) Gihyo, like the hair bonnet...

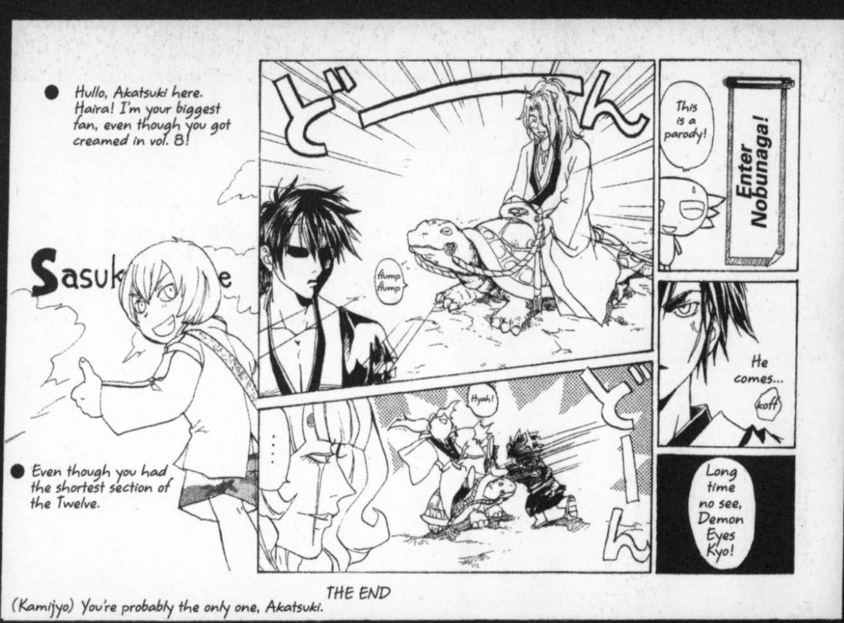
Enter Nobunaga!
This is a parody!
He comes...
koff
Long time no see, Demon Eyes Kyo!
flump flump
Hyah!
....
Hullo, Akatsuki here. Haira! I'm your biggest fan, even though you got creamed in vol. 8!
Even though you had the shortest section of the Twelve.
THE END
(Kamijyo) You're probably the only one, Akatsuki.

Souma Akatsuki

■ ***Thank you for the letters and drawings for the staff! We all have fun reading them! (Don't worry–they all get where they're supposed to go!)***

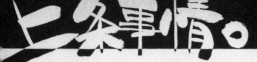

The Endless Quiet Battle

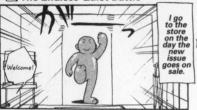

I go to the store on the day the new issue goes on sale.
Welcome!
MAGAJIN
SCORE 0-7
The battle contin- ues...

I read all letters and postcards! Even the backs and the edges! Your letters are my last defense when I lose hope! See you in the next (double digit) volume!

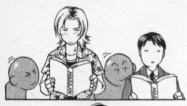

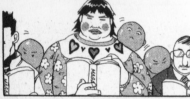

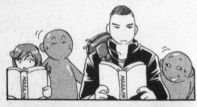

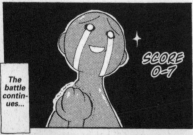

CHALLENGE AKIMINE KAMIJYO

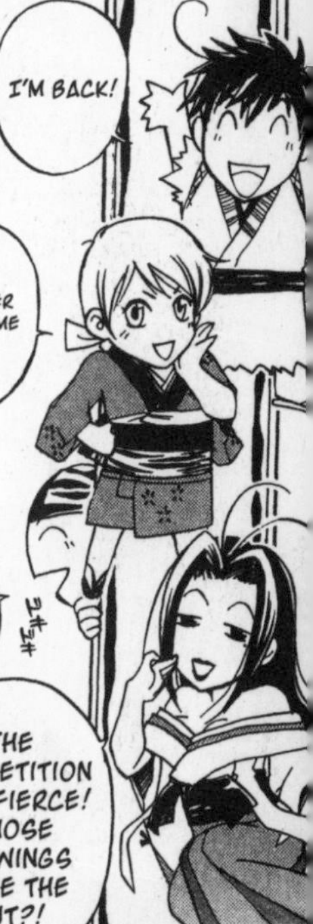
I'M BACK!
REMEMBER TO DRAW ME CUTE!
AM I IN HERE?
THE COMPETITION WAS FIERCE! WHOSE DRAWINGS MADE THE CUT?!

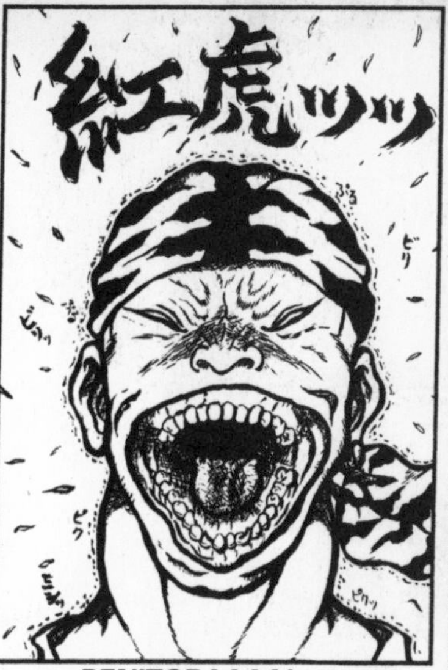
紅虎ッッッ

BENITORAAAA!
[Kinou / Nagasaki]
No comment! (Amazing!)

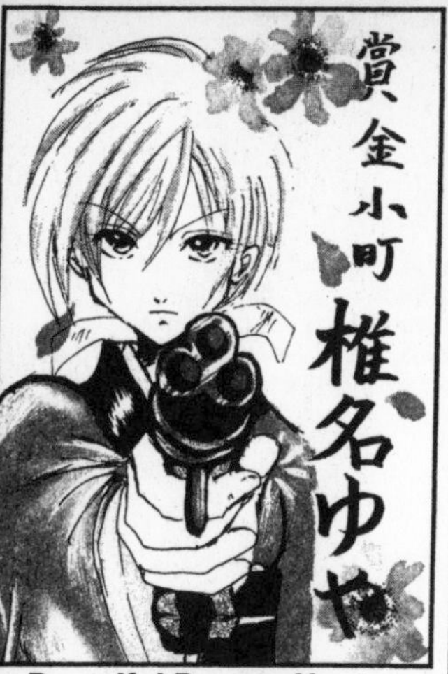
賞金小町
椎名ゆや

Beautiful Bounty Hunter Shiina Yuya
[Yuki / Shizuoka]
This is what they mean by "strong eyes."

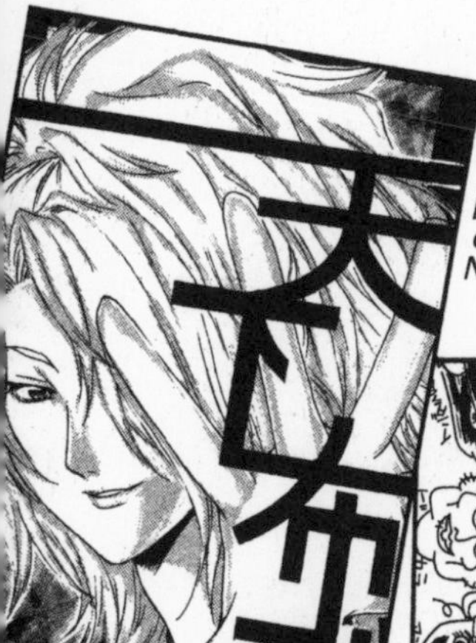
天下布武

[Kitabayashi Yukari / Nagano]
A beaut!
TENKAFUBU!
[NOTE: "military rule of all under heaven" - Nobunaga's slogan]

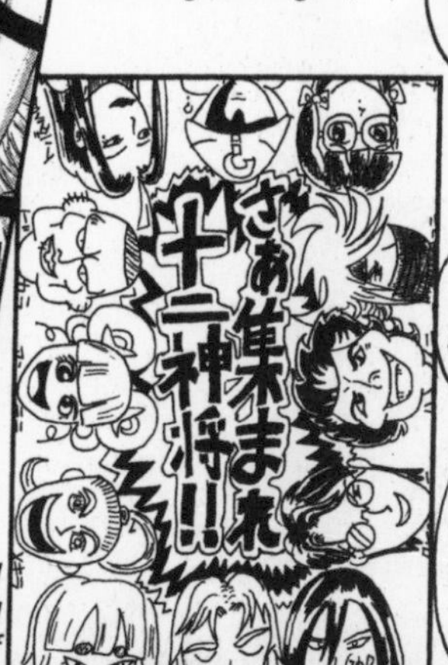
さぁ集まれ十二神将!!

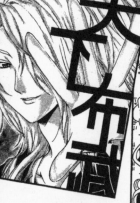

Now--Twelve, Unite!
[Kashiba Yuji / Osaka]
We never did have all of them together, did we?

THANK YOU
FOR ALL
THE AMAZING ART!
PLEASE KEEP
SENDING IT!

Message from the Editor:

♡

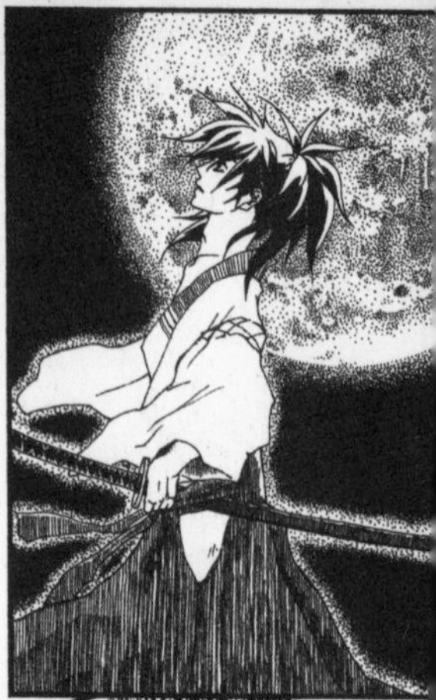

We're not getting enough pictures of Kyo! (...Why?!) Arise, challengers!

[Oyuu / Wakayama] *I can feel the tension! Good work!*

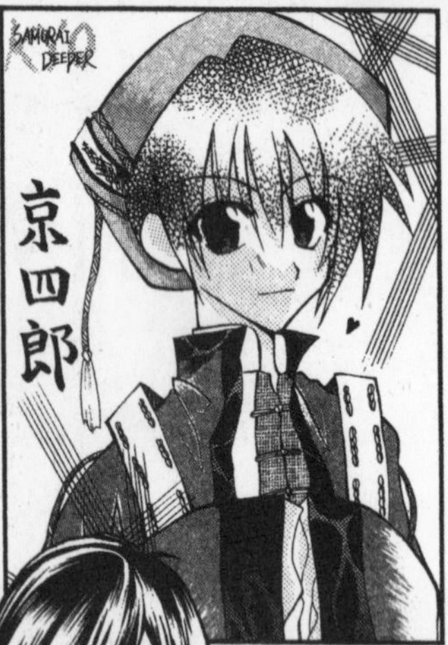
SAMURAI DEEPER KYO
京四郎

Kyoshiro
[Kamimura Chijin / Aomori] *Very spiffy. Is that his uniform?*

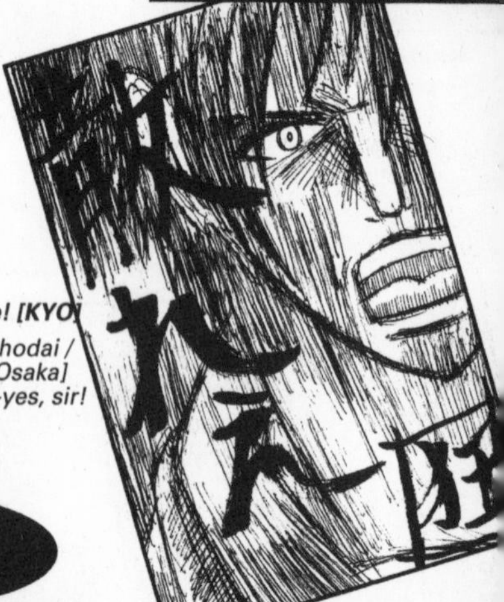

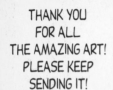

Dieeee! [KYO]
[Kisa Shodai / Osaka] *Y-yes, sir!*

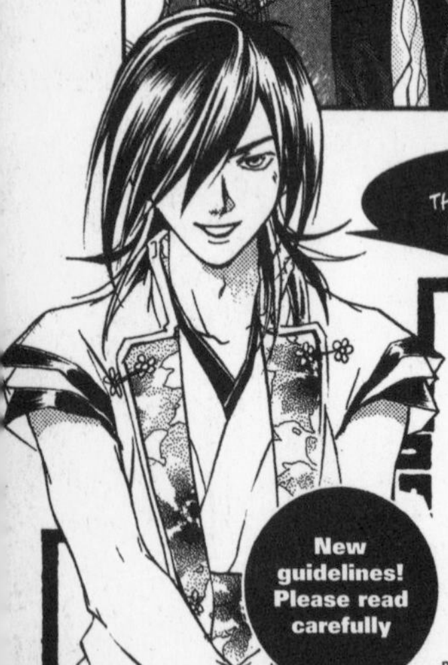
IT SEEMS
THE LADIES LIKE TO
DRAW ME BEST!

New guidelines! Please read carefully

How to submit:
1) Send your work via regular mail (NOT e-mail) to:

SAMURAI DEEPER KYO FAN MAIL
C/O TOKYOPOP
5900 WILSHIRE BLVD., SUITE 2000
LOS ANGELES, CA 90036

2) All work should be in black-and-white and no larger than 8.5" x 11". (And try not to fold it too many times!) 3) Anything you send will not be returned. If you want to keep your original, it's fine to send us a copy. 4) Please include your full name, age, city and state for us to print with your work. If you'd rather us use a pen name, please include that too. 5) IMPORTANT: If you're under the age of 18, you must have your parent's permission in order for us to print your work. Any submissions without a signed note of parental consent will not be used. 6) For full details, please check out *http://www.tokyopop.com/aboutus/fanart.php*

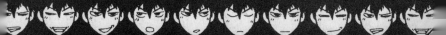

Dale H.
Marito, IL

Chibi-Akira-chan! Move over Zatoichi! Finally a blind swordsman you can put in your pocket! But does he give massages?

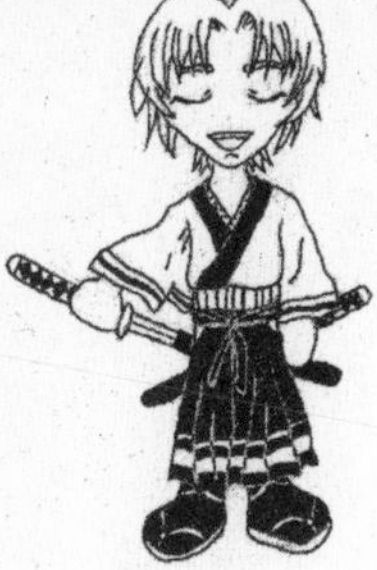

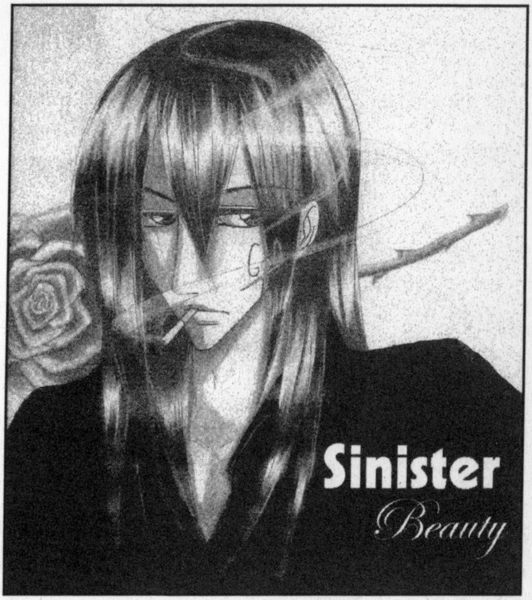
Sinister
Beauty

Amanda P.
Age 17
Gastonia, NC

Hey, shouldn't this art go to Saiyuki fan mail? ...oh! That cross-shaped scar, the "undying" beauty... Of course, it's Shindara! Nice to see one of the Twelve getting a little love. He does look like Gojyo...doesn't he?

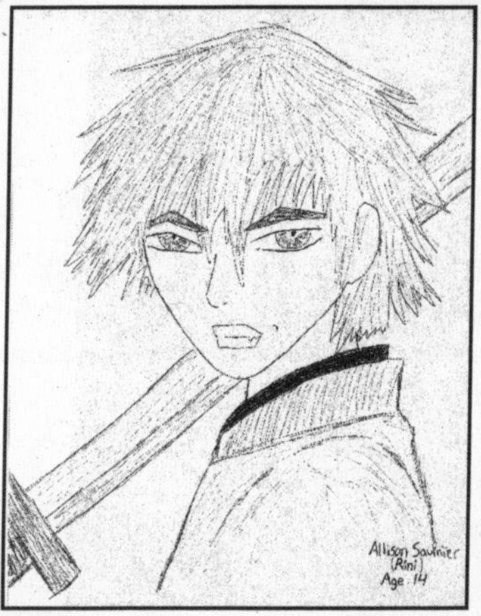
Allison Saulnier
(Rini)
Age. 14

Allison S. (Rini)
Age 14
Grand Junction, CO

Kyo looks pissed! Better not say anything rude or he might gut me! Nice eyes, Rini.

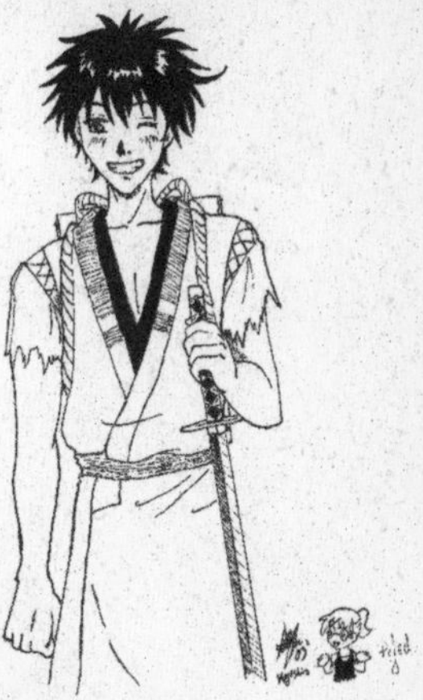

Shannon M.
Marietta, GA

Kyoshiro! You're back at last! But will you ever smile? Thank you for this beautiful trip down memory lane, Sha-chan!

Mike R.
Brooklyn, NY

You know the problem with wielding a 5-shaku long katana? They're so dang hard to unsheathe! Thanks for the pic, Mike!

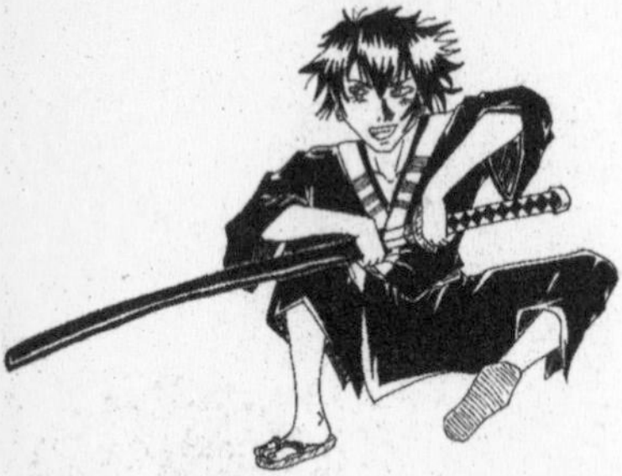

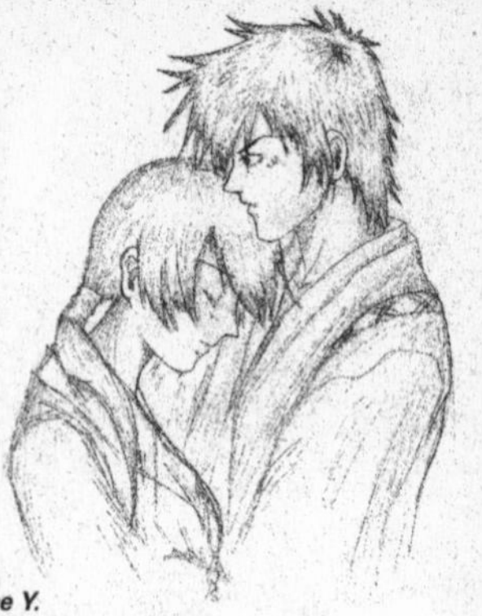

Grace Y.
Age 18
Fresno, CA

A tender moment...will it ever come to pass? Beautiful work, Grace.

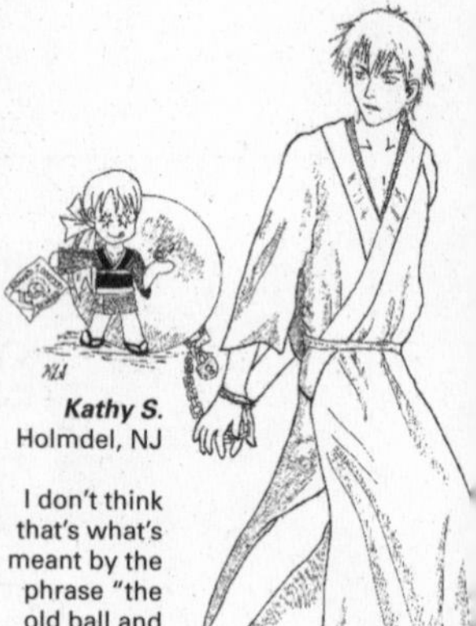

Kathy S.
Holmdel, NJ

I don't think that's what's meant by the phrase "the old ball and chain." Poor Kyo...

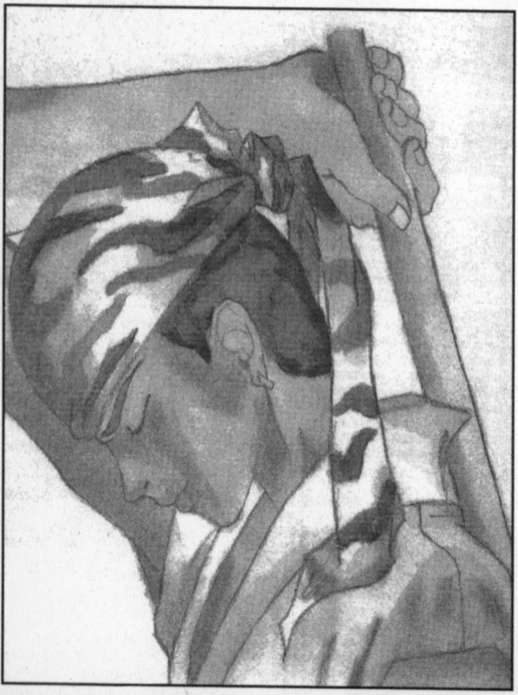

Tara Y.
Age 22
Palisades Park, NJ

The softer side of Benitora. I guess the ladies like the "Tiger," too!

Cherubella T.
Age 14
Pasadena, MD

The gang's all here! Well, the current gang. Just wait for a couple more volumes—Kyo's posse becomes a virtual army!

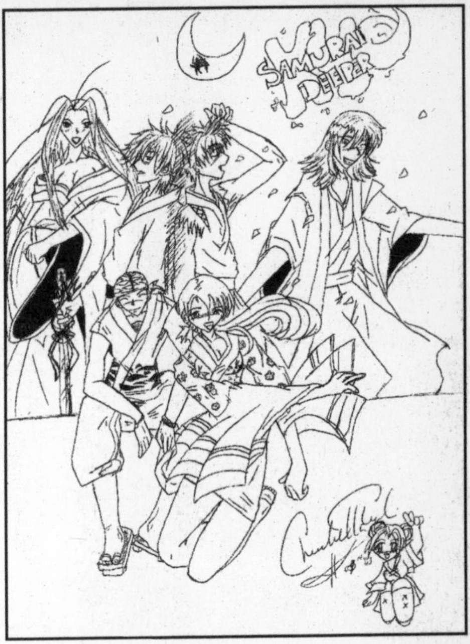
SAMURAI DEEPER

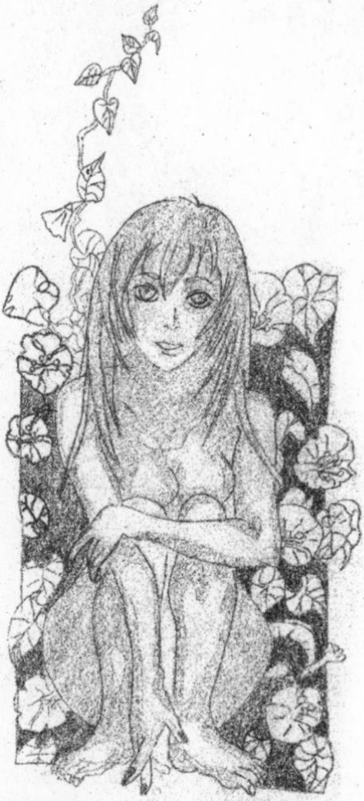

Dong N.
Age 13
Westminister, CA

Whoa! Yuya's smokin'! Are you sure this isn't meant for Maxim magazine?

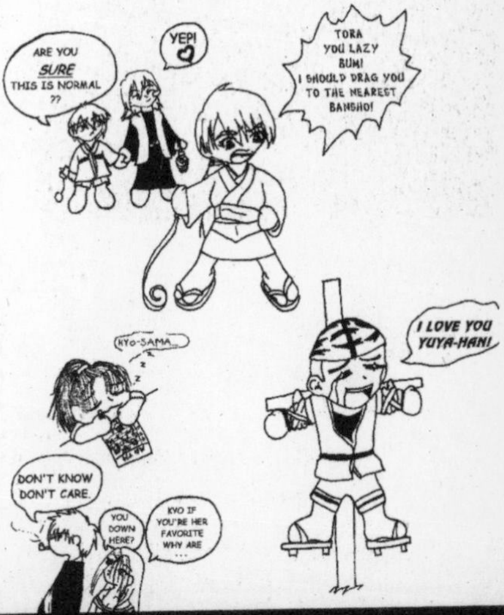
TORA YOU LAZY BUM! I SHOULD DRAG YOU TO THE NEAREST BANSHO!
YEP! ♡
ARE YOU SURE THIS IS NORMAL ??
I LOVE YOU YUYA-HAN!
KYO-SAMA...
KYO IF YOU'RE HER FAVORITE WHY ARE ...
YOU DOWN HERE?
DON'T KNOW DON'T CARE.

Kimberly H.
Age 13

Chibi-fest! Cute, cute, cute!
PS- Thanks for the "cookies."

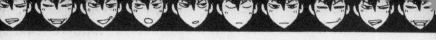

Lisa O.
Age 43
Everett, WA

Women love the Yukimura, ne?
Super sexy.

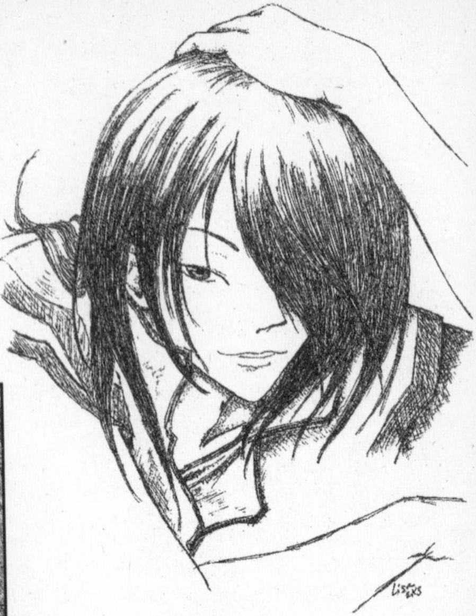

Maria K.
Age 15
Kissimmee, FL

A "kissing" picture
from Kissimmee, Florida?
What are the odds?
Very sensual picture,
Maria.

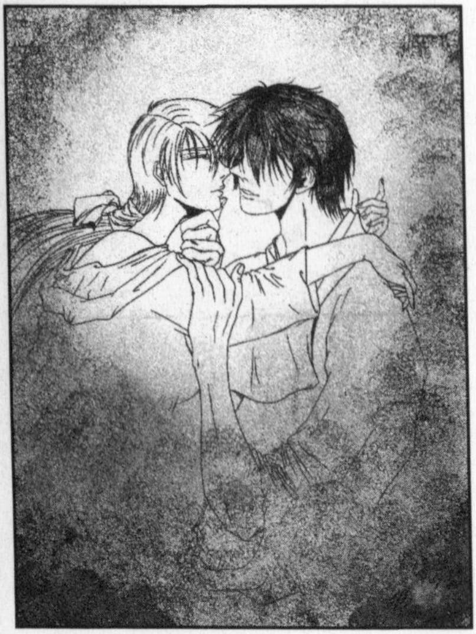

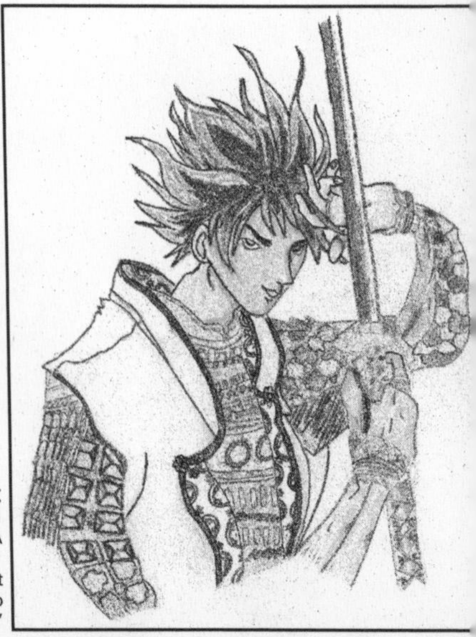

Christopher T.
Age 11
Westminister, CA

If this Kyo were an action figure, it
would be "Ceremonial Armor Kyo
with Burning Fury Action!"

GLOSSARY

Akechi Mitsuhide—(1526-1582) One of Nobunaga's generals who betrayed Nobunaga at Honnoji temple. Unfortunately for Akechi, he died just two weeks later, earning the nickname "The 13-Day Shogun."

Aokigahara—"The Sea of Trees." The forest at the base of Mt. Fuji. Its reputation for being haunted endures to this day.

Edo Era—(1603-1868) Japan's "Golden Era" of political and economic stability after the civil wars of the Sengoku Era. During the Edo Era, all of Japan would be ruled by one Shogun. *Samurai Deeper Kyo* takes place at the start of the Edo Era.

Fushimi Castle—Prior to Sekigahara, Ishida Mitsunari (a warlord and Tokugawa rival) launched an attack on Fushimi Castle where Tokugawa Ieyasu was based. Hearing of the attack, Tokugawa and his troops fled. He left behind less than 2,000 men under the leadership of Torii Mototada to defend the keep against Ishida's 50,000 men. Torii managed to hold off the attackers for nearly two weeks before he was beheaded. His loyal men committed *seppuku* rather than face capture or death at the hands of the enemy.

-han—The "-san" suffix as said with Benitora's accent.

Honnoji no Hen—The uprising led by Nobunaga's retainer Akechi Mitsuhide at Honnoji Temple, Kyoto, which led to the death of Nobunaga.

Kagemusha—Literally "shadow warrior." A kagemusha is a body double for a political or military leader, intended to protect him or her from potential assassins. Sanada Yukimura's kagemusha is currently in Kudoyama with Sakuya.

Kansai-ben—Regional dialect of the Kansai area (incl. Osaka, Kyoto, Kobe). Benitora speaks in this dialect, known for its fast-paced diction and unique slang.

Kazusa-no-suke—"Lord of Kazusa." Nobunaga's title. Kazusa is the former name for the area that is now Chiba Prefecture, where Nobunaga had his base of power.

Mumyou-Jinpuu-Ryuu—Kyo's combat style. *"Mumyou"* means absence of light, and *"Jinpuu"* is an alternate reading of the kanji for *"kamikaze,"* or "divine wind."

Oda Nobunaga—(1534-1582) One of Japan's most famous and controversial historical figures. During the Sengoku Era, he attempted to unite all of Japan under his rule, mercilessly killing all who opposed him—including countless Buddhist monks. He was also the first Japanese leader to embrace Western culture, including modern warfare (firearms and iron-clad ships) and Christianity. For all his brutality, Nobunaga was also a patron of the arts and culture.

-san—The most common honorific. Equivalent to Mr./Mrs.

Sanada Ju-Yuushi—The Sanada Ten. The ten elite warriors who served Sanada Yukimura and have since passed into legend.

Sanada Yukimura—The son of Sanada Masayuki, who fought against Tokugawa at Sekigahara. Yukimura's brother, Nobuyuki (see SDK vol. 4), sided with Tokugawa and was able to use his influence to save his brother and father's lives. Sanada Yukimura continued his father's fight against Tokugawa after Sekigahara.

Sekigahara—The greatest battle in Japanese history, the Battle of Sekigahara took place in the fall of 1600 and ended years of civil war.

Sarutobi Sasuke—A historical member of the Sanada Ten and a legendary ninja.

Sengoku Era—(1467-1568/1615) The "Warring States" period of Japanese history during which the country was split between warring factions. It came to an end when Tokugawa created a unified government in Edo, ushering in the Edo Era.

Tenkafubu—"Military rule of all under heaven." Nobunaga's slogan, seen on the battlefield banners on pg. 13.

Tokugawa Hidetada—(1579-1632) Tokugawa Ieyasu's son and heir, here fictionalized as Benitora. Some...liberties were taken with the historical figure.

Tokugawa Ieyasu—(1543-1616) The first shogun of the Edo Era who united all of Japan under one ruler following the battle of Sekigahara. The historical Ieyasu merely commanded the Iga ninjas; in SDK, Ieyasu is one-and-the-same with legendary ninja Hattori Hanzo, leader of the Iga ninjas.

Uzumasa Movie Village—Operated by Toei, one of Japan's largest movie studios, the Uzumasa Movie Village is a combination working studio and theme park. Guests can watch films being made or enjoy special shows, which are put on in the studio's elaborate period sets.

*errata: In SDK vol. 7, the descriptions for Tokugawa Hidetada and Tokugawa Ieyasu were inadvertently switched. They are correctly described here. We apologize for any confusion.

SAMURAI DEEPER KYO NEXT!!

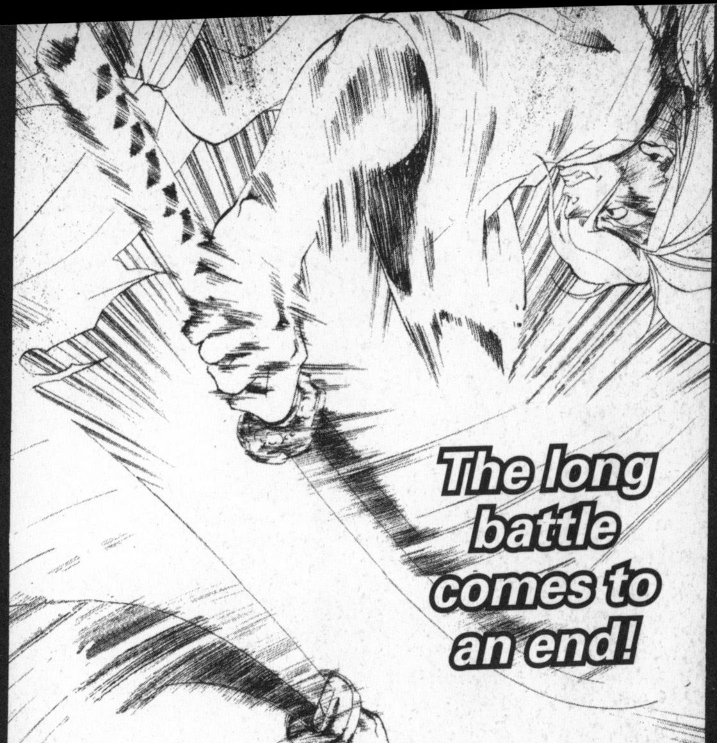

The earth-shaking SDK Volume 10! Don't miss it!

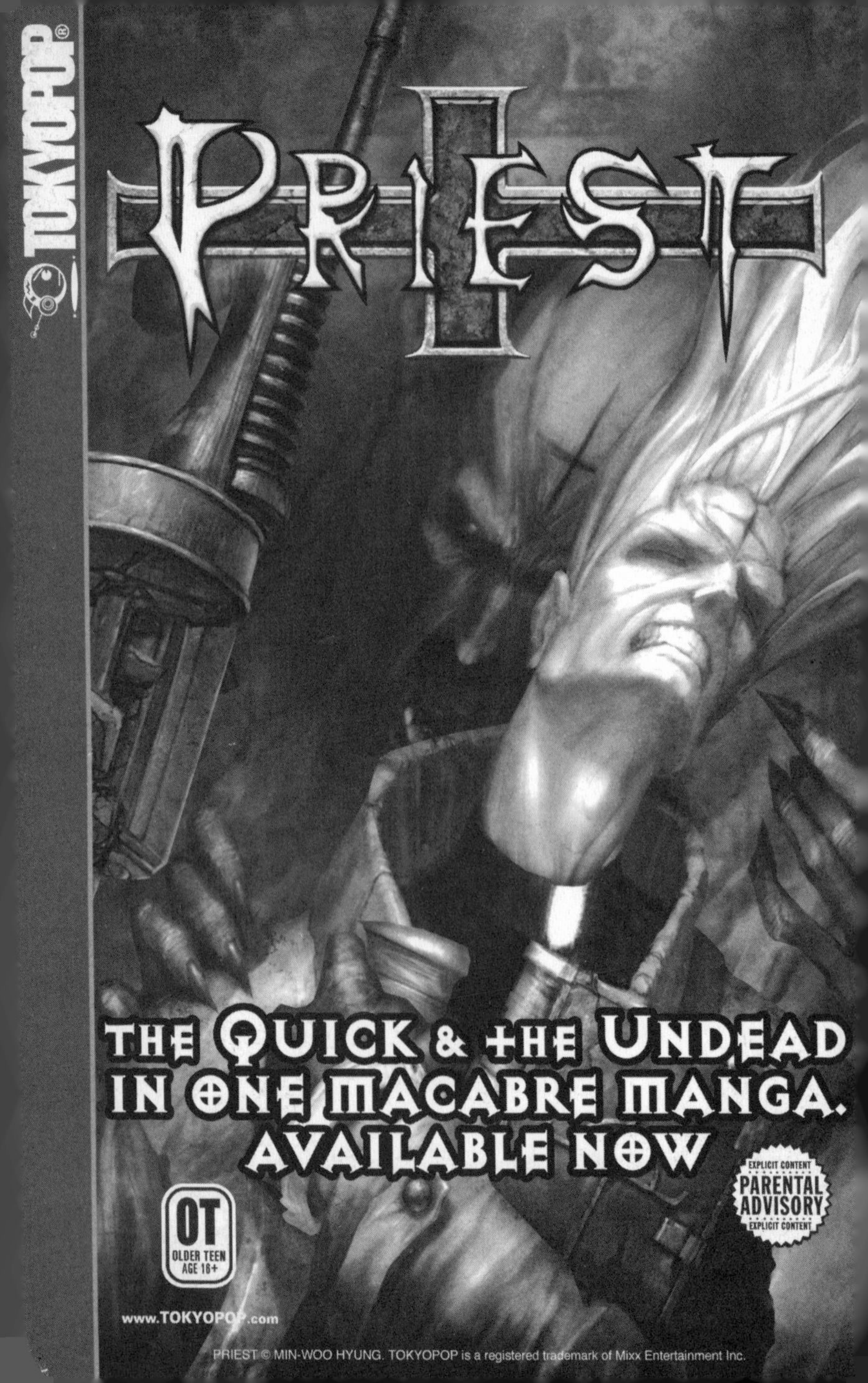

TOKYOPOP
PRIEST
THE QUICK & THE UNDEAD
IN ONE MACABRE MANGA.
AVAILABLE NOW
OT
OLDER TEEN
AGE 18+
EXPLICIT CONTENT
PARENTAL ADVISORY
EXPLICIT CONTENT
www.TOKYOPOP.com
PRIEST © MIN-WOO HYUNG. TOKYOPOP is a registered trademark of Mixx Entertainment Inc.

Jing is STILL the King!

The fresh, new adventures of Jing and his feisty, feathered friend Kir

KING OF BANDITS

王ドロボウ JING™

By YUICHI KUMAKURA

TWILIGHT TALES

T TEEN AGE 13+

Jing: King of Bandits - Twilight Tales: © 2004 Yuichi Kumakura

www.TOKYOPOP.com

TOKYOPOP®

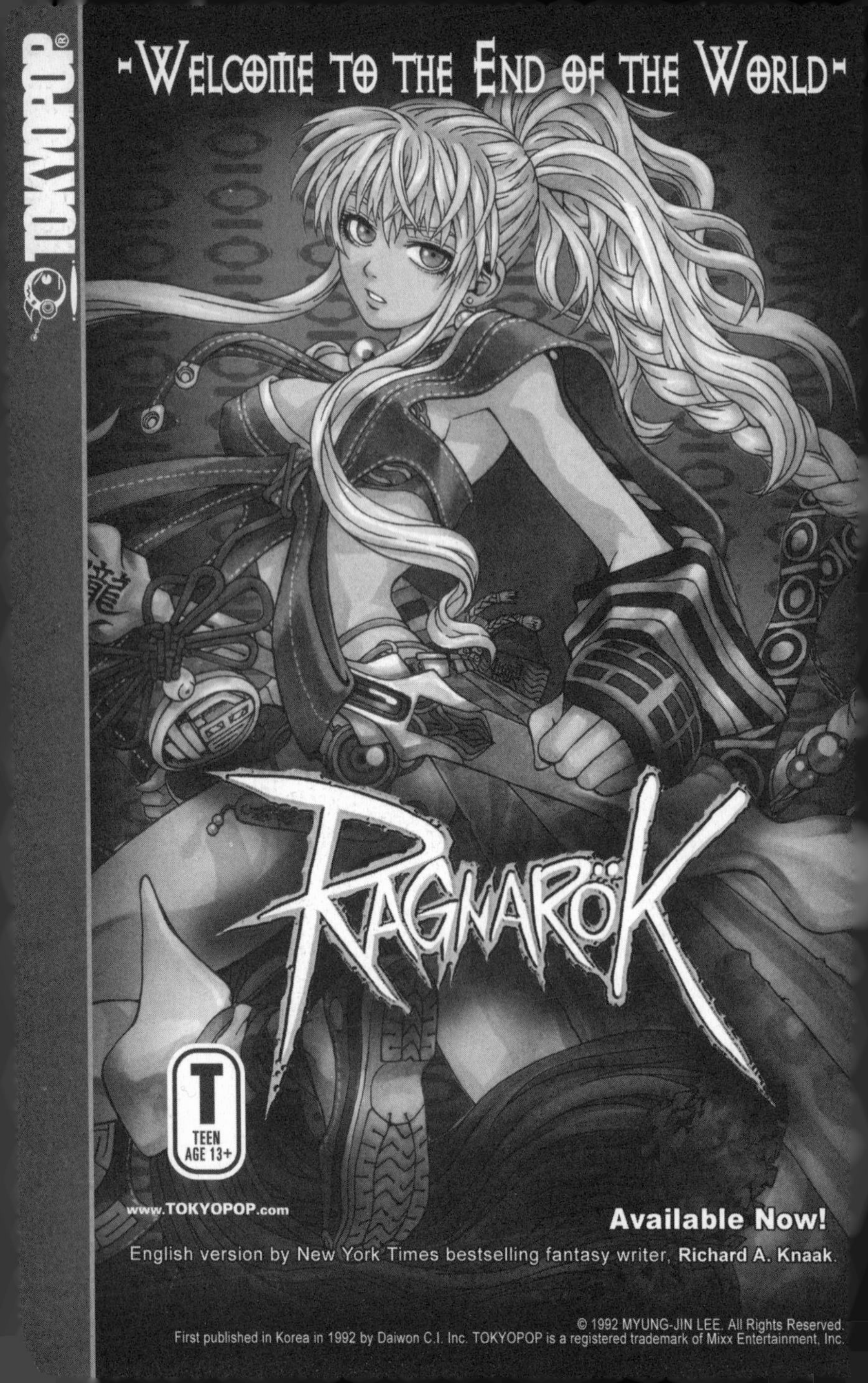

TOKYOPOP
-WELCOME TO THE END OF THE WORLD-
RAGNARÖK
T TEEN AGE 13+
www.TOKYOPOP.com
Available Now!
English version by New York Times bestselling fantasy writer, Richard A. Knaak.
© 1992 MYUNG-JIN LEE. All Rights Reserved.
First published in Korea in 1992 by Daiwon C.I. Inc. TOKYOPOP is a registered trademark of Mixx Entertainment, Inc.

SAIYUKI™

come get some.

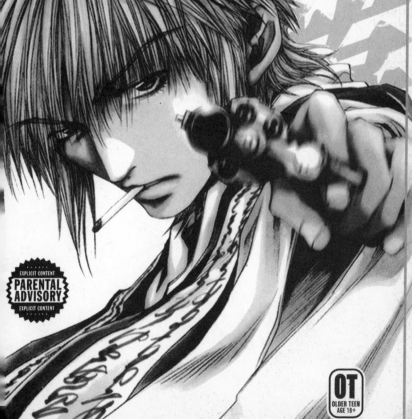

PARENTAL ADVISORY
EXPLICIT CONTENT
EXPLICIT CONTENT

OT
OLDER TEEN
AGE 16+

SAIYUKI ©2002 Kazuya Minekura / ISSAISHA Inc. ©2004 TOKYOPOP Inc. All rights reserved.   www.TOKYOPOP.com

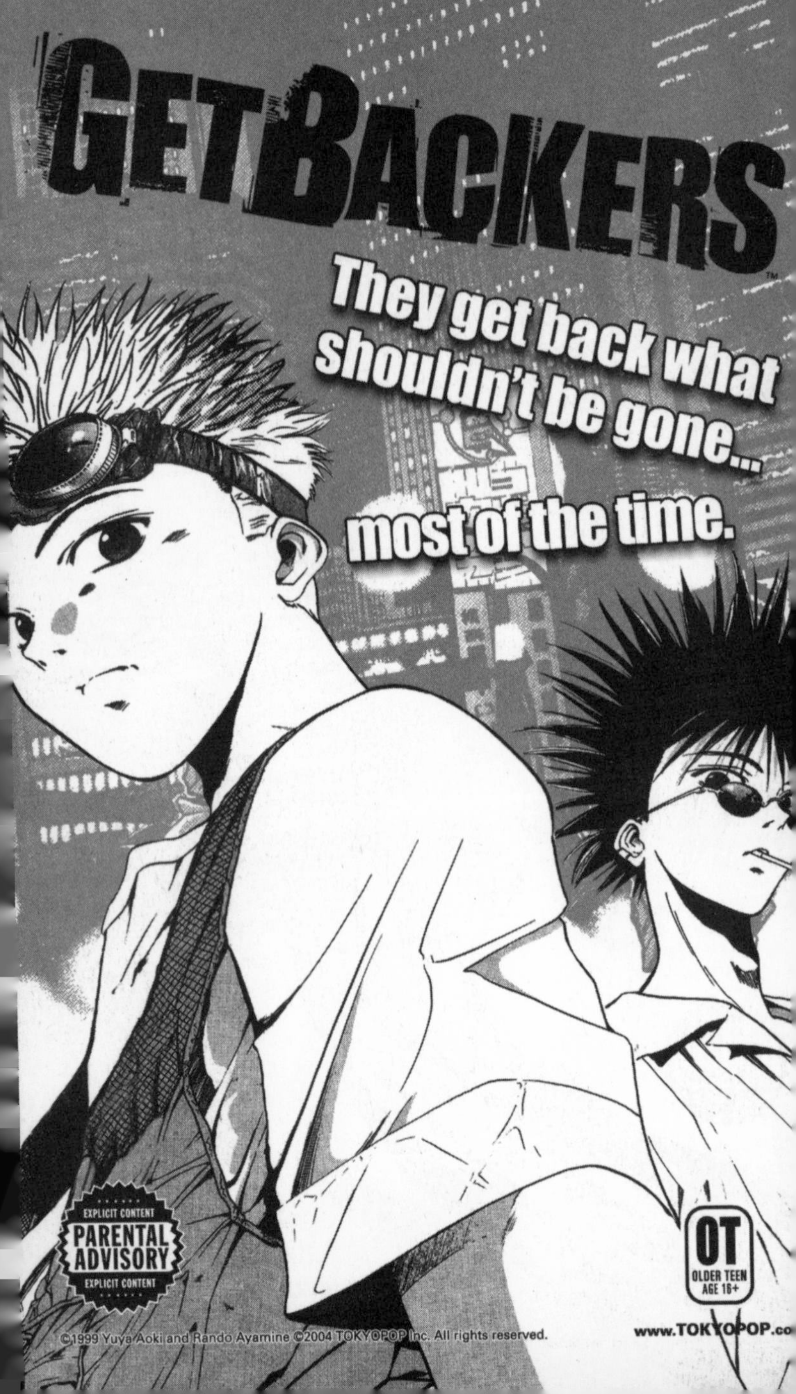
GETBACKERS™
They get back what shouldn't be gone...
most of the time.
EXPLICIT CONTENT
PARENTAL ADVISORY
EXPLICIT CONTENT
OT
OLDER TEEN AGE 16+
©1999 Yuya Aoki and Rando Ayamine ©2004 TOKYOPOP Inc. All rights reserved.
www.TOKYOPOP.co

ALSO AVAILABLE FROM TOKYOPOP

PET SHOP OF HORRORS
PITA-TEN
PLANET LADDER
PLANETES
PRIEST
PRINCESS AI
PSYCHIC ACADEMY
QUEEN'S KNIGHT, THE
RAGNAROK
RAVE MASTER
REALITY CHECK
REBIRTH
REBOUND
REMOTE
RISING STARS OF MANGA
SABER MARIONETTE J
SAILOR MOON
SAINT TAIL
SAIYUKI
SAMURAI DEEPER KYO
SAMURAI GIRL REAL BOUT HIGH SCHOOL
SCRYED
SEIKAI TRILOGY, THE
SGT. FROG
SHAOLIN SISTERS
SHIRAHIME-SYO: SNOW GODDESS TALES
SHUTTERBOX
SKULL MAN, THE
SNOW DROP
SORCERER HUNTERS
STONE
SUIKODEN III
SUKI
THREADS OF TIME
TOKYO BABYLON
TOKYO MEW MEW
TOKYO TRIBES
TRAMPS LIKE US
UNDER THE GLASS MOON
VAMPIRE GAME
VISION OF ESCAFLOWNE, THE
WARRIORS OF TAO
WILD ACT
WISH
WORLD OF HARTZ
X-DAY
ZODIAC P.I.

NOVELS

CLAMP SCHOOL PARANORMAL INVESTIGATORS
SAILOR MOON
SLAYERS

ART BOOKS

ART OF CARDCAPTOR SAKURA
ART OF MAGIC KNIGHT RAYEARTH, THE
PEACH: MIWA UEDA ILLUSTRATIONS

ANIME GUIDES

COWBOY BEBOP
GUNDAM TECHNICAL MANUALS
SAILOR MOON SCOUT GUIDES

TOKYOPOP KIDS

STRAY SHEEP

CINE-MANGA™

ALADDIN
CARDCAPTORS
DUEL MASTERS
FAIRLY ODDPARENTS, THE
FAMILY GUY
FINDING NEMO
G.I. JOE SPY TROOPS
GREATEST STARS OF THE NBA: SHAQUILLE O'NEAL
GREATEST STARS OF THE NBA: TIM DUNCAN
JACKIE CHAN ADVENTURES
JIMMY NEUTRON: BOY GENIUS, THE ADVENTURES OF
KIM POSSIBLE
LILO & STITCH: THE SERIES
LIZZIE MCGUIRE
LIZZIE MCGUIRE MOVIE, THE
MALCOLM IN THE MIDDLE
POWER RANGERS: DINO THUNDER
POWER RANGERS: NINJA STORM
PRINCESS DIARIES 2
RAVE MASTER
SHREK 2
SIMPLE LIFE, THE
SPONGEBOB SQUAREPANTS
SPY KIDS 2
SPY KIDS 3-D: GAME OVER
TEENAGE MUTANT NINJA TURTLES
THAT'S SO RAVEN
TOTALLY SPIES
TRANSFORMERS: ARMADA
TRANSFORMERS: ENERGON

You want it? We got it!
A full range of TOKYOPOP
products are available now at:
www.TOKYOPOP.com/shop

06.21.04T

ALSO AVAILABLE FROM TOKYOPOP®

MANGA

.HACK//LEGEND OF THE TWILIGHT
@LARGE
ABENOBASHI: MAGICAL SHOPPING ARCADE
A.I. LOVE YOU
AI YORI AOSHI
ANGELIC LAYER
ARM OF KANNON
BABY BIRTH
BATTLE ROYALE
BATTLE VIXENS
BOYS BE...
BRAIN POWERED
BRIGADOON
B'TX
CANDIDATE FOR GODDESS, THE
CARDCAPTOR SAKURA
CARDCAPTOR SAKURA - MASTER OF THE CLOW
CHOBITS
CHRONICLES OF THE CURSED SWORD
CLAMP SCHOOL DETECTIVES
CLOVER
COMIC PARTY
CONFIDENTIAL CONFESSIONS
CORRECTOR YUI
COWBOY BEBOP
COWBOY BEBOP: SHOOTING STAR
CRAZY LOVE STORY
CRESCENT MOON
CROSS
CULDCEPT
CYBORG 009
D•N•ANGEL
DEMON DIARY
DEMON ORORON, THE
DEUS VITAE
DIABOLO
DIGIMON
DIGIMON TAMERS
DIGIMON ZERO TWO
DOLL
DRAGON HUNTER
DRAGON KNIGHTS
DRAGON VOICE
DREAM SAGA
DUKLYON: CLAMP SCHOOL DEFENDERS
EERIE QUEERIE!
ERICA SAKURAZAWA: COLLECTED WORKS
ET CETERA
ETERNITY
EVIL'S RETURN
FAERIES' LANDING
FAKE
FLCL
FLOWER OF THE DEEP SLEEP
FORBIDDEN DANCE
FRUITS BASKET

G GUNDAM
GATEKEEPERS
GETBACKERS
GIRL GOT GAME
GIRLS EDUCATIONAL CHARTER
GRAVITATION
GTO
GUNDAM BLUE DESTINY
GUNDAM SEED ASTRAY
GUNDAM WING
GUNDAM WING: BATTLEFIELD OF PACIFISTS
GUNDAM WING: ENDLESS WALTZ
GUNDAM WING: THE LAST OUTPOST (G-UNIT)
HANDS OFF!
HAPPY MANIA
HARLEM BEAT
HYPER RUNE
I.N.V.U.
IMMORTAL RAIN
INITIAL D
INSTANT TEEN: JUST ADD NUTS
ISLAND
JING: KING OF BANDITS
JING: KING OF BANDITS - TWILIGHT TALES
JULINE
KARE KANO
KILL ME, KISS ME
KINDAICHI CASE FILES, THE
KING OF HELL
KODOCHA: SANA'S STAGE
LAMENT OF THE LAMB
LEGAL DRUG
LEGEND OF CHUN HYANG, THE
LES BIJOUX
LOVE HINA
LUPIN III
LUPIN III: WORLD'S MOST WANTED
MAGIC KNIGHT RAYEARTH I
MAGIC KNIGHT RAYEARTH II
MAHOROMATIC: AUTOMATIC MAIDEN
MAN OF MANY FACES
MARMALADE BOY
MARS
MARS: HORSE WITH NO NAME
MINK
MIRACLE GIRLS
MIYUKI-CHAN IN WONDERLAND
MODEL
MOURYOU KIDEN
MY LOVE
NECK AND NECK
ONE
ONE I LOVE, THE
PARADISE KISS
PARASYTE
PASSION FRUIT
PEACH GIRL
PEACH GIRL: CHANGE OF HEART

06.21.04T

KAMIJŌ, AKIMINE.
SAMURAI DEEPER KYO, V.11

C2004.
37565024745555 CENT

P9-AEW-780

This is the back of the book.
You wouldn't want to spoil a great ending!

This book is printed "manga-style," in the authentic Japanese right-to-left format. Since none of the artwork has been flipped or altered, readers get to experience the story just as the creator intended. You've been asking for it, so TOKYOPOP® delivered: authentic, hot-off-the-press, and far more fun!

DIRECTIONS

If this is your first time reading manga-style, here's a quick guide to help you understand how it works.

It's easy... just start in the top right panel and follow the numbers. Have fun, and look for more 100% authentic manga from TOKYOPOP®!

品質第一公式商品
100%
AUTHENTIC
MANGA
品質第一公式商品